Editors/Advisory Board

Members of the Advisory Board are instrumental in the final selection of articles for each edition of ANNUAL EDITIONS. Their review of articles for content, level, currentness, and appropriateness provides critical direction to the editor and staff. We think that you will find their careful consideration well reflected in this volume.

D0074386

Staff

Preface

In publishing ANNUAL EDITIONS we recognize the enormous role played by the magazines, newspapers, and journals of the public press in providing current, first-rate educational information in a broad spectrum of interest areas. Many of these articles are appropriate for students, researchers, and professionals seeking accurate, current material to help bridge the gap between principles and theories and the real world. These articles, however, become more useful for study when those of lasting value are carefully collected, organized, indexed, and reproduced in a low-cost format, which provides easy and permanent access when the material is needed. That is the role played by ANNUAL EDITIONS.

This eighth "Annual Editions: Archaeology," has been compiled by its two new editors, with the intent of presenting a vivid overview of the field of archaeology as practiced today. It is our hope that these readings in keeping with its pervious editions will make the old bones, shards of pottery, and stone tools of the past pop into the present. The book's purpose is to present an approach in which archaeologists speak for themselves of their own special experiences. The student is shown that archaeology is a historical, living, and public science. The idea is to show the student the necessary basics to enable the student to transform passive learning into active learning. This way, information is both perceived and conceptualized. Hopefully, the light bulb will go on when students read these articles.

This book is organized into five units, each of which contains several articles on various themes on "doing" archaeology. At the beginning of the book a table of contents provides a short synopsis of each article. This is followed by a topic guide that cross-references general areas of interest as they appear in the different articles. At the end of the book is a comprehensive index. In addition, there are Internet References that can be used to further explore the above articles. Each unit is introduced by an overview that provides both commentary on the unit topic and key points to provoke thought and discussion. It is highly recommended that the student read these unit overviews. They are presented for the student with humor and contain challenges and even puzzles to solve. The organization of this book is both suggestive and subjective. The articles may be assigned or read in any fashion that is deemed desirable. Each article stands on its own and may be assigned in conjunction with or in contrast to any other reading. "Annual Editions: Archaeology 06/07" may serve as a supplement to a standard textbook for both introductory and graduate archaeology courses. It may also be used in general, undergraduate, or graduate courses in anthropology. The lay reader in anthropology may also find the collection of readings insightful.

It is the desire of those involved in the production of this book that each edition be a valuable and provocative teaching tool. We welcome your criticisms, advice, and suggestions in order to carefully hone new editions into a finer artifact of education. We suggest you use the postage-paid form at the end of this book for your comments and article ratings. We would be most grateful for the time you take to give us your feedback. Each year these comments and ratings are carefully read by the editors and the advisory board in creating the next edition. Your responses would truly be appreciated and seriously considered.

Mari Pritchard Parker
Editor

Elvio Angeloni
Editor

To The Instructor

What Are Annual Editions?

Annual Editions are an exciting instructional tool—diverse and challenging. Published by *McGraw-Hill Contemporary Learning Series*, *Annual Editions* are a collection of the most interesting, informative, and important articles related to a particular subject area. Every article has been carefully chosen from a broad range of the public press including magazines, professional journals, and major newspapers. The latest information and research is supplemented by enduring articles, essays, and important basic documents.

Annual Editions bring topics into sharp focus for students—a focus that no textbook can match! The amount of material available in today's information-oriented society is staggering. With *Annual Editions*, the problem of how to sort through this mountain of material is solved. *Annual Editions* offer the *best* from the current press. Every article has been carefully reviewed by professional editors, an academic editor, and an *Annual Editions* Advisory Board. *Annual Editions* are updated annually, which guarantees that students are exposed to the latest ideas that are shaping the discipline.

How Can Annual Editions Be Used in the Classroom?

- For Supplementary Reading
- As a Basic Text
- As a Starting Point for Student Research
- For Independent Study
- For Extra Credit or Make-Up Work

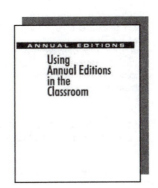

This handy supplement provides a wealth of ideas for easily and inexpensively incorporating the best of the current press into your instructional program.

Ask your McGraw-Hill Sales Representative for a copy today!

ISBN 0-07-254844-4

Instructor's Resource Guide for

A comprehensive Instructor's Resource Guide is available for every *Annual Editions* title. A must for every teacher, this instructor's resource guide contains:

- Summaries of each article
- Over 100 multiple-choice test questions, including study guide web questions
- Hundreds of essay and discussion questions

Ask your McGraw-Hill Sales Representative for a copy today!

ISBN 0-07-351613-9

Additionally, the question bank in each Instructor's Resource Guide is also available online as an ASCII text file. To access these banks, contact your McGraw-Hill Sales Representative or refer to the title page of the *printed* Instructor's Resource Guide; there you will find a boxed paragraph explaining how to access the ASCII file for the book you are using. The steps are quite simple: enter our Internet address, **http://www.mhcls.com/irg**, then enter the unique 5-digit password that is provided at the beginning of the guide.

Contents

UNIT 1
About Archaeologists and Archaeology

1. **The Awful Truth About Archaeology,** Dr. Lynne Sebastian, *The SAA Archaeological Record,* March 2003

"You're an Archaeologist! That sounds soooo exciting!" Of course it sounds exciting because of the hyperbole and mystic surrounding archaeologists perpetuated by TV shows, movies, and novels—professional archaeologists know better! *The process of discovery is slow, tedious, and frustrating* when nothing is found. Digging square holes in the ground and carefully measuring artifacts, cataloging, taking notes, and hopefully something meaningful about the past gets published.   3

2. **Distinguished Lecture in Archaeology: Communication and the Future of American Archaeology,** Jeremy A. Sabloff, *American Anthropologist,* December 1998

Jeremy Sabloff discusses the role that archaeology should play in **public education** and the need for archaeologists to communicate more effectively with **relevant writing** for the public. He further suggests the need to recognize **nonacademic archaeologists** and to focus on **action archaeology** or what is more usually termed **public archaeology**.   5

3. **All the King's Sons,** Douglas Preston, *The New Yorker,* January 22, 1996

A well-told narrative of **modern archaeology**, Douglas Preston's article is based on **scientific archaeology**. It is not, however, a typical "scientific" or "monograph" report common to **academic archaeology**. This tale of archaeology is wish fulfillment for students or laypersons of archaeology because it is about a spectacular find—the biggest archaeological site in **Egypt** since King Tut's tomb. No "blah, blah Egypt, blah, blah dummy," here.   11

4. **Antiquities Sleuth has a Fraud Mandate,** Jacqueline Trestcott, *The Washington Post,* March 29, 2005

It is a given that **most museums have fakes** in their collections. By using certifiably genuine objects as her guide, Jane MacLaren Walsh of the Smithsonian Institute is establishing a **database** to guide those trying to **spot fraudulent antiquities**. What complicates the search for authenticity is that some of the forgeries are so old that they too qualify as antiques.   22

The concepts in bold italics are developed in the article. For further expansion, please refer to the Topic Guide and the Index.

UNIT 2
Problem Oriented Archaeology

The concepts in bold italics are developed in the article. For further expansion, please refer to the Topic Guide and the Index.

UNIT 3
Techniques in Archaeology

The concepts in bold italics are developed in the article. For further expansion, please refer to the Topic Guide and the Index.

UNIT 4
Historical Archaeology

The concepts in bold italics are developed in the article. For further expansion, please refer to the Topic Guide and the Index.

UNIT 5
Contemporary Archaeology

The concepts in bold italics are developed in the article. For further expansion, please refer to the Topic Guide and the Index.

The concepts in bold italics are developed in the article. For further expansion, please refer to the Topic Guide and the Index.

The concepts in bold italics are developed in the article. For further expansion, please refer to the Topic Guide and the Index.

Topic Guide

This topic guide suggests how the selections in this book relate to the subjects covered in your course. You may want to use the topics listed on these pages to search the Web more easily.

On the following pages a number of Web sites have been gathered specifically for this book. They are arranged to reflect the units of this *Annual Edition*. You can link to these sites by going to the student online support site at *http://www.mhcls.com/online/*.

ALL THE ARTICLES THAT RELATE TO EACH TOPIC ARE LISTED BELOW THE BOLD-FACED TERM.

About archaeologists and archaeology

1. The Awful Truth About Archaeology
2. Distinguished Lecture in Archaeology: Communication and the Future of American Archaeology
3. All the King's Sons
5. Prehistory of Warfare
7. The Littlest Human
8. Who's On First?
9. The Slow Birth of Agriculture
10. Archaeologists Rediscover Cannibals
17. Through Dirt to the Past
21. Simulating Ancient Societies
23. City of the Hawk
29. Archaeology from the Dark Side
30. Ownership and Control of Ethnographic Materials
31. Last Word on Kennewick Man?
32. Guardians of the Dead
33. Thracian Gold Fever
36. Earth Movers
39. Space: The Final [Archaeological] Frontier

Art and religion

3. All the King's Sons
10. Archaeologists Rediscover Cannibals
23. City of the Hawk
24. The Lost Goddess of Israel
27. Israel's Mysterious Stone
28. Legacy of the Crusades
32. Guardians of the Dead

Burials, reburials and human remains

8. Who's On First?
10. Archaeologists Rediscover Cannibals
12. New Women of the Ice Age
18. High-Tech "Digging"
20. Profile of an Anthropologist: No Bone Unturned
23. City of the Hawk
25. Secrets of the Medici
26. Living Through the Donner Party
28. Legacy of the Crusades
31. Last Word on Kennewick Man?
32. Guardians of the Dead
33. Thracian Gold Fever
34. In Flanders Fields
35. The Past as Propaganda

Ceramic analysis

23. City of the Hawk
24. The Lost Goddess of Israel
33. Thracian Gold Fever
36. Earth Movers

Classical and biblical archaeology

3. All the King's Sons
9. The Slow Birth of Agriculture
16. The Maya Collapses
18. High-Tech "Digging"
23. City of the Hawk
24. The Lost Goddess of Israel
27. Israel's Mysterious Stone
28. Legacy of the Crusades
29. Archaeology from the Dark Side
33. Thracian Gold Fever

Cognitive and ideological archaeology

2. Distinguished Lecture in Archaeology: Communication and the Future of American Archaeology
29. Archaeology from the Dark Side

Cultural Resource Management (CRM)

4. Antiquities Sleuth has a Fraud Mandate
18. High-Tech "Digging"
30. Ownership and Control of Ethnographic Materials
31. Last Word on Kennewick Man?
32. Guardians of the Dead
34. In Flanders Fields
39. Space: The Final [Archaeological] Frontier

Epistemology (method and theory)

1. The Awful Truth About Archaeology
2. Distinguished Lecture in Archaeology: Communication and the Future of American Archaeology
3. All the King's Sons
8. Who's On First?
9. The Slow Birth of Agriculture
12. New Women of the Ice Age
13. Woman The Toolmaker
21. Simulating Ancient Societies
25. Secrets of the Medici
29. Archaeology from the Dark Side

Internet References

The following internet sites have been carefully researched and selected to support the articles found in this reader. The easiest way to access these selected sites is to go to our student online support site at *http://www.mhcls.com/online/*.

AE: Archaeology

The following sites were available at the time of publication. Visit our Web site—we update our student online support site regularly to reflect any changes.

General Sources

Anthropology Resources on the Internet
http://www.socsciresearch.com/r7.html

This site provides extensive Internet links that are primarily of anthropological relevance. *The Education Index* rated it "one of the best education-related sites on the Web."

Archaeological Institute of America
http://www.archaeological.org

This home page of the AIA describes the purpose of the nonprofit organization. Review this site for information about AIA and AIA/IAA–Canada and other archaeological-research institutions and organizations around the world.

How Humans Evolved
http://www.wwnorton.com/college/anthro/bioanth/

This site presents a good overview of human evolution, with links to *Science* and *Nature* magazines, access to e-mail chat groups, and other topics of archaeological interest.

Library of Congress
http://www.loc.gov

Examine this extensive Web site to learn about resource tools, library services/resources, exhibitions, and databases in many different subfields of archaeology.

The New York Times
http://www.nytimes.com/

Browsing through the extensive archives of the *New York Times* will provide you with a wide array of articles and information related to archaeology.

USD Anthropology
http://www.usd.edu/anth/

Many topics can be accessed from this site, such as South Dakota archaeology. Repatriation and reburial are just a few examples of the variety of information available.

UNIT 1: About Archaeologists and Archaeology

Anthropology, Archaeology, and American Indian Sites on the Internet
http://dizzy.library.arizona.edu/library/teams/sst/anthro/

This Web page points out a number of Internet sites of interest to archaeologists. Visit this page for links to electronic journals and more.

GMU Anthropology Department
http://www.gmu.edu/departments/anthro/

Look over this site for current listings of scientific papers dealing with anthropological and archaeological studies. The site provides a number of interesting links, such as a listing of archaeological fieldwork opportunities.

Smithsonian Institution Web Site
http://www.si.edu/

This site, which will provide access to many of the enormous resources of the Smithsonian, will give you a sense of the scope of anthropological and archaeological inquiry today.

UNIT 2: Problem Oriented Archaeology

Archaeology Links (NC)
http://www.arch.dcr.state.nc.us/links.htm#stuff

North Carolina Archaeology provides this site, which has many links to sites of interest to archaeologists, such as the paleolithic painted cave at Vallon-Pont-d'Arc (Ardeche).

Archaeology Magazine
http://www.archaeology.org

This home page of *Archaeology* magazine, the official publication of the AIA, provides information about current archaeological events, staff picks of Web sites, and access to selected articles from current and past editions of the magazine.

UNIT 3: Techniques in Archaeology

American Anthropologist
http://www.aaanet.org

Check out this site—the home page of the American Anthropology Association—for general information about archaeology and anthropology as well as access to a wide variety of articles.

NOVA Online/Pyramids—The Inside Story
http://www.pbs.org/wgbh/nova/pyramid/

Take a virtual tour of the pyramids at Giza through this interesting site. It provides information on the pharaohs for whom the tombs were built and follows a team of archaeologists as they excavate a bakery that fed the pyramid builders.

UNIT 4: Historical Archaeology

GIS and Remote Sensing for Archaeology: Burgundy, France
http://www.informatics.org/france/france.html

This project has been an ongoing collaboration between Dr. Scott Madry from the Center for Remote Sensing and Spatial Analysis at Rutgers University and many other researchers. A period of over 2,000 years in the Arroux River Valley region of Burgundy is being analyzed to understand long-term interaction between the different cultures and the physical environment.

Petra Great Temple/Technology
http://www.brown.edu/Departments/Anthropology/Petra/excavations/technology.html

The introduction of a field reporting system using computers in fieldwork holds promise for resolving the dilemma between recording much information or recording accurate data. At this site, surveying is done using a computer-controlled theodolite and ground-penetrating radar.

Radiocarbon Dating for Archaeology

http://www.rlaha.ox.ac.uk/orau/index.html

This Web site describes the advantages inherent in using radiocarbon dating to promote mass spectrometry over the older decay counting method.

Zeno's Forensic Page

http://forensic.to/forensic.html

A complete list of resources on forensics is here. It includes DNA/serology sources and databases, forensic-medicine anthropology sites, and related areas.

UNIT 5: Contemporary Archaeology

Archaeology and Anthropology: The Australian National University

http://online.anu.edu.au/AandA/

Browse through this home page of the Anthropology and Archaeology Departments of the Australian National University for information about topics in Australian and regional archaeology and to access links to other resource centers.

WWW: Classical Archaeology

http://www.archaeology.org/wwwarky/classical.html

This site provides information and links regarding ancient Greek and Roman archaeology.

Al Mashriq-Archaeology in Beirut

http://almashriq.hiof.no/base/archaeology.html

At this site the links to the fascinating excavations taking place in Beirut can be explored. Reports from the site, background material, discussion of the importance of the site, and information on other Lebanese sites are included.

American Indian Ritual Object Repatriation Foundation

http://www.repatriationfoundation.org/

Visit this home page of the American Indian Ritual Object Repatriation Foundation, which aims to assist in the return of sacred ceremonial material to the appropriate American Indian nation, clan, or family, and to educate the public.

ArchNet—WWW Virtual Library

http://archnet.asu.edu/archnet/

ArchNet serves as the World Wide Web Virtual Library for Archaeology. This site can provide you with access to a broad variety of archaeological resources available on the Internet, categorized by geographic region and subject.

Current Archaeology

http://www.archaeology.co.uk

This is the home page of *Current Archaeology,* Great Britain's leading archaeological magazine. Its various sections provide links about archaeology in Britain.

National Archeological DataBase

http://www.cast.uark.edu/other/nps/nagpra/nagpra.html

Examine this site from the Archeology and Ethnography Program of the NAD to read documents related to the Native American Graves Protection and Repatriation Act.

Society for Archaeological Sciences

http://www.socarchsci.org/

The Society for Archaeological Sciences provides this site to further communication among scholars applying methods from the physical sciences to archaeology.

We highly recommend that you review our Web site for expanded information and our other product lines. We are continually updating and adding links to our Web site in order to offer you the most usable and useful information that will support and expand the value of your Annual Editions. You can reach us at: *http://www.mhcls.com/annualeditions/.*

UNIT 1

About Archaeologists and Archaeology

Unit Selections

1. **The Awful Truth About Archaeology**, Dr. Lynne Sebastian
2. **Distinguished Lecture in Archaeology: Communication and the Future of American Archaeology**, Jeremy A. Sabloff
3. **All the King's Sons**, Douglas Preston
4. **Antiquities Sleuth has a Fraud Mandate**, Jacqueline Trestcott

Key Points to Consider

- How does modern archeology differ from archeology of the Nineteenth Century and why? Give some examples of what is meant by archeological methods, fieldwork, theory, and ethics.

- How is culture viewed by anthropology?

- What is the general relationship between anthropology and archeology? Please give specific examples.

- What is public archeology? How could archeologists better communicate with the public? What role should archeology play in public education? Give some examples.

- What is the difference between academic and non-academic archeologists? What is the potential for non-academic archeologists?

- What is the biggest find in Egypt since King Tut-ankh-Amun's tomb? Why is digging in Egypt considered to be a cliché among archeologists? Is this an example of academic archeology? Give some examples.

- How is it possible to distinguish the fakes from the genuine objects in today's museums?

Student Website

www.mhcls.com/online

Internet References

Further information regarding these websites may be found in this book's preface or online.

Anthropology, Archaeology, and American Indian Sites on the Internet
http://dizzy.library.arizona.edu/library/teams/sst/anthro/

GMU Anthropology Department
http://www.gmu.edu/departments/anthro/

Smithsonian Institution Web Site
http://www.si.edu/

Is there a difference between archaeology and anthropology? No, archaeology as practiced in the Americas is anthropology. Its goal is to reconstruct culture based on the material remains left from the human groups of the past.

If human behavior were a baseball game, the anthropologist would be in the broadcaster's booth. But long before the game was over, in a seeming paradox, the anthropologist would run into the stands to be a spectator, chow down on a good fresh steamy mustard-covered hot dog, and then rush onto the field to be a player and catch a high fly to left field. This is the eccentric nature of anthropology. This is why anthropology is so interesting.

If one compares anthropology, psychology, sociology, and history as four disciplines that study human nature, anthropology is the one that takes the giant step back and uses a 360-degree panoramic camera. The psychologist stands nose to nose with the individual person, the sociologist moves back for the group shot, and the historian goes back in time as well as space. However, the anthropologist does all these things, standing well behind the others, watching and measuring, using the data of all these disciplines but recombining them into the uniqueness of the anthropological perspective: much the way meiosis generates novel genetic combinations.

Anthropology is the science of human behavior that studies all humankind, starting with our biological and evolutionary origins as cultural beings and continuing with the diversification of our cultural selves. Humankind is the single species that has evolved culture as our unique way of adapting to the world. Academically, anthropology is divided into the four major fields, cultural, physical, linguistics, and archaeology. Anthropologists hold in common a generally shared concept of culture. The basic tenet that anthropologists share is to generate a behavioral science that can explain the differences and similarities between cultures. In order to achieve this, anthropologists view people within a cross-cultural perspective. This encompasses comparing the parts and parcels of all cultures, present and past, with each other. This is the holistic approach of anthropology: considering all things in all their manifestations. A grand task, indeed. One that requires, above all, learning to ask the "right" questions.

What is culture? Culture is the unique way in which our species adapts to its total environment. Total environment includes everything that affects human beings—the physical environment, plants, animals, the weather, beliefs, values, a passing insult, or an opportunistic virus. Everything possible that human beings are capable of is by culture. Culture is the human adaptive system. It is an ecology in which all people live in groups defined by time, space, and place. They pass on shared values and beliefs through common language(s), and manipulate things in their environment through tool use and tool making. Cultures change and evolve through time. And perhaps most enigmatically cultures, all cultures, be they high civilizations or small tribes, do eventually cease to exist.

Archaeology is the subfield of anthropology that studies these extinct cultures. Archaeologists dig up the physical remains, the tools, the houses, the garbage, and the utensils of once-living cultures. And from this spare database, archaeologists attempt to reconstruct these past cultures in their material, social, and ideological aspects. Is this important to anthropology? Yes, this is anthropology because these once-living cultures represent approximately ninety-eight percent of all cultures that have ever existed. They tell us where we have been, when we are there again, and where we might go in the future.

How do archaeologists do this? Today the mass media is the major source of the epistemology in the modern world and thus underscores cultural values as well as creating the necessary cultural myths by which all humans must live. The media is as much a response to our demands as we are to its manipulations. Its themes play a medley in our minds over and over again, until they fade into our unconscious only to be recycled again, pulled up, and laid before us like the ice cream man's musical chimes of our childhood. But the media mind is characterized by fuzzy thinking and credulity. The essence of archaeology is scientific thinking and skepticism. If minds are trained to be articulate, thought and action will follow suit. Scientific thinking involves a very strict set of rules and regulations that test the veracity of conclusions. A kind of operationalized language emerges, codified similarly to mathematics, that allows apples to be compared to apples.

Postmodernists may argue that knowledge is only knowable in a relative sense. But we know what we know in a very real and pragmatic sense because we are, after all, humans—the cultural animal. It is our way of knowing and surviving. Let us proceed now to see how archaeologists ply their magical trade.

The Awful Truth about Archaeology

Dr. Lynne Sebastian

"Ohhhh! You're an Archaeologist! That sounds soooo exciting!" Whenever I tell someone on a plane or at a dinner party what I do for a living, this is almost always the response that I get. Either that, or they want to talk to me about dinosaurs, and I have to explain gently that it is paleontologists who do dinosaurs; archaeologists study people who lived long ago.

The reason people think archaeology must be exciting is that they have spent WAY too much time watching The *Curse of the Mummy*, *Indiana Jones* and the *Temple of Doom*, and *Lara Croft, Tomb Raider* (do you suppose that she actually has that printed on her business cards?). Perhaps it is a flaw in my character or a lapse in my professional education, but I have never once recovered a golden idol or been chased through the jungle by thugs, and I appear to have been absent from graduate school on the day that they covered bullwhips, firearms, and the martial arts. I have not even, so far as I can tell, suffered from a curse, although I have had few nasty encounters with serpents, scorpions, and lightening.

I'm sure that members of every profession are exasperated by the way that they are portrayed in movies and on television, and archaeologists are no exception. Every time we see Sydney Fox (*Relict Hunter*, another great job title) fly off to an exotic country, follow the clues on the ancient map, and rip-off some fabulous object to bring home to the museum, we want to root for the bad guys who are trying to bring her career to an abrupt and permanent halt.

What would really happen if a mysterious man wearing an eye patch showed up at Sydney's university office and gave her the map, just before expiring as a result of slow-acting poison? Well, of course, first there would be a lot of unpleasantness with the campus police … but leaving that aside, she would spend months writing grant proposals to get funding for a research expedition and more months getting the needed permits and authorizations from the government of the exotic country. Then she would have to persuade the Dean and her department Chair to give her release time from teaching. And when she and her research team finally arrived in the exotic country, they would spend months meticulously mapping the site, painstakingly removing thin layers of soil from perfectly square holes, and recording every stone, every bit of stained earth, every piece of debris that they encountered, using photos, maps, sketches, and detailed written notes. Finally, at the end of the field season, the team would return to the university with 70 boxes of broken pottery, bits of stone, and all manner of scientific samples to be washed and cataloged and analyzed. And in the end, all that material would be returned to a musuem in the exotic country.

Now, of course, nobody would want to watch a TV show where even the beauteous Sydney did all that, but this kind of tedious, detailed work is one important aspect of "real" archaeology. Just about every archaeologist that I know has a copy of an old Calvin and Hobbs cartoon somewhere in his or her office. In it, Calvin, who has spent an exhausting day doing a make-believe archaeological excavation in his backyard, turns to Hobbs in disgust and says, "Archaeology has to be the most mind-numbing job in the world!!" And some days it is. Worse yet, it is detailed work that involves a lot of paperwork and delicate instruments but has to be done outdoors in every sort of adverse weather. When it is 20 degrees and you are hunched down in a square hole in the ground trying to write a description of layers of dirt with a pen that keeps freezing solid or when the wind is blowing sheets of sand straight sideways into your face while you are lying on your stomach using a dental pick to expose a broken shell bracelet so you can photograph it before you remove it - these are experiences that can cause a person to question her career choice.

But you know what? Archaeology really IS exciting, and not for any of the reasons that Indy or Lara would suggest. Archaeology is exciting because it connects with the past in a way that nothing else can, and sometimes that connection can be stunningly immediate and personal. I worked one year on the Hopi Reservation in Arizona, excavating a site that was going to be destroyed by road construction. We found that one of the three "pithouses" or semi-subterranean structures on the site appeared to have been cleaned out and closed up, presumably in the expectation that someone would return to live in it again. A flat slab had been placed over the ventilator opening, perhaps to keep out dirt and debris and critters, and the slab was sealed in place with wet mud. But no one came back, and eventually the small pithouse burned.

When we excavated the pithouse, we found the imprint of human hands, perfectly preserved in the mud, which had been hardened by the fire. That little house was built in AD 805, but I could reach out and place my hands in those handprints left there by someone a thousand years before. And more important, the Hopi school children who visited the site could place their small hands in those prints made by one of their ancestors, 50 generations removed. We lifted each one of the children into the pithouse, and let them do just that—like children everywhere, they were astonished that they were being encouraged to touch rather than being forbidden to do so.

Afterward we sat together on the site and talked about what life was like for that Hisatsinom (the Hopi term for the people we call Anasazi) person. We talked about food and looked at the burned corn kernels and the squash seeds that we had found. We talked about shelter and tools and looked at the three houses and the broken bits of stone and bone and pottery that we were recovering from the trash areas at the site. One of the houses had burned while it was occupied, and we looked at the fragments of the rolled up sleeping mats and baskets of corn and other possessions that the people had lost. We talked about the family that had lived there, how much the parents loved their children and how they must have worried about providing for them after such a terrible loss. And we talked about the migration stories that are a central part of Hopi oral history, and about what the Hopi elders had told us about the place of this particular site in those stories. I like to think that those children, who reached back across the centuries and touched the hand of their fifty-times-great grandmother, came away with a stronger sense of who they were and where they came from and a richer understanding of the oral traditions of their people.

But what if I had been not me, Dr. Science, purveyor of meticulous and mind-numbing archaeological techniques, but rather Lara Croft, Tomb Raider? If Lara had been rooting about in this site, searching for "treasures," she would have quickly dismissed that small pithouse, although she might have smashed that burned mud with the handprints in order to rip away the slab and check for hidden goodies behind it.

No, she would have focused on the other house, the one that burned while it was being used. She would have pulled out all those burned roof beams whose pattern of rings enabled us to learn that the houses were built in AD 805, probably using them for her campfire. She would have crushed the remnants of the burned sleeping mats and baskets of corn. She would never have noticed the stone griddle still in place on the hearth or the grease stains left by the last two corn cakes cooking on it when the fire started. She would have kicked aside the broken pieces of the pottery vessels that were crushed when the burning roof fell, the same pots that we put back together in the lab in order to estimate the size of the family and to recover traces of the items stored and cooked in them.

No, Lara would have missed all that we learned about that site and the people who made their homes there. Instead, she would have seized the single piece of pottery that didn't break in the fire and clutching it to her computer enhanced bosom, she would have stolen away into the night, narrowly escaping death and destruction at the hands of the rival gang of looters.

Is archaeology the most mind-numbing pursuit in the world, as Calvin claims? Or is it "sooo exciting" as my airline seatmates always exclaim? Both. And much more. What Lara and Indy and the others don't know is that archaeology is not about things, it is about people. It is about understanding life in the past, about understanding who we are and where we came from—not just where we came from as a particular cultural group, but what we share with all people in this time and in all the time that came before.

Lynne Sebastian is Director of Historic Preservation with the SRI Foundation, a private nonprofit dedicated to historic preservation, and an adjunct assistant professor of Anthropology at UNM. She is a former New Mexico State Archaeologist and State Historic Preservation Office, and she is currently the President of the Society for American Archaeology.

Distinguished Lecture in Archeology: Communication and the Future of American Archaeology

What follows is the revised text of the Distinguished Lecture in Archeology, presented at the 95th Annual Meeting of the American Anthropological Association, held in San Francisco, California, November, 1996.

Jeremy A. Sabloff

University of Pennsylvania Museum of Archaeology and Anthropology Philadelphia, PA 19104

I offer these remarks with somewhat ambivalent feelings. While it is an honor indeed to be asked to give the Archaeology Division's Distinguished Lecture, I nevertheless must admit that it is a daunting challenge. I have looked at many of the superb Distinguished Lectures that have been presented to you in recent years and subsequently published in the *American Anthropologist* and am very impressed with what our colleagues have had to say. Most of the recent talks have focused on aspects of the ongoing debates on modern archaeological theory and methods. I certainly could have continued this tradition, because, as many of you know, I have strong feelings about this topic. However, I decided to pursue a different, more general tack, which I hope you will agree is of equal importance.

In a few short years, we will be entering a new millennium. Will American archaeology survive in the twenty-first century? Of course it will. But will it continue to thrive in the new millennium? The answer to this question is a more guarded "yes." There are various causes for concern about the future health of archaeology. I would like to examine one of these concerns and offer some suggestions as to how this concern might be eased.

My theme will be archaeologists' communication with the public—or lack thereof—and, more specifically, the relevance of archaeology to non-professionals. In thinking about this theme, which has been a particular interest and concern of mine, it struck me how one of my favorite cartoons provided an important insight into the whole question of archaeological communication. I know that many of you have your office doors or bulletin boards festooned with a host of "Calvin and Hobbes," "Shoe," "Bloom County," "Doonesbury," or "Far Side" drawings that unerringly seem to pinpoint many of life's enduring paradoxes and problems. In particular, the "Far Side" cartoons by Gary Larson, who is now lamentably in early retirement like several of our master cartoonists, often resonate well with archaeologists' sensibilities. This cartoon, while not specifically targeting archaeologists or cultural anthropologists, as Larson often did pinpoint a central concern of my discussion.

While archaeologists may think they are talking clearly to the public, what the latter often hears, I believe, is "blah, blah, blah, *tomb,* blah, blah, blah *sacrifice,* blah, blah, blah, arrowhead."

I will argue that the field of American archaeology, despite some significant progress in the past decade, is still failing to effectively tell the public about how modern anthropological archaeology functions and about the huge gains archaeologists have made in understanding the development of ancient cultures through time and space.

More than 25 years ago, John Fritz and Fred Plog ended their article on "The Nature of Archaeological Explanation" (1970:412) with the famous assertion that "We suggest that unless archaeologists find ways to make their research increasingly relevant to the modern world, the modern world will find itself increasingly capable of getting along without archaeologists." Although Fritz and Plog had a very particular definition of relevance in mind relating to the development of laws of culture change, as did Fritz in his important article on "Relevance, Archaeology, and Subsistence Theory" (1973), if one adopts a broader view of the term *relevance,* then the thrust of their statement is just as important today—if not more so—than it was in 1970.

How can this be true? Archaeology appears to be thriving, if one counts number of jobs, money spent on archaeological field research, course enrollments, publications, and public fascination with the subject as measured in media coverage. But is the public interest, or, better yet, the public's interest, being served properly and satisfied in a productive and responsible fashion? With some important exceptions, I unfortunately would answer "no." Why do I think this to be the case?

In the nineteenth century, archaeology played an important public and intellectual role in the fledgling United States. Books concerned wholly or in part with archaeology were widely read and, as Richard Ford has indicated clearly in his article on "Archeology Serving Humanity" (1973), archaeology played an important part in overthrowing the then-dominant Biblical view of human development in favor of Darwinian evolutionary theory. Empirical archaeological research, which excited public interest and was closely followed by the public, was able to provide data that indicated that human activities had considerable antiquity and that archaeological studies of the past could throw considerable light on the development of the modern world.

As is the case in most disciplines, as archaeology became increasingly professionalized throughout the nineteenth century and as academic archaeology emerged in the late-nineteenth and early-twentieth centuries, the communications gap between professionals and the public grew apace. This gap was accentuated because amateurs had always played an important part in the archaeological enterprise. As late as the 1930s, before academic archaeology really burgeoned, the gap between most amateurs and professionals was still readily bridgeable, I believe. The first article in *American Antiquity,* for example, was written by an amateur, and, as I have discussed in detail elsewhere, the founders of the journal hoped that it "would provide a forum for communication between these two groups" (Sabloff 1985:228). However, even a quick look today at *American Antiquity* will indicate that those earlier hopes have been dashed. It may be a terrific journal for professionals, but much of it would be nearly incomprehensible to non-professionals, except perhaps to the most devoted amateurs.

In 1924, Alfred Vincent Kidder published his landmark book *An Introduction to the Study of Southwestern Archaeology.* This highly readable volume both made key advances in scholarly understanding of the ancient Southwest and was completely accessible to the general public. As Gordon Willey (1967:299) has stated: "It is a rarity in that it introduces systematics to a field previously unsystematized, and, at the same time, it is vitally alive and unpedantic.... He wrote a book that was romantic but not ridiculous, scrupulously close to the facts but not a boring recital of them." How many regional archaeological syntheses could have that said of them today? Happily, the answer is not "none," and there is some evidence of a positive trend in the publication of more popularly oriented regional and site syntheses (see, for instance, Kolata 1993; Plog 1997; or Schele and Freidel 1990, among others). Marcus and Flannery's (1996) recent book on Zapotec civilization is a superb example of how such accessible writing can be combined with a clear, theoretically sophisticated approach, as well.

Kidder also was deeply concerned about the relevance of archaeology to the contemporary world and was not shy about expressing his belief that archaeology could and should play an important social role in the modern world (a view which is paralleled today by some post-processual [e.g., Hodder et al. 1995] and feminist [e.g., Spector 1993] concerns with humanizing archaeological narratives). Kidder's views were most clearly expressed by him at a 1940 symposium at the American Philosophical Society on "Characteristics of American Culture and Its Place in General Culture." As Richard Woodbury (1973:171) notes: "Kidder presented one of his most eloquent pleas for the importance of the anthropological understanding of the past through the techniques of archaeology." Kidder (1940:528), for example, states: "it is good for an archaeologist to be forced to take stock, to survey his field, to attempt to show what bearing his delvings into the past may have upon our judgement of present day life; and what service, if any, he renders the community beyond filling the cases of museums and supplying material for the rotogravure sections of the Sunday papers." Lamentably, his prescription for the practitioners of archaeology has not been well filled in the past half century.

The professionalization of archaeology over the course of this century obviously has had innumerable benefits. In the most positive sense, the discipline has little resemblance to the archaeology of 100 years ago. With all the advances in method, theory, and culture historical knowledge, archaeologists are now in a position to make important and useful statements about cultural adaptation and development that should have broad intellectual appeal. Ironically, though, one aspect of the professionalization of the discipline, what can be termed the academization of archaeology, is working against such broad dissemination of current advances in archaeological understanding of cultures of the past. The key factor, I am convinced, is that since World War II, and especially in the past few decades as archaeology rapidly expanded as an academic subject in universities and colleges throughout this country, the competition for university jobs and the institutional pressures to publish in quantity, in general, and in peer review journals, in particular, has led in part to the academic devaluation of popular writing and communication with the general public. Such activities just don't count or, even worse, count against you.

In addition, I believe that it is possible that some archaeologists, in their desire to prove the rigor and scientific standing of the discipline within the academy and among their non-anthropological colleagues and university administrators, have rejected or denigrated popular writing because it might somehow taint archaeology with a nonscientific "softness" from which they would like to distance the field.

If popular writing is frowned upon by some academics, then popularization in other media, such as television, can be treated even more derisively by these scholars, and consequently too few archaeologists venture into these waters. Why should the best known "archaeologist" to the public be an unrepentant looter like Indiana Jones? Is he the role model we want for our profession? When I turn on the television to watch a show with archaeological content, why should I be more than likely to see Leonard Nimoy and the repeated use of the term *mysterious?* It should be professional archaeologists routinely helping to write and perhaps even hosting many of the archaeology shows on television, not just—at best—popular science writers and Hollywood actors. In sum, I strongly feel that we need more accessible writing, television shows, videos, CD-ROMs, and the like with archaeologists heavily involved in all these enterprises.

Forty years ago, Geoffrey Bibby, in his best-selling book *The Testimony of the Spade,* wrote in his foreword (1956:vii):

> It has long been customary to start any book that can be included under the comprehensive heading of "popular science" with an apology from the author to his fellow scientists for his desertion of the icy uplands of the research literature for the supposedly lower and supposedly lush fields of popular representation. This is not an apology, and it is not directed to archaeologists. In our day, when the research literature of one branch of knowledge has become all but incomprehensible to a researcher in another branch, and when the latest advances within any science can revolutionize—or end—our lives within a decade, the task of interpreting every science in language

that can be understood by workers in other fields is no longer—if it ever was—a slightly disreputable sideline, but a first-priority duty.

Bibby was making a point that is similar to one made years ago by C. P. Snow (1959) that scholars in different disciplines do not read or are unable to read each others' works, but should! However, I believe that Bibby's argument can easily be expanded to include the lay public, which should be able to readily find out what archaeologists are doing. If they are interested in the subject, and they have no accessible professionally written sources to turn to—like *The Testimony of the Spade*—is it any surprise that they turn to highly speculative, non-professional sources? Unfortunately, Bibby's wise call has gone relatively unheeded. Where are all the *Testimony of the Spades* of this generation, or even the *Gods, Graves, and Scholars* (Ceram 1951)?

But even encouraging communication between archaeologists and the general public is not sufficient, I believe, to dispel the lack of popular understanding about the modern archaeological enterprise and the potential importance of archaeological knowledge. With all the problems that the world faces today, the conflicts and ethnic strife, the innumerable threats to the environment, and the inadequacy of food supplies in the face of rising populations, there never has been a more propitious time for archaeology's new insights into the nature of human development and diversity in time and space to be appreciated by people in all walks of life. In order for better communication to have a useful impact, I believe that the profession has to heed Fritz and Plog's call and strive to be relevant. Moreover, we should pursue relevance in both the general and specific senses of the term. In its broadest sense, *relevance* is "to the purpose; pertinent," according to *The American College Dictionary,* while in its more narrow definition, relevance according to *The Oxford English Dictionary,* means "pertinency to important current issues."

All things being equal, archaeology could be justified on the basis of its inherent interest. But all things are rarely equal, and therefore archaeological activities and their relevance to today's world do need justification. To what is archaeology pertinent? In the general sense, archaeology's main claim to relevance is its revelation of the richness of human experience through the study and understanding of the development of past cultures over the globe. Among the goals of such study is to foster awareness and respect of other cultures and their achievements. Archaeology can make itself relevant—pertinent—by helping its audiences appreciate past cultures and their accomplishments.

Why should we actively seek to fulfill such a goal? I firmly believe in the lessons of history. By appreciating the nature of cultures both past and present, their uniqueness and their similarities, their development, and their adaptive successes and failures, we have a priceless opportunity to better grapple with the future than is possible without such knowledge. For example, as many of you are aware, I have long argued that new understandings of the decline of Classic Maya civilization in the southern Maya lowlands in the eighth century A.D. can shed important light on the ability of the ancient Maya to sustain a complex civilization in a tropical rain-forest environment for over a millennium and the reasons why this highly successful adapta-

tion ultimately failed (see Sabloff 1990). The potential implications for today's world are profound.

This form of striving for relevance is powerful and should have great appeal to the public, but it is not necessarily sufficient in terms of outreach goals for general audiences. Archaeology also needs to attempt to be relevant, where possible, in the narrower sense, too. As some of our colleagues in the Maya area, for instance, begin to take the new archaeological insights about sustainable agriculture and the potential for demographic growth and begin to directly apply them to modern situations, then archaeology clearly is becoming pertinent "to important current issues" (see, for example, Rice and Rice 1984).

In relation to this latter goal, I would argue that we need more "action archaeology," a term first coined by Maxine Klehidienst and Patty Jo Watson (1956) more than four decades ago (in the same year that *Testimony of the Spade* first appeared), but which I use in a more general way to convey the meaning of archaeology working *for* living communities, not just *in* them. One compelling example of such action archaeology is the field research of my colleague Clark Erickson, who has identified the remains of raised field agriculture in the Bolivian Amazon and has been studying the raised fields and other earthworks on the ground. He has been able to show that there was a complex culture in this area in Precolumbian times. Erickson also is working with local peasants in his field study area to show them how Precolumbian farmers successfully intensified their agricultural production and to indicate how the ancient raised field and irrigation techniques might be adapted to the modern situation so as to improve the current economic picture (see Erickson 1998). This is just one example of many that could be cited, including the close collaboration between archaeologists and Native American groups in, for example, the innovative research of my colleague Robert Preucel (1998) at Cochiti Pueblo, or in organizations like the Zuni Archaeological Project (see Anyon and Ferguson 1995), in the many pathbreaking modern garbage projects initiated by William L. Rathje and his colleagues (Rathje and Murphy 1992), in the thoughtful archaeological/environmental development project initiated by Anabel Ford and her collaborators at El Pilar in Belize and Guatemala (Ford 1998), or in cooperative projects between archaeologists and members of the local communities in locations such as Labrador or Belize that have been reported on by Stephen Loring and Marilyn Masson in recent Archeology Division sections of the *AAA Newsletter* (October and November 1996). However, we need many more examples of such work. They should be the rule, not the exception.

This kind of work in archaeology parallels the continued growth of action anthropology among our cultural colleagues. The potential for collaboration among archaeologists and cultural anthropologists in this regard, as advocated, for example, by Anne Pybum and Richard Wilk (1995), is quite strong. Explorations of the possibilities of such cooperation should be particularly appropriate and of great importance to the Archeology Division of the American Anthropological Association, which I know is interested in integrating archaeology within a general anthropological focus, and I urge the Division to pursue such an endeavor. Applied anthropology in its action form need not—and should not—be restricted to cultural anthropology.

It is depressing to note that the academic trend away from public communication appears to be increasing just as public interest in archaeology seems to be reaching new heights. Whatever the reasons for this growing interest, and clearly there are many potential reasons that could be and have been cited, including a turn to the past in times of current uncertainties, New Age ideological trends, or the growing accessibility of archaeological remains through travel, television, and video, there is no doubt that there is an audience out there that is thirsting for information about the past. But it does not appear that this interest is being well served, given the ratio of off-the-wall publications to responsible ones that one can find in any bookstore. I have written elsewhere (Sabloff 1982:7) that "Unfortunately, one of the prices we must pay for the privilege of sharing a free marketplace of ideas is the possibility that some writers will write unfounded speculation, some publishers will publish them, some bookstores will sell them, and some media will sensationalize them. In this way, unfounded speculations become widely spread among the general population of interested readers." I went on to suggest that "Perhaps the best solution to this problem is to help readers to become aware of the standards of scientific research so that scientific approaches can be better appreciated and pseudoscientific approaches can be read critically" (p. 7).

In order for this solution to work, however, archaeologists need to compete effectively in this free market. Why must we always run into the most outrageous pseudo-archaeology books (what Stephen Williams [1991] has termed "fantastic archaeology") in such visible places as airport news shops? I simply refuse to believe that among the large pool of professional archaeological writing talent that there aren't some of our colleagues who can write books that can replace *Chariots of the Gods?* (Von Däniken 1970). If we abandon much of the field of popular writing to the fringe, we should not be surprised at all that the public often fails to appreciate the significance of what we do. So what? Why does it matter if many archaeologists don't value public communication and much of the public lacks an understanding of archaeology and what archaeologists do and accomplish? There are two principal answers to this question, I believe. First, I strongly feel that we have a moral responsibility to educate the public about what we do. Good science and public education not only are compatible but should go hand in hand. The overwhelming majority of us, whether in the academic, government or business world, receive at least some public support in our work. I believe that we have a responsibility to give back to the public that provides us with grants, or contracts, or jobs. We need to share with them our excitement in our work and our insights into how peoples of the past lived and how our understandings of the past can inform us about the present and future; and we need to share all this in ways that everyone from young schoolchildren to committed amateur archaeologists can understand and appreciate.

Moreover, the better the public understands and appreciates what we do, what we know, and how we come to know it, the better it can assess the uses and—unfortunately—the abuses of archaeology, especially in political contexts. In this age of exploding ethnic conflicts, a public that has been educated to understand the nature of archaeological research and is thus able to cast a critical eye on how archaeological findings are used in modern political arenas clearly is preferable to people who lack such understanding. On a global scale, the use of archaeological myths in some of the former Soviet republics by various ethnic groups to justify repression of others is just one example—unfortunately!—of many kinds of abuses of archaeological data that could be cited (see Kohl and Fawcett 1995).

Second, there are eminently practical reasons for emphasizing and valuing public communication. Namely—and obviously—it is in our enlightened self-interest! As governmental, academic, and corporate budgets grow tighter and tighter, we are increasingly vying with innumerable groups and people, many with very compelling causes and needs, for extremely competitive dollars. If we don't make our case to the public about the significance of our work, then, in Fritz and Plog's (1970) words, we will surely find our public increasingly capable of getting along without us. How many of our representatives in Congress or in state legislatures really understand what archaeologists do and what they can contribute to the modern world? How many of them get letters from constituents extolling the virtues of the archaeological enterprise and urging them to support archaeological research both financially and through legislation? Unless we educate and work with our many publics, we are certain to find our sources of support, many of which have been taken for granted in recent years, rapidly drying up.

Let's turn our attention from the general problem to potential solutions. How can American archaeologists rectify the situation just described and particularly promote more popular writing by professional scholars? One answer is deceptively simple: we need to change our value system and our reward system within the academy. Just as Margaret Mead and other great anthropological popularizers have been sneered at by some cultural anthropologists, so colleagues like Brian Fagan, who has done so much to reach out to general readers (see, for example, Fagan 1977, 1984, 1987, 1991, and 1995, among many others), are often subject to similar snide comments. We need to celebrate those who successfully communicate with the public, not revile them. Ideally, we should have our leading scholars writing for the public, not only for their colleagues. Some might argue that popular writing would be a waste of their time. To the contrary, I would maintain that such writing is part of our collective academic responsibility. Who better to explain what is on the cutting edge of archaeological research than the field's leading practitioners? Moreover, we need to develop a significant number of our own Stephen Jay Goulds or Stephen Hawkings, not just a few.

Why do some scholars look down at archaeologists who are perceived as popularizers? There are probably a host of reasons, but one of them definitely is pure jealousy. Some archaeologists are jealous of their colleagues who successfully write popular books and articles because of the latter's writing skills. They also are jealous, I believe, of the visibility that popular communication brings those who enter this arena, and they are jealous of the monetary rewards that sometimes accompany popular success. But since such jealousy is not socially acceptable, it tends to be displaced into negative comments on the scholarly abilities of the popularizers.

Not only do we need to change our value system so that public communication is perceived in a positive light, more particularly, we need to change the academic evaluation and reward system for archaeologists (and others!), so that it gives suitable recognition to popular writing and public outreach. Clearly, these activities also can be counted as public service. But they further merit scholarly recognition. I also would include the curation of museum exhibits in this regard, especially ones that include catalogs or CD-ROMs that are accessible to broad audiences. Effective writing for general audiences requires excellent control of the appropriate theoretical, methodological, and substantive literature and the ability to comprehend and articulate clearly the core issues of the archaeology of an area, time period, or problem, and therefore should be subject to the same kind of qualitative academic assessment that ideally goes on today in any academic tenure, promotion, or hiring procedure. However, such a development would go against the current pernicious trend that features such aspects as counting peer-review articles and use of citation indices. I strongly believe that the growing reliance on numbers of peer-review articles and the denigration of both popular and non-peer-review writing needs to be reversed. As in so many areas of life, quantity is being substituted for quality, while the measurement of quality becomes increasingly problematic. As the former editor of a major peer-review journal, as well as the editor of many multi-author volumes, I can assure you that the quality of chapters in edited books—often discounted as non-peer-reviewed writings—can be and frequently are of as high or higher quality than peer-reviewed articles. However, many faculty and administrators appear to be looking for formulae that shortchange the qualitative evaluation of research and writing, no matter what form of publication. The whole academic system of evaluation for hiring, tenure, promotion, and salary raises needs to be rethought. In my opinion it is headed in the wrong direction, and the growing trend away from qualitative evaluation is especially worrisome.

As a call to action, in order to encourage popular writing among academics, particularly those with tenure, all of us need to lobby university administrators, department chairs, and colleagues about the value and importance of written communication with audiences beyond the academy. Academics should be evaluated on their popular as well as their purely academic writings. Clearly, what is needed is a balance between original research and popular communication. In sum, evaluations should be qualitative, not quantitative.

Concerning non-academic archaeologists, we need to raise the perceived value of general publications and public outreach in the cultural resource management arm of the profession and work toward having public reporting be routinely included in scopes of work of as many cultural resource management contracts as is feasible. In some areas, fortunately, such as in the National Parks Service or in some Colonial archaeological settings, such outreach already is valued. Positive examples like this need to be professionally publicized and supported.

I would be remiss if I didn't point out that there clearly is a huge irony here. The academic world obviously is becoming increasingly market-oriented with various institutions vying for perceived "stars" in their fields with escalating offers of high salaries, less teaching, better labs, more research funds, and so on, and most academics not only are caught up in this system but have bought into it. At the same time, those scholars who are most successful in the larger marketplace of popular ideas and the popular media and who make dollars by selling to popular audiences are frequently discounted and denigrated by the self-perceived "true scholars," who often have totally bought into the broad academic market economy and are busy playing this narrower market game!

To conclude, I hope that I have been able to stimulate some thought about what might appear to be a very simple problem but which in reality is quite complicated. In order to fulfill what I believe is one of archaeology's major missions, that of public education, we need to make some significant changes in our professional modes of operation. The Archeology Division can form a common cause with many other units of the American Anthropological Association to realize this goal. This is a four-field problem with four-field solutions! The Society for American Archaeology has just endorsed public education and outreach as one of the eight principles of archaeological ethics. This Division can also play a key role in such endeavors by working within the American Anthropological Association and using its influence to help change the emphases of our professional lives and the reward systems within which we work. To reiterate, I strongly believe that we must change our professional value system so that public outreach in all forms, but especially popular writing, is viewed and supported in highly positive terms. We need to make this change. There are signs that the pendulum of general communication in the field of American archaeology is starting to swing in a positive direction. Let us all work to push it much further!

I am sure that we all have heard the clarion call to the American public—"will you help me to build a bridge the twenty-first century"—many, many times. It is my belief that, unfortunately, the bridge to the twenty-first century will be a shaky one indeed for archaeology and anthropology—perhaps even the proverbial bridge to nowhere!— unless we tackle the communication problem with the same energy and vigor with which we routinely debate the contentious issues of contemporary archaeological theory that past lecturers to this group have delineated for you. The fruits of our research and analyses have great potential relevance for the public at large. The huge, exciting strides in understanding the past that anthropological archaeology has made in recent years need to be brought to the public's attention both for our sakes and theirs.

NOTES

Acknowledgments. I am honored that I was asked to deliver the Archeology Division's 1996 Distinguished Lecture and grateful to the Archeology Division for its kind invitation to deliver this important talk. I wish to acknowledge the growing list of colleagues, only a few of which have been cited above, who have accepted the crucial challenge of writing for general public. May your numbers multiply! I also wish thank Paula L. W. Sabloff, Joyce Marcus, and the reviewer for this journal for their many insightful and helpful comments and suggestions, only some of which I have been able to take advantage of, that have certainly improved the quality of paper.

REFERENCES CITED

Anyon, Roger, and T. J. Ferguson 1995 Cultural Resources Management at the Pueblo of Zuni, N.M., U.S.A. Antiquity 69 (266):913–930.

Bibby, Geoffrey 1956 The Testimony of the Spade. New York: Alfred A. Knopf.

Ceram, C. W. 1951 Gods, Graves, and Scholars: The Story of Archaeology. New York: Alfred A. Knopf.

Erickson, Clark L. 1998 Applied Archaeology and Rural Development: Archaeology's Potential Contribution to the Future. *In* Crossing Currents: Continuity and Change in Latin America. M. Whiteford and S. Whiteford, eds. Pp. 34–45. Upper Saddle, NJ: Prentice-Hall.

Fagan, Brian M. 1977 Elusive Treasure: The Story of Early Archaeologists in the Americas. New York: Scribners. 1984 The Aztecs. New York: W. H. Freeman. 1987 The Great Journey: The Peopling of Ancient America. London: Thames and Hudson. 1991 Kingdoms of Gold, Kingdoms of Jade: The Americas before Columbus. London: Thames and Hudson. 1995 Time Detectives: How Archaeologists Use Technology to Recapture the Past. New York: Simon and Schuster.

Ford, Anabel, ed. 1998 The Future of El Pilar: The Integrated Research and Development Plan for the El Pilar Archaeological Reserve for Flora and Fauna, Belize-Guatemala. Department of State Publication 10507, Bureau of Oceans. and International Environmental and Scientific Affairs, Washington, DC.

Ford, Richard I. 1973 Archeology Serving Humanity. *In* Research and Theory in Current Archeology. Charles L. Redman, ed. Pp. 83–94. New York: John Wiley.

Fritz, John M. 1973 Relevance, Archeology, and Subsistence Theory. *In* Research and Theory in Current Archaeology. Charles L. Redman, ed. Pp. 59–82. New York: John Wiley.

Fritz, John M., and Fred Plog 1970 The Nature of Archaeological Explanation. American Antiquity 35:405–12.

Hodder, Ian, Michael Shanks, Alexandra Alexandri, Victor Buchli, John Carman, Jonathan Last, and Gavin Lucas, eds. 1995 Interpreting Archaeology: Finding Meaning in the Past. New York: Routledge.

Kidder, Alfred V. 1924 An Introduction to the Study of Southwestern Archaeology, with a Preliminary Account of the Excavations at Pecos. Papers of the Southwestern Expedition, No. 1. Published for the Department of Archaeology, Phillips Academy, Andover. New Haven, CT: Yale University Press. 1940 Looking Backward. Proceedings of the American Philosophical Society 83:527–537.

Kleindienst, Maxine R., and Patty Jo Watson 1956 'Action Archaeology': The Archaeological Inventory of a Living Community. Anthropology Tomorrow 5:75–78.

Kohl, Philip L., and Clare Fawcett, eds. 1995 Nationalism, Politics, and the Practice of Archaeology. Cambridge: Cambridge University Press.

Kolata, Alan L. 1993 The Tiwanaku: Portrait of an Andean Civilization. Cambridge: Blackwell.

Marcus, Joyce, and Kent V. Flannery 1996 Zapotec Civilization: How Urban Society Evolved in Mexico's Oaxaca Valley. New York: Thames and Hudson.

Plog, Stephen 1997 Ancient Peoples of the American Southwest. London: Thames and Hudson.

Preucel, Robert W. 1998 The Kotyiti Research Project: Report of the 1996 Field Season. Report submitted to the Pueblo of Cochiti and the USDA Forest Service, Santa Fe National Forest, Santa Fe, NM.

Pyburn, Anne, and Richard Wilk 1995 Responsible Archaeology Is Applied Anthropology. *In* Ethics in American Archaeology: Challenges for the 1990s. Mark J. Lynott and Alison Wylie, eds. Pp. 71–76. Washington, DC: Society for American Archaeology.

Rathje, William L., and Cullen Murphy 1992 Rubbish!: The Archaeology of Garbage. New York: HarperCollins.

Rice, Don S., and Prudence M. Rice 1984 Lessons from the Maya. Latin American Research Review 19(3):7–34.

Sabloff, Jeremy A. 1982 Introduction. *In* Archaeology: Myth and Reality. Jeremy A. Sabloff, ed. Pp. 1–26. Readings from Scientific American. San Francisco: W. H. Freeman. 1985 American Antiquity's First Fifty Years: An Introductory Comment. American Antiquity 50:228–236. 1990: The New Archaeology and the Ancient Maya. A Scientific American Library Book. New York: W. H. Freeman.

Schele, Linda, and David A. Freidel 1990 A Forest of Kings: The Untold Story of the Ancient Maya. New York: Morrow.

Snow, C. P. 1959 The Two Cultures and the Scientific Revolution. Cambridge: Cambridge University Press.

Spector, Janet 1993 What This Awl Means: Feminist Archaeology at a Wahpeton Dakota Village. St. Paul: Minnesota Historical Society Press.

Von Däniken, Erich 1970 Chariots of the Gods? New York: G. P. Putnam's Sons.

Willey, Gordon R. 1967 Alfred Vincent Kidder, 1885–1963. *In* Biographical Memoirs, vol. 39. Published for the National Academy of Sciences. New York: Columbia University Press.

Williams, Stephen 1991 Fantastic Archaeology: The Wild Side of North American Prehistory. Philadelphia: University of Pennsylvania Press.

Woodbury, Richard B. 1973 Alfred V. Kidder. New York Columbia University Press.

From *American Anthropologist*, 100:4, December 1998, pp. 869-875. © 1998 by the American Anthropological Association. Reproduced by permission. Not for further reproduction.

Annals of Archaeology

All the King's Sons

The biggest archeological find in Egypt since King Tut's tomb is also the most unusual: it may explain the fate of most of Ramesses II's fifty-two sons, New Kingdom funerary practices, and pharaonic sex. What does it feel like to be the first person to enter such a place in three thousand years?

By Douglas Preston

On February 2, 1995, at ten in the morning, the archeologist Kent R. Weeks found himself a hundred feet inside a mountain in Egypt's Valley of the Kings, on his belly in the dust of a tomb. He was crawling toward a long-buried doorway that no one had entered for at least thirty-one hundred years. There were two people with him, a graduate student and an Egyptian workman; among them they had one flashlight.

To get through the doorway, Weeks had to remove his hard hat and force his large frame under the lintel with his toes and fingers. He expected to enter a small, plain room marking the end of the tomb. Instead, he found himself in a vast corridor, half full of debris, with doorways lining either side and marching off into the darkness. "When I looked around with the flashlight," Weeks recalled later, "we realized that the corridor was tremendous. I didn't know *what* to think." The air was dead, with a temperature in excess of a hundred degrees and a humidity of one hundred per cent. Weeks, whose glasses had immediately steamed up, was finding it hard to breathe. With every movement, clouds of powder arose, and turned into mud on the skin.

The three people explored the corridor, stooping, and sometimes crawling over piles of rock that had fallen from the ceiling. Weeks counted twenty doorways lining the hundred-foot hallway,

some opening into whole suites of rooms with vaulted ceilings carved out of the solid rock of the mountain. At the corridor's end, the feeble flashlight beam revealed a statue of Osiris, the god of resurrection: he was wearing a crown and holding crossed flails and sceptres; his body was bound like that of a mummy. In front of Osiris, the corridor came to a T, branching into two transverse passageways, each of them eighty feet long and ending in what looked like a descending staircase blocked with debris. Weeks counted thirty-two additional rooms off those two corridors.

The tomb was of an entirely new type, never seen by archeologists before. "The architecture didn't fit any known pattern," Weeks told me. "And it was so *big*. I just couldn't make sense of it." The largest pharaonic tombs in the Valley contain ten or fifteen rooms at most. This one had at least sixty-seven—the total making it not only the biggest tomb in the Valley but possibly the biggest in all Egypt. Most tombs in the Valley of the Kings follow a standard architectural plan—a series of consecutive chambers and corridors like a string of boxcars shot at an angle into the bedrock, and ending with the burial vault. This tomb, with its T shape, had a warren of side chambers, suites, and descending passageways. Weeks knew from earlier excavations that the tomb was the resting place for at least four sons of Ramesses II, the pha-

raoh also known as Ramesses the Great—and, traditionally, as simply Pharaoh in the Book of Exodus. Because of the tomb's size and complexity, Weeks had to consider the possibility that it was a catacomb for as many as fifty of Ramesses' fifty-two sons—the first example of a royal family mausoleum in ancient Egypt.

Weeks had discovered the tomb's entrance eight years earlier, after the Egyptian government announced plans to widen the entrance to the Valley to create a bus turnaround at the end of an asphalt road. From reading old maps and reports, he had recalled that the entrance to a lost tomb lay in the area that was to be paved over. Napoleon's expedition to Egypt had noted a tomb there, and a rather feckless Englishman named James Burton had crawled partway inside it in 1825. A few years later, the archeologist Sir John Gardner Wilkinson had given it the designation KV5, for Kings' Valley Tomb No. 5, when he numbered eighteen tombs there. Howard Carter—the archeologist who discovered King Tutankhamun's tomb in 1922, two hundred feet farther on—dug two feet in, decided that KV5's entrance looked unimportant, and used it as a dumping ground for debris from his other excavations, thus burying it under ten feet of stone and dirt. The location of the tomb's entrance was quickly forgotten.

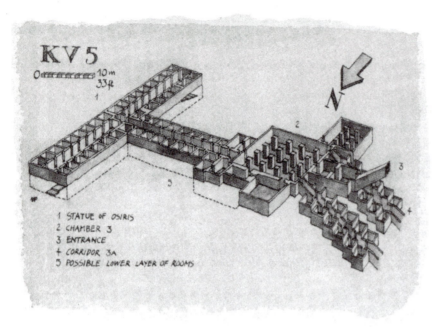

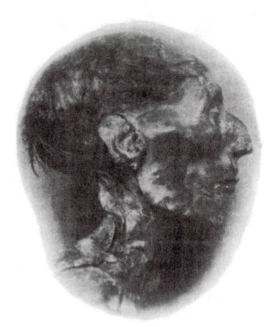

A floor plan of KV5, which may be the largest tomb in Egypt and the only royal mausoleum. Ramesses II, the master builder of Thebes, now rests in the Cairo Museum

©Matteo Pericoli

Egyptian Museum of Antiquities, Cairo

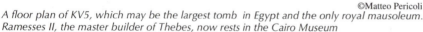

It took about ten days of channelling through Carter's heaps of debris for Weeks and his men to find the ancient doorway of KV5, and it proved to be directly across the path from the tomb of Ramesses the Great. The entrance lay at the edge of the asphalt road, about ten feet below grade and behind the rickety booths of T-shirt venders and fake-scarab-beetle sellers.

Plans for the bus turnaround were cancelled, and, over a period of seven years, Weeks and his workmen cleared half of the first two chambers and briefly explored a third one. The tomb was packed from floor to ceiling with dirt and rocks that had been washed in by flash floods. He uncovered finely carved reliefs on the walls, which showed Ramesses presenting various sons to the gods, with their names and titles recorded in hieroglyphics. When he reached floor level, he found thousands of objects: pieces of faience jewelry, fragments of furniture, a wooden fist from a coffin, human and animal bones, mummified body parts, chunks of sarcophagi, and fragments of the canopic jars used to hold the mummified organs of the deceased—all detritus left by ancient tomb robbers.

The third chamber was anything but modest. It was about sixty feet square, one of the largest rooms in the Valley, and was supported by sixteen massive stone pillars arranged in four rows. Debris filled the room to within about two feet of the ceiling, allowing just enough space for Weeks to wriggle around. At the back of the chamber, in the axis of the tomb, Weeks noticed an almost buried doorway. Still believing that the tomb was like others in the Valley, he assumed that the doorway merely led to a small, dead-end annex, so he didn't bother with it for several years—not until last February, when he decided to have a look.

Immediately after the discovery, Weeks went back to a four-dollar-a-night pension he shared with his wife, Susan, in the mud village of Gezira Bairat, showered off the tomb dust, and took a motorboat across the Nile to the small city of Luxor. He faxed a short message to Cairo, three hundred miles downriver. It was directed to his major financial supporter, Bruce Ludwig, who was attending a board meeting at the American University in Cairo, where Weeks is a professor. It read, simply, "Have made wonderful discovery in Valley of the Kings. Await your arrival."

Ludwig instantly recognized the significance of the fax and the inside joke it represented: it was a close paraphrase of the telegram that Howard Carter had sent to the Earl of Carnarvon, his financial supporter, when he discovered Tutankhamun's tomb. Ludwig booked a flight to Luxor.

"That night, the enormousness of the discovery began to sink in," Weeks recalled. At about two o'clock in the morning, he turned to his wife and said, "Susan, I think our lives have changed forever."

The discovery was announced jointly by Egypt's Supreme Council of Antiquities, which oversees all archeological work in the country, and the American University in Cairo, under whose aegis Weeks was working. It became the biggest archeological story of the decade, making the front page of the *Times* and the cover of *Time*. Television reporters descended on the site. Weeks had to shut down the tomb to make the talk-show circuit. The London newspapers had a field day: the *Daily Mail* headlined its story "PHARAOH'S 50 SONS IN MUMMY OF ALL TOMBS," and one tabloid informed its readers that texts in the tomb gave a date for the Second Coming and the end of the world, and also revealed cures for AIDS and cancer.

The media also wondered whether the tomb would prove that Ramesses II was indeed the pharaoh referred to in Exodus. The speculation centered on Amun-her-khopshef, Ramesses' firstborn son, whose name is prominent on KV5's wall. According to the Bible, in order to force Egypt to free the Hebrews from bondage the Lord visited a number of disasters on the land, including the killing of all firstborn Egyptians from the pharaoh's son on down. Some scholars believe that if Amun-her-khopshef's remains are found it may be possible to show at what age and how he died.

Book publishers and Hollywood producers showed great interest in Weeks's story. He didn't respond at first, dismissing inquiries with a wave of the hand. "It's all *kalam fadi*," he said, using the Arabic phrase for empty talk. Eventually, however, so many offers poured in that he engaged an agent at William Morris to handle them; a book proposal will be submitted to publishers later this month.

In the fall, Weeks and his crew decided to impose a partial media blackout on the excavation site—the only way they could get any work done, they felt—but they agreed to let me accompany them near the end of the digging season. Just before I arrived, in mid-November, two mysterious descending corridors, with dozens of new chambers, unexpectedly came to light, and I had the good fortune to be the only journalist to see them.

The Valley of the Kings was the burial ground for the pharaohs of the New Kingdom, the last glorious period of Egyptian history. It began around 1550 B.C., when the Egyptians expelled the foreign Hyksos rulers from Lower Egypt and reëstablished a vast empire, stretching across the Middle East to Syria. It lasted half a millennium. Sixty years before Ramesses, the pharaoh Akhenaten overthrew much of the Egyptian religion and decreed that thenceforth Egyptians should worship only one god—Light, whose visible symbol was Aten, the disk of the sun. Akhenaten's

revolution came to a halt at his death. Ramesses represented the culmination of the return to tradition. He was an exceedingly conservative man, who saw himself as the guardian of the ancient customs, and he was particularly zealous in erasing the heretic pharaoh's name from his temples and stelae, a task begun by his father, Seti I. Because Ramesses disliked innovation, his monuments were notable not for their architectural brilliance but for their monstrous size. The New Kingdom began a slow decline following his rule, and finally sputtered to an end with Ramesses XI, the last pharaoh buried in the Valley of the Kings.

The discovery of KV5 will eventually open for us a marvellous window on this period. We know almost nothing about the offspring of the New Kingdom pharaohs or what roles they played. After each eldest prince ascended the throne, the younger sons disappeared so abruptly from the record that it was once thought they were routinely executed. The burial chambers' hieroglyphics, if they still survive, may give us an invaluable account of each son's life and accomplishments. There is a remote possibility—it was suggested to me by the secretary-general of the Supreme Council of Antiquities, Professor Abdel-Halim Nur el-Din, who is an authority on women in ancient Egypt—that Ramesses' daughters might be buried in KV5 as well. (Weeks thinks the possibility highly unlikely.) Before Weeks is done, he will probably find sarcophagi, pieces of funerary offerings, identifiable pieces of mummies, and many items with hieroglyphics on them. The tomb will add a new chapter to our understanding of Egyptian funerary traditions. And there is always a possibility of finding an intact chamber packed with treasure.

Ramesses the Great's reign lasted an unprecedented sixty-seven years, from 1279 to 1213 B.C. He covered the Nile Valley from Nubia to the delta with magnificent temples, statuary, and stelae, which are some of the grandest monuments the world has ever seen. Among his projects were the enormous forecourt at Luxor Temple; the Ramesseum; the cliffside temples of Abu Simbel; the great Hall of Columns at Karnak; and the city of Pi-Ramesse. The two "vast and

trunkless legs of stone" with a "shattered visage" in Shelley's poem "Ozymandias" were those of Ramesses—fragments of the largest statue in pharaonic history. Ramesses outlived twelve of his heirs, dying in his early nineties. The thirteenth crown prince, Merneptah, became pharaoh only in his sixties.

By the time Ramesses ascended the throne, at twenty-five, he had fathered perhaps ten sons and as many daughters. His father had started him out with a harem while he was still a teenager, and he had two principal wives, Nefertari and Istnofret. He later added several Hittite princesses to his harem, and probably his sister and two daughters. It is still debated whether the incestuous marriage of the pharaohs were merely ceremonial or actually consummated. If identifiable remains of Ramesses' sons are found in KV5, it is conceivable that DNA testing might resolve this vexing question.

In most pharaonic monuments we find little about wives and children, but Ramesses showed an unusual affection for his family, extolling the accomplishments of his sons and listing their names on numerous temple walls. All over Egypt, he commissioned statues of Nefertari (not to be confused with the more famous Nefertiti, who was Akhenaten's wife), "for whose sake the very sun does shine." When she died, in Year 24 of his reign, Ramesses interred her in the most beautiful tomb yet discovered in the Valley of the Queens, just south of the Valley of the Kings. The tomb survived intact, and its incised and painted walls are nearly as fresh as the day they were fashioned. The rendering of Nefertari's face and figure perhaps speaks most eloquently of Ramesses' love for her. She is shown making her afterlife journey dressed in a diaphanous linen gown, with her slender figure emerging beneath the gossamer fabric. Her face was painted using the technique of chiaroscuro—perhaps the first known example in the history of art of a human face being treated as a three-dimensional volume. The Getty Conservation Institute recently spent millions restoring the tomb. The Getty recommended that access to the tomb be restricted, in order to preserve it, but the Egyptian government has opened it to tourists, at thirty-five dollars a head.

The design of royal tombs was so fixed by tradition that they had no architect, at least as we use that term today. The tombs were laid out and chiselled from ceiling to floor, resulting in ceiling dimensions that are precise and floor dimensions that can vary considerably. All the rooms and corridors in a typical royal tomb had names, many of which we still do not fully understand: the First God's Passage, Hall of Hindering, Sanctuaries in Which the Gods Repose. The burial chamber was often called the House of Gold. Some tombs had a Hall of Truth, whose murals showed the pharaoh's heart being weighed in judgment by Osiris, with the loathsome god Ammut squatting nearby, waiting to devour it if it was found wanting. Many of the reliefs were so formulaic that they were probably taken from copybooks. Yet even within this rigid tradition breathtaking flights of creativity and artistic expression can be found.

Most of the tombs in the Valley were never finished: they took decades to cut, and the plans usually called for something more elaborate than the pharaoh could achieve during his rule. As a result, the burial of the pharaoh was often a panicky, ad-hoc affair, with various rooms in the tomb being adapted for other purposes, and decorations and texts painted in haste or omitted completely. (Some of the most beautiful inscriptions were those painted swiftly; they have a spontaneity and freshness of line rivalling Japanese calligraphy.)

From the time of Ramesses II on, the tombs were not hidden: their great doorways, which were made of wood, could be opened. It is likely that the front rooms of many tombs were regularly visited by priests to make offerings. This may have been particularly true of KV5, where the many side chambers perhaps served such a purpose. The burial chambers containing treasure, however, were always sealed.

Despite all the monuments and inscriptions that Ramesses left us, it is still difficult to bridge the gap of thirty-one hundred years and see Ramesses as a person. One thing we do know: the standard image of the pharaoh, embodied in

Shelley's "frown, and wrinkled lip, and sneer of cold command," is a misconception. One of the finest works from Ramesses' reign is a statue of the young king now in the Museo Egizio, in Turin. The expression on his face is at once compassionate and other-worldly, not unlike that of a Giotto Madonna; his head is slightly bowed, as if to acknowledge his role as both leader and servant. This is not the face of a tyrant-pharaoh who press-ganged his people into building monuments to his greater glory. Rather, it is the portrait of a ruler who had his subjects' interests at heart, and this is precisely what the archeological and historical records suggest about Ramesses. Most of the Egyptians who labored on the pharaoh's monuments did so proudly and were, by and large, well compensated. There is a lovely stela on which Ramesses boasts about how much he has given his workers, "so that they work for me with their full hearts." Dorothea Arnold, the head curator of the Egyptian Department at the Metropolitan Museum, told me, "The pharaoh was *believed* in. As to whether he was beloved, that is beside the point: he was *necessary*. He was life itself. He represented everything good. Without him there would be nothing."

Final proof of the essential humanity of the pharaonic system is that it survived for more than three thousand years. (When Ramesses ascended the throne, the pyramids at Giza were already thirteen hundred years old.) Egypt produced one of the most stable cultural and religious traditions the world has ever seen.

Very little lives in the Valley of the Kings now. It is a wilderness of stone and light—a silent, roofless sepulchre. Rainfall averages a quarter inch per year, and one of the hottest natural air temperatures on earth was recorded in the surrounding mountains. And yet the Valley is a surprisingly intimate place. Most of the tombs lie within a mere forty acres, and the screen of cliffs gives the area a feeling of privacy. Dusty paths and sun-bleached, misspelled signs add a pleasant, ramshackle air.

The Valley lies on the outskirts of the ancient city of Thebes, now in ruins. In a six-mile stretch of riverbank around the city, there are as many temples, palaces, and monuments as anywhere else on earth, and the hills are so pockmarked with the yawning pits and doorways of ancient tombs that they resemble a First World War battlefield. It is dangerous to walk or ride anywhere alone. Howard Carter discovered an important tomb when the horse he was riding broke through and fell into it. Recently, a Canadian woman fell into a tomb while hiking and fractured her leg; no one could hear her screams, and she spent the days leading up to her death writing postcards. One archeologist had to clear a tomb that contained a dead cow and twenty-one dead dogs that had gone in to eat it.

Almost all the tombs lying open have been pillaged. A papyrus now in Italy records the trial of someone who robbed KV5 itself in 1150 B.C. The robber confessed under torture to plundering the tomb of Ramesses the Great and then going "across the path" to rob the tomb of his sons. Ancient plunderers often vandalized the tombs they robbed, possibly in an attempt to destroy the magic that supposedly protected them. They smashed everything, levered open sarcophagi, ripped apart mummies to get at the jewelry hidden in the wrappings, and sometimes threw objects against the walls with such force that they left dents and smudges of pure gold.

Nobody is sure why this particular valley, three hundred miles up the Nile from the pyramids, was chosen as the final resting place of the New Kingdom pharaohs. Egyptologists theorize that the sacred pyramidal shape of el-Qurn, the mountain at the head of the Valley of the Kings, may have been one factor. Another was clearly security: the Valley is essentially a small box canyon carved out of the barren heart of a desert mountain range; it has only one entrance, through a narrow gorge, and the surrounding cliffs echo and magnify any sounds of human activity, such as the tapping of a robber's pick on stone.

Contrary to popular belief, the tombs in the Valley are not marked with curses. King Tut's curse was invented by Arthur Weigall, an Egyptologist and journalist at the *Daily Mail,* who was furious that Carnarvon had given the London *Times* the exclusive on the discovery. Royal tombs did not need curses to protect them. Priests guarded the Valley night and day, and thieves knew exactly what awaited them if they were caught: no curse could compete with the fear of being impaled alive. "There are a few curses on some private tombs and in some legal documents," James Allen, an Egyptologist with the Metropolitan Museum, told me. "The most extreme I know of is on a legal document of the Ramesside Period. It reads, 'As for the one who will violate it, he shall be seized for Amun-Ra. He shall be for the flame of Sekhmet. He is an enemy of Osiris, lord of Abydos, and so is his son, for ever and ever. May donkeys fuck him, may donkeys fuck his wife, may his wife fuck his son.'"

Some scholars today, looking back over the past two hundred years of archeological activity, think a curse might have been a good idea: most of the archeology done in the Valley has been indistinguishable from looting. Until the nineteen-sixties, those who had concessions to excavate there were allowed to keep a percentage of the spoils as "payment" for their work. In the fever of the treasure hunt, tombs were emptied without anyone bothering to photograph the objects found or to record their positions in situ, or even to note which tomb they came from. Items that had no market value were trashed. Wilkinson, the man who gave the tombs their numbers, burned three-thousand-year-old wooden coffins and artifacts to heat his house. Murals and reliefs were chopped out of walls. At dinner parties, the American lawyer Theodore M. Davis, who financed many digs in the Valley, used to tear up necklaces woven of ancient flowers and fabric to show how strong they were after three thousand years in a tomb. Pyramids were blasted open with explosives, and one tomb door was bashed in with a battering ram. Even Carter never published a proper scientific report on Tut's tomb. It is only in the last twenty-five years that real archeology has come to Egypt, and KV5 will be one of the first tombs in the Valley of the Kings to be entirely excavated and documented according to proper archeological techniques.

Fortunately, other great archeological projects remain to be carried out with the new techniques. The Theban Necropolis is believed to contain between four thousand and five thousand tombs, of which only four hundred have been given numbers. More than half of the royal tombs in the Valley of the Kings have not been fully excavated, and of these only five have been properly documented. There are mysterious blocked passageways, hollow floors, chambers packed with debris, and caved-in rooms. King Tut's was by no means the last undiscovered pharaonic tomb in Egypt. In the New Kingdom alone, the tombs of Amosis, Amenhotep I, Tuthmosis II, and Ramesses VIII have never been identified. The site of the burial ground for the pharaohs of the entire Twenty-first Dynasty is unknown. And the richness and size of KV5 offer the tantalizing suggestion that other princely tombs of its kind are lying undiscovered beneath the Egyptian sands; Ramesses would surely not have been the only pharaoh to bury his sons in such style.

Work at KV5 in the fall season proceeds from six-thirty in the morning until one-thirty in the afternoon. Every day, to get to KV5 from my hotel in Luxor, I cross the Nile on the public ferry, riding with a great mass of fellaheen—men carrying goats slung around their necks, children lugging sacks of eggplants, old men squatting in their djellabas and smoking cigarettes or eating *leb* nuts— while the ancient diesel boat wheezes and blubs across the river. I am usually on the river in time to catch the sun rising over the shattered columns of Luxor Temple, along the riverbank. The Nile is still magical—crowded with feluccas, lined with date palms, and bearing on its current many clumps of blooming water hyacinths.

The ferry empties its crowds into a chaos of taxis, camels, donkeys, children begging for baksheesh, and hopeful guides greeting every tourist with a hearty "Welcome to Egypt!" In contrast to the grand hotels and boulevards of Luxor, the west bank consists of clusters of mud villages scattered among impossibly green fields of cane and clover, where the air is heavy with smoke and the droning prayers of the muezzin. Disembarkation is followed by a harrowing high-speed taxi ride to the Valley, the driver weaving past donkey carts and herds of goats, his sweaty fist pounding the horn.

On the first day of my visit, I find Kent Weeks sitting in a green canvas tent at the entrance to KV5 and trying to fit together pieces of a human skull. It is a cool Saturday morning in November. From the outside, KV5 looks like all the other tombs— a mere doorway in a hillside. Workmen in a bucket brigade are passing baskets filled with dirt out of the tomb's entrance and dumping them in a nearby pile, on which two men are squatting and sifting through the debris with small gardening tools. "Hmm," Weeks says, still fiddling with the skull. "I had this together a moment ago. You'll have to wait for our expert. He can put it together just like that." He snaps his fingers.

"Whose skull is it?"

"One of Ramesses' sons, I hope. The brown staining on it—here—shows that it might have come from a mummified body. We'll eventually do DNA comparisons with Ramesses and other members of his family."

Relaxing in the tent, Weeks does not cut the dapper, pugnacious figure of a Howard Carter, nor does he resemble the sickly, elegant Lord Carnarvon in waistcoat and watch chain. But because he is the first person to have made a major discovery in the Valley of the Kings since Carter, he is surely in their class. At fifty-four, he is handsome and fit, his ruddy face peering at the world through thick square glasses from underneath a Tilley hat. His once crisp shirt and khakis look like hell after an hour in the tomb's stifling atmosphere, and his Timberland shoes have reached a state of indescribable lividity from tomb dust.

Weeks has the smug air of a man who is doing the most interesting thing he could possibly do in life. He launches into his subject with such enthusiasm that one's first impulse is to flee. But as he settles back in his rickety chair with the skull in one hand and a glass of *yansoon* tea in the other, and yarns on about lost tombs, crazy Egyptologists, graver-obbers, jackal-headed gods, mummies, secret passageways, and the mysteries of the Underworld, you begin to succumb. His conversation is laced with obscene sallies delivered with a schoolboy's relish, and you can tell he has not been to any gender-sensitivity training seminars. He can be disconcertingly blunt. He characterized one archeologist as "ineffectual, ridiculously inept, and a wonderful source of comic relief," another as "a raving psychopath," and a third as "a dork, totally off the wall." When I asked if KV5 would prove that Ramesses was the Biblical Pharaoh, he responded with irritation: "I can almost guarantee you that we will *not* find anything in KV5 bearing on the Exodus question. All the speculation in the press assumed there *was* an exodus and that it was described accurately in the Bible. I don't believe it. There may have been Israelites in Egypt, but I sincerely doubt Exodus is an exact account of what occurred. At least I *hope* it wasn't—with the Lord striking down the firstborn of Egypt and turning the rivers to blood."

His is a rarefied profession: there are only about four hundred Egyptologists in the world, and only a fraction of them are archeologists. (Most are art historians and philologists.) Egyptology is a difficult profession to break into; in a good year, there might be two job openings in the United States. It is the kind of field where the untimely death of a tenured figure sets the photocopying machines running all night.

"From the age of eight, I had no doubt: I wanted to be an Egyptologist," Weeks told me. His parents—one a policeman, the other a medical librarian—did not try to steer him into a sensible profession, and a string of teachers encouraged his interest. When Weeks was in high school, in Longview, Washington, he met the Egyptologist Ahmed Fakhry in Seattle, and Fakhry was so charmed by the young man that he invited him to lunch and mapped out his college career.

In 1963, Weeks's senior year at the University of Washington, one of the most important events in the history of Egyptology took place. Because of the construction of the High Dam at Aswan,

the rising waters of the Nile began to flood Nubia; they would soon inundate countless archeological sites, including the incomparable temples of Abu Simbel. UNESCO and the Egyptian and Sudanese governments issued an international plea for help. Weeks immediately wrote to William Kelly Simpson, a prominent Egyptologist at Yale who was helping to coördinate the salvage project, and offered his services. He received plane tickets by return mail.

"The farthest I'd been away from home was Disneyland, and here I was going to Nubia," Weeks said. "The work had to be done fast: the lake waters were already rising. I got there and suddenly found myself being told, 'Take these eighty workmen and go dig that ancient village.' The nearest settlement was Wadi Halfa, ninety miles away. The first words of Arabic I learned were 'Dig no deeper' and 'Carry the baskets faster.'"

Weeks thereafter made a number of trips to Nubia, and just before he set out on one of them he invited along as artist a young woman he had met near the mummy case at the University of Washington museum—Susan Howe, a solemn college senior with red hair and a deadpan sense of humor.

"We lived on the river on an old rat-infested dahabeah," Susan told me. "My first night on the Nile, we were anchored directly in front of Abu Simbel, parked right in front of Ramesses' knees. It was all lit up, because work was going on day and night." An emergency labor force was cutting the temple into enormous blocks and reassembling it on higher ground. "After five months, the beer ran out, the cigarettes ran out, the water was really hot, the temperature was a hundred and fifteen degrees in the shade, and there were terrible windstorms. My parents were just *desperate* to know when I was coming home. But I thought, Ah! This is the life! It was so romantic. The workmen sang songs and clapped every morning when we arrived. So we wrote home and gave our parents ten days' notice that we were going to get married."

They have now been married twenty-nine years. Susan is the artist and illustrator for many of Kent's projects, and has also worked for other archeologists in Egypt. She spends much of her day in

front of KV5, in the green tent, wearing a scarf and peach-colored Keds, while she makes precise scale drawings of pottery and artifacts. In her spare time, she wanders around Gezira Bairat, painting exquisite watercolors of doorways and donkeys.

Weeks eventually returned to Washington to get his M.A., and in 1971 he received a Ph.D. from Yale; his dissertation dealt with ancient Egyptian anatomical terminology. He landed a plum job as a curator in the Metropolitan Museum's Egyptian Department. Two years later, bored by museum work, he quit and went back to Egypt, and was shortly offered the directorship of Chicago House, the University of Chicago's research center in Luxor. The Weekses have two children, whom they reared partly in Egypt, sending them to a local Luxor school. After four years at Chicago House, Weeks took a professorship at Berkeley, but again the lure of Egypt was too strong. In 1987, he renounced tenure at Berkeley, took a large pay cut, and went back to Egypt as a professor of Egyptology at the American University in Cairo, where he has been ever since.

While in Nubia, Weeks excavated an ancient working-class cemetery, pulling some seven thousand naturally desiccated bodies out of the ground. In a study of diet and health, he and a professor of orthodontics named James Harris X-rayed many of these bodies. Then Weeks and Harris persuaded the Egyptian government to allow them to X-ray the mummies of the pharaohs, by way of comparison. A team of physicians, orthodontists, and pathologists studied the royal X-rays, hoping to determine such things as age at death, cause of death, diet, and medical problems. They learned that there was surprisingly little difference between the two classes in diet and health.

One finding caused an uproar among Egyptologists. The medical team had been able to determine ages at death for most of the pharaohs, and in some cases these starkly contradicted the standard chronologies of the Egyptologists. The mystery was eventually solved when the team consulted additional ancient papyri, which told how, in the late New Kingdom, the high priests realized that many of the tombs in the Valley of the Kings had been robbed. To prevent further desecration, they gathered up almost all the royal mummies (missing only King Tut) and reburied them in two caches, both of which were discovered intact in the nineteenth century. "What we think happened is that the priests let the name dockets with some of the mummies fall off and put them back wrong," Weeks told me. It is also possible that the mixup occurred when the mummies were moved down the river to Cairo in the nineteenth century.

The team members analyzed the craniofacial characteristics of each mummy and figured out which ones looked most like which others. (Most of the pharaohs were related.) By combining these findings with age-at-death information, they were able to restore six of the mummies' proper names.

Weeks' second project led directly to the discovery of KV5. In 1979, he began mapping the entire Theban Necropolis. After an overview, he started with the Valley of the Kings. No such map had ever been done before. (That explains how KV5 came to be found and then lost several times in its history.) The Theban Mapping Project is to include the topography of the Valley and the three-dimensional placement of each tomb within the rock. The data are being computerized, and eventually Weeks will re-create the Valley on CD-s, which will allow a person to "fly" into any tomb and view in detail the murals and reliefs on its walls and ceilings.

Some Egyptologists I spoke with consider the mapping of the Theban Necropolis to be the most important archeological project in Egypt, KV5 notwithstanding. A map of the Valley of the Kings is desperately needed. Some tombs are deteriorating rapidly, with murals cracking and falling to the floors, and ceilings, too, collapsing. Damage has been done by the opening of the tombs to outside air. (When Carter opened King Tut's tomb, he could actually hear "strange rustling, murmuring, whispering sounds" of objects as the new air began its insidious work of destruction. In other tombs, wooden objects turned into "cigar-ash.") Greek, Roman, and early European tourists explored the

tombs with burning torches—and even lived in some tombs—leaving an oily soot on the paintings. Rapid changes in temperature and humidity generated by the daily influx of modern-day tourists have caused even greater damage, some of it catastrophic.

The gravest danger of all comes from flooding. Most of the tombs are now wide open. Modern alterations in the topography, such as the raising of the valley floor in order to build paths for the tourists, have created a highway directing floodwaters straight into the mouths of the tombs. A brief rain in November of 1994 generated a small flash flood that tore through the Valley at thirty miles an hour and damaged several tombs. It burst into the tomb of Bay, a vizier of the New Kingdom, with such force that it churned through the decorated chambers and completely ruined them. Layers of debris in KV5 indicate that a major flash flood occurs about once every three hundred years. If such a flood occurred tomorrow, the Valley of the Kings could be largely destroyed.

There is no master plan for preserving the Valley. The most basic element in such a plan is the completion of Weeks's map. Only then can preservationists monitor changes in the tombs and begin channelling and redirecting floodwaters. For this reason, some archeologists privately panicked when Weeks found KV5. "When I first heard about it," one told me, "I thought, Oh my God, that's it, Kent will never finish the mapping project."

Weeks promises that KV5 will not interfere with the Theban Mapping Project. "Having found the tomb, we've got an obligation to leave it in a good, stable, safe condition," he says. "And we have an obligation to publish. Public interest in KV5 has actually increased funding for the Theban Mapping Project."

At 9 A.M., the workmen laboring in KV5—there are forty-two of them—begin to file out and perch in groups on the hillside, to eat a breakfast of bread, tomatoes, green onions, and a foul cheese called *misht*. Weeks rises from his chair, nods to me, and asks, "Are you ready?"

We descend a new wooden staircase into the mountain and enter Chamber 1, where we exchange our sun hats for hard hats. The room is small and only half cleared. Visible tendrils of humid, dusty air waft in from the dim recesses of the tomb. The first impression I have of the tomb is one of shocking devastation. The ceilings are shot through with cracks, and in places they have caved in, dropping automobile-size pieces of rock. A forest of screw jacks and timbers holds up what is left, and many of the cracks are plastered with "tell-tales"—small seals that show if any more movement of the rock occurs.

The reliefs in Chamber 1 are barely visible, a mere palimpsest of what were once superbly carved and painted scenes of Ramesses and his sons adoring the gods, and panels of hieroglyphics. Most of the damage here was the result of a leaky sewer pipe that was laid over the tomb about forty years ago from an old rest house in the Valley. The leak caused salt crystals to grow and eat away the limestone walls. Here and there, however, one can still see traces of the original paint.

The decorations on the walls of the first two rooms show various sons being presented to the gods by Ramesses, in the classic Egyptian pose: head in profile, shoulders in frontal view, and torso in three-quarters view. There are also reliefs of tables laden with offerings of food for the gods, and hieroglyphic texts spelling out the names and titles of several sons and including the royal cartouche of Ramesses.

A doorway from Chamber 2 opens into Chamber 3—the Pillared Hall. It is filled with dirt and rock almost to the ceiling, giving one a simultaneous impression of grandeur and claustrophobia. Two narrow channels have been cut through the debris to allow for the passage of the workmen. Many of the pillars are split and shattered, and only fragments of decorations remain—a few hieroglyphic characters, an upraised arm, part of a leg. Crazed light from several randomly placed bulbs throws shadows around the room.

I follow Weeks down one of the channels. "This room is in such dangerous condition that we decided not to clear it," he says. "We call this channel the Mubarak trench. It was dug so that President Mubarak could visit the tomb without having to creep around on his hands and knees." He laughs.

When we are halfway across the room, he points out the words "James Burton 1825" smoked on the ceiling with the flame of a candle: it represents the Englishman's farthest point of penetration. Not far away is another graffito—this one in hieratic, the cursive form of hieroglyphic writing. It reads "Year 19"—the nineteenth year of Ramesses' reign. "This date gives us a *terminus ante quem* for the presence of Ramesses' workmen in this chamber," Weeks says.

He stops at one of the massive pillars. "And here's a mystery," he says, "Fifteen of the pillars in this room were cut from the native rock, but this one is a fake. The rock was carefully cut away—you can see chisel marks on the ceiling—and then the pillar was rebuilt out of stone and plastered to look like the others. Why?" He gives the pillar a sly pat. "Was something very large moved in here?"

I follow Weeks to the end of the trench—the site of the doorway that he crawled through in February. The door has been cleared, and we descend a short wooden staircase to the bottom of the great central corridor. It is illuminated by a string of naked light bulbs, which cast a yellow glow through a pall of dust. The many doors lining both sides of the corridor are still blocked with debris, and the stone floor is covered with an inch of dust.

At the far end of the corridor, a hundred feet away, stands the mummiform statue of Osiris. It is carved from the native rock, and only its face is missing. Lit from below, the statue casts a dramatic shadow on the ceiling. I try to take notes, but my glasses have fogged up, and sweat is dripping onto my notebook, making the ink run off the page. I can only stand and blink.

Nothing in twenty years of writing about archeology has prepared me for this great wrecked corridor chiseled out of the living rock, with rows of shattered doorways opening into darkness, and ending in the faceless mummy of Osiris. I feel like a trespasser, a voyeur, grazing

into the sacred precincts of the dead. As I stare at the walls, patterns and lines begin to emerge from the shattered stone: ghostly figures and faint hieroglyphics; animal-headed gods performing mysterious rites. Through doorways I catch glimpses of more rooms and more doorways beyond. There is a presence of death in this wrecked tomb that goes beyond those who were buried here; it is the death of a civilization.

With most of the texts on the walls destroyed or still buried under debris, it is not yet possible to determine what function was served by the dozens of side chambers. Weeks feels it likely, however, that they were *not* burial chambers, because the doorways are too narrow to admit a sarcophagus. Instead, he speculates they were chapels where the Theban priests could make offerings to the dead sons. Because the tomb departs so radically from the standard design, it is impossible even to speculate what the mysterious Pillared Hall or many of the other antechambers were for.

Weeks proudly displays some reliefs on the walls, tracing with his hand the figure of Isis and her husband, Osiris, and pointing out the ibis-headed god Thoth. "Ah!" he cries. "And here is a *wonderful* figure of Anubis and Hathor!" Anubis is the jackal-headed god of mummification, and Hathor a goddess associates with the Theban Necropolis. These were scenes to help guide Ramesses' sons through the rituals, spells, and incantations that would insure them a safe journey through the realm of death. The reliefs are exceedingly difficult to see; Susan Weeks told me later that she has sometimes had to stare at a wall for long periods—days, even—before she could pick out the shadow of a design. She is now in the process of copying these fragmentary reliefs on Mylar film, to help experts who will attempt to reconstruct the entire wall sequence and its accompanying test, and so reveal to us the purpose of the room or the corridor. KV5 will only yield up its secrets slowly, and with great effort.

"Here's Ramesses and one of his sons," Weeks says, indicating two figures standing hand in hand. "But, alas, the name is gone. Very disappointing!" He charges off down the corridor, raising

a trail of dust, and comes to a halt at the statue of Osiris, poking his glasses back up his sweating nose. "Look at this. Spectacular! A three-dimensional statue of Osiris is very rare. Most tombs depict him painted only. We dug around the base here trying to find the face, but instead we found a lovely offering of nineteen clay figs."

He makes a ninety-degree turn down the left transverse corridor, snaking around a cave-in. The corridor runs level for some distance and then plunges down a double staircase with a ramp in the middle, cut from the bedrock, and ends in a wall of bedrock. Along the sides of this corridor we have passed sixteen more partly blocked doors.

"Now, here is something new," Weeks says. "You're the first outsider to see this. I hoped that this staircase would lead to the burial chambers. This kind of ramp was usually built to slide the sarcophagi down. But look! The corridor just ends in a blank wall. Why in the world would they build a staircase and ramp going nowhere? So I decided to clear the two lowest side chambers. We just finished last week."

He ushers me into one of the rooms. There is no light; the room is large and very hot.

"They were empty," Weeks says.

"Too bad."

"Take a look at this floor."

"Nice." Floors do not particularly excite me.

"It happens to be the finest plastered floor in the Valley of the Kings. They went to enormous trouble with this floor, laying down three coats of plaster at different times, in different colors. Why?" He pauses. "Now stamp on the floor."

I thump the floor. There is a hollow reverberation that shakes not only the floor but the entire room. "Oh, my God, there's something underneath there!" I exclaim.

"*Maybe,*" Weeks says, a large smile gathering on his face. "Who knows? It could be a natural cavity or crack, or it might be a passageway to a lower level."

"You mean there might be sealed burial chambers below?"

Weeks smiles again. "Let's not get ahead of ourselves. Next June, we'll drill some test holes and do it properly."

We scramble back to the Osiris statue. "Now I'm going to take you to our latest discovery," Weeks says. "This is intriguing. *Very* fascinating."

We make our way through several turns back to the Pillared Hall. Weeks leads me down the other trench, which ends at the southwest corner of the hall. Here, earlier in the month, the workmen discovered a buried doorway that opened onto a steep descending passageway, again packed solid with debris. The workmen have now cleared the passageway down some sixty feet, exposing twelve more side chambers, and are still at work.

We pause at the top of the newly excavated passageway. A dozen screw jacks with timbers hold up its cracked ceiling. The men have finished breakfast and are back at work, one man picking away at the wall of debris at the bottom of the passageway while another scoops the debris into a basket made out of old tires. A line of workmen then pass the basket up the corridor and out of the tomb.

"I've called this passageway 3A," Weeks says. He drops his voice. "The incredible thing is that this corridor is heading toward the tomb of Ramesses himself. If it connects, that will be extraordinary. No two tombs were ever deliberately connected. This tomb just gets curiouser and curiouser."

Ramesses' tomb, lying a hundred feet across the Valley, was also wrecked by flooding and is now being excavated by a French team. "I would dearly love to surprise them," Weeks says. "To pop out one day and say *'Bonjour! C'est moi!'* I'd love to beat the French into their own tomb."

I follow him down the newly discovered corridor, slipping and sliding on the pitched floor. "Of course," he shouts over his shoulder, "the sons might also be buried *underneath* their father! We clearly haven't found the burial chambers yet, and it is my profound hope that one way or another this passageway will take us there."

We come to the end, where the workmen are picking away at the massive wall of dirt that blocks the passage. The forty-two men can remove about nine tons of dirt a day.

At the bottom, Weeks introduces me to a tall, handsome Egyptian with a black mustache and wearing a baseball cap on

backward. "This is Muhammad Mahmud," Weeks says. "One of the senior workmen."

I shake his hand. "What do you hope to find down here?"

"Something very nice, *inshallah.*"

"What's in these side rooms?" I ask Weeks. All the doorways are blocked with dirt.

Weeks shrugs. "We haven't been in those rooms yet."

"Would it be possible... " I start to ask.

He grins. "You mean, would you like to be the first human being in three thousand years to enter a chamber in an ancient Egyptian tomb? Maybe Saturday."

As we are leaving the tomb, I am struck by the amount of work still unfinished. Weeks has managed to dig out only three rooms completely and clear eight others partway—leaving more than eighty rooms entirely untouched. What treasures lie under five or ten feet of debris in those rooms is anyone's guess. It will take from six to ten more years to clear and stabilize the tomb, and then many more years to publish the findings from it. As we emerge from the darkness, Weeks says, "I know what I'll be doing for the rest of my life."

One morning, I find a pudgy, bearded man sitting in the green tent and examining, Hamlet-like, the now assembled skull. He is the paleontologist Elwyn Simons, who has spent decades searching the sands of the Faiyum for primate ancestors of human beings. Susan Weeks once worked for him, and now he is a close friend of the couple, dropping in on occasion to look over bones from the tomb. Kent and Susan are both present, waiting to hear his opinions about the skull's sex. (Only DNA testing can confirm whether it's an actual son of Ramesses, of course.)

Simons rotates the skull, pursing his lips. "Probably a male, because it has fairly pronounced brow ridges," he says. "This"—he points to a hole punched in the top of the cranium—"was made post mortem. You can tell because the edges are sharp and there are no suppressed fractures."

Simons laughs, and sets the skull down. "You can grind this up and put it in your soup, Kent."

When the laughter has died down, I venture that I didn't get the joke.

"In the Middle ages, people filled bottles with powdered mummies and sold it as medicine," Simons explains.

"Or mummies were burned to power the railroad," Weeks adds. "I don't know how many miles you get per mummy, do you, Elwyn?"

While talk of mummies proceeds, a worker brings a tray of tea. Susan Weeks takes the skull away and puts another bone in front of Simons.

"That's the scapula of an artiodactyl. Probably a cow. The camel hadn't reached Egypt by the Nineteenth Dynasty."

The next item is a tooth.

"Artiodactyl again," he says, sipping his tea. "Goat or gazelle."

The identification process goes on.

The many animal bones found in KV5 were probably from offerings for the dead: valley tombs often contained sacrificed bulls, mummified baboons, birds, and cats, as well as steaks and veal chops.

Suddenly, Muhammad appears at the mouth of the tomb. "Please, Dr. Kent," he says, and starts telling Weeks in Arabic that the workers have uncovered something for him to see. Weeks motions for me to follow him into the dim interior. We put on our hard hats and duck through the first chambers into Corridor 3A. A beautiful set of carved limestone steps has appeared where I saw only rubble a few days before. Weeks kneels and brushes the dirt away, excited about the fine workmanship.

Muhammad and Weeks go to inspect another area of the tomb, where fragments of painted and carved plaster are being uncovered. I stay to watch the workmen digging in 3A. After a while, they forget I am there and begin singing, handing the baskets up the long corridor, their bare feet white with dust. A dark hole begins to appear between the top of the debris and the ceiling. It looks as if one could crawl inside and perhaps look farther down the corridor.

"May I take a look in there?" I ask.

One of the workmen hoists me up the wall of dirt, and I lie on my stomach and wriggle into the gap. I recall that archeologists sometimes sent small boys into tombs through holes just like this.

Unfortunately, I am not a small boy, and in my eagerness I find myself thoroughly wedged. It is pitch-black, and I wonder why I thought this would be exciting.

"Pull me out!" I yell.

The Egyptians heave on my legs, and I come sliding down with a shower of dirt. After the laughter subsides, a skinny man named Nubie crawls into the hole. In a moment, he is back out, feet first. He cannot see anything; they need to dig more.

The workmen redouble their efforts, laughing, joking, and singing. Working in KV5 is a coveted job in the surrounding villages; Weeks pays his workmen four hundred Egyptian pounds a month (about a hundred and twenty-five dollars), four times what a junior inspector of antiquities makes and perhaps three times the average monthly income of an Egyptian family. Weeks is well liked by his Egyptian workers, and is constantly bombarded with dinner invitations from even his poorest laborers. While I was there, I attended three of these dinners. The flow of food was limitless, and the conversation competed with the bellowing of a water buffalo in an adjacent room or the braying of a donkey tethered at the door.

After the hole has been widened a bit, Nubie goes up again with a light and comes back down. There is great disappointment: it looks as though the passageway might come to an end. Another step is exposed in the staircase, along with a great deal of broken pottery. Weeks returns and examines the hole himself, without comment.

As the week goes by, more of Corridor 3A is cleared, foot by foot. The staircase in 3A levels out to a finely made floor, more evidence that the corridor merely ends in a small chamber. On Wednesday, however, Weeks emerges from the tomb smiling. "Come," he says.

The hole in 3A has now been enlarged to about two feet in diameter. I scramble up the dirt and peer inside with a light, choking on the dust. As before, the chiselled ceiling comes to an abrupt end, but below it lies what looks like a shattered door lintel.

"It's got to be a door," Weeks says, excited. "I'm afraid we're going to have to halt for the season at that doorway. We'll break through next June."

Later, outdoors, I find myself coughing up flecks of mud.

"Tomb cough," Weeks says cheerfully.

On Thursday morning, Weeks is away on business, and I go down into the tomb with Susan. At the bottom of 3A, we stop to watch Ahmed Mahmud Hassan, the chief supervisor of the crew, sorting through some loose dirt at floor level. Suddenly, he straightens up, holding a perfect alabaster statuette of a mummy.

"Madame," he says, holding it out.

Susan begins to laugh. "Ahmed, that's beautiful. Did you get that at one of the souvenir stalls?"

"No," he says. "I just found it." He points to the spot. "Here."

She turns to me. "They once put a rubber cobra in here. Everyone was terrified, and Muhammad began beating it with a rock."

"Madame," Ahmed says. "Look, please." By now, he is laughing, too.

"I see it," Susan says. "I hope it wasn't too expensive."

"Madame, please."

Susan takes it, and there is a sudden silence. "It's real," she says quietly.

"This is what I was telling Madame," Ahmed says, still laughing.

Susan slowly turns it over in her hands. "It's beautiful. Let's take it outside."

In the sunlight, the statuette glows. The head and shoulders still have clear traces of black paint, and the eyes look slightly crossed. It is an *ushabti,* a statuette that was buried only with the dead, meant to spare the deceased toil in the afterlife: whenever the deceased was called upon to do work, he would send the *ushabti* in his place.

That morning, the workmen also find in 3A a chunk of stone. Weeks hefts it. "This is very important," he says.

"How?"

"It's a piece of a sidewall of a sarcophagus that probably held one of Ramesses' sons. It's made out of serpentine, a valuable stone in ancient Egypt." He pulls out a tape measure and marks off the thickness of the rim. "It's eight-point-five centimetres, which, doubled, gives seventeen centimetres. Add to that the width of an average pair of human shoulders, and perhaps an inner coffin,

and you could not have fitted this sarcophagus through any door to any of the sixty side chambers in that tomb." He pauses. "So, you see, this piece of stone is one more piece of evidence that we have yet to find the burial chambers."

Setting the stone down with a thud on a specimen mat, he dabs his forehead. He proceeds to lay out a theory about KV5. Ramesses had an accomplished son named Khaemwaset, who became the high priest of an important cult that worshipped a god represented by a sacred bull. In Year 16, Khaemwaset began construction of the Serapeum, a vast catacomb for the bulls, in Saqqara. The original design of the Serapeum is the only one that remotely resembles KV5's layout, and it might have been started around the same time. In the Serapeum, there are two levels: an upper level of offering chapels and a lower level for burials. "But," Weeks adds, throwing open his arms, "until we find the burial chambers it's *all* speculation."

On Friday, Bruce Ludwig arrives—a great bear of a man with white hair and a white beard. Dressed like an explorer, he is lugging a backpack full of French wine for the team.

Unlike Lord Carnarvon and other wealthy patrons who funded digs in the Valley of the Kings, Ludwig is a self-made man. His father owned a grocery store in South Dakota called Ludwig's Superette. Bruce Ludwig made his money in California real estate and is now a partner in a firm managing four billion dollars in pension funds. He has been supporting Weeks and the Theban Mapping Project for twelve years.

Over the past three, he has sunk a good deal of his own money into the project and has raised much more among his friends. Nevertheless, the cost of excavation continually threatens to outstrip the funds at hand. "The thing is, it doesn't take a Rockefeller or a Getty to be involved," he told me over a bottle of Château Lynch-Bages. "What I like to do is show other successful people that it won't cost a fortune and that it's just hugely rewarding. Buildings crumble and fall down, but when you put something in the books, it's there forever."

Ludwig's long-term support paid off last February, when he became one of the first people to crawl into the recesses of KV5. There may be better moments to come. "When I discover that door covered with unbroken Nineteenth Dynasty seals," Weeks told me, joking, "you bet I'll hold off until Bruce can get here."

Saturday, the workers' taxi picks the Weekses and me up before sunrise and then winds through a number of small villages, collecting workers as it goes along.

The season is drawing to a close, and Susan and Kent Weeks are both subdued. In the last few weeks, the probable number of rooms in the tomb has increased from sixty-seven to ninety-two, with no end in sight. Everyone is frustrated at having to lock up the tomb now, leaving the doorway at the bottom of 3A sealed, the plaster floor unplumbed, the burial chambers still not found, and so many rooms unexcavated.

Weeks plans to tour the United States lecturing and raising more funds. He estimates that he will need a quarter of a million dollars per year for the indefinite future in order to do the job right.

As we drive alongside sugarcane fields, the sun boils up over the Nile Valley through a screen of palms, burning into the mists lying on the fields. We pass a man driving a donkey cart loaded with tires, and whizz by the Colossi of Memnon, two enormous wrecked statues standing alone in a farmer's field. The taxi begins the climb to a village once famous for tomb robbing, some of whose younger residents now work for Weeks. The houses are completely surrounded by the black pits of tombs. The fragrant smell of dung fires drifts through the rocky streets.

Along the way, I talk with Ahmed, the chief supervisor. A young man with a handsome, aristocratic face, who comes from a prominent family in Gezira Bairat, he has worked for Weeks for about eight years. I ask him how he feels about working in the tomb.

Ahmed thinks for a moment, then says, "I forget myself in this tomb. It is so vast inside."

"How so?"

"I feel at home there. I know this thing. I can't express the feeling, but it's not so strange for me to be in this tomb. I feel something in there about myself. I am descended from these people who built this tomb. I can feel their blood is in me."

When we arrive in the Valley of the Kings, an inspector unlocks the metal gate in front of the tomb, and the workers file in, with Weeks leading the way. I wait outside to watch the sunrise. The tourists have not arrived, and if you screen out some signs you can imagine the Valley as it might have appeared when the pharaohs were buried here three thousand years ago. (The venders and rest house were moved last year.) As dawn strikes el-Qurn and invades the upper reaches of the canyon walls, a soft, peach-colored lights fills the air. The encircling cliffs lock out the sounds of the world; the black doorways of the tombs are like dead eyes staring out; and one of the guard huts of the ancient priests can still be seen perched at the cliff edge. The whole Valley becomes a slowly changing play of light and color, mountain and sky, unfolding in absolute stillness. I am given a brief, shivery insight into the sacredness of this landscape.

At seven, the tourists begin to arrive, and the spell is dispersed. The Valley rumbles to life with the grinding of diesel engines, the frantic expostulations of venders, and the shouting of guides leading groups of tourists. KV5 is the first tomb in the Valley, and the tourists begin gathering at the rope, pointing and taking pictures, while the guides impart the most preposterous misinformation about the tomb: that Ramesses had four hundred sons by only two wives, that there are eight hundred rooms in the tomb, that the greedy Americans are digging for gold but won't find any. Two thousand tourists a day stand outside the entrance to KV5.

I go inside and find Weeks in 3A, supervising the placement of more screw jacks and timbers. When he has finished, he turns to me. "You ready?" He points to the lowest room in 3A. "This looks like a good one for you to explore."

One of the workmen clears away a hole at the top of the blocked door for me to crawl through, and then Muhammad gives me a leg up. I shove a caged light bulb into the hold ahead of me and wriggle through. I can barely fit.

In a moment, I am inside. I sit up and look around, the light throwing my distorted shadow against the wall. There is three feet of space between the top of the debris and the ceiling, just enough for me to crawl around on my hands and knees. The room is about nine feet square, the walls finely chiselled from the bedrock. Coils of dust drift past the light. The air is just breathable.

I run my fingers along the ancient chisel marks, which are as fresh as if they were made yesterday, and I think of workmen who carved out this room, three millennia ago. Their only source of light would have been the dim illumination from wicks burning in a bowl of oil salted to reduce smoke. There was no way to tell the passage of time in the tomb: the wicks were cut to last eight hours, and when they guttered it meant that the day's work was done. The tombs were carved from the ceiling downward, the workers whacking off flakes of limestone with flint choppers, and then finishing the walls and ceilings with copper chisels and sandstone abrasive. Crouching in the hot stone chamber, I suddenly get a powerful sense of the enormous religious faith of the Egyptians. Nothing less could have motivated an entire society to pound these tombs out of rock.

Much of the Egyptian religion remains a mystery to us. It is full of contradictions, inexplicable rituals, and impenetrable texts. Amid the complexity, one simple fact stands out: it was a great human bargain with death. Almost everything that ancient Egypt has left us—the pyramids, the tombs, the temples—represents an attempt to overcome that awful mystery at the center of all our lives.

A shout brings me back to my senses.

"Find anything?" Weeks calls out.

"The room's empty," I say. "There's nothing in here but dust."

From *The New Yorker*, January 22, 1996, pp. 44-54, 56-59. © 1996 by Douglas Preston. Reprinted by permission of the author.

Antiquities Sleuth Has a Fraud Mandate

For antiquities sleuth Jane MacLaren Walsh, tiny marks by the maker can betray the fakes.

Jacqueline Trescott

Most museums have fakes in their collections. This is a reality to which they don't want to bring attention. Jane MacLaren Walsh, however, loves to turn the material legacy of the past over and over in her strong hands. As an art detective, it's both her research and her reverie. She fingers a tube of jade as narrow as a soda straw and wonders about its maker, the artist who worked some 3,500 years ago and thought to carve a snake like the one crawling near the fire.

Then she thinks of the other craftsmen who, roughly 200 years ago, created forgeries of such antiquities so convincing that today they nestle in the world's finest museums.

Walsh sits in a sunny office at the National Museum of Natural History and wonders if the next wonderful piece of allegedly pre-Columbian art that comes through the door will be real or a fake. Beneath her short wave of soft silver hair is pale skin reddened by the sun of Mexico, where she has just been examining the bounty from a dig.

An anthropologist with the Smithsonian for 35 years, Walsh finds a certain joy in being stumped and a delicious satisfaction in spotting a forgery.

It's not easy to find objects that are certifiably genuine to judge others against. But Walsh and sleuths in Britain and Mexico have three pre-Columbian collections that they regard as beyond reproach: The Museo del Templo Mayor in Mexico City has the results of an accidental discovery in the 1970s of an ancient Aztec temple. The artifacts represent the last period of pre-Columbian art, from about A.D. 700–1500. The British Museum has a collection of Mayan jades that date from A.D. 100–900. And the Smithsonian has holdings from an Olmec site at La Venta, Mexico, where anthropologist Matthew Williams Stirling, working from 1938–1946, found a cache dated from 900 to 200 B.C.

"They were selected because they are documented. They came from controlled scientific excavations," says Walsh. "We know for certain that they are authentic, and because of the cultures and sites, we know what time periods they come from."

Walsh is creating a computerized reference base, meant to guide those trying to spot fraudulent antiquities. After studying the holes and markings on genuine items in the three museums,

she examines suspect artifacts with advanced scanners for the telltale marks of relatively modern equipment.

"In excavations you don't find the tools because [the figures] were offerings to the gods," Walsh says. The workshop where they were made was somewhere else. So the indoor anthropologist has to ask hundreds of questions as she turns over an object. "What did they use to make that hole?" she says, looking at an Olmec ear ornament, dated from 900 to 400 B.C. Could the ancient craftsmen have used bamboo? Or cactus thorns or small bones or flint or quartz?

What complicates the search for authenticity is that some of the forgeries are also antiques.

"Fakes have been made, I think, since early in the 1800s. Some people think they begin even earlier. After the wars of independence starting in 1810, all of Mexico was opened up to travelers from Europe and America," she explains. "So when lots of travelers came in, they were fascinated by the presence of ruins and wanted to take home souvenirs. They created a demand, and as usual, somebody else created a supply."

Although Walsh was born in the Bronx, her interest in Mesoamerican archaeology and history was kindled when her father's foreign service career took the family to Mexico. In high school, she often went to the museum that had been made out of the home of Diego Rivera and Frida Kahlo. There she fell in love with its paintings, folk art and antiquities. Even after her family moved on, she stayed to earn her degrees from the University of the Americas in Mexico City. Later she got a PhD from Catholic University in Washington.

She focused on the pre-Columbian world. "The beauty of the collections is that they are like libraries, they tell you so much," says Walsh. And at Natural History, which has the largest scientific staff of any museum in the world, the collections yielded plenty of authentic examples that she could use to debunk frauds.

She uses all sorts of equipment in her detective work. An up-to-the-minute Apple computer is on one side of her office, where she can manipulate high-resolution images. Many of these come from the museum's labs, which are equipped with CT scanners, X-ray machines and scanning electron microscopes. But advanced technology goes only so far: She has also created tools using materials available to ancient artisans.

Walsh picks up a piece of obsidian, shiny and sharp, and shows how it might have been used. "This volcanic glass is the fifth hardest mineral there is," she says. A fake, by contrast, often shows evidence of a hard metal tool. "With modern tools, you get these regular, clean lines, very sharp, very narrow. If you see impressions left by a tool that didn't exist" at the time, she says, "you know it is a fake." A high polish may also signal the use of modern tools.

She thinks of those very old hands. "Of all the documented Olmec jades that I've looked at, I haven't seen evidence of hollow drills yet," Walsh says, pointing out the jades were probably drilled with a solid pointed stone. Later, after the Olmec period, other cultures used bird bones and bamboo-like reeds for hollow drills.

And there Walsh stops. "I don't want the fakers to know what to avoid," she says.

Tracking how ancient carvers worked has led Walsh down some curious trails, including experimenting with a mouse bone as a drill bit. "The rodent bone worked very well. The mouse had tough small bones, and I used it to drill with sand," she says. She also tried rabbit bones she took home from a dinner out. Then there was a duck, eaten for dinner, its bones then donated to science.

"It worked pretty well as a drill. Ducks and rabbits and mice all would have been available to pre-Columbian peoples, and since they would have used what they could find, I tried to use what I could find too," says Walsh. Once the bones are cleaned and sharpened, she goes over to the mineralogy department at the museum and with another colleague runs tests using mechanical drills that more or less duplicate the motion of an ancient hand drill.

"He runs them at a relatively slow speed to simulate a bow or hand drill. Using quartz sand we see how long it takes to drill into some samples of jade and jadeite," says Walsh.

Some cases are clear-cut: She was certain about a purported Aztec crystal skull. One arrived at the Smithsonian in 1992 from an anonymous donor. The alarm bells went off, since Walsh knew that New Age practitioners bragged about the powers of these objects and people were creating them to serve a special market.

But had they ever really existed?

"It was a class of artifact never dug up," she says. Working with Margaret Sax at the British Museum, she created a test with molds of the lines and drill holes. Under the microscope, her first inkling was verified.

"One of the things that was obvious about the crystal skulls was that the carving was done by a wheel, or a rotary saw. No pre-Columbian carver had such a tool, so we felt it had to be after European contact," says Walsh. She also investigated how the crystal skulls had made their way into the British Museum and the Musee de l'Homme in Paris. The same dealer had sold both, and the skulls had originated in Germany.

More often, she finds pieces she is 90 percent sure are counterfeit, but is reluctant to render a verdict until she's finally completed her database. In this way she hopes she will someday be able to offer other art sleuths an authentic road map to fakes.

UNIT 2
Problem Oriented Archaeology

Unit Selections

Key Points to Consider

- Explain the causes of primitive warfare. Is warfare endemic to the human species?
- Who is the "Iceman?" What is the archeological evidence that identifies him?
- What is H. floresiensis? Where does it belong on our family tree and why?
- Compare the major theories as to when modern humans migrated to the New World. Please cite the archaeological evidence.
- What new methods have been used by archaeologists to show that people began cultivating crops before they embraced full-scale farming? Cite examples.
- What was the advantage of the projectile point as compared to tips of hand-thrown spears? What impact did this technological innovation have on human evolution?
- What is the archaeological evidence for human cannibalism? How widespread has it been?
- What role did women play in hunting and gathering in Ice Age Europe? How does this view run contrary to what has been thought?
- What does archaeology tell us about women as tool-makers in the Ice Age? Cite the archaeological evidence.
- What is a "garbologist?" What kind of archaeology do they do? Cite examples.
- What does the excavation of present hunter-gatherer peoples tell us about their past? Use the example of the Bushmen.
- What factors were involved in the collapse of Mayan civilization? What lessons does this hold for the modern world?

Student Website
www.mhcls.com/online

Internet References
Further information regarding these websites may be found in this book's preface or online.

Archaeology Links (NC)
http://www.arch.dcr.state.nc.us/links.htm#stuff

Archaeology Magazine
http://www.archaeology.org

What are the goals of archaeology? What kinds of things motivate well-educated people to go out and dig square holes in the ground and sift through their diggings like flour for a cake? How do they know where to dig? What are they looking for? What do they do with the things they find? Let us drop in on an archaeology class at Metropolis University.

"Good afternoon, class, I'm Dr. Penny Pittmeyer. Welcome to Introductory Archaeology. Excuse me, young lady. Yes, you in the back, wearing the pith helmet. I don't think you'll need to bring that shovel to class this semester. We aren't going to be doing any digging."

A moan like that of an audience that had just heard a bad pun sounded throughout the classroom. Eyes bugged out, foreheads receded, sweat formed on brow ridges, and mouths formed into alphabet-soup at this pronouncement.

"That's right, no digging. You are here to learn about archaeology."

"But archaeology is digging. So what are we going to do all semester? Sheesh!" protested a thin young man with stern, steel granny glasses and a straight, scraggly beard, wearing a stained old blue work shirt and low slung 501's with an old, solid, and finely tooled leather belt and scuffed cowboy boots. A scratched trowel jutted from his right back pocket where the seam was half torn away.

Dr. Pittmeyer calmly surveyed the class and quietly repeated, "You are here to learn about archaeology." In a husky, compelling voice, she went on. "Archaeology is not digging, nor is it just about Egyptian ruins or lost civilizations. It's a science. First you have to learn the basics of that science. Digging is just a technique. Digging comes later. Digging comes after you know why you are going to dig."

"No Egyptian ruins," a plaintive echo resonated through the still classroom.

"You can have your ruins later. Take a class in Egyptian archaeology—fine, fine! But this class is the prerequisite to all those other classes. I hate to be the one to tell you this, people, but there ain't no Indiana Jones! I would have found him by now if there were." Dr. Pittmeyer said this with a slightly lopsided smile. But a veiled look in her light eyes sent an "uh-oh" that the students felt somewhere deep in their guts. They knew that the woman had something to teach them. And teach them she would!

Dr. Pittmeyer half sat on the old desk at the front of the classroom. Leaning one elbow on the podium to her right, she picked up a tall, red, opaque glass, and took a long and satisfying drink from it. Behind her large-framed black glasses, her eyes brightened noticeably. She wiped away an invisible mustache from her upper lip and settled onto the desk, holding the red glass in her left hand and letting it sway slightly as she unhurriedly looked over the students. Her left eyebrow rose unconsciously. The quiet lengthened so that the students filling out the Day-Glo-orange drop cards stopped writing, conscious of the now-loud silence in the room.

"O.K! LET'S GO!" Dr. Pittmeyer said with a snap like a whip singing over their heads. The startled students went straight-backed in unison.

"Archaeology is a science, ladies and gentlemen. It's part of the larger science of anthropology. The goals of both are to understand and predict human behavior. Let's start by looking at an area or subfield of archaeology that we may designate as problem-oriented archaeology. Humans evolved in Africa, Asia, and Europe, or what we refer to as the Old World."

Dr. Pittmeyer simultaneously turned out the lights and clicked on an overhead projector and wrote rapidly with a harshly bright purple pen in a hieroglyphic-like scrawl. Dangling from her neck was a microphone that was plugged into a speaker that was then plugged back into the overhead projector which in turn was plugged into an old, cracked socket, the single electric outlet offered by the ancient high-ceilinged asbestos-filled room.

Doubtful students suddenly felt compelled to take notes in the dim light provided by the irregularities of old-fashioned thick blinds that did not quite close completely.

"In the New World, in the Americas, from Alaska down to the tip of Tierra del Fuego, we only have well documented evidence that the first people lived here about 15,000-11,000 years ago. In Contrast people have been living in the Old World for 200,000 years or more—people in the sense of Homo sapiens.

"So what took them so long to get here?" a perplexed female voice asked.

"Please let me point out that your question contains a very telling assumption. You said what took them so long to get here.

The question is moot because these early peoples were not trying to get here. We're talking about the Paleolithic era—people were migratory. They hunted and collected their food every day. They followed their food resources usually in seasonal patterns that moved them around but within fairly local areas. So it is a non-question. Let me explain, please.

"In archaeology, you have to ask the right questions before you can get any useful answers. That is why archaeologists dig—not to make discoveries, but to answer questions. Now here's what I want you to do. Go home and try to think yourself back into the Paleolithic. Its 35,000 years ago, and mostly you hang out with your family and other close relatives. You get your food and shelter on a daily basis, and you have some free time, too. Everyone cooperates to survive. The point is that wherever you are, you are there. There is no place to try to get to. There is no notion of private property or ownership of land. Nobody needs to conquer anybody. There are no cities, no freeways, no clocks, and no rush. Think about it. It's a concept of life without measurements or urgencies."

"But they must have been pretty stupid back that long ago!" the young man with the beard, now nibbling his trowel, protested.

"Please think about that assumption! No, these were people just like you and me. If they were here today, they probably could program their VCRs. These were people with many skills and accomplishments. They met their needs as we meet ours. But they had something we might envy. They were already there no matter where they were! There's a lot to be learned from our prehistoric ancestors.

"But, frankly, tomorrow's another day." Alone in the classroom, Dr. Penny Pittmeyer finished her soda and allowed her eyes to glaze over as the forgotten Day-Glo-orange drop cards fluttered to the floor. She stared far back in time where she saw intelligent people living a simple life in peace—or so she hoped.

Prehistory *of* Warfare

Humans have been at each others' throats since the dawn of the species.

by STEVEN A. LEBLANC

IN THE EARLY 1970s, working in the El Morro Valley of west-central New Mexico, I encountered the remains of seven large prehistoric pueblos that had once housed upwards of a thousand people each. Surrounded by two-story-high walls, the villages were perched on steep-sided mesas, suggesting that their inhabitants built them with defense in mind. At the time, the possibility that warfare occurred among the Anasazi was of little interest to me and my colleagues. Rather, we were trying to figure out what the people in these 700-year-old communities farmed and hunted, the impact of climate change, and the nature of their social systems—not the possibility of violent conflict.

One of these pueblos, it turned out, had been burned to the ground; its people had clearly fled for their lives. Pottery and valuables had been left on the floors, and bushels of burned corn still lay in the storerooms. We eventually determined that this site had been abandoned, and that immediately afterward a fortress had been built nearby. Something catastrophic had occurred at this ancient Anasazi settlement, and the survivors had almost immediately, and at great speed, set about to prevent it from happening again.

Thirty years ago, archaeologists were certainly aware that violent, organized conflicts occurred in the prehistoric cultures they studied, but they considered these incidents almost irrelevant to our understanding of past events and people. Today, some of my colleagues are realizing that the evidence I helped uncover in the El Morro Valley is indicative warfare endemic throughout the entire Southwest, with its attendant massacres, population decline, and area abandonments that forever changed the Anasazi way of life.

When excavating eight-millennia-old farm villages in southeastern Turkey in 1970, I initially marveled how similar modern villages were to ancient ones, which were occupied at a time when an abundance of plants and animals made warfare quite unnecessary. Or so I thought. I knew we had discovered some plaster sling missiles (one of our workmen showed me how shepherds used slings to hurl stones at predators threatening their sheep). Such missiles were found at many of these sites, often in great quantities, and were clearly not intended for protecting flocks of sheep; they were exactly the same size and shape as later Greek and Roman sling stones used for warfare.

The so-called "donut stones" we had uncovered at these sites were assumed to be weights for digging sticks, presumably threaded on a pole to make it heavier for digging holes to plant crops. I failed to note how much they resembled the round stone heads attached to wooden clubs—maces—used in many places of the world exclusively for fighting and still used ceremonially to signify power. Thirty years ago, I was holding mace heads and sling missiles in my hands, unaware of their use as weapons of war.

We now know that defensive walls once ringed many villages of this era, as they did the Anasazi settlements. Rooms were massed together behind solid outside walls and were entered from the roof. Other sites had mud brick defensive walls, some with elaborately defended gates. Furthermore, many of these villages had been burned to the ground, their inhabitants massacred, as indicated by nearby mass graves.

Certainly for those civilizations that kept written records or had descriptive narrative art traditions, warfare is so clearly present that no one can deny it. Think of Homer's *Iliad* or the Vedas of South India, or scenes of prisoner sacrifice on Moche pottery. There is no reason to think that warfare played any less of a role in prehistoric societies for which we have no such records, whether they be hunter-gatherers or farmers. But most scholars studying these cultures still are not seeing it. They should assume warfare occurred among the people they study, just as they assume religion and art were a normal part of human culture. Then they could ask more interesting questions, such as: What form did warfare take? Can warfare explain some of the material found in the archaeological record? What were people fighting over and why did the conflicts end?

Today, some scholars know me as Dr. Warfare. To them, I have the annoying habit of asking un-politic questions about their research. I am the one who asks why the houses at a particular site were jammed so close together and many catastrophically burned. When I suggest that the houses were crowded behind defensive walls that were not found because no one was looking for them, I am not terribly appreciated. And I don't win any popularity contests when I suggest that twenty-mile-wide zones with no sites in them imply no-man's lands—clear evidence for warfare—to archaeologists who have explained a region's history without mention of conflict.

> Scholars should assume warfare occurred among the people they study, just as they assume religion was a normal part of human culture. Then they would ask more interesting questions, such as: What form did warfare take? Why did people start and stop fighting?

Virtually all the basic textbooks on archaeology ignore the prevalence or significance of past warfare, which is usually not discussed until the formation of state-level civilizations such as ancient Sumer. Most texts either assume or actually state that for most of human history there was an abundance of available resources. There was no resource stress, and people had the means to control population, though how they accomplished this is never explained. The one archaeologist who has most explicitly railed against this hidden but pervasive attitude is Lawrence Keeley of the University of Illinois, who studies the earliest farmers in Western Europe. He has fund ample evidence of warfare as farmers spread west, yet most of his colleagues still believe the expansion was peaceful and his evidence a minor aberration, as seen in the various papers in Barry Cunliffe's *The Oxford Illustrated Prehistory of Europe* (1994) or Douglas Price's *Europe's First Farmers* (2000). Keeley contends that "prehistorians have increasingly pacified the past," presuming peace or thinking up every possible alternative explanation for the evidence they cannot ignore. In his *War Before Civilization* (1996) he accused archaeologists of being in denial on the subject.

Witness archaeologist Lisa Valkenier suggesting in 1997 that hilltop constructions along the Peruvian coast are significant because peaks are sacred in Andean cosmology. Their enclosing walls and narrow guarded entries may have more to do with restricting access to the *huacas*, or sacred shrines, on top of the hills than protecting defenders and barring entry to any potential attackers. How else but by empathy can one formulate such an interpretation in an area with a long defensive wall and hundreds of defensively located fortresses, some still containing piles of sling missiles ready to be used; where a common

artistic motif is the parading and execution of defeated enemies; where hundreds were sacrificed; and where there is ample evidence of conquest, no-man's lands, specialized weapons, and so on?

A talk I gave at the Mesa Verde National Park last summer, in which I pointed out that the over 700-year-old cliff dwellings were built in response to warfare, raised the hackles of National Park Service personnel unwilling to accept anything but the peaceful Anasazi message peddled by their superiors. In fact, in the classic book *Indians of Mesa Verde*, published in 1961 by the park service, author Don Watson first describes the Mesa Verde people as "peaceful farming Indians," and admits that the cliff dwellings had a defensive aspect, but since he had already decided that the inhabitants were peaceful, the threat must have been from a new enemy—marauding nomadic Indians. This, in spite of the fact that there is ample evidence of Southwestern warfare for more than a thousand years before the cliff dwellings were built, and there is no evidence for the intrusion of nomadic peoples at this time.

Of the hundreds of research projects in the Southwest, only one—led by Jonathan Haas and Winifred Creamer of the Field Museum and Northern Illinois University, respectively—deliberately set out to research prehistoric warfare. They demonstrated quite convincingly that the Arizona cliff dwellings of the Tsegi Canyon area (known best for Betatakin and Kiet Siel ruins) were defensive, and their locations were not selected for ideology or because they were breezier and cooler in summer and warmer in the winter, as was previously argued by almost all Southwestern archaeologists.

For most prehistoric cultures, one has to piece together the evidence for warfare from artifactual bits and pieces. Most human history involved foragers, and so they are particularly relevant. They too were not peaceful. We know from ethnography that the Inuit (Eskimo) and Australian Aborigines engaged in warfare. We've also discovered remains of prehistoric bone armor in the Arctic, and skeletal evidence of deadly blows to the head are well documented among the prehistoric Aborigines. Surprising to some is the skeletal evidence for warfare in prehistoric California, once thought of as a land of peaceful acorn gatherers. The prehistoric people who lived in southern Californian had the highest incident of warfare deaths known anywhere in the world. Thirty percent of a large sample of males dating to the first centuries A.D. had wounds or died violent deaths. About half that number of women had similar histories. When we remember that not all warfare deaths leave skeletal evidence, this is a staggering number.

There was nothing unique about the farmers of the Southwest. From the Neolithic farmers of the Middle East and Europe to the New Guinea highlanders in the twentieth century, tribally organized farmers probably had the most intense warfare of any type of society. Early villages in China, the Yucatán, present-day Pakistan, and Micronesia were well fortified. Ancient farmers in coastal Peru had plenty of forts. All Polynesian societies had warfare, from the smallest islands like Tikopia, to Tahiti, New Zealand (more than four thousand prehistoric forts), and Hawaii. No-man's lands separated farming settlements in Okinawa, Oaxaca, and the southeastern United States. Such societies took trophy heads and cannibalized their enemies. Their skeletal remains show ample evidence of violent deaths. All well-studied prehistoric farming societies had warfare. They may have had intervals of peace, but over the span of hundreds of years there is plenty of evidence for real, deadly warfare.

When farmers initially took over the world, they did so as warriors, grabbing land as they spread out from the Levant through the Middle East into Europe, or from South China down through Southeast Asia. Later complex societies like the Maya, the Inca, the Sumerians, and the Hawaiians were no less belligerent. Here, conflict took on a new dimension. Fortresses, defensive walls hundreds of miles long, and weapons and armor expertly crafted by specialists all gave the warfare of these societies a heightened visibility.

> Demonstrating the prevalence of warfare is not an end in itself. It is only the first step in understanding why there was so much of it, why it was "rational" for everyone to engage in it all the time. I believe the question of warfare links to the availability of resources.

There is a danger in making too much of the increased visibility of warfare we see in these complex societies. This is especially true for societies with writing. When there are no texts, it is easy to see no warfare. But the opposite is true. As soon as societies can write, they write about warfare. It is not a case of literate societies having warfare for the first time, but their being able to write about what had been going on for a long time. Also, many of these literate societies link to European civilization in one way or another, and so this raises the specter of Europeans being warlike and spreading war to inherently peaceful people elsewhere, a patently false but prevalent notion. Viewing warfare from their perspective of literate societies tells us nothing about the thousands of years of human societies that were not civilizations—that is, almost all of human history. So we must not rely too much on the small time slice represented by literate societies if we want to understand warfare in the past.

The Maya were once considered a peaceful society led by scholarly priests. That all changed when the texts written by their leaders could be read, revealing a long history of warfare and conquest. Most Mayanists now accept that there was warfare, but many still resist dealing with its scale or implications. Was there population growth that resulted in resource depletion, as throughout the rest of the world? We would expect the Maya to have been fighting each other over valuable farmlands as a consequence, but Mayanist Linda Schele concluded in 1984 that "I do not think it [warfare] was territorial for the most part,"

this even though texts discuss conquest, and fortifications are present at sites like El Mirador, Calakmul, Tikal, Yaxuná, Uxmal, and many others from all time periods. Why fortify them, if no one wanted to capture them?

Today, more Maya archaeologists are looking at warfare in a systematic way, by mapping defensive features, finding images of destruction, and dating these events. A new breed of younger scholars is finding evidence of warfare throughout the Maya past. Where are the no-man's lands that almost always open up between competing states because they are too dangerous to live in? Warfare must have been intimately involved in the development of Maya civilization, and resource stress must have been widespread.

Demonstrating the prevalence of warfare is not an end in itself. It is only the first step in understanding why there was so much, why it was "rational" for everyone to engage in it all the time. I believe the question of warfare links to the availability of resources.

During the 1960s, I lived in Western Samoa as a Peace Corps volunteer on what seemed to be an idyllic South Pacific Island—exactly like those painted by Paul Gauguin. Breadfruit and coconut groves grew all around my village, and I resided in a thatched-roof house with no walls beneath a giant mango tree. If ever there was a Garden of Eden, this was it. I lived with a family headed by an extremely intelligent elderly chief named Sila. One day, Sila happened to mention that the island's trees did not bear fruit as they had when he was a child. He attributed the decline to the possibility that the presence of radio transmissions had affected production, since Western Samoa (now known as Samoa) had its own radio station by then. I suggested that what had changed was not that there was less fruit but that there were more mouths to feed. Upon reflection, Sila decided I was probably right. Being an astute manager, he was already taking the precaution of expanding his farm plots into some of the last remaining farmable land on the island, at considerable cost and effort, to ensure adequate food for his growing family. Sila was aware of his escalating provisioning problems but was not quite able to grasp the overall demographic situation. Why was this?

The simple answer is that the rate of population change in our small Samoan village was so gradual that during an adult life span growth was not dramatic enough to be fully comprehended. The same thing happens to us all the time. Communities grow and change composition, and often only after the process is well advanced do we recognize just how significant the changes have been—and we have the benefit of historic documents, old photographs, long life spans, and government census surveys. All human societies can grow substantially over time, and all did whenever resources permitted. The change may seem small in one person's lifetime, but over a couple of hundred years, populations can and do double, triple, or quadruple in size.

The consequences of these changes become evident only when there is a crisis. The same can be said for environmental changes. The forests of Central America were being denuded and encroached upon for many years, but it took Hurricane Mitch, which ravaged most of the region in late October 1998, to produce the dramatic flooding and devastation that fully demonstrated the magnitude of the problem: too many people cutting down the forest and farming steep hillsides to survive. The natural environment is resilient and at the same time delicate, as modern society keeps finding out. And it was just so in the past.

From foragers to farmers to more complex societies, when people no longer have resource stress they stop fighting. When climate greatly improves, warfare declines. The great towns of Chaco Canyon were built during an extended warm–and peaceful–period.

These observations about Mother Nature are incompatible with popular myths about peaceful people living in ecological balance with nature in the past. A peaceful past is possible only if you live in ecological balance. If you live in a Garden of Eden surrounded by plenty, why fight? By this logic, warfare is a sure thing when natural resources run dry. If someone as smart as Sila couldn't perceive population growth, and if humans all over Earth continue to degrade their environments, could people living in the past have been any different?

A study by Canadian social scientists Christina Mesquida and Neil Wiener has shown that the greater the proportion of a society is composed of unmarried young men, the greater the likelihood of war. Why such a correlation? It is not because the young men are not married; it is because they cannot get married. They are too poor to support wives and families. The idea that poverty breeds war is far from original. The reason poverty exists has remained the same since the beginning of time: humans have invariably overexploited their resources because they have always outgrown them.

There is another lesson from past warfare. It stops. From foragers to farmers, to more complex societies, when people no longer have resource stress they stop fighting. When the climate greatly improves, warfare declines. For example, in a variety of places the medieval warm interval of ca. 900–1100 improved farming conditions. The great towns of Chaco Canyon were built at this time, and it was the time of archaeologist Stephen Lekson's *Pax Chaco*—the longest period of peace in the Southwest. It is no accident that the era of Gothic cathedrals was a response to similar climate improvement. Another surprising fact is that the amount of warfare has declined over time. If we count

the proportion of a society that died from warfare, and not the size of the armies, as the true measure of warfare, then we find that foragers and farmers have much higher death rates—often approaching 25 percent of the men—than more recent complex societies. No complex society, including modern states, ever approached this level of warfare.

If warfare has ultimately been a constant battle over scarce resources, then solving the resource problem will enable us to become better at ridding ourselves of conflict.

There have been several great "revolutions" in human history: control of fire, the acquisition of speech, the agricultural revolution, the development of complex societies. One of the most recent, the Industrial Revolution, has lowered the birth rate and increased available resources. History shows that peoples with strong animosities stop fighting after adequate resources are established and the benefits of cooperation recognized. The Hopi today are some of the most peaceful people on earth, yet their history is filled with warfare. The Gebusi of lowland New Guinea, the African !Kung Bushmen, the Mbuti Pygmies of central Africa, the Sanpoi and their neighbors of the southern Columbia River, and the Sirionno of Amazonia are all peoples who are noted for being peaceful, yet archaeology and historical accounts provide ample evidence of past warfare. Sometimes things changed in a generation; at other times it took longer. Adequate food and opportunity does not instantly translate into peace, but it will, given time.

The fact that it can take several generations or longer to establish peace between warring factions is little comfort for those engaged in the world's present conflicts. Add to this a recent change in the decision-making process that leads to war. In most traditional societies, be they forager bands, tribal farmers, or even complex chiefdoms, no individual held enough power to start a war on his own. A consensus was needed; pros and cons were carefully weighed and hotheads were not tolerated. The risks to all were too great. Moreover, failure of leadership was quickly recognized, and poor leaders were replaced. No Hitler or Saddam Hussein would have been tolerated. Past wars were necessary for survival, and therefore were rational; too often today this is not the case. We cannot go back to forager-band-type consensus, but the world must work harder at keeping single individuals from gaining the power to start wars. We know from archaeology that the amount of warfare has declined markedly over the course of human history and that peace can prevail under the right circumstances. In spite of the conflict we see around us, we are doing better, and there is less warfare in the world today than there ever has been. Ending it may be a slow process, but we are making headway.

©2003 *by* STEVEN A. LEBLANC. *Portions of this article were taken from his book* Constant Battles, *published in April 2003 by St. Martin's Press. LeBlanc is director of collections at Harvard University's Peabody Museum of Archaeology and Ethnology. For further reading visit* www.archaeology.org.

The Iceman Reconsidered

Where was the Iceman's home and what was he doing at the high mountain pass where he died? Painstaking research—especially of plant remains found with the body—contradicts many of the initial speculations

By James H. Dickson, Klaus Oeggl and Linda L. Handley

On a clear day in September 1991 a couple hiking along a high ridge in the Alps came upon a corpse melting out of the ice. When they returned to the mountain hut where they were staying, they alerted the authorities, who assumed the body was one of the missing climbers lost every year in the crevasses that crisscross the glaciers of the region. But after the remains were delivered to nearby Innsbruck, Austria, Konrad Spindler, an archaeologist from the University there, ascertained that the corpse was prehistoric. The victim, a male, had died several thousand years ago. Spindler and other scientists deduced that his body and belongings had been preserved in the ice until a fall of dust from the Sahara and an unusually warm spell combined to melt the ice, exposing his head, back and shoulders.

No well-preserved bodies had ever been found in Europe from this period, the Neolithic, or New Stone Age. The Iceman is much older than the Iron Age men from the Danish peat bogs and older even than the Egyptian royal mummies. Almost as astounding was the presence of a complete set of clothes and a variety of gear.

In the ensuing excitement over the discovery, the press and researchers offered many speculations about the ancient man. Spindler hypothesized

> THE ICEMAN was discovered in a rocky hollow high in the Alps, in the zone of perennial snow and ice. Pressure from the overlying ice had removed a piece of the scalp. His corpse lay draped over a boulder. Contrary to earlier assumptions, evidence indicates it had floated into that position during previous thaws.

an elaborate disaster theory. He proposed that the man had fled to safety in the mountains after being injured in a fight at his home village. It was autumn, Spindler went on, and the man was a shepherd who sought refuge in the high pastures where he took his herds in summer. Hurt and in a state of exhaustion, he fell asleep and died on the boulder on which he was found five millennia later. The beautiful preservation of the body, according to this account, was the result of a fall of snow that protected the corpse from scavengers, followed by rapid freeze-drying.

Because the uniqueness of the discovery had not been immediately evident, the corpse was torn from the ice in a way that destroyed much archaeological information and damaged the body itself. A more thorough archaeological excavation of the site took place in the summer of 1992 and produced much valuable evidence, including an abundance or organic material (seeds, leaves, wood, mosses). This material added greatly to the plant remains, especially mosses, already washed from the clothes during the conservation process. Now, after a decade of labor-intensive research by us and other scientists on these plant remains and on samples taken from the Iceman's intestines, some hard facts are revising those first, sketchily formed impressions and replacing them with a more substantiated story.

> Ötzi had been WARMLY DRESSED in leggings, loincloth and jacket made of the hide of deer and goat, and a cape made of grass and bast.

Who Was He?

THE HIKERS HAD DISCOVERED the body at 3,210 meters above sea level in the Ötztal Alps, which led to the popular humanizing nickname Ötzi. A mere 92 meters south of the Austrian-Italian border, the shallow, rocky hollow that sheltered the body is near the pass called Hauslabjoch between Italy's Schnalstal (Val Senales in Italian) and the Ventertal in Austria [*see map on the next page*]. Ötzi lay in an awkward position, draped prone over a boulder, his left arm sticking out to the right, and his right hand trapped under a large stone. His gear and clothing, also frozen or partially frozen in the ice, were scattered around him, some items as far as several meters away. Radiocarbon dates from three different laboratories made both on plant remains found with the body and on samples of Ötzi's tissues and gear all confirm that he lived about 5,300 years ago.

Certain other features of Ötzi were relatively easy to discover as well. At 159 centimeters (5'2.5"), he was a small man, as many men in Schnalstal vicinity are today. Bone studies show he was 46 years old, an advanced age for people of his time. DNA analysis indicates his origin in central-northern Europe, which may seem obvious, but it differentiates him from Mediterranean people, whose lands lie not too far distant to the south.

In an unusual congenital anomaly, his 12th ribs are missing. His seventh and eighth left ribs had been broken and had healed in his lifetime. According to Peter Vanezis of the University of Glasgow, his right rib cage is deformed and there are possible fractures of the third and fourth ribs. These changes happened after he died, as did a fracture of the left arm. That these breakages occurred after death is among the considerable evidence that casts doubt on the early disaster theory. So does the finding that an area of missing scalp was caused by pressure, not by a blow or decay.

Holding aside the unanswered questions concerning Ötzi' death and whether it was violent or not, several sound reasons suggest that he had not been in the best of health when he died. Although most of his epidermis (the outer layer of the skin), hair and fingernails are gone, probably having decayed as a result of exposure to water during occasional thaws, his remains still offer something of a health record for modern investigators. Examination of the only one of his fingernails to have been found revealed three Beau's lines, which develop when the nails stop growing and then start again. These lines show that he had been very ill three times in the last six months of his life and that the final episode, about two months before his death, was the most serious and lasted at least two weeks. Horst Aspöck of the University of Vienna found that he had an infestation of the intestinal parasite whipworm, which can cause debilitating diarrhea and even dysentery, although we do not know how bad his infestation was.

Overview/A New Look at an Ancient Man

The most current research indicates that the Iceman:

- May have lived near where Juval Castle now stands in southern Tyrol (Italy)
- Ate a varied diet of primitive wheat, other plants and meat
- Was 46 years old and had not been in the best of health
- Died in the spring, not in the autumn as previously thought
- May have been killed by being shot in the back with an arrow
- Did not expire on the boulder where he was found, as was believed, but floated into position there during occasional thaws

---

Moreover, many simple, charcoal-dust tattoos are visible on the layer of skin under the missing epidermis. These marks were certainly not decorative and were probably therapeutic. Several are on or close to Chinese acupuncture points and at places where he could have suffered from arthritis—the lower spine, right knee and ankle. This coincidence has led to claims of treatment by acupuncture. Yet, according to Vanezis and Franco Tagliaro of the University of Rome, x-rays show little if any sign of arthritis.

The little toe of his left foot reveals evidence of frostbite. Ötzi's teeth are very worn, a reflection of his age and diet. Remains of two human fleas were found in his clothes. No lice were seen, but because his epidermis had been shed, any lice may have been lost.

What Was His Gear Like?

TURNING TO ÖTZI'S clothing and gear, scientists have learned not only about Ötzi himself but about the community in which he lived. The items are a testament of how intimately his people knew the rocks, fungi, plants and animals in their immediate surroundings. And we can see that they also knew how to obtain resources from farther afield, such as flint and copper ore. This knowledge ensured that Ötzi was extremely well equipped, each object fashioned from the material best suited to its purpose.

He had been warmly dressed in three layers of clothing—leggings, loincloth and jacket made of the hide of deer and goat, and a cape made of grass and bast, the long, tough fibers from the bark of the linden tree. His hat was bearskin, and his shoes, which were insulated with grass, had bearskin soles and goatskin uppers

He had carried a copper ax and a dagger of flint from near Lake Garda, about 150 kilometers to the south. The handle of the dagger was ash wood, a material still used for handles today because it does not splinter easily. His unfinished longbow was carved from yew, the best wood for such a purpose because of its great tensile strength. The famous English longbows used to defeat the

THE ROUTE THE ICEMAN MAY HAVE TAKEN

THE AREA WHERE the Iceman was found (*red circle*) straddles the frontier between Austria and Italy. At first thought to lie in Austria, the body was taken to Innsbruck. Later, however, authorities determined that the site falls just over the border in Italy, where the Iceman now resides in a specially prepared museum at Bolzano. Based mainly on botanical remains preserved with the body, the authors speculate that the Iceman's last journey (*red line*) may have been from the area near Juval Castle through the Schnalstal and finally the steep climb up the Tisental (*profile below*). Dickson and his fellow fieldworkers have surveyed this region for the 80 species of mosses and liverworts found with the Iceman and extracted from the sand and gravel in the hollow; only about 20 of the species grow around the site now. The moss found in largest amount adhering to the clothing is *Neckera complanata* (*green circles indicate where it grows today*). The greatest concentration of this moss and the presence of many of the other plants found with the Iceman occur to the south of the site, at Juval Castle, where there is archaeological evidence of a prehistoric settlement. This spot may have been his home.

Vent

Ventertal

GERMANY

Innsbruck

AUSTRIA

Bolzano

AREA OF DETAIL

ITALY

Lake Garda

Verona

Venice

Po River

N

Niedertal

ÖTZTAL ALPS

Hauslabjoch

Ötzi Site

Finailspitze

AUSTRIA

Border

Tisental
(Val di Tisa)

ITALY

1 KILOMETER

Vernagt Reservoir
(Vernago)

Schnalstal
(Val Senales)

Possible route of Iceman

Neckera complanata
moss sites

Vinschgau
(Val Venosta)

Juval Castle

Map © RobWood/Wood Ronsaville Harlin, Inc.

Courtesy of James H. Dickson, University of Glasgow

Elevation Profile

Finailspitze
3,514 meters

Ötzi
Site

Tisental

Niedertal

Vent

Vernagt
Reservoir

Ventertal

Juval Castle

Schnalstal

ITALY

AUSTRIA

Vinschgau

Height [meters]: 4,000 / 3,500 / 3,000 / 2,500 / 2,000 / 1,500 / 1,000 / 500 / 0

Distance (kilometers): 0 5 10 15 20 25 30 35

French at Agincourt some 4,000 years later were made of yew. A hide quiver contained 14 arrows, only two of which had feathers and flint arrowheads attached, but these two were broken. Thirteen of the arrow shafts were made of wayfaring tree, which produces long, straight, rigid stems of suitable diameter; one was partly of wayfaring tree and partly of dogwood.

On hide thongs, he carried two pierced pieces of BIRCH BRACKET FUNGUS, known to contain pharmacologically active compounds.

A belted pouch contained a tinder kit, which held a bracket fungus that grows on trees, known as the true tinder fungus, and iron pyrites and flints for making sparks. A small tool for sharpening the flints was also found with the body. On hide thongs, Ötzi carried two pierced pieces of birch bracket fungus; it is known to contain pharmacologically active compounds (triterpens) and so may have been used medicinally. There were also the fragments of a net, the frame of a backpack, and two containers made of birch bark; one held both charcoal and leaves of Norway maple—perhaps it originally transported embers wrapped in the leaves.

Where Was He From?

IN THIS PART OF THE ALPS, the valleys run north and south between towering ranges of mountains. Thus, the question of Ötzi's homeland resolves itself into north versus south rather than east versus west. The botanical evidence points to the south. A Neolithic site has been discovered at Juval, a medieval castle at the southern end of the Schnalstal, more than 2,000 meters lower but only 15 kilo-

meters from the hollow as the crow flies. Archaeologists have not excavated the site in modern times, and there has been no radiocarbon dating, but Juval is the nearest place to the hollow where a number of the flowering plants and mosses associated with Ötzi now grow. We have no reason to suppose that they did not grow there in prehistoric times, and so perhaps that is the very place where Ötzi lived.

When his clothes were conserved, the washing revealed many plant fragments, including a mass of the large woodland moss *Neckera complanata*. This moss and others he had carried grow to the north and to the south of where he was found, but the southern sources are much closer. *N. complanata* grows in some abundance near Juval. Wolfgang Hofbauer of the Fraunhofer Institute for Building Physics in Valley, Germany, has discovered that this moss grows, in more moderate amounts, at Vernagt (Vernago), just 1,450 meters lower than the site and only five kilometers away. And most recently, Alexandra Schmidl of the University of Innsbruck Botanical Institute discovered small leaf fragments of the moss *Anomodon viticulosus* in samples taken from the stomach. This woodland moss grows with *N. complanata* in lowermost Schnalstal.

If Juval was not his home, signs of Neolithic occupation at other locations in the immediately adjacent Vinschgau (Val Venosta), the valley of the River Etsch (Adige), offer other possibilities. In contrast, to the north, the nearest known Stone Age settlements are many tens of kilometers away, and we are not aware of any Neolithic settlements in the Ventertal or elsewhere in the Ötztal. If Ötzi's home was indeed in lowermost Schnalstal or in Vinschgau, then his community lived in a region of mild, short, largely snow-free winters, especially so if the climate was then slightly warmer.

Investigations by Wolfgang Müller of the Australian National

University of the isotopic composition of the Iceman's tooth enamel suggest that he had grown up in one area but spent the last several decades of his life in a different place. Investigating stable isotopes and trace elements, Jurian Hoogewerff of the Institute of Food Research in Norwich, England, and other researchers have claimed that Ötzi probably spent most of his final years in the Ventertal or nearby valleys to the north. If these deductions can be substantiated, they are intriguing developments.

What Did He Eat?

THE ONGOING STUDIES of the plant remains in samples taken from the digestive tract provide direct evidence of some of Ötzi's last meals. One of us (Oeggl) has detected bran of the primitive wheat called einkorn, so fine that it may well have been ground into flour for baking bread rather than having been made into a gruel. Microscopic debris of as yet unidentified types shows that he had eaten other plants as well. And Franco Rollo and his team at the University of Camerino in Italy, in their DNA studies of food residues in the intestines, have recognized both red deer and alpine ibex (wild goat). Splinters of ibex neck bones were also discovered close to Ötzi's body. A solitary but whole sloe lay near the corpse as well. Sloes are small, bitter, plumlike fruit, and Ötzi may have been carrying dried sloes as provisions.

Several types of moss were recovered from the digestive tract. There is virtually no evidence that humans have ever eaten mosses, certainly not as a staple of their diet. But 5,000 and more years ago no materials were manufactured for wrapping, packing, stuffing or wiping. Mosses were highly convenient for such purposes, as many archaeological discoveries across Europe have revealed: various mosses in Viking and medieval cesspits were clearly used as toilet paper. Had Ötzi's provisions been wrapped in moss, that would neatly explain, as an accidental ingestion, the several leaves and leaf fragments of *N. complanata* recovered from the samples taken from the gut.

Analyzing archaeological remains of bone and hair for their abundances of the stable isotopes of carbon and nitrogen (carbon 13 and nitrogen 15) can provide information about a person's diet. Nitrogen 15 can reveal the extent to which the individual relied on animal or plant protein. Carbon 13 can indicate the type of food plant the person ate and whether seafood or terrestrial carbon was an important part of the diet.

The isotopic data agree with the other evidence that Ötzi ate a mixed diet of plants and animals. He obtained about 30 percent of his dietary nitrogen from animal protein and the rest from plants. This value is consistent with those found in hunter-gatherer tribes living today. The data also indicate that seafood was probably not a component of his diet, a finding that makes sense because of the great distance to the sea.

What Was He Doing There?

TO THIS DAY, in what may be an ancient custom, shepherds take their flocks from the Schnalstal up to high pastures in the Ötztal in June and bring them down again in September. The body was found near one of the traditional routes, which is why early theories held that he was a shepherd. Nothing about his clothing or equipment, however, proves that he had done such work. No wool was on or around his person, no dead collie by his feet, no crook in his hand. Some support for the shepherd hypothesis comes from the grass and bast cape, which has modern parallels in garments worn by shepherds in the Balkans, but that alone is not conclusive; for all we know, it was standard dress for travelers at that time.

Analysis of the few strands of Ötzi's hair that survived reveals very high values of both arsenic and copper. The published explanation (also

given independently on television) was that he had taken part in the smelting of copper. But Geoffrey Grime of the University of Surrey in England now considers that these exceptional levels may have resulted from the action of metal-fixing bacteria after Ötzi died and that the copper was *on,* not *in,* the hair. Further support for the possibility of copper having attached itself to the hair after death comes from the presence of the moss *Mielichhoferia elongata,* called copper moss, which spreads preferentially on copper-bearing rocks. It has been found growing at the site by one of us (Dickson) and, independently, by Ronald D. Porley of the U.K. government agency English Nature.

Another hypothesis is that Ötzi was a hunter of alpine ibex; the longbow and quiver of arrows may support this notion. If, however, he had been actively engaged in hunting at the time of his death, why is the bow unfinished and unstrung and all but two of the arrows without heads and feathers and those two broken?

Other early ideas about Ötzi are that he was an outlaw, a trader of flint, a shaman or a warrior. None of these has any solid basis, unless the pieces of bracket fungus he was carrying had medicinal or spiritual use for a shaman.

How Did He Die?

IN JULY 2001 Paul Gostner and Eduard Egarter Vigl of the Regional Hospital of Bolzano in Italy announced that x-rays had revealed an arrowhead in Ötzi's back under the left shoulder. This assertion has led to numerous statements in the media that Ötzi was murdered and to claims from Gostner and Egarter Vigl that it is "now proven that Ötzi did not die a natural death, nor due to exhaustion or frostbite alone." Although three-dimensional reconstructions of the object, which is 27 millimeters long and 18 millimeters wide, exist, requests by Vanezis and Tagliaro for the object to be removed to show convincingly that it is an ar-

rowhead are still unanswered. Furthermore, it must be removed in a way that makes clear what fatal damage it might have done.

The arrowhead need not have caused death. Many people stay alive after foreign objects such as bullets have entered their bodies. A notable archaeological example is the Cascade spear point in the right pelvis of the famous Kennewick Man in North America; it had been there long enough for the bone to begin healing around it.

Even more recently, in a statement to the media, Egarter Vigl has reported that Ötzi's right hand reveals a deep stab wound. No scientific publication of this finding has been made yet.

At What Time of Year?

INITIAL REPORTS PLACED the season of death in autumn. The presence of the sloe, which ripens in late summer, near the body and small pieces of grain in Ötzi's clothing, presumed to have lodged there during harvest threshing, formed the basis for these reports. But strong botanical evidence now indicates that Ötzi died in late spring or early summer. Studies by Oeggl of a tiny sample of food residue from Ötzi's colon have revealed the presence of the pollen of a small tree called hop hornbeam. Strikingly, much of that pollen has retained its cellular contents, which normally decay swiftly. This means that Ötzi might have ingested airborne pollen or drunk water containing freshly shed pollen shortly before he died. The hop hornbeam, which grows up to about 1,200 meters above sea level in the Schnalstal, flowers only in late spring and early summer.

As for the sloe found near his body, if Ötzi had been carrying sloes dried like prunes, the drying could have taken place some time before his journey. Small bits of grain also keep indefinitely, and a few scraps could have been carried inadvertently in his clothes for a long period.

What We Know

MORE THAN 10 YEARS after the discovery of the oldest, best-preserved human body, interpretations about who he was and how he came to rest in a rocky hollow high in the Alps have changed greatly. Just as important, we see that much careful research still needs to be done. The studies of the plant remains-the pollen, seeds, mosses and fungi found both inside and outside the body-have already disclosed a surprising number of Ötzi's secrets. We are aware of his omnivorous diet, his intimate knowledge of his surroundings, his southern domicile, his age and state of health, the season of his death, and something of his environment. Perhaps one of the most surprising reinterpretations is that Ötzi did not die on the boulder on which

he was found. Rather he had floated there during one of the temporary thaws known to have occurred over the past 5,000 years. The positioning of the body, with the left arm stuck out awkwardly to the right and the right hand trapped under a stone, and the missing epidermis both suggest this conclusion. So does the fact that some of his belongings lay several meters distant, as if they had floated away from the body.

But we do not know and may never know what reason Ötzi had for being at a great altitude in the Alps. And we may never understand exactly how he died. An autopsy would be too destructive to be carried out. In the absence of this kind of proof, we cannot completely exclude the possibility that perhaps Ötzi died elsewhere and was carried

to the hollow where the hikers found him 5,000 years later.

THE AUTHORS *JIM DICKSON, KLAUS OEGGL* and *LINDA HANDLEY* share an interest in the plants that the Tyrolean Iceman may have used in his daily life. Dickson, professor of archaeobotany and plant systematics at the University of Glasgow, is recipient of the Neill Medal of the Royal Society of Edinburgh. He has written more than 150 papers and five books, including *Plants and People in Ancient Scotland* (Tempus Publishing, 2000), which he co-authored with his late wife, Camilla. Oeggl is professor of botany at the University of Innsbruck in Austria. He is an expert in archaeobotany and co-editor of the book *The Iceman and His Natural Environment* (Springer-Verlag, 2000). Handley, an ecophysiologist at the Scottish Crop Research Institute in Invergowrie, near Dundee, Scotland, specializes in the study of stable isotopes of carbon and nitrogen in plants and soils.

THE LITTLEST HUMAN

A spectacular find in Indonesia reveals that a strikingly different hominid shared the earth with our kind in the not so distant past

By Kate Wong

On the island of Flores in Indonesia, villagers have long told tales of a diminutive, upright-walking creature with a lopsided gait, a voracious appetite, and soft, murmuring speech.

They call it *ebu gogo*, "the grandmother who eats anything." Scientists' best guess was that macaque monkeys inspired the *ebu gogo* lore. But last October, an alluring alternative came to light. A team of Australian and Indonesian researchers excavating a cave on Flores unveiled the remains of a lilliputian human—one that stood barely a meter tall—whose kind lived as recently as 13,000 years ago.

The announcement electrified the paleoanthropology community. *Homo sapiens* was supposed to have had the planet to itself for the past 25 millennia, free from the company of other humans following the apparent demise of the Neandertals in Europe and *Homo erectus* in Asia. Furthermore, hominids this tiny were known only from fossils of australopithecines (Lucy and the like) that lived nearly three million years ago—long before the emergence of *H. sapiens*. No one would have predicted that our own species had a contemporary as small and primitive-looking as the little Floresian. Neither would anyone have guessed that a creature with a skull the size of a grapefruit might have possessed cognitive capabilities comparable to those of anatomically modern humans.

Isle of Intrigue

THIS IS NOT THE FIRST TIME Flores has yielded surprises. In 1998 archaeologists led by Michael J. Morwood of the University of New England in Armidale, Australia, reported having discovered crude stone artifacts some 840,000 years old in the Soa Basin of central Flores. Although no human remains turned up with the tools, the implication was that *H. erectus*, the only hominid known to have lived in Southeast Asia during that time, had crossed the deep waters separating Flores from Java.

Overview/Mini Humans

- Conventional wisdom holds that *Homo sapiens* has been the sole human species on the earth for the past 25,000 years. Remains discovered on the Indonesian island of Flares have upended that view.
- The bones are said to belong to a dwarf species of *Homo* that lived as recently as 13,000 years ago.
- Although the hominid is as small in body and brain as the earliest humans, it appears to have made sophisticated stone tools, raising questions about the relation between brain size and intelligence.
- The find is controversial, however—some experts wonder whether the discoverers have correctly diagnosed the bones and whether anatomically modern humans might have made those advanced artifacts.

To the team, the find showed *H. erectus* to be a seafarer, which was startling because elsewhere *H. erectus* had left behind little material culture to suggest that it was anywhere near capable of making watercraft. Indeed, the earliest accepted date for boat-building was 40,000 to 60,000 years ago, when modern humans colonized Australia. (The other early fauna on Flores probably got there by swimming or accidentally drifting over on flotsam. Humans are not strong enough swimmers to have managed that voyage, but skeptics say they may have drifted across on natural rafts.)

Hoping to document subsequent chapters of human occupation of the island, Morwood and Radien P. Soejono of the Indonesian Center for Archaeology in Jakarta turned their attention to a large limestone cave called Liang Bua located in western Flores. Indonesian archaeologists had been excavating the cave intermittently since the 1970s, depending on funding availability, but workers had penetrated only the uppermost deposits. Morwood and Soejono set their sights on reaching bedrock and began digging in July 2001. Before long, their team's efforts turned up abundant stone tools and bones of a pygmy version of an extinct elephant relative known as *Stegodon*. But it was not until nearly the end of the third season of fieldwork that diagnostic hominid material in the form of an isolated tooth surfaced. Morwood brought a cast of the tooth back to Armidale to show to his department colleague Peter Brown. "It was clear that while the premolar was broadly humanlike, it wasn't from a modern human," Brown recollects. Seven days later Morwood received word that the Indonesians had recovered a skeleton. The Australians boarded the next plane to Jakarta.

Peculiar though the premolar was, nothing could have prepared them for the skeleton, which apart from the missing arms was largely complete. The pelvis anatomy revealed that the individual was bipedal and probably a female, and the tooth eruption and wear indicated that it was an adult. Yet it was only as tall as a modern three-year-old, and its brain was as small as the smallest australopithecine brain known. There were other primitive traits as well, including the broad pelvis and the long neck of the femur. In other respects, however, the specimen looked familiar. Its small teeth and narrow nose, the overall shape of the braincase and the thickness of the cranial bones all evoked *Homo*.

Brown spent the next three months analyzing the enigmatic skeleton, catalogued as LB1 and affectionately nicknamed the Hobbit by some of the team members, after the tiny beings in J.R.R. Tolkien's *The Lord of the Rings* books. The decision about how to classify it did not come easily. Impressed with the characteristics LB1 shared with early hominids such as the australopithecines, he initially proposed that it represented a new genus of human. On further consideration, however, the similarities to *Homo* proved more persuasive. Based on the 18,000-year age of LB1, one might have reasonably expected the bones to belong to *H. sapiens*, albeit a very petite representative. But when Brown and his colleagues considered the morphological characteristics of small-bodied modern humans—including normal ones, such as pygmies, and abnormal ones, such as pituitary dwarfs—LB1 did not seem to fit any of those descriptions. Pygmies have small bodies and large brains—the result of delayed growth during puberty, when the brain has already attained its full size. And individuals with genetic disorders that produce short stature and small brains have a range of distinctive features not seen in LB1 and rarely reach adulthood, Brown says. Conversely, he notes, the Flores skeleton exhibits archaic traits that have never been documented for abnormal small-bodied *H. sapiens*.

DWARFS AND GIANTS tend to evolve on islands, with animals larger than rabbits shrinking and animals smaller than rabbits growing. The shifts appear to be adaptive responses to the limited food supplies available in such environments. *Stegodon*, an extinct proboscidean, colonized Flores several times, dwindling from elephant to water buffalo proportions. Some rats, in contrast, became rabbit-sized over time. *H. floresiensis* appears to have followed the island rule as well. It is thought to be a dwarfed descendant of *H. erectus*, which itself was nearly the size of a modern human.

What LB1 looks like most, the researchers concluded, is a miniature *H. erectus*. Describing the find in the journal *Nature*, they assigned LB1 as well as the isolated tooth and an arm bone from older deposits to a new species of human, *Homo floresiensis*. They further argued that it was a descendant of *H. erectus* that had become marooned on Flores and evolved in isolation into a dwarf species, much as the elephant-like *Stegodon* did.

Biologists have long recognized that mammals larger than rabbits tend to shrink on small islands, presumably as an adaptive response to the limited food supply. They have little to lose by doing so, because these environments harbor few predators. On Flores, the only sizable predators were the Komodo dragon and another, even larger monitor lizard. Animals smaller than rabbits, on the other hand, tend to attain brobdingnagian proportions—perhaps because bigger bodies are more energetically efficient than small ones. Liang Bua has yielded evidence of that as well, in the form of a rat as robust as a rabbit.

But attributing a hominid's bantam size to the so-called island rule was a first. Received paleoanthropological wisdom holds that culture has buffered us humans from many of the selective pressures that mold other creatures—we cope with cold, for example, by building fires and making clothes, rather than evolving a proper pelage. The discovery of a dwarf hominid species indicates that, under the right conditions, humans can in fact respond in the same, predictable way that other large mammals do when the going gets tough. Hints that *Homo* could deal with resource fluxes in this manner came earlier in 2004 from the discovery of a relatively petite *H. erectus* skull from Olorgesailie in Kenya, remarks Richard Potts of the Smithsonian Institution, whose team recovered the bones. "Getting small is one of the things *H. erectus* had in its biological tool kit," he says, and the Flores hominid seems to be an extreme instance of that.

SHARED FEATURES between LB1 and members of our own genus led to the classification of the Flores hominid as *Homo*, despite its tiny brain size. Noting that the specimen most closely resembles *H. erectus*, the researchers posit that it is a new species, *H. floresiensis*, that dwarfed from a *H. erectus* ancestor. *H. floresiensis* differs from *H. sapiens* in having, among other characteristics, no chin, a relatively projecting face, a prominent brow and a low braincase.

Curiouser and Curiouser

H. FLORESIENSIS's teeny brain was perplexing. What the hominid reportedly managed to accomplish with such a modest organ was nothing less than astonishing. Big brains are a hallmark of human evolution. In the space of six million to seven million years, our ancestors more than tripled their cranial capacity, from some 360 cubic centimeters in *Sahelanthropus*, the earliest putative hominid, to a whopping 1,350 cubic centimeters on average in modern folks. Archaeological evidence indicates that behavioral complexity increased correspondingly. Experts were thus fairly certain that large brains are a prerequisite for advanced cultural practices. Yet whereas the pea-brained australopithecines left behind only crude stone tools at best (and most seem not to have done any stone working at all), the comparably gray-matter-impoverished *H. floresiensis* is said to have manufactured implements that exhibit a level of sophistication elsewhere associated exclusively with *H. sapiens*.

The bulk of the artifacts from Liang Bua are simple flake tools struck from volcanic rock and chert, no more advanced than the implements made by late australopithecines and early *Homo*. But mixed in among the pygmy *Stegodon* remains excavators found a fancier set of tools, one that included finely worked points, large blades, awls and small blades that may have been hafted for use as spears. To the team, this association suggests that *H. floresiensis* regularly hunted *Stegodon*. Many of the *Stegodon* bones are those of young individuals that one *H. floresiensis* might have been able to bring down alone. But some belonged to adults that weighed up to half a ton, the hunting and transport of which must have been a coordinated group activity—one that probably required language, surmises team member Richard G. ("Bert") Roberts of the University of Wollongong in Australia.

The discovery of charred animal remains in the cave suggests that cooking, too, was part of the cultural repertoire of *H. floresiensis*. That a hominid as cerebrally limited as this one might have had control of fire gives pause. Humans are not thought to have tamed flame until relatively late in our collective cognitive development: the earliest unequivocal evidence of fire use comes from 200,000-year-old hearths in Europe that were the handiwork of the large-brained Neandertals.

If the *H. floresiensis* discoverers are correct in their interpretation, theirs is one of the most important paleoanthropological finds in decades. Not only does it mean that another species of human coexisted with our ancestors just yesterday in geological terms, and that our genus is far more variable than expected, it raises all sorts of questions about brain size and intelligence. Perhaps it should come as no surprise, then, that controversy has accompanied their claims.

Classification Clash

IT DID NOT TAKE LONG for alternative theories to surface. In a letter that ran in the October 31 edition of Australia's *Sunday Mail*, just three days after the publication of the *Nature* issue containing the initial reports, paleoanthropologist Maciej Henneberg of the University of Adelaide countered that a pathological condition known as microcephaly (from the Greek for "small brain") could explain LB1's unusual features. Individuals afflicted with the most severe congenital form of microcephaly, primordial microcephalic dwarfism, die in childhood. But those with milder forms, though mentally retarded, can survive into adulthood. Statistically comparing the head and face dimensions of LB1 with those of a 4,000-year-old skull from Crete that is known to have

Awl

Blade

Centimeters

Point

ADVANCED IMPLEMENTS appear to have been the handiwork of *H. floresiensis*. Earlier hominids with brains similar in size to that of *H. floresiensis* made only simple flake tools at most. But in the same stratigraphic levels as the hominid remains at Liang Bua, researchers found a suite of sophisticated artifacts—including awls, blades and points—exhibiting a level of complexity previously thought to be the sole purview of *H. sapiens*.
© Mark Moore, Ph.D./University of New England, Armidale, Australia

belonged to a microcephalic, Henneberg found no significant differences between the two. Furthermore, he argued, the isolated forearm bone found deeper in the deposit corresponds to a height of 151 to 162 centimeters—the stature of many modern women and some men, not that of a dwarf—suggesting that larger-bodied people, too, lived at Liang Bua. In Henneberg's view, these findings indicate that LB1 is more likely a microcephalic *H. sapiens* than a new branch of *Homo*.

Susan C. Antón of New York University disagrees with that assessment. "The facial morphology is completely different in microcephalic [modern] humans," and their body size is normal, not small, she says. Antón questions whether LB1 warrants a new species, however. "There's little in the shape that differentiates it from *Homo erectus*," she notes. One can argue that it's a new species, Antón allows, but the difference in shape between LB1 and *Homo erectus* is less striking than that between a Great Dane and a Chihuahua. The possibility exists that the LB1 specimen is a *H. erectus* individual with a pathological growth condition stemming from microcephaly or nutritional deprivation, she observes.

But some specialists say the Flores hominid's anatomy exhibits a more primitive pattern. According to Colin P. Groves of the Australian National University and David W. Cameron of the University of Sydney, the small brain, the long neck of the femur and other characteristics suggest an ancestor along the lines of *Homo habilis*, the earliest member of our genus, rather than the more advanced *H. erectus*. Milford H. Wolpoff of the University of Michigan at Ann Arbor wonders whether the Flores find might even represent an offshoot of *Australopithecus*. If LB1 is a descendant of *H. sapiens* or *H. erectus*, it is hard to imagine how natural selection left her with a brain that's even smaller than expected for her height, Wolpoff says. Granted, if she descended from *Australopithecus*, which had massive jaws and teeth, one has to account for her relatively delicate jaws and dainty dentition. That, however, is a lesser evolutionary conundrum than the one posed by her tiny brain, he asserts. After all, a shift in diet could explain the reduced chewing apparatus, but why would selection downsize intelligence?

Finding an australopithecine that lived outside of Africa—not to mention all the way over in Southeast Asia—18,000 years ago would be a first. Members of this group were thought to have died out in Africa one and a half million years ago, never having left their mother continent. Perhaps, researchers reasoned, hominids needed long, striding limbs, large brains and better technology before they could venture out into the rest of the Old World. But the recent discovery of 1.8 million-year-old *Homo* fossils at a site called Dmanisi in the Republic of Georgia refuted that explanation—the Georgian hominids were primitive and small and utilized tools like those australopithecines had made a million years before. Taking that into consideration, there is no a priori reason why australopithecines (or habilines, for that matter) could not have colonized other continents.

Troubling Tools

YET IF *AUSTRALOPITHECUS* made it out of Africa and survived on Flores until quite recently, that would raise the question of why no other remains supporting that scenario have turned up in the region. According to Wolpoff, they may have: a handful of poorly studied Indonesian fossils discovered in the 1940s have been variously classified as *Australopithecus, Meganthropus* and, most recently, *H. erectus*. In light of the Flores find, he says, those remains deserve reexamination.

Many experts not involved in the discovery back Brown and Morwood's taxonomic decision, however. "Most of the differences [between the Flores hominid and known members of *Homo*], including apparent similarities to australopithecines, are almost certainly related to very small body mass," declares David R. Begun of the University of Toronto. That is, as the Flores people dwarfed from *H. erectus*, some of their anatomy simply converged on that of the likewise little australopithecines. Because LB1 shares some key derived features with *H. erectus* and some with other members of *Homo*, "the most straightforward option is to call it a new species of *Homo*," he remarks. "It's a fair and reasonable interpretation," *H. erectus* expert G. Philip Rightmire of Binghamton University agrees. "That was quite a little experiment in Indonesia."

Even more controversial than the position of the half-pint human on the family tree is the notion that it made those advanced-looking tools. Stanford University paleoanthropologist Richard Klein notes that the artifacts found near LB1 appear to include few, if any, of the sophisticated types found elsewhere in the cave. This brings up the possibility that the modern-looking tools were produced by modern humans, who could have occupied the cave at a different time. Further excavations are necessary to determine the stratigraphic relation between the implements and the hominid remains, Klein opines. Such efforts may turn up modern humans like us. The question then, he says, will be whether there were two species at the site or whether modern humans alone occupied Liang Bua—in which case LB1 was simply a modern who experienced a growth anomaly.

Stratigraphic concerns aside, the tools are too advanced and too large to make manufacture by a primitive, diminutive hominid likely, Groves contends. Although the Liang Bua implements allegedly date back as far as 94,000 years ago, which the team argues makes them too early to be the handiwork of *H. sapiens*, Groves points out that 67,000-year-old tools have turned up in Liujiang, China, and older indications of a modern human presence in the Far East might yet emerge. "*H. sapiens*, once it was out of Africa, didn't take long to spread into eastern Asia," he comments.

"At the moment there isn't enough evidence" to establish that *H. floresiensis* created the advanced tools, concurs Bernard Wood of George Washington University. But as a thought experiment, he says, "let's pretend that they did." In that case, "I don't have a clue about brain size and ability," he confesses. If a hominid with no more gray matter than a chimp has can create a material culture like this one, Wood contemplates, "why did it take people such a bloody long time to make tools" in the first place?

"If *Homo floresiensis* was capable of producing sophisticated tools, we have to say that brain size doesn't add up to much," Rightmire concludes. Of course, humans today exhibit considerable variation in gray matter volume, and great thinkers exist at both ends of the spectrum. French writer Jacques Anatole Francois Thibault (also known as Anatole France), who won the 1921 Nobel Prize for Literature, had a cranial capacity of only about 1,000 cubic centimeters; England's General Oliver Cromwell had more than twice that. "What that means is that once you get the brain to a certain size, size no longer matters, it's the organization of the brain," Potts states. At some point, he adds, "the internal wiring of the brain may allow competence even if the brain seems small."

LB1's brain is long gone, so how it was wired will remain a mystery. Clues to its organization may reside on the interior of the braincase, however. Paleontologists can sometimes obtain latex molds of the insides of fossil skulls and then create plaster endocasts that reveal the morphology of the organ. Because LBI's bones are too fragile to withstand standard casting procedures, Brown is working on creating a virtual endocast based on CT scans of the skull that he can then use to generate a physical endocast via stereolithography, a rapid prototyping technology.

"If it's a little miniature version of an adult human brain, I'll be really blown away," says paleoneurologist Dean Falk of the University of Florida. Then again, she muses, what happens if the convolutions look chimplike? Specialists have long wondered whether bigger brains fold differently simply because they are bigger or whether the reorganization reflects selection for increased cognition. "This specimen could conceivably answer that," Falk observes.

Return to the Lost World

SINCE SUBMITTING their technical papers to *Nature*, the Liang Bua excavators have reportedly recovered the remains of another five or so individuals, all of which fit the *H. floresiensis* profile. None are nearly so complete as LB1, whose long arms turned up during the most recent field season. But they did unearth a second lower jaw that they say is identical in size and shape to LB1's. Such duplicate bones will be critical to their case that they have a population of these tiny humans (as opposed to a bunch of scattered bones from one person). That should in turn dispel concerns that LB1 was a diseased individual.

Additional evidence may come from DNA: hair samples possibly from *H. floresiensis* are undergoing analysis at the University of Oxford, and the hominid teeth and bones may contain viable DNA as well. "Tropical environments are not the best for long-term preservation of DNA, so we're not holding our breath," Roberts remarks, "but there's certainly no harm in looking."

The future of the bones (and any DNA they contain) is uncertain, however. In late November, Teuku Jacob of the Gadjah Mada University in Yogyakarta, Java, who was not involved in the discovery or the analyses, had the delicate specimens transported from their repository at the Indonesian Center for Archaeology to his own laboratory with Soejono's assistance. Jacob, the dean of Indonesian paleoanthropology, thinks LB1 was a microcephalic and allegedly ordered the transfer of it and the new, as yet undescribed finds for examination and safekeeping, despite strong objections from other staff members at the center. At the time this article was going to press, the team was waiting for Jacob to make good on his promise to return the remains to Jakarta by January 1 of this year, but his reputation for restricting scientific access to fossils has prompted pundits to predict that the bones will never be studied again.

Efforts to piece together the *H. floresiensis* puzzle will proceed, however. For his part, Brown is eager to find the tiny hominid's large-bodied forebears. The possibilities are three-fold, he notes. Either the ancestor dwarfed on Flores (and was possibly the maker of the 840,000-year-old Soa Basin tools), or it dwindled on another island and later reached Flores, or the ancestor was small before it even arrived in Southeast Asia. In fact, in many ways, LB1 more closely resembles African *H. erectus* and the Georgian hominids than the geographically closer Javan *H. erectus*, he observes. But whether these similarities indicate that *H. floresiensis* arose from an earlier *H. erectus* foray into Southeast Asia than the one that produced Javan *H. erectus* or are merely coincidental results of the dwarfing process remains to be determined. Future excavations may connect the dots. The team plans to continue digging on Flores and Java and will next year begin work on other Indonesian islands, including Sulawesi to the north.

The hominid bones from Liang Bua now span the period from 95,000 to 13,000 years ago, suggesting to the team that the little Floresians perished along with the pygmy *Stegodon* because of a massive volcanic eruption in the area around 12,000 years ago, although they may have survived later farther east. If *H. erectus* persisted on nearby Java until 25,000 years ago, as some evidence suggests, and *H. sapiens* had arrived in the region by 40,000 years ago, three human species lived cheek by jowl in Southeast Asia for at least 15,000 years. And the discoverers of *H. floresiensis* predict that more will be found. The islands of Lombok and Sumbawa would have been natural stepping-stones for hominids traveling from Java or mainland Asia to Flores. Those that put down roots on these islands may well have set off on their own evolutionary trajectories.

Perhaps, it has been proposed, some of these offshoots of the *Homo* lineage survived until historic times. Maybe they still live in remote pockets of Southeast Asia's dense rain forests, awaiting (or avoiding) discovery. On Flores, oral histories hold that the *ebu gogo* was still in existence when Dutch colonists settled there in the 19th century. And Malay folklore describes another small, humanlike being known as the *orang pendek* that supposedly dwells on Sumatra to this day.

"Every country seems to have myths about these things," Brown reflects. "We've excavated a lot of sites around the world, and we've never found them. But then [in September 2003] we found LB1." Scientists may never know whether tales of the *ebu gogo* and *orang pendek* do in fact recount actual sightings of other hominid species, but the newfound possibility will no doubt spur efforts to find such creatures for generations to come.

Kate Wong is editorial director of ScientificAmerican.com.

Who's On First?

There's still no end to the controversy over when and how humans populated the New World.

By Anna Curtenius Roosevelt

Alittle less than 13,000 years ago, as the Ice Age was drawing to a close, big-game hunters crossed the Bering land bridge from Siberia into the Americas. By 12,000 years ago, they had made their way south from the interior of Alaska through an ice-free corridor to the high plains of North America. Hunting effectively by using spears tipped with fluted, flaked stone points (called Clovis points, after an archaeological site in New Mexico), these Paleoindians decimated the game herds of the plains in less than a thousand years. Some then migrated farther south through the highlands of Central America and the Andes, reaching the tip of South America about 10,000 years ago, just as global warming and rising sea levels marked the end of the Ice Age, or Pleistocene epoch. Only then did people spread to the coasts and big rivers; develop new varieties of triangular, stemmed points; and begin to subsist on small game, fish, shellfish, and wild plants. The game-poor tropical forests remained off-limits until after New World peoples had developed agriculture, about 5,000 years ago.

This attractively simple tale, still enshrined in some textbooks, is unraveling as a result of archaeological evidence accumulated over the past two decades. Nearly seventy years after excavations first revealed the Clovis big game hunting culture, new sites and new dates in both North and South America are challenging Clovis's claim to priority. But a new consensus has not yet emerged. Instead, scholars are engaging in acrimonious public disputes while dramatic press releases with conflicting claims incite the media.

Two new books on the first Americans offer to clarify the picture. One is by Thomas D. Dillehay, the T. Marshall Hahn Jr. Professor of Anthropology at the University of Kentucky, Lexington; the other is by E. James Dixon, the curator of archaeology at the Denver Museum of Natural History. Both books are definitely worth reading, but they require considerable effort and a critical eye. Both use terms and dating criteria inconsistently and contain inaccuracies or out-of date information that will confuse the general reader.

Although the books differ in several respects—for one thing, Dillehay's emphasizes South American discoveries, while Dixon's focuses more on North America and the Clovis sites—both take it for granted that people entered the New World before the rise of Clovis culture. The idea of an earlier migration is not new. For more than thirty years, Alan Bryan and Ruth Gruhn, as well as other archaeologists, have argued that people who lacked projectile points for big-game hunting entered the Americas more than 30,000 years ago. Recurring claims for such early cultures have been based on a handful of sites, along with analyses of Native American linguistic and genetic diversity suggesting that people have lived in the New World for a long time. But with the exception of evidence for the Nenana culture (known from several sites in central Alaska), the data supporting all pre-Clovis cultures have failed to withstand careful scrutiny. C. Vance Haynes and others have shown that the sites in question do not provide a consistent series of early dates that are securely tied to unambiguous evidence of human presence.

Neither Dillehay nor Dixon can marshal a consistent pattern of evidence for an arrival prior to 12,000 years ago. The new claims for pre-Clovis sites are no stronger than the old ones, and the old ones continue to circulate despite their evident flaws. A number of the sites championed by one or both authors—for example, Putu and Bluefish Caves—have no evidence of human presence at an early date. Some, such as Meadowcroft Rockshelter, have questionable dates due to possible contamination, and others, such as Cactus Hill, a new site in Virginia, have inconsistent dates, vague stratigraphy, and inadequate artifact

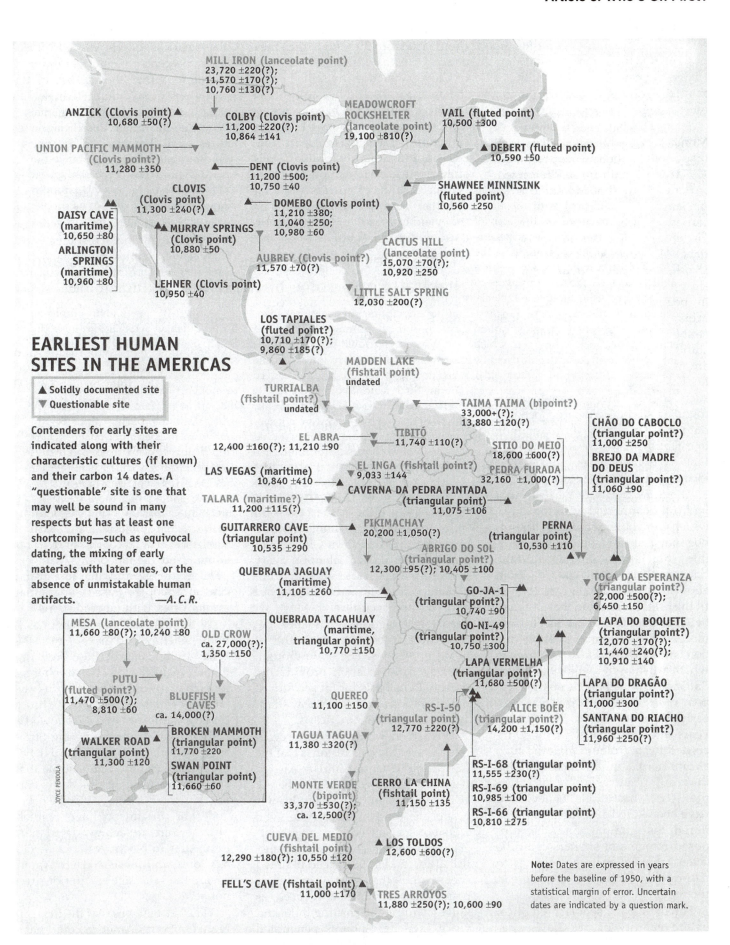

MILL IRON (lanceolate point)
23,720 ±220(?);
11,570 ±170(?);
10,760 ±130(?)

ANZICK (Clovis point) ▲
10,680 ±50(?)

COLBY (Clovis point)
11,200 ±220(?);
10,864 ±141

MEADOWCROFT
ROCKSHELTER
(lanceolate point)
19,100 ±810(?)

VAIL (fluted point)
10,500 ±300

UNION PACIFIC MAMMOTH
(Clovis point?) ▼
11,280 ±350

DEBERT (fluted point)
10,590 ±50

DENT (Clovis point)
11,200 ±500;
10,750 ±40

SHAWNEE MINNISINK
(fluted point)
10,560 ±250

CLOVIS
(Clovis point)
11,300 ±240(?) ▲

DOMEBO (Clovis point)
11,210 ±380;
11,040 ±250;
10,980 ±60

DAISY CAVE
(maritime)
10,650 ±80

MURRAY SPRINGS
(Clovis point)
10,880 ±50

ARLINGTON
SPRINGS
(maritime)
10,960 ±80

AUBREY (Clovis point)
11,570 ±70(?)

CACTUS HILL
(lanceolate point)
15,070 ±70(?);
10,920 ±250

LEHNER (Clovis point)
10,950 ±40

LITTLE SALT SPRING
12,030 ±200(?)

LOS TAPIALES
(fluted point?)
10,710 ±170(?);
9,860 ±185(?)

EARLIEST HUMAN
SITES IN THE AMERICAS

▲ Solidly documented site
▼ Questionable site

Contenders for early sites are
indicated along with their
characteristic cultures (if known)
and their carbon 14 dates. A
"questionable" site is one that
may well be sound in many
respects but has at least one
shortcoming—such as equivocal
dating, the mixing of early
materials with later ones, or the
absence of unmistakable human
artifacts.   —A.C.R.

MADDEN LAKE
(fishtail point)
undated

TURRIALBA
(fishtail point?)
undated

TAIMA TAIMA (bipoint?)
33,000+(?);
13,880 ±120(?)

CHÃO DO CABOCLO
(triangular point?)
11,000 ±250

EL ABRA
12,400 ±160(?); 11,210 ±90

TIBITÓ
11,740 ±110(?)

SITIO DO MEIO
18,600 ±600(?)

BREJO DA MADRE
DO DEUS
(triangular point?)
11,060 ±90

LAS VEGAS (maritime)
10,840 ±410

EL INGA (fishtail point?)
9,033 ±144

PEDRA FURADA
32,160 ±1,000(?)

TALARA (maritime?)
11,200 ±115(?)

CAVERNA DA PEDRA PINTADA
(triangular point)
11,075 ±106

GUITARRERO CAVE
(triangular point)
10,535 ±290

PIKIMACHAY
20,200 ±1,050(?)

PERNA
(triangular point)
10,530 ±110

ABRIGO DO SOL
(triangular point?)
12,300 ±95(?); 10,405 ±100

QUEBRADA JAGUAY
(maritime)
11,105 ±260

TOCA DA ESPERANZA
(triangular point?)
22,000 ±500(?);
6,450 ±150

MESA (lanceolate point)
11,660 ±80(?); 10,240 ±80

OLD CROW
ca. 27,000(?);
1,350 ±150

QUEBRADA TACAHUAY
(maritime,
triangular point)
10,770 ±150

GO-JA-1
(triangular point?)
10,740 ±90

GO-NI-49
(triangular point?)
10,750 ±300

LAPA DO BOQUETE
(triangular point?)
12,070 ±170(?);
11,440 ±240(?);
10,910 ±140

PUTU
(fluted point?)
11,470 ±500(?);
8,810 ±60

BLUEFISH ▼
CAVES
ca. 14,000(?)

LAPA VERMELHA
(triangular point?)
11,680 ±500(?)

LAPA DO DRAGÃO
(triangular point?)
11,000 ±300

QUEREO
11,100 ±150

RS-I-50
(triangular point)
12,770 ±220(?)

ALICE BOËR
(triangular point?)
14,200 ±1,150(?)

SANTANA DO RIACHO
(triangular point?)
11,960 ±250(?)

WALKER ROAD ▲
(triangular point)
11,300 ±120

BROKEN MAMMOTH
(triangular point)
11,770 ±220

SWAN POINT
(triangular point)
11,660 ±60

TAGUA TAGUA
11,380 ±320(?)

RS-I-68 (triangular point)
11,555 ±230(?)

RS-I-69 (triangular point)
10,985 ±100

RS-I-66 (triangular point)
10,810 ±275

MONTE VERDE
(bipoint)
33,370 ±530(?);
ca. 12,500(?)

CERRO LA CHINA
(fishtail point)
11,150 ±135

CUEVA DEL MEDIO
(fishtail point)
12,290 ±180(?); 10,550 ±120

LOS TOLDOS
12,600 ±600(?)

FELL'S CAVE (fishtail point) ▲
11,000 ±170

TRES ARROYOS
11,880 ±250(?); 10,600 ±90

Note: Dates are expressed in years
before the baseline of 1950, with a
statistical margin of error. Uncertain
dates are indicated by a question mark.

JOYCE PENDOLA

samples that disqualify them from scientific acceptance, at least for the present. (On the accompanying map, I have indicated which early sites I think do—and which I think do not-meet stringent criteria.)

Even Dillehay's Chilean site of Monte Verde-which he, Dixon, and many others believe to be about 12,500 years old-can be challenged. (After these two books went to press, the magazine *Discovering Archaeology* carried an acerbic article by Stuart Fiedel criticizing the quality of the data.) As Fiedel, Dena Dincauze, Tom Lynch, and I have pointed out, this site presents many problems. Located in boggy terrain along a stream, Monte Verde has discontinuous stratigraphy, suggesting a mixing of strata. Few of the objects unearthed are indisputably tools, and there are no flakes from the manufacture of such tools. Three narrow points found at Monte Verde are tapered at both ends, a "bipoint" form common in established sites in Chile and Peru that have more recent dates—Holocene rather than Pleistocene.

The tools at Monte Verde cannot be firmly connected with the dates, which were obtained on the basis of bog material, not from incontrovertible artifacts or food plants. And the dates are too widely spaced—from about 14,000 to 12,000 years ago—to fit the brief occupation that Dillehay believes the site represents. Furthermore, the site contains possible carbon contaminants, such as bitumen, which are known to make materials dated by the carbon 14 method appear older than they are (two very early dates of more than 33,000 years ago are typical of those recorded for petroleum material such as bitumen). Human traces could be the result of intrusion by later peoples. The mastodons believed to have been killed and eaten could be mired fossil fauna, and the supposed remains of shelters could be snags from fallen trees—similar to natural deposits found elsewhere in the region.

For their part, scholars skeptical of the validity of pre-Clovis sites typically fail to apply the same rigorous criteria to the Clovis sites they *do* accept. As a consequence, the age of Clovis, which many still claim is the ancestor to all other cultures in the New World, has been exaggerated. It is regularly put at 11,500 or sometimes even 12,000 years old, but no indisputably valid Clovis site has such early carbon 14 dates. (When carbon 14 results are that old, they turn out to be from sites that yield only isolated single dates, dates with a margin of error greater than 300 years, or dates based on carbon that has no certain connection with a human presence.) Even Dixon, despite his preClovis yearnings, perpetuates this exaggeration of Clovis's antiquity.

The earliest migrants used various resources and habitats; only some of them hunted big game.

The inconsistent treatment of dates has given the false impression of a rapid wave of colonization by groups descended from Clovis peoples and has drawn attention away from numerous valid sites that are contemporaneous with Clovis but very different culturally Most archaeologists ignore such sites because they do not have the cachet of being pre-Clovis. For now, though, their age and location provide the most reliable basis for an account of the migrations and ecological adaptations of the first Americans.

What, then, would be a more accurate picture? My conclusion is that the first people to venture into the eastern Bering Strait region, a bit before 12,000 years ago, may have been a group like the Nenana people, who were not specialized big-game hunters but rather foragers of small game, fish, fruits, and nuts. Instead of fluted spear-points they made triangular points that they probably used as knives. During the ensuing thousand years, their descendants penetrated

diverse ecological zones throughout the Americas. Clovis was only one of these descendant cultures and not, therefore, either the earliest in the Americas or a culture that set an adaptive pattern for the hemisphere. None of the other descendant cultures were characterized by specialized big-game hunting.

No one type of environment seems to have been colonized before others, and people did not create one single style of artifact or survive on one particular kind of resource. Most Clovis-age peoples in the far north lacked fluted points; they used microblade tools (small blades struck off a prepared core) to hunt and gather a variety of resources. Even the Clovis fluted point (with its shallow channel on one or both sides and its parallel edges), which spread widely in the interior continental United States, is conclusively associated with big-game hunting only in the high plains. In South America, by about 11,000 years ago, specialized maritime foragers had already settled the Pacific coast, guanaco hunters were living in the southern grasslands, and riverine tropical-forest foragers inhabited the eastern lowlands. The peoples of the far south used fishtail points with expanded stems, and the forest and coastal peoples used triangular points, often with tapered stems.

With their pre-Clovis emphasis, both Dillehay and Dixon miss the broad significance of these sites, and neither manages to sketch a coherent picture of colonization that fits the pattern of current data. Dixon argues that the earliest migrants followed a coastal route from the Bering Strait region southward to Tierra del Fuego, yet he cannot demonstrate that coastal sites were occupied any earlier than interior sites. As Ted Goebel and John Erlandson have pointed out, there are no securely dated maritime sites in North America as old as Clovis, and those in South America are the same age as interior sites, not older.

Dillehay believes that the first migrants in South America could have been pre-Clovis big-game hunters who arrived at least 15,000 years ago and used fishtail projectile points. However, he can identify no fishtail-point sites earlier than 11,000 years ago, and these are in the far south, not the north, as would be expected. And, as he admits, few early South American human sites include the bones of now-extinct Ice Age game animals. In addition, Dillehay distinguishes another South American tradition of foragers with only unifacial tools (made by flaking one side), but no such culture has been shown to exist. All the sites that have been adequately sampled and dated yield bifacial as well as unifacial tools.

Both authors try to make sense of the current heated debate about the biological origins of the first Americans, a debate with political and racial overtones. Some archaeologists argue that modern-day Native Americans are significantly different physically from the Paleoindians—and that Paleoindian sites are therefore not subject to the Native American Graves Protection and Repatriation Act (NAGPRA). They suggest that the very first New World peoples were of European origin and that modern-day Native Americans descend principally from later waves of migrants from Asia. The long and narrow prehistoric crania, such as that belonging to Kennewick Man (discovered in Washington State), are taken to be Caucasoid, while Solutrean tools from France are proposed as precursors of Clovis points. However, this cranial shape and the relevant tool traits are found in Asia as well. Citing studies of teeth, Dixon rightly points to maritime northeastern Asia rather than to Europe for the origin of Paleoindians. Dillehay is ambivalent, but gives some credence to claims of Australian or African affinities—such as for a woman's skull found at Lapa Vermelha, Brazil—but these claims are weak on both geographical and chronological grounds.

All modern groups differ significantly from their distant ancestors. With more precise studies, the cultural and biological links of living Native Americans to the Paleoindians are becoming clearer. Although some groups, such as the Umatilla in Washington State, want to prevent future research on Paleoindians, members of other groups, such as the Tlingit, welcome the new information about their predecessors. From my own experience with Paleoindian archaeology, I'd say that present-day Native Americans have much to gain, and nothing to fear, from continuing research.

Anna Curtenius Roosevelt is a professor of anthropology at the University of Illinois, Chicago, and the curator of archaeology at the Field Museum of Natural History.

The Slow Birth of Agriculture

New methods show that around the world, people began cultivating some crops long before they embraced full-scale farming, and that crop cultivation and village life often did not go hand in hand

Heather Pringle

According to early Greek storytellers, humans owe the ability to cultivate crops to the sudden generosity of a goddess. Legend has it that in a burst of goodwill, Demeter, goddess of crops, bestowed wheat seeds on a trusted priest, who then crisscrossed Earth in a dragon-drawn chariot, sowing the dual blessings of agriculture and civilization.

For decades, archaeologists too regarded the birth of agriculture as a dramatic transformation, dubbed the Neolithic Revolution, that brought cities and civilization in its wake. In this scenario, farming was born after the end of the last Ice Age, around 10,000 years ago, when hunter-gatherers settled in small communities in the Fertile Crescent, a narrow band of land arcing across the Near East. They swiftly learned to produce their own food, sowing cereal grains and breeding better plants. Societies then raised more children to adulthood, enjoyed food surpluses, clustered in villages, and set off down the road to civilization. This novel way of life then diffused across the Old World.

But like many a good story, over time this tale has fallen beneath an onslaught of new data. By employing sensitive new techniques—from sifting through pollen cores to measuring minute shape changes in ancient cereal grains—researchers are building a new picture of agricultural origins. They are pushing back the dates of both plant domestication and animal husbandry around the world, and many now view the switch to an agrarian lifestyle as a long, complex evolution rather than a dramatic revolution.

The latest evidence suggests, for example, that hunter-gatherers in the Near East first cultivated rye fields as early as 13,000 years ago.[*] But for centuries thereafter, they continued to hunt wild game and gather an ever-decreasing range of wild plants, only becoming full-blown farmers living in populous villages by some 8500 B.C. And in some cases, villages appear long before intensive agriculture. "The transition from hunters and gatherers to agriculturalists is not a brief sort of thing," says Bruce Smith, an expert on agricultural origins at the Smithsonian Institution's National Museum of Natural History in Washington, D.C. "It's a long developmental process"—and one that did not necessarily go hand in hand with the emergence of settlements.

Similar stories are emerging in South America, Mesoamerica, North America, and China. Although cultivation may have been born first in the Near East, the latest evidence suggests that people on other continents began to domesticate the plants they lived with—squash on the tropical coast of Ecuador and rice along the marshy banks of the Yangtze in China, for example—as early as 10,000 to 11,000 years ago, thousands of years earlier than was thought and well before the first signs of farming villages in these regions. To many researchers, the timing suggests that worldwide environmental change—climate fluctuations at the end of the Ice Age—may well have prompted cultivation, although they are still pondering exactly how this climate change spurred people around the world to begin planting seeds and reaping their bounty.

CULTIVATING THE GREEN HELL

Perhaps the most dramatic and controversial new discoveries in ancient agriculture have emerged from the sultry lowland rainforests of Central and South America. These forests, with their humid climate, poor soils, and profusion of pests, were long considered an unlikely place for ancient peoples to embark upon the sweaty toil of farming, says Dolores Piperno, an archaeobotanist at the Smithsonian Tropical Research Institution in Balboa, Panama. "If people were going to have a hard time living in [these forests], how were they ever going to develop agriculture there?" she asks. And most research suggested that these forest dwellers were relative latecomers to agriculture, first cultivating crops between 4000 to 5000 years ago.

But tropical forests harbor the wild ancestors of such major food crops as manioc and yams. Back in the 1950s, American cultural geographer Carl Sauer speculated that these regions were early centers of plant domestication, but there was little evidence to support the idea, as the soft fruit and starchy root crops of these regions rapidly rot away in the acid soils. The better preserved evidence found in arid regions, such as seeds from grain crops in the Near East, captured the attention of most archaeologists.

In the early 1980s, however, Piperno and colleague Deborah Pearsall, an archaeobotanist from the University of Missouri, Columbia, began searching the sediments of rainforest sites in Panama and Ecuador for more enduring plant remnants. They focused on phytoliths, microscopic silica bodies that form when plants take up silica from groundwater. As the silica gradually fills plant cells, it assumes their distinctive size and shape. Piperno and Pearsall came up with ways to distinguish phytoliths from wild and domestic species—domestic plants, for example, have larger fruits and seeds, and hence larger cells and phytoliths. Then they set about identifying specimens from early archaeological sites.

This spring, after nearly 20 years of research, the team published its findings in a book entitled *The Origins of Agriculture in the Lowland Neotropics*. In one study, they measured squash phytoliths from a sequence of layers at Vegas Site 80, a coastal site bordering the tropical forest of southwestern Ecuador. From associated shell fragments as well as the carbon trapped inside the phytoliths themselves, they were able to carbon-date the microfossils. A sharp increase in phytolith size indicated that early Ecuadorians had domesticated squash, likely *Cucurbita moschata*, by 10,000 years ago—some 5000 years earlier than some archaeologists thought farming began there. Such timing suggests, she notes, that people in the region began growing their own plants after much local game went extinct at the end of the last Ice Age and tropical forest reclaimed the region. "I think that's the key to the initiation of agriculture here," says Piperno. If this find holds up, the Ecuador squash rivals the oldest accepted evidence of plant domestication in the Americas—the seeds of another squash, *C. pepo*, excavated from an arid Mexican cave and directly dated to 9975 years ago (*Science*, 9 May 1997, pp. 894 and 932).

The phytolith technique is also pushing back the first dates for maize cultivation in the Americas, says Piperno. Phytoliths taken from sediment samples from Aguadulce rock-shelter in central Panama by Piperno and her colleagues and carbondated both directly and by analyzing shells from the same strata imply that maize cultivation began there as early as 7700 years ago. That's not only more than 2500 years earlier than expected in a rainforest site, it's also 1500 years earlier than the first dates for maize cultivation anywhere in the

more arid parts of the Americas. Almost certainly, the oldest partially domesticated maize at the site came from somewhere else, because the wild ancestor of corn is known only from a narrow band of land in Mexico. But the squash data raise important questions, says Piperno, about where agriculture first emerged in the Americas. "Clearly tropical forest is in the ball game."

But the community is split over whether to accept the phytolith evidence. Some critics question the dating of the phytoliths themselves, saying that carbon from other sources could have become embedded in the cracks and crevices on the fossil surfaces, skewing the results. Others such as Gayle Fritz, an archaeobotanist at Washington University in St. Louis, point out that the shells and other objects used to support the dates may not be the same age as the phytoliths. "I would be as thrilled as anyone else to push the dates back," says Fritz, "but my advice now is that people should be looking at these as unbelievable."

However, proponents such as Mary Pohl, an archaeologist at Florida State University in Tallahassee, note that the Piperno team typically supports its claims with multiple lines of evidence, so that even if one set of dates is suspect, the body of work makes it clear that some domestication took place startlingly early in the rainforest. "The data seem irrefutable to my mind," she says.

If so, they overturn some basic assumptions about the relationship between village life and agriculture in the tropical forest. For years, says Piperno, researchers believed that the first farmers there lived in villages, like the well-studied Neolithic grain farmers of the Near East. "Because settled village life is just not seen in [this part of the] Americas until 5000 years ago, [researchers thought] that means food production was late too," says Piperno. "But it doesn't work." In her view, farming in the region came long before village life. For thousands of years, she says, "you had slash-and-burn agriculture instead of settled village agriculture."

TAMING WILD RICE

At the same time as early Americans may have been planting their first squash, hunter-gatherers some 16,000 kilometers east along the banks of the Yangtze River were beginning to cultivate wild rice, according to new studies by archaeobotanist

Zhijun Zhao of the Smithsonian Tropical Research Institution and colleagues. Rice, the most important food crop in the world, was long thought to have been cultivated first around 6500 years ago in southern Asia, where the climate is warm enough to support luxuriant stands of wild rice. But in the 1980s, ancient bits of charred rice turned up in a site along the banks of the middle Yangtze River, in the far northern edge of the range of wild rice today. Directly carbon-dated to 8000 years ago, these grains are the oldest known cultivated rice and suggest that the center of rice cultivation was actually farther north.

Now the dates have been pushed back even farther, revealing a long, gradual transition to agriculture, according to work in press in *Antiquity* by Zhao. He has analyzed a sequence of abundant rice phytoliths from a cave called Diaotonghuan in northern Jiangxi Province along the middle Yangtze, which was excavated by Richard MacNeish, research director at the Andover Foundation for Archaeological Research in Massachusetts, and Yan Wenming, a Peking University archaeologist in Beijing.

Radiocarbon dates for the site seemed to have been contaminated by groundwater, so Zhao constructed a relative chronology based on ceramic and stone artifacts of known styles and dates found with the phytoliths. In recent weeks, Zhao has further refined his *Antiquity* chronology as a result of a joint study with Piperno on paleoecological data from lake sediments in the region.

To trace the work of ancient cultivators at the site, he distinguished the phytoliths of wild and domesticated rice by measuring minute differences in the size of a particular type of cell in the seed covering. With this method, which Zhao pioneered with Pearsall, Piperno, and others at the University of Missouri, "we can get a 90% accuracy," he says.

By counting the proportions of wild and domesticated rice fossils, Zhao charted a gradual shift to agriculture. In a layer dated to at least 13,000 years ago, the phytoliths show that hunter-gatherers in the cave were dining on wild rice. But by 12,000 years ago, those meals abruptly ceased—Zhao suspects because the climate became colder and the wild grain, too tender for such conditions, vanished from this region. Studies of the Greenland ice cores have revealed a global cold spell called the Younger Dryas from about 13,000 to 11,500 years ago. Zhao's own studies of phytoliths and pollen in lake sediments from the region reveal that warmth-loving vegetation began retreating from this region around 12,000 years ago.

As the big chill waned, however, rice returned to the region. And people began dabbling in something new around 11,000 years ago—sowing, harvesting, and selectively breeding rice. In a zone at Diaotonghuan littered with sherds from a type of crude pottery found in three other published sites in the region and radiocarbon-dated to between 9000 and 13,000 years ago, Zhao found the first domesticated rice phytoliths—the oldest evidence of rice cultivation in the world. But these early Chinese cultivators were still hunting and gathering, says Zhao. "The cave at that time is full of animal bones—mainly deer and wild pig—and wild plants," he notes. Indeed, it was another 4000 years before domestic rice dominated wild rice to become the dietary staple, about 7000 years ago.

It makes sense that the transition to farming was slow and gradual and not the rapid switch that had been pictured, says MacNeish. "Once you learn to plant the stuff, you must learn to get a surplus and to get the best hybrid to rebreed this thing you're planting," he notes. "And when this begins to happen, then very gradually your population begins going up. You plant a little bit more and a little bit more." At some point, he concludes, the hunter-gatherers at sites like Diaotonghuan were unable to gather enough wild food to support their burgeoning numbers and so had little choice but to embrace farming in earnest.

THE CRADLE OF CIVILIZATION

In the Near East, archaeologists have been studying early agriculture for decades, and it was here that the idea of the Neolithic Revolution was born. Yet even here, it seems there was a long and winding transition to agriculture. And although settled village life appeared early in this region, its precise connection to farming is still obscure.

The latest findings come from Abu Hureyra, a settlement east of Aleppo, Syria, where the inhabitants were at least semisedentary, occupying the site from at least early spring to late autumn, judging from the harvest times of more than 150 plant species identified there to date. Among the plant remains are seeds of cultivated rye, distinguished from wild grains by their plumpness and much larger size.

University College London archaeobotanists Gordon Hillman and Susan Colledge have now dated one of those seeds to some 13,000 years ago, according to unpublished work they presented at a major international workshop in September. If the date is confirmed, this rye will be the oldest domesticated cereal grain in the world.

These dates are nearly a millennium earlier than previous evidence for plant domestication. And the rye is not even the first sign of cultivation at the Abu Hureyra site: Just before the appearance of this domestic grain, the team found a dramatic rise in seed remains from plants that typically grow among crops as weeds. All this occurs some 2500 years before the most widely accepted dates for full-scale agriculture and populous villages in the Near East. Although the semisedentism of the inhabitants fits with earlier ideas, the long time span contradicts ideas of a rapid agricultural "revolution."

The early date for plant domestication in the Near East is not entirely unexpected, says Ofer Bar-Yosef of Harvard University. For example, inhabitants of Ohallo II in what is now Israel had made wild cereal seeds a major part of their diets as early as 17,000 B.C., according to published work by Mordechai Kislev, an archaeobotanist at Bar Ilan University in Ramat-Gan, Israel. Moreover, as close observers of nature, these early foragers were almost certain to have noticed that a seed sown in the ground eventually yielded a plant with yet more seeds. "These people knew their fauna and flora very well," says Bar-Yosef, "and they probably played with planting plants long before they really switched into agriculture."

Just what spurred hunter-gatherers to begin regularly sowing seeds and cultivating fields, however, remains unclear. For several years, many Near Eastern experts have favored the theory that climate change associated with the Younger Dryas was the likely trigger. Bar-Yosef, for example, suggests that inhabitants of the Fertile Crescent first planted cereal fields in order to boost supplies of grain when the Younger Dryas cut drastically into wild harvests. And at Abu Hureyra, Hillman thinks that the drought accompanying the Younger Dryas was a key factor. Before the jump in weeds and the appearance of domestic rye, the inhabitants relied on wild foods as starch staples. Over time, they turned to more and more drought-resistant plants—and even these dwindled in abundance. So "progressive desiccation could

indeed have been the impetus for starch cultivation," says Hillman.

But new dates for the cold spell in the Near East paint a more complex view. At the Netherlands workshop, Uri Baruch, a palynologist at the Israel Antiquities Authority in Jerusalem, and Syze Bottema, a palynologist at the Groningen Institute of Archeology in the Netherlands, announced that they had redated a crucial pollen core at Lake Hula in northern Israel. Their original published estimate put a retreat in the region's deciduous oak forest—due to cool, dry conditions believed to be the local manifestation of the Younger Dryas—starting about 13,500 years ago. But after correcting for contamination by old carbon dissolved in the lake water, they found that the cold spell in the Near East was a bit later, starting around 13,000 years ago and ending around 11,500 years ago.

These dates suggest that farmers of Abu Hureyra may have begun cultivating rye before the Younger Dryas set in, at the very end of the warm, moist interval that preceded it. "The domesticated rye dates and the pollen core don't match up so well at this time," says Mark Blumler, a geographer at the State University of New York, Binghamton.

Moreover, others point out that the clearest evidence for the domestication of grains such as wheat and barley in the Near East comes around 10,500 years ago, after the Younger Dryas had waned and the climate had improved again. By then, says George Willcox, an archaeobotanist at the Institut de Prehistoire Orientale in St-Paul-le-Jeune, France, other factors could have contributed to the transition. Hunter-gatherers in the region, for example, had settled year-round in small villages between 12,300 and 10,500 years ago. There, he says, rising human populations and overexploitation of wild foods could have driven people to take up farming. "Because people at this time appear to be living in one place," says Willcox, "they could use up all the resources in a particular area."

Putting the evidence from around the world together, a new picture of the origins of agriculture begins to emerge. In the Near East, some villages were born before agriculture and may even have forced its adoption in some cases. But elsewhere—China, North America, and Mesoamerica—plants were cultivated and domesticated by nomadic hunter-gatherers, perhaps to increase their yield during the dramatic climate shifts that accompanied the final phase of the last Ice Age. Either way, it no longer makes sense to suppose a strong causal link between farming and settled village life, Piperno says.

Indeed, in many regions, settled agriculturalists emerged only centuries or millennia after cultivation, if at all. Many ancient peoples simply straddled the middle ground between foraging and farming, creating economies that blended both. "For so long, we've put everybody in black boxes" as farmers or hunter-gatherers, notes Joanna Casey, an archaeologist at the University of South Carolina, Columbia, and a specialist in agricultural origins in western Africa. But mixed cultivation and foraging is not necessarily a step "on the way" to full-scale farming—it was a long-term lifestyle for many groups. "These societies in the middle ground are certainly not failures," says the Smithsonian's Smith. "They are not societies that stum-

bled or stuttered or got frozen developmentally. They're societies that found an excellent long-term solution to their environmental challenges."

Eventually, for reasons still unclear, many of the early domesticators did become true agriculturalists—by 10,500 years ago in the Near East, 7000 years ago in China, and later in the Americas and Africa. And during this transition, human populations did indeed soar, and hamlets became villages. Archaeological sites in the intensively studied Fertile Crescent, for example, increased more than 10-fold in size, from 0.2 hectares to 2.0 to 3.0 hectares, during this period of transition. The combination of settlement and reliable food probably brought about "a longer period of fertility for the now better fed

women," says Bar-Yosef, setting the stage for cities and civilization.

So it seems that the ancient Greek legends got it half right when they told how seeds fell throughout the world, sparking independent centers of domestication on many continents. But cities and civilization did not necessarily arrive at the same time as the seeds. Demeter's priest apparently gave out only one blessing at a time.

---

*All dates are calendar years.

†The Transition From Foraging to Farming in Southwest Asia, Groningen, the Netherlands, 7–11 September.

Heather Pringle is a science writer in Vancouver, British Columbia.

Archaeologists Rediscover Cannibals

At digs around the world, researchers have unearthed strong new evidence that people ate their own kind from the early days of human evolution through recent prehistory

When Arizona State University bio-archaeologist Christy G. Turner II first looked at the jumbled heap of bones from 30 humans in Arizona in 1967, he was convinced that he was looking at the remains of a feast. The bones of these ancient American Indians had cut marks and burns, just like animal bones that had been roasted and stripped of their flesh. "It just struck me that here was a pile of food refuse," says Turner, who proposed in *American Antiquity* in 1970 that these people from Polacca Wash, Arizona, had been the victims of cannibalism.

But his paper was met with "total disbelief," says Turner. "In the 1960s, the new paradigm about Indians was that they were all peaceful and happy. So, to find something like this was the antithesis of the new way we were supposed to be thinking about Indians"—particularly the Anasazi, thought to be the ancestors of living Pueblo Indians. Not only did Turner's proposal fly in the face of conventional wisdom about the Anasazi culture, but it was also at odds with an emerging consensus that earlier claims of cannibalism in the fossil record rested on shaky evidence. Where earlier generations of archaeologists had seen the remains of cannibalistic feasts, current researchers saw bones scarred by ancient burial practices, war, weathering, or scavenging animals.

To Turner, however, the bones from Polacca Wash told a more disturbing tale, and so he set about studying every prehistoric skeleton he could find in the Southwest and Mexico to see if it was an isolated event. Now, 30 years and 15,000 skeletons later, Turner is putting the final touches on a 1500-page book to be published next year by the University of Utah press in which he says, "Cannibalism was practiced intensively for almost four centuries" in the Four Corners region. The evidence is so strong that Turner says "I would bet a year of my salary on it."

He isn't the only one now betting on cannibalism in prehistory. In the past decade, Turner and other bioarchaeologists have put together a set of clear-cut criteria for distinguishing the marks of cannibalism from other kinds of scars. "The analytical rigor has increased across the board," says paleoanthropologist Tim D. White of the University of California, Berkeley. Armed with the new criteria, archaeologists are finding what they say are strong signs of cannibalism throughout the fossil record. This summer, archaeologists are excavating several sites in Europe where the practice may have occurred among our ancestors, perhaps as early as 800,000 years ago. More recently, our brawny cousins, the Neandertals, may have eaten each other. And this behavior wasn't limited to the distant past—strong new evidence suggests that in addition to the Anasazi, the Aztecs of Mexico and the people of Fiji also ate their own kind in the past 2500 years.

These claims imply a disturbing new view of human history, say Turner and others. Although cannibalism is still relatively rare in the fossil record, it is frequent enough to imply that extreme hunger was not the only driving force. Instead of being an aberration, practiced only by a few prehistoric Donner Parties, killing people for food may have been standard human behavior—a means of social control, Turner suspects, or a mob response to stress, or a form of infanticide to thin the ranks of neighboring populations.

Not surprisingly, some find these claims hard to stomach: "These people haven't explored all the alternatives," says archaeologist Paul Bahn, author of the *Cambridge Encyclopedia* entry on cannibalism. "There's no question, for example, that all kinds of weird stuff is done to human remains in mortuary practice"—and in warfare. But even the most prominent skeptic of earlier claims of cannibalism, cultural anthropologist William Arens of the State University of New York, Stony Brook, now admits the case is stronger: "I think the procedures are sounder, and there is more evidence for cannibalism than before."

White learned how weak most earlier scholarship on cannibalism was in 1981, when he first came across what he thought might be a relic of the practice—a massive skull of an early human ancestor from a site called Bodo in Ethiopia. When he got his first look at this 600,000-year-old skull on a museum table, White noticed that it had a series of fine, deep cut marks on its cheekbone and inside its eye socket, as if it had been defleshed. To confirm his suspicions, White wanted to compare the marks with a "type collection" for cannibalism—a carefully studied assemblage of bones showing how the signature of cannibalism differs from damage by animal gnawing, trampling, or excavation.

"We were naïve at the time," says White, who was working with archaeol-

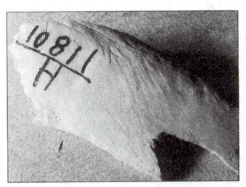

PHOTOS BY: C. TURNER/ARIZONA STATE UNIVERSITY

Cannibals house? The Peasco Blanco great house at Chaco Canyon, New Mexico, where some bones bear cut marks (upper left); others were smashed, perhaps to extract marrow.

ogist Nicholas Toth of Indiana University in Bloomington. They learned that although the anthropological literature was full of fantastic tales of cannibalistic feasts among early humans at Zhoukoudian in China, Krapina cave in Croatia, and elsewhere, the evidence was weak—or lost.

Indeed, the weakness of the evidence had already opened the way to a backlash, which was led by Arens. He had deconstructed the fossil and historical record for cannibalism in a book called *The Man-Eating Myth: Anthropology and Anthropophagy* (Oxford, 1979). Except for extremely rare cases of starvation or insanity, Arens said, none of the accounts of cannibalism stood up to scrutiny—not even claims that it took place among living tribes in Papua New Guinea (including the Fore, where cannibalism is thought to explain the spread of the degenerative brain disease kuru). There were no reliable eye witnesses for claims of cannibalism, and the archaeological evidence was circumstantial. "I

didn't deny the existence of cannibalism," he now says, "but I found that there was no good evidence for it. It was bad science."

T . D. WHITE/BERKELEY

Unkind cuts. A Neandertal bone from Vindija Cave, Croatia.

Physical anthropologists contributed to the backlash when they raised doubts about what little archaeological evidence there was (*Science,* 20 June 1986, p.

1479). Mary Russell, then at Case Western Reserve University in Cleveland, argued, for example, that cut marks on the bones of 20 Neandertals at Krapina Cave could have been left by Neandertal morticians who were cleaning the bones for secondary burial, and the bones would have been smashed when the roof caved in, for example. In his 1992 review in the *Cambridge Encyclopedia,* Bahn concluded that cannibalism's "very existence in prehistory is hard to swallow."

RISING FROM THE ASHES

But even as some anthropologists gave the ax to Krapina and other notorious cases, a new, more rigorous case for cannibalism in prehistory was emerging, starting in the American Southwest. Turner and his late wife, Jacqueline Turner, had been systematically studying tray after tray of prehistoric bones in museums and private collections in the United States and Mexico. They had identified a pattern of bone processing in several hundred specimens that showed little respect for the dead. "There's no known mortuary practice in the Southwest where the body is dismembered, the head is roasted and dumped into a pit unceremoniously, and other pieces get left all over the floor," says Turner, describing part of the pattern.

White, meanwhile, was identifying other telltale signs. To fill the gap he discovered when he looked for specimens to compare with the Bodo skull, he decided to study in depth one of the bone assemblages the Turners and others had cited. He chose Mancos, a small Anasazi pueblo on the Colorado Plateau from A.D. 1150, where archaeologists had recovered the scattered and broken remains of at least 29 individuals. The project evolved into a landmark book, *Prehistoric Cannibalism at Mancos* (Princeton, 1992). While White still doesn't know why the Bodo skull was defleshed—"it's a black box," he says—he extended the blueprint for identifying cannibalism.

In his book, White describes how he painstakingly sifted through 2106 bone fragments, often using an electron microscope to identify cut marks, burn traces, percussion and anvil damage, disarticulations, and breakages. He reviewed how to distinguish marks left by butchering from those left by animal gnawing, trampling, or other wear and tear. He also proposed a new category of bone damage, which he called "pot polish"—shiny abrasions on bone tips that come from being stirred in pots (an idea he tested by stirring deer bones in a replica of an Anasazi pot). And he outlined how to compare the remains of suspected victims with those of ordinary game animals at other sites to see if they were processed the same way.

When he applied these criteria to the Mancos remains, he concluded that they were the leavings of a feast in which 17 adults and 12 children had their heads cut off, roasted, and broken open on rock anvils. Their long bones were broken—he believes for marrow—and their vertebral bodies were missing, perhaps crushed and boiled for oil. Finally, their bones were dumped, like animal bones.

In their forthcoming book, the Turners describe a remarkably similar pattern

of bone processing in 300 individuals from 40 different bone assemblages in the Four Corners area of the Southwest, dating from A.D. 900 to A.D. 1700. The strongest case, he says, comes from bones unearthed at the Peñasco Blanco great house at Chaco Canyon in New Mexico, which was the highest center of the Anasazi culture and, he argues, the home of cannibals who terrorized victims within 100 miles of Chaco Canyon, where most of the traumatized bones have been excavated. "Whatever drove the Anasazi to eat people, it happened at Chaco," says Turner.

The case for cannibalism among the Anasazi that Turner and White have put together hasn't swayed all the critics. "These folks have a nice package, but I don't think it proves cannibalism," says Museum of New Mexico archaeologist Peter Bullock. "It's still just a theory."

But even critics like Bullock acknowledge that Turner and White's studies, along with work by the University of Colorado, Boulder's, Paolo Villa and colleagues at another recent site, Fontbrégoua Cave in southeastern France (*Science,* 25 July 1986, p. 431), have raised the standards for how to investigate a case of cannibalism. In fact, White's book has become the unofficial guidebook for the field, says physical anthropologist Carmen Pijoan at the Museum of Anthropology in Mexico City, who has done a systematic review of sites in Mexico where human bones were defleshed. In a forthcoming book chapter, she singles out three sites where she applied diagnostic criteria outlined by Turner, White, and Villa to bones from Aztec and other early cultures and concludes that all "three sites, spread over 2000 years of Mexican prehistory, show a pattern of violence, cannibalism, and sacrifice through time."

White's book "is my bible," agrees paleontologist Yolanda Fernandez-Jalvo of the Museum of Natural History in Madrid, who is analyzing bones that may be the oldest example of cannibalism in the fossil record—the remains of at least six individuals who died 800,000 years ago in an ancient cave at Atapuerca in northern Spain.

AGE-OLD PRACTICES

The Spanish fossils have caused considerable excitement because they may represent a new species of human ancestor (*Science,* 30 May, pp. 1331 and 1392). But they also show a pattern familiar from the more recent sites: The bones are highly fragmented and are scored with cut marks, which Fernandez-Jalvo thinks were made when the bodies were decapitated and the bones defleshed. A large femur was also smashed open, perhaps for marrow, says Fernandez-Jalvo, and the whole assemblage had been dumped, like garbage. The treatment was no different from that accorded animal bones at the site. The pattern, says Peter Andrews, a paleoanthropologist at The Natural History Museum, London, is "pretty strong evidence for cannibalism, as opposed to ritual defleshing." He and others note, however, that the small number of individuals at the site and the absence of other sites of similar antiquity to which the bones could be compared leave room for doubt.

A stronger case is emerging at Neandertal sites in Europe, 45,000 to more than 130,000 years old. The new criteria for recognizing cannibalism have not completely vindicated the earlier claims about Krapina Cave, partly because few animal bones are left from the excavation of the site in 1899 to compare with the Neandertal remains. But nearby Vindija Cave, excavated in the 1970s, did yield both animal and human remains. When White and Toth examined the bones recently, they found that both sets showed cut marks, breakage, and disarticulation, and had been dumped on the cave floor. It's the same pattern seen at Krapina, and remarkably similar to that at Mancos, says White, who will publish his conclusions in a forthcoming book with Toth. Marseilles prehistorian Alban DeFleur is finding that Neandertals may also have feasted on their kind in the Moula-Guercy Cave in the Ardeche region of France, where animal and Neandertal bones show similar processing. Taken together, says White, "the evidence from Krapina, Vindija, and Moula is strong."

Not everyone is convinced, however. "White does terrific analysis, but he hasn't proved this is cannibalism," says Bahn. "Frankly, I don't see how he can unless you find a piece of human gut [with human bone or tissue in it]." No matter how close the resemblance to butchered animals, he says, the cut marks and other bone processing could still be the result of mortuary practices. Bullock adds that warfare, not cannibalism, could explain the damage to the bones.

White, however, says such criticism resembles President Clinton's famous claim about marijuana: "Some [although not all] of the Anasazi and Neandertals processed their colleagues. They skinned them, roasted them, cut their muscles off, severed their joints, broke their long bones on anvils with hammerstones, crushed their spongy bones, and put the pieces into pots." Borrowing a line from a review of his book, White says: "To say they didn't eat them is the archaeological equivalent of saying Clinton lit up and didn't inhale."

White's graduate student David De-Gusta adds that he has compared human bones at burial sites in Fiji and at a nearby trash midden from the last 2000 years. The intentionally buried bones were less fragmentary and had no bite marks, burns, percussion pits, or other signs of food processing. The human bones in the trash midden, however, were processed like those of pigs. "This site really challenges the claim that these assemblages of bones are the result of mortuary ritual," says DeGusta.

After 30 years of research, Turner says it is a modern bias to insist that cannibalism isn't part of human nature. Many other species eat their own, and our ancestors may have had their own "good" reasons—whether to terrorize subject peoples, limit their neighbors' offspring, or for religious or medicinal purposes. "Today, the only people who eat other people outside of starving are the crazies," says Turner. "We're dealing with a world view that says this is bad and always has been bad.... But in the past, that view wasn't necessarily the group view. Cannibalism could have been an adaptive strategy. It has to be entertained."

—**Ann Gibbons**

Modern Humans Made Their Point

Ann Gibbons

Long before guns gave European explorers a decisive advantage over indigenous peoples, our ancestors had their own technological innovation that allowed them to dominate the Stone Age competition: the projectile point, launched from bows or spear throwers. Paleolithic hunters shooting spears or arrows tipped with these small stone points could stay at a safe distance while hunting a wide assortment of prey—or other humans, says archaeologist John Shea of Stony Brook University in New York. Projectile launchers might even be the key to modern humans' triumph when they entered the Neandertal territory of Europe about 40,000 years ago, Shea proposed in his talk. Neandertals lacked projectiles until it was too late, and they could heft their heavier spears only as far as they could throw them. "Projectile points were such an important invention, like gunpowder, that it would have given the bearers a huge advantage," says archaeologist Alison Brooks of George Washington University in Washington, D.C.

In two separate studies, Shea and Brooks showed that modern humans were using lightweight points associated with projectile launchers by 40,000 years ago. Shea and Brooks both think these new weapons were invented first in Africa, although they disagree about the timing. They agree that modern humans had a technological advantage when they left Africa and spread around the globe. "These lightweight points show up more than 50,000 years ago in Africa," says Stan Ambrose of the University of Illinois, Urbana-Champaign, who heard Shea's talk. "They may have helped modern humans get out of Africa."

The challenge in pinpointing when projectiles were invented is that few of the launchers themselves survive, because they were made of materials that disintegrate over time. The oldest known bow is only 11,000 years old, and the oldest known spear thrower is about 18,000 years old, but archaeologists suspect that the technology is much older. So they try to distinguish projectile points from those used on the tips of hand-thrown spears. One criterion is size: Projectile points must be small and light to soar fast enough to kill. "You wouldn't go up to a Cape buffalo with those tiny points on a thrusting spear," says Brooks.

Shea and Brooks each surveyed points from around the world, setting an upper limit on the size and weight of points considered projectiles. Shea set an upper limit on cross sections at the tip, whereas Brooks set a limit on weight. Shea found that projectile points were widespread by 40,000 years ago; earlier points didn't meet his criteria. He proposed that the points were developed for warfare and may have hastened the extinction of Neandertals.

Brooks found that points from 50,000 to 90,000 years ago in three regions of Africa met her criteria. She noted that there was a "grammar and an order" to assembling these tools—one that required extensive social networks in order to exchange technology and specialized materials. She thinks that projectiles made modern humans more efficient hunters who could shoot small game and live in varied terrain. "They didn't have to kill [Neandertals]," says Brooks. "They just had to outcompete them."

New Women of the Ice Age

Forget about hapless mates being dragged around by macho mammoth killers. The women of Ice Age Europe, it appears, were not mere cavewives but priestly leaders, clever inventors, and mighty hunters.

By Heather Pringle

THE BLACK VENUS OF DOLNÍ VESTONICE, A SMALL, splintered figurine sensuously fashioned from clay, is an envoy from a forgotten world. It is all soft curves, with breasts like giant pillows beneath a masked face. At nearly 26,000 years old, it ranks among the oldest known portrayals of women, and to generations of researchers, it has served as a powerful—if enigmatic—clue to the sexual politics of the Ice Age.

Excavators unearthed the Black Venus near the Czech village of Dolní Vestonice in 1924, on a hillside among charred, fractured mammoth bones and stone tools. (Despite its nickname, the Black Venus is actually reddish—it owes its name to the ash that covered it when it was found.) Since the mid-nineteenth century, researchers had discovered more than a dozen similar statuettes in caves and open-air sites from France to Russia. All were cradled in layers of earth littered with stone and bone weaponry, ivory jewelry, and the remains of extinct Ice Age animals. All were depicted naked or nearly so. Collectively, they came to be known as Venus figurines, after another ancient bare-breasted statue, the Venus de Milo. Guided at least in part by prevailing sexual stereotypes, experts interpreted the meaning of the figurines freely. The Ice Age camps that spawned this art, they concluded, were once the domain of hard-working male hunters and secluded, pampered women who spent their days in idleness like the harem slaves so popular in nineteenth-century art.

Over the next six decades, Czech archeologists expanded the excavations at Dolní Vestonice, painstakingly combing the site square meter by square meter. By the 1990s they had unearthed thousands of bone, stone, and clay artifacts and had wrested 19 radiocarbon dates from wood charcoal that sprinkled camp floors. And they had shaded and refined their portrait of Ice Age life. Between 29,000 and 25,000 years ago, they concluded, wandering bands had passed the cold months of the year repeatedly at Dolní Vestonice. Armed with short-range spears, the men appeared to have been specialists in hunting tusk-wielding mammoths and other big game, hauling home great mountains of meat to feed their dependent mates and children. At night men feasted on mammoth steaks, fed their fires with mammoth bone, and fueled their sexual fantasies with tiny figurines of women carved from mammoth ivory and fired from clay. It was the ultimate man's world.

Or was it? Over the past few months, a small team of American archeologists has raised some serious doubts. Amassing critical and previously overlooked evidence from Dolní Vestonice and the neighboring site of Pavlov, Olga Soffer, James Adovasio, and David Hyland now propose that human survival there had little to do with manly men hurling spears at big-game animals. Instead, observes Soffer, one of the world's leading authorities on Ice Age hunters and gatherers and an archeologist at the University of Illinois in Champaign-Urbana, it depended largely on women, plants, and a technique of hunting previously invisible in the archeological evidence—net hunting. "This is not the image we've always had of Upper Paleolithic macho guys out killing animals up close and personal," Soffer explains. "Net hunting is communal, and it involves the labor of children and women. And this has lots of implications."

MANY OF THESE IMPLICATIONS MAKE HER CONservative colleagues cringe because they raise serious questions about the focus of previous studies. European archeologists have long concentrated on analyzing broken stone tools and butchered big-game bones, the most plentiful and best preserved relics of the Upper Paleolithic era (which stretched from 40,000 to 12,000 years ago). From these analyses, researchers have developed theories about how these societies once hunted and gathered food. Most researchers ruled out the possibility of women hunters for biological reasons. Adult females, they reasoned, had to devote themselves to breast-feeding and tending infants. "Human babies have always been immature and dependent," says Soffer. "If women are the people who are always involved with biological reproduction and the rearing of the young, then that is going to constrain their behavior. They have to provision that child. For fathers, provisioning is optional."

To test theories about Upper Paleolithic life, researchers looked to ethnography, the scientific description of modern and historical cultural groups. While the lives of modern hunters do not exactly duplicate those of ancient hunters, they supply valuable clues to universal human behavior. "Modern ethnography cannot be used to clone the past," says Soffer. "But people have always had to solve problems. Nature and social relationships present problems to people. We use ethnography to look for theoretical insights into human behavior, test them with ethnography, and if they work, assume that they represent a universal feature of human behavior."

But when researchers began turning to ethnographic descriptions of hunting societies, they unknowingly relied on a very incomplete literature. Assuming that women in surviving hunting societies were homebodies who simply tended hearths and suckled children, most early male anthropologists spent their time with male informants. Their published ethnographies brim with descriptions of males making spears and harpoons and heaving these weapons at reindeer, walruses, and whales. Seldom do they mention the activities of women. Ethnography, it seemed, supported theories of ancient male big-game hunters. "When they talked about primitive man, it was always 'he,'" says Soffer. "The 'she' was missing."

Recent anthropological research has revealed just how much Soffer's colleagues overlooked. By observing women in the few remaining hunter-gatherer societies and by combing historical accounts of tribal groups more thoroughly, anthropologists have come to realize how critical the female half of the population has always been to survival. Women and children have set snares, laid spring traps, sighted game and participated in animal drives and surrounds—forms of hunting that endangered neither young mothers nor their offspring. They dug starchy roots and collected other plant carbohydrates essential to survival. They even hunted, on occasion, with the projectile points traditionally deemed men's weapons. "I found references to Inuit women carrying bows and arrows, especially the blunt arrows that were used for hunting birds," says Linda Owen, an archeologist at the University of Tübingen in Germany.

The revelations triggered a volley of new research. In North America, Soffer and her team have found tantalizing evidence of the hunting gear often favored by women in historical societies. In Europe, archeobotanists are analyzing Upper Paleolithic hearths for evidence of plant remains probably gathered by women and children, while lithics specialists are poring over stone tools to detect new clues to their uses. And the results are gradually reshaping our understanding of Ice Age society. The famous Venus figurines, say archeologists of the new school, were never intended as male pornography: instead they may have played a key part in Upper Paleolithic rituals that centered on women. And such findings, pointing toward a more important role for Paleolithic women than had previously been assumed, are giving many researchers pause.

Like many of her colleagues, Soffer clearly relishes the emerging picture of Upper Paleolithic life. "I think life back then was a hell of a lot more egalitarian than it was with your later peasant societies," she says. "Of course the Paleolithic women were pulling their own weight." After sifting through Ice Age research for nearly two decades, Soffer brings a new critical approach to the notion—flattering to so many of her male colleagues—of mighty male mammoth hunters. "Very few archeologists are hunters," she notes, so it never occurred to most of them to look into the mechanics of hunting dangerous tusked animals. They just accepted the ideas they'd inherited from past work.

But the details of hunting bothered Soffer. Before the fifth century B.C., no tribal hunters in Asia or Africa had ever dared make their living from slaying elephants; the great beasts were simply too menacing. With the advent of the Iron Age in Africa, the situation changed. New weapons allowed Africans to hunt elephants and trade their ivory with Greeks and Romans. A decade ago, keen to understand how prehistoric bands had slaughtered similar mammoths, Soffer began studying Upper Paleolithic sites on the Russian and Eastern European plains. To her surprise, the famous mammoth bone beds were strewn with cumbersome body parts, such as 220-pound skulls, that sensible hunters would generally abandon. Moreover, the bones exhibited widely differing degrees of weathering, as if they had sat on the ground for varying lengths of time. To Soffer, it looked suspiciously as if Upper Paleolithic hunters had simply camped next to places where the pachyderms had perished naturally—such as water holes or salt licks—and mined the bones for raw materials.

"If one of these Upper Paleolithic guys killed a mammoth, and occasionally they did, they probably didn't stop talking about it for ten years."

Soffer began analyzing data researchers had gathered describing the sex and age ratios of mammoths excavated from four Upper Paleolithic sites. She found many juveniles, a smaller number of adult females, and hardly any males. The distribution mirrored the death pattern other researchers had observed at African water holes, where the weakest animals perished closest to the water and the strongest farther off. "Imagine the worst time of year in Africa, which is the drought season," explains Soffer. "There is no water, and elephants need an enormous amount. The ones in the worst shape—your weakest, your infirm, your young—are going to be tethered to that water before they die. They are in such horrendous shape, they don't have any extra energy to go anywhere. The ones in better shape would wander off slight distances and then keel over farther away. You've got basket cases and you've got ones that can walk 20 feet."

To Soffer, the implications of this study were clear. Upper Paleolithic bands had pitched their camps next to critical resources such as ancient salt licks or water holes. There the men spent more time scavenging bones and ivory from mammoth carcasses then they did risking life and limb by attacking 6,600-pound pachyderms with short-range spears. "If one of these

Upper Paleolithic guys killed a mammoth, and occasionally they did," concedes Soffer dryly, "they probably didn't stop talking about it for ten years."

But if Upper Paleolithic families weren't often tucking into mammoth steaks, what were they hunting and how? Soffer found the first unlikely clue in 1991, while sifting through hundreds of tiny clay fragments recovered from the Upper Paleolithic site of Pavlov, which lies just a short walk from Dolní Vestonice. Under a magnifying lens, Soffer noticed something strange on a few of the fragments: a series of parallel lines impressed on their surfaces. What could have left such a regular pattern? Puzzled, Soffer photographed the pieces, all of which had been unearthed from a zone sprinkled with wood charcoal that was radiocarbon-dated at between 27,000 and 25,000 years ago.

W HEN SHE RETURNED HOME, SOFFER HAD THE film developed. And one night on an impulse, she put on a slide show for a visiting colleague, Jim Adovasio. "We'd run out of cable films," she jokes. Staring at the images projected on Soffer's refrigerator, Adovasio, an archeologist at Mercyhurst College in Pennsylvania and an expert on ancient fiber technology, immediately recognized the impressions of plant fibers. On a few, he could actually discern a pattern of interlacing fibers— weaving.

Without a doubt, he said, he and Soffer were gazing at textiles or basketry. They were the oldest—by nearly 7,000 years—ever found. Just how these pieces of weaving got impressed in clay, he couldn't say. "It may be that a lot of these [materials] were lying around on clay floors," he notes. "When the houses burned, the walked-in images were subsequently left in the clay floors."

Soffer and Adovasio quickly made arrangements to fly back to the Czech Republic. At the Dolní Vestonice branch of the Institute of Archeology, Soffer sorted through nearly 8,400 fired clay pieces, weeding out the rejects. Adovasio made positive clay casts of 90. Back in Pennsylvania, he and his Mercyhurst colleague David Hyland peered at the casts under a zoom stereomicroscope, measuring warps and wefts. Forty-three revealed impressions of basketry and textiles. Some of the latter were as finely woven as a modern linen tablecloth. But as Hyland stared at four of the samples, he noted something potentially more fascinating: impressions of cordage bearing weaver's knots, a technique that joins two lengths of cord and that is commonly used for making nets of secure mesh. It looked like a tiny shred of a net bag, or perhaps a hunting net. Fascinated, Soffer expanded the study. She spent six weeks at the Moravian Museum in Brno, sifting through the remainder of the collections from Dolní Vestonice. Last fall, Adovasio spied the telltale impression of Ice Age mesh on one of the new casts.

The mesh, measuring two inches across, is far too delicate for hunting deer or other large prey. But hunters at Dolní Vestonice could have set nets of this size to capture hefty Ice Age hares, each carrying some six pounds of meat, and other fur-bearers such as arctic fox and red fox. As it turns out, the bones of hares and foxes litter camp floors at Dolní Vestonice and

Pavlov. Indeed, this small game accounts for 46 percent of the individual animals recovered at Pavlov. Soffer, moreover, doesn't rule out the possibility of turning up bits of even larger nets. Accomplished weavers in North America once knotted mesh with which they captured 1,000-pound elk and 300-pound bighorn sheep. "In fact, when game officials have to move sheep out west, it's by nets," she adds. "You throw nets on them and they just lie down. It's a very safe way of hunting."

Illustration by Ron Miller

NETS MADE ICE AGE HUNTING safe enough for entire communities to participate, and they captured everything from hares and foxes to deer and sheep.

In many historical societies, she observes, women played a key part in net hunting since the technique did not call for brute strength nor did it place young mothers in physical peril. Among Australian aborigines, for example, women as well as men knotted the mesh, laboring for as much as two or three years on a fine net. Among native North American groups, they helped lay out their handiwork on poles across a valley floor. Then the entire camp joined forces as beaters. Fanning out across the valley, men, women, and children alike shouted and screamed, flushing out game and driving it in the direction of the net. "Everybody and their mother could participate," says Soffer. "Some people were beating, others were screaming or holding the net. And once you got the net on these animals, they were immobilized. You didn't need brute force. You could club them, hit them any old way."

People seldom returned home empty-handed. Researchers living among the net-hunting Mbuti in the forests of Congo report that they capture game every time they lay out their woven traps, scooping up 50 percent of the animals encountered. "Nets are a far more valued item in their panoply of food-producing things than bows and arrows are," says Adovasio. So lethal are these traps that the Mbuti generally rack up more meat than they can consume, trading the surplus with neighbors. Other net hunters traditionally smoked or dried their catch and stored it for leaner times. Or they polished it off immediately in large ceremonial feasts. The hunters of Dolní Vestonice and Pavlov, says Soffer, probably feasted during ancient rituals. Archeologists unearthed no evidence of food storage pits at either site. But there is much evidence of ceremony. At Dolní Vestonice, for example, many clay figurines appear to have been ritually destroyed in secluded parts of the site.

Soffer doubts that the inhabitants of Dolní Vestonice and Pavlov were the only net makers in Ice Age Europe. Camps stretching from Germany to Russia are littered with a notable abundance of small-game bones, from hares to birds like ptarmigan. And at least some of their inhabitants whittled bone tools that look much like the awls and net spacers favored by historical net makers. Such findings, agree Soffer and Adovasio, reveal just how shaky the most widely accepted reconstructions of Upper Paleolithic life are. "These terribly stilted interpretations," says Adovasio, "with men hunting big animals all the time and the poor females waiting at home for these guys to bring home the bacon—what crap."

Illustration by Ron Miller

ONCE ANIMALS were caught in the nets, hunters could beat them to death with whatever was handy.

In her home outside Munich, Linda Owen finds other faults with this traditional image. Owen, an American born and raised, specializes in the microscopic analysis of stone tools. In her years of work, she often noticed that many of the tools made by hunters who roamed Europe near the end of the Upper Paleolithic era, some 18,000 to 12,000 years ago, resembled pounding stones and other gear for harvesting and processing plants. Were women and children gathering and storing wild plant foods?

Most of her colleagues saw little value in pursuing the question. Indeed, some German archeologists contended that 90 percent of the human diet during the Upper Paleolithic era came from meat. But as Owen began reading nutritional studies, she saw that heavy meat consumption would spell death. To stoke the body's cellular engines, human beings require energy from protein, fat, or carbohydrates. Of these, protein is the least efficient. To burn it, the body must boost its metabolic rate by 10 percent, straining the liver's ability to absorb oxygen. Unlike carnivorous animals, whose digestive and metabolic systems are well adapted to a meat-only diet, humans who consume more than half their calories as lean meat will die from protein poisoning. In Upper Paleolithic times, hunters undoubtedly tried to round out their diets with fat from wild game. But in winter, spring, and early summer, the meat would have been very lean. So how did humans survive?

Owen began sifting for clues through anthropological and historical accounts from subarctic and arctic North America. These environments, she reasoned, are similar to that of Ice Age Europe and pose similar challenges to their inhabitants. Even in the far north, Inuit societies harvested berries for winter storage and gathered other plants for medicines and for fibers. To see if any of the flora that thrived in Upper Paleolithic Europe could be put to similar uses, Owen drew up a list of plants economically important to people living in cold-climate regions of North America and Europe and compared it with a list of species that botanists had identified from pollen trapped in Ice Age sediment cores from southern Germany. Nearly 70 plants were found on both lists. "I came up with just a fantastic list of plants that were available at that time. Among others, there were a number or reeds that are used by the Eskimo and subarctic people in North America for making baskets. There are a lot of plants with edible leaves and stems, and things that were used as drugs and dyes. So the plants were there."

The chief plant collectors in historical societies were undoubtedly women. "It was typically women's work," says Owen. "I did find several comments that the men on hunting expeditions would gather berries or plants for their own meals, but they did not participate in the plant-gathering expeditions. They might go along, but they would be hunting or fishing."

Were Upper Paleolithic women gathering plants? The archeological literature was mostly silent on the subject. Few archeobotanists, Owen found, had ever looked for plant seeds and shreds in Upper Paleolithic camps. Most were convinced such efforts would be futile in sites so ancient. At University College London, however, Owen reached a determined young archeobontanist, Sarah Mason, who had analyzed a small sample of charcoal-like remains from a 26,390-year-old hearth at Dolní Vestonice.

The sample held more than charcoal. Examining it with a scanning electron microscope, Mason and her colleagues found fragments of fleshy plant taproots with distinctive secretory cavities—trademarks of the daisy and aster family, which boasts several species with edible roots. In all likelihood, women at Dolní Vestonice had dug the roots and cooked them into starchy meals. And they had very likely simmered other plant foods too. Mason and her colleagues detected a strange pulverized substance in the charred sample. It looked as if the women had either ground plants into flour and then boiled the results to make gruel or pounded vegetable material into a mush for their babies. Either way, says Soffer, the results are telling. "They're stuffing carbohydrates."

Owen is pursuing the research further. "If you do look," she says, "you can find things." At her urging, colleagues at the University of Tübingen are now analyzing Paleolithic hearths for botanical remains as they unearth them. Already they have turned up more plants, including berries, all clearly preserved after thousands of years. In light of these findings, Owen suggests that it was women, not men, who brought home most of the calories to Upper Paleolithic families. Indeed, she estimates that if Ice Age females collected plants, bird eggs, shellfish, and edible insects, and if they hunted or trapped small game and participated in the hunting of large game—as northern women did in historical times—they most likely contributed 70 percent of the consumed calories.

Illustration by Ron Miller

THE CLAY FIGURINES at Dolní Vestonice may have been used in divination rituals.

Moreover, some women may have enjoyed even greater power, judging from the most contentious relics of Ice Age life: the famous Venus figurines. Excavators have recovered more than 100 of the small statuettes, which were crafted between 29,000 and 23,000 years ago from such enduring materials as bone, stone, antler, ivory, and fired clay. The figurines share a strange blend of abstraction and realism. They bare prominent breasts, for example, but lack nipples. Their bodies are often minutely detailed down to the swaying lines of their backbones and the tiny rolls of flesh—fat folds—beneath their shoulder blades, but they often lack eyes, mouths, and any facial expression. For years researchers viewed them as a male art form. Early anthropologists, after all, had observed only male hunters carving stone, ivory, and other hard materials. Females were thought to lack the necessary strength. Moreover, reasoned experts, only men would take such loving interest in a woman's body. Struck by the voluptuousness of the small stone, ivory, and clay bodies, some researchers suggested they were Ice Age erotica, intended to be touched and fondled by their male makers. The idea still lingers. In the 1980s, for example, the well-known American paleontologist Dale Guthrie wrote a scholarly article comparing the postures of the figurines with the provocative poses of *Playboy* centerfolds.

But most experts now dismiss such contentions. Owen's careful scouring of ethnographic sources, for example, revealed that women in arctic and subarctic societies did indeed work stone and ivory on occasion. And there is little reason to suggest the figurines figured as male erotica. The Black Venus, for example, seems to have belonged to a secret world of ceremony and ritual far removed from everyday sexual life.

THE EVIDENCE, SAYS SOFFER, LIES IN THE RAW material from which the Black Venus is made. Clay objects sometimes break or explode when fired, a process called thermal-shock fracturing. Studies conducted by Pamela Vandiver of the Smithsonian Institution have demonstrated that the Black Venus and other human and animal figurines recovered from Dolní Vestonice—as well as nearly 2,000 fired ceramic pellets that litter the site—were made from a local clay that is resistant to thermal-shock fracturing. But many of the figurines, including the celebrated Black Venus, bear the distinctive jagged branching splinters created by thermal shock. Intriguingly, the fired clay pellets do not.

Curious, Vandiver decided to replicate the ancient firing process. Her analysis of the small Dolní Vestonice kilns revealed that they had been fired to temperatures around 1450 degrees Fahrenheit—similar to those of an ordinary hearth. So Vandiver set about making figurines of local soil and firing them in a similar earthen kiln, which a local archeological crew had built nearby. To produce thermal shock, she had to place objects larger than half an inch on the hottest part of the fire; moreover, the pieces had to be so wet they barely held their shape.

To Vandiver and Soffer, the experiment—which was repeated several times back at the Smithsonian Institution—suggests that thermal shock was no accident. "Stuff can explode naturally in the kiln," says Soffer, "or you can make it explode. Which was going on at Dolní Vestonice? We toyed with both ideas. Either we're dealing with the most inept potters, people with two left hands, or they are doing it on purpose. And we reject the idea that they were totally inept, because other materials didn't explode. So what are the odds that this would happen only with a very particular category of objects?"

These exploding figurines could well have played a role in rituals, an idea supported by the location of the kilns. They are situated far away from the dwellings, as ritual buildings often are. Although the nature of the ceremonies is not clear, Soffer speculates that they might have served as divination rites for discerning what the future held. "Some stuff is going to explode. Some stuff is not going to explode. It's evocative, like picking petals off a daisy. She loves me, she loves me not."

Moreover, ritualists at Dolní Vestonice could have read significance into the fracturing patterns of the figurines. Many historical cultures, for example, attempted to read the future by a related method called scapulimancy. In North America, Cree ceremonialists often placed the shoulder blade, or scapula, of a desired animal in the center of a lodge. During the ceremonies, cracks began splintering the bone: a few of these fractures leaked droplets of fat. To Cree hunters, this was a sign that they would find game if they journeyed in the direction indicated by the cracks.

Venus figurines from other sites also seem to have been cloaked in ceremony. "They were not just something made to look pretty," says Margherita Mussi, an archeologist at the University of Rome-La Sapienza who studies Upper Paleolithic figurines. Mussi notes that several small statuettes from the Grimaldi Cave carvings of southern Italy, one of the largest troves of Ice Age figurines ever found in Western Europe, were carved from rare materials, which the artists obtained with great difficulty, sometimes through trade or distant travel. The statuettes were laboriously whittled and polished, then rubbed with ocher, a pigment that appears to have had ceremonial significance, suggesting that they could have been reserved for special events like rituals.

The nature of these rites is still unclear. But Mussi is convinced that women took part, and some archeologists believe they stood at the center. One of the clearest clues, says Mussi, lies in a recently rediscovered Grimaldi figurine known as Beauty and the Beast. This greenish yellow serpentine sculpture portrays two arched bodies facing away from each other and joined at the head, shoulders, and lower extremities. One body is that of a Venus figurine. The other is a strange creature that combines the triangular head of a reptile, the pinched waist of a wasp, tiny arms, and horns. "It is clearly not a creature of this world," says Mussi.

The pairing of woman and supernatural beast, adds Mussi, is highly significant. "I believe that these women were related to the capacity of communicating with a different world," she says. "I think they were believed to be the gateway to a different dimension." Possessing powers that far surpassed others in their communities, such women may have formed part of a spiritual elite, rather like the shamans of ancient Siberia. As intermediaries between the real and spirit worlds, Siberian shamans were said to be able to cure illnesses and intercede on behalf of others for hunting success. It is possible that Upper Paleolithic women performed similar services for their followers.

Although the full range of their activities is unlikely ever to be known for certain, there is good reason to believe that Ice Age women played a host of powerful roles—from plant collectors and weavers to hunters and spiritual leaders. And the research that suggests those roles is rapidly changing our mental images of the past. For Soffer and others, these are exciting times. "The data do speak for themselves," she says finally. "They answer the questions we have. But if we don't envision the questions, we're not going to see the data."

HEATHER PRINGLE *lives in Vancouver, British Columbia. "I love how this article overturns the popular image of the role of women in the past," says Pringle, who specializes in writing about archeology. "It was fun to write and a delight to research." Pringle is the author of* In Search of Ancient North America.

WOMAN
THE TOOLMAKER

A day in the life of an Ethiopian woman who scrapes
hides the old-fashioned way.

by STEVEN A. BRANDT *and* KATHRYN WEEDMAN

ON THE EDGE OF THE WESTERN ESCARPMENT of the Ethiopian Rift Valley, we sit in awe, not of the surrounding environment—some of the world's most spectacular scenery—but of an elderly woman deftly manufacturing stone scrapers as she prepares food, answers an inquisitive child, and chats with a neighbor. She smiles at us, amused and honored by our barrage of questions and our filming of her activities.

In our world of electronic and digital gadgetry, it is surprising to meet someone who uses stone tools in their everyday life. Yet, over the past three decades, researchers have identified a handful of ethnic groups in Ethiopia's southern highlands whose artisans live by making stone scrapers and processing animal hides.

In 1995, with colleagues from Ethiopia's Authority for Research and Conservation of Cultural Heritage and the University of Florida, we surveyed the highlands and, much to our surprise, identified hundreds of stone tool makers in ten different ethnic groups.

The Konso, one group we surveyed, grow millet and other crops on terraces and raise livestock that provide the skins for the hide workers. While hide working in virtually all of the other groups is conducted by men who learn from their fathers, among the Konso the hide workers are women, taught by their mothers or other female relatives.

In archaeological writings, scholarly and popular, stone toolmaking has generally been presented as a male activity; *Man the Toolmaker* is the title of one classic work. This is despite the fact that Australian Aboriginal, North American Inuit (Eskimo), and Siberian women, among others, have been reported in recent times to have made flaked-stone artifacts. The Konso hide workers are probably the only women in the world still making stone tools on a regular basis. They provide a unique opportunity for ethnoarchaeology, the study of the material remains of contemporary peoples. In the past two summers, our team returned to study the women hide workers, following them with our notebooks and cameras, and observing them as they went through their daily lives.

One Konso woman we studied is Sokate, a respected and energetic grandmother now in her 70s. Our many questions amuse Sokate, but she is polite and patient with us. When we ask why only 31 of the 119 Konso hide workers are men, she can only laugh and say that hide working has always been women's work.

AFTER AN EARLY MORNING RAIN, Sokate strides through her village's terraced millet fields to the same riverbed in which her mother and grandmother searched for chert, a flakeable stone similar to flint. She uses a digging stick to pry stones loose. After almost an hour, Sokate picks up a small nodule of chert. She places it on a large, flat basalt rock. Lifting another large piece of basalt, she brings it down onto the nodule several times, striking off many pieces. Sokate selects ten of the flakes and places them into the top ruffle of her skirt, folding it into her waistband. She also tucks in three pieces of usable quartz, found with the aid of accompanying children.

Returning home, Sokate is greeted by children, goats, and chickens. She picks up the iron tip of a hoe, and, sitting on a goat hide in front of her house, strikes flakes off a chert nodule she collected earlier. She then picks up a wooden bowl filled with scraper components—wooden handles, used stone scrapers, small, unused flakes—and puts the new chert and quartz flakes in it. Moving to the hearth area in front of her house, she takes a flake from the bowl. Resting the flake directly along the edge of a large basalt block that serves as a hearthstone and an anvil, she strikes the flake's edges with the hoe tip, shaping it into a scraper that will fit into the socket of the wooden handle. Although she has access to iron, Sokate tells us that she prefers using stone because it is sharper, more controllable, and easier to resharpen than iron, or even glass. But not all Konso hide workers share her opinion, and in fact, there are now only 21 of them who still use stone regularly.

She places the handle, passed down to her from her mother, into the ashes of the hearth, warming the acacia tree gum (mastic) that holds the scraper in its socket. When the mastic becomes pliable, Sokate pulls the old, used-up scraper out of the socket, then places the end of the handle back into the ashes. After a few minutes, she takes it out and removes some of the old mastic with a stick. On an earthenware sherd, she mixes fresh resin she collected earlier in the day with ashes and heats it. Winding it onto a stick, she drips it into the socket. Sokate then puts a new scraper into the socket, patting the resin down around it with her index finger, making certain that it is set at the proper 90-degree angle to the haft.

Local farmers and other artisans bring Sokate hides to scrape, paying her with grain or money. The morning she is going to scrape a cow hide, Sokate brushes it with a mixture of water and juice from the enset plant, or false banana. If the hide is too dry, removing the fat from its inner side is difficult. After the hide is saturated, she latches one end of it to a tree or post so the hide is slightly above the ground. Squatting or kneeling, she holds the hide taut with her feet to facilitate scraping it. Then with both hands holding the wooden handle, she scrapes the cow hide in long strokes, using a "pull" motion. Goat hides are laid flat on the ground with Sokate sitting with one leg on top of the hide and the other underneath to keep it taut. She scrapes a got hide with short strokes and a "push" motion away from her body, giving better control of the scraper with the thin goat skin.

Sokate removes the fatty inner layer, shaving off long strips in a rhythmic motion. When the edge of her tool becomes dull, usually after about 60 strokes, she resharpens it. Most of the small chips she removes from the scraper to resharpen it fall into a wooden bowl or gourd. Her barefoot grandchildren periodically dump the sharp chips onto the communal trash pile just outside the village. Sokate uses the scraper until it becomes too dull for scraping and too small to resharpen further. She'll wear out two or three scraping a single cattle hide, one or two for a goat hide.

After Sokate scrapes the hide, she spreads a reddish, oily paste of ground castor beans and pieces of red ocher over it. She then folds the hide over and works the mixture into it. After a few days, the skin is soft. Cow hides are then made into bedding, sandals, straps, belts, and musical instruments, while goat hides are made into bags and (now much more rarely) clothing. During harvest time, the demand for goat hides increases because more bags are

> Many hide-working activities take place in Konso compounds, which are often surrounded by stone walls. A broken pot on the roof indicates the father of a household is a first-born son, a person of higher status.

needed to carry agricultural goods. Sokate then sends her granddaughter to tell the hide's owner that it is ready.

SOKATE AND THE OTHER Ethiopian hide workers say they are proud of their profession, as they play important economic and social roles within their villages. In addition to hide working, they may also be responsible for announcing births, deaths, and meetings, and for performing puberty initiation ceremonies and other ritual activities. Despite the usefulness of their craft and other duties in the community, Konso hide workers and other artisans, such as ironsmiths and potters, have low social status. Farmers hold them in low esteem and consider them polluted, probably because their crafts involve contact with items that are thought to be impure, like the skins of dead animals. They cannot marry outside of their artisan group, usually cannot own land, and are often excluded from political and judicial life.

Clearly, the Konso hide workers are a rich source of information from which we can address a range of questions: Can excavations of abandoned hide worker compounds provide insights into the identification of social inequality and ranking? How and in what social contexts is stone toolmaking learned? Can we differentiate women's activities from men's on the basis of stone tools?

There is a sense of urgency in our work. Many of the hide workers are elderly and have not taught their children their craft; the influx of plastic bags and Western furnishings have greatly reduced demand for their products. And many of the hide workers have abandoned the use of stone in favor of bottle glass: why hike two hours for chert when you can just walk down the road and pick up pieces of glass? We want to complete our study of the Konso hide workers as soon as possible and begin studying other groups in southern Ethiopia whose hide workers are still using flaked stone, for after 2.5 million years of stone tool use and probably more than 100,000 years of scraping hides with stone, humanity's first and longest-lasting cultural tradition is rapidly being lost.

STEVEN A. BRANDT *and* KATHRYN WEEDMAN *are in the department of anthropology at the University of Florida, Gainseville. Their work is supported by funds from the National Science Foundation.*

Yes, Wonderful Things

William Rathje and Cullen Murphy

On a crisp October morning not long ago the sun ascended above the Atlantic Ocean and turned its gaze on a team of young researchers as they swarmed over what may be the largest archaeological site in the world. The mound they occupied covers three thousand acres and in places rises more than 155 feet above a low-lying island. Its mass, estimated at 100 million tons, and its volume, estimated at 2.9 billion cubic feet, make it one of the largest man-made structures in North America. And it is known to be a treasure trove—a Pompeii, a Tikal, a Valley of the Kings—of artifacts from the most advanced civilization the planet has ever seen. Overhead sea gulls cackled and cawed, alighting now and then to peck at an artifact or skeptically observe an archaeologist at work. The surrounding landscape still supported quail and duck, but far more noticeable were the dusty, rumbling wagons and tractors of the New York City Department of Sanitation.

The site was the Fresh Kills landfill, on Staten Island, in New York City, a repository of garbage that, when shut down, in the year 2005, will have reached a height of 505 feet above sea level, making it the highest geographic feature along a fifteen-hundred-mile stretch of the Atlantic seaboard running north from Florida all the way to Maine. One sometimes hears that Fresh Kills will have to be closed when it reaches 505 feet so as not to interfere with the approach of aircraft to Newark Airport, in New Jersey, which lies just across the waterway called Arthur Kill. In reality, though, the 505-foot elevation is the result of a series of calculations designed to maximize the landfill's size while avoiding the creation of grades so steep that roads built upon the landfill can't safely be used.

Fresh Kills was originally a vast marshland, a tidal swamp. Robert Moses's plan for the area, in 1948, was to dump enough garbage there to fill the marshland up—a process that would take, according to one estimate, until 1968—and then to develop the site, building houses, attracting light industry, and setting aside open space for recreational use. ("The Fresh Kills landfill project," a 1951 report to Mayor Vincent R. Impelliteri observed, "cannot fail to affect constructively a wide area around it. It is at once practical and idealistic.") Something along these lines may yet happen when Fresh Kills is closed. Until then, however, it is the largest active landfill in the world. It is twenty-five times the size of the Great Pyramid of Khufu at Giza, forty times the size of the Temple of the Sun at Teotihuacan. The volume of Fresh Kills is approaching that of the Great Wall of China, and by one estimate will surpass it at some point in the next few years. It is the sheer physical stature of Fresh Kills in the hulking world of landfills that explains why archaeologists were drawn to the place.

To the archaeologists of the University of Arizona's Garbage Project, which is now entering its twentieth year, landfills represent valuable lodes of information that may, when mined and interpreted, produce valuable insights—insights not into the nature of some past society, of course, but into the nature of our own. Garbage is among humanity's most prodigious physical legacies to those who have yet to be born; if we can come to understand our discards, Garbage Project archaeologists argue, then we will better understand the world in which we live. It is this conviction that prompts Garbage Project researchers to look upon the steaming detritus of daily existence with the same quiet excitement displayed by Howard Carter and Lord George Edward Carnarvon at the unpillaged, unopened tomb of Tutankhamun.

"Can you see anything?" Carnarvon asked as Carter thrust a lighted candle through a hole into the gloom of the first antechamber. "Yes," Carter replied. "Wonderful things."

Garbage archaeology can be conducted in several ways. At Fresh Kills the method of excavation involved a mobile derrick and a thirteen-hundred-pound bucket auger, the latter of which would be sunk into various parts of the landfill to retrieve samples of garbage from selected strata. At 6:15 a.m. Buddy Kellett of the company Kellett's Well Boring, Inc., which had assisted with several previous Garbage Project landfill digs, drove one of the company's trucks, with derrick and auger collapsed for travel, straight up the steep slope of one of the landfill mounds. Two-thirds of the way up, the Garbage Project crew directed Kellett to a small patch of level ground. Four hydraulic posts were deployed from the stationary vehicle, extending outward to keep it safely moored. Now the derrick was raised. It supported a long metal rod that in turn housed two other metal rods; the apparatus, when pulled to its full length, like a telescope, was capable of penetrating the landfill to a depth of ninety-seven feet—enough at this particular spot to go clear through its bottom and into the original marsh that Fresh Kills had been (or into what was left of it). At the end of the rods was the auger, a large bucket made of high-tension steel: four feet high, three feet in diameter, and open at the bottom like a cookie cutter, with six graphite-and-steel teeth around the bottom's circumference. The bucket would spin at about thirty revolutions per minute and with such force that virtually nothing could impede its descent. At a Garbage Project excavation in Sunnyvale, California, in 1988, one of the first things the bucket hit in the cover dirt a few feet below the surface of the Sunnyvale Landfill was the skeleton of a car. The bucket's teeth snapped the axle, and drilled on.

The digging at Fresh Kills began. Down the whirring bucket plunged. Moments later it returned with a gasp, laden with garbage that, when released, spewed a thin vapor into the chill autumnal air. The smell was pungent, somewhere between sweet and disagreeable. Kellett's rig operator, David Spillers, did his job with the relaxation that comes of familiarity, seemingly oblivious to the harsh grindings and sharp clanks. The rest of the archaeological crew, wearing cloth aprons and heavy rubber gloves, went about their duties with practiced efficiency and considerable speed. They were veteran members of the Garbage Project's A-Team—its landfill-excavating arm—and had been through it all before.

Again a bucketful of garbage rose out of the ground. As soon as it was dumped Masakazu Tani, at the time a Japanese graduate student in anthropology at the University of Arizona (his Ph.D. thesis, recently completed, involves identifying activity areas in ancient sites on the basis of distributions of litter), plunged a thermometer into the warm mass. "Forty-three degrees centigrade," Tani called out. The temperature (equivalent to 109.4 degrees Fahrenheit) was duly logged. The garbage was then given a brusque preliminary examination to determine its generic source and, if possible, its date of origin. In this case the presence of telltale domestic items, and of legible newspapers, made both tasks easy. Gavin Archer, another anthropologist and a research associate of the Garbage Project, made a notation in the running log that he would keep all day long: "Household, circa 1977." Before the next sample was pulled up Douglas Wilson, an anthropologist who specializes in household hazardous waste, stepped up to the auger hole and played out a weighted tape measure, eventually calling out, "Thirty-five feet." As a safety precaution, Wilson, like any other crew member working close to the sunken shaft on depth-measure duty, wore a leather harness tethered to a nearby vehicle. The esophagus created by the bucket auger was just large enough to accept a human being, and anyone slipping untethered a story or two into this narrow, oxygen- starved cavity would die of asphyxiation before any rescue could be attempted.

Most of the bucketfuls of garbage received no more attention than did the load labeled "Household, circa 1977." Some basic data were recorded for tracking purposes, and the garbage was left on a quickly

accumulating backdirt pile. But as each of what would finally be fourteen wells grew deeper and deeper, at regular intervals (either every five or every ten feet) samples were taken and preserved for full-dress analysis. On those occasions Wilson Hughes, the methodical and serenely ursine co-director and field supervisor of the Garbage Project, and the man responsible for day-to-day logistics at the Fresh Kills dig, would call out to the bucket operator over the noise of the engine: "We'll take the next bucket." Then Hughes and Wilson would race toward the rig in a running crouch, like medics toward a helicopter, a plywood sampling board between them. Running in behind came a team of microbiologists and civil engineers assembled from the University of Oklahoma, the University of Wisconsin, and Procter & Gamble's environmental laboratory. They brought with them a variety of containers and sealing devices to preserve samples in an oxygen-free environment—an environment that would allow colonies of the anaerobic bacteria that cause most of the biodegradation in landfills (to the extent that biodegradation occurs) to survive for later analysis. Behind the biologists and engineers came other Garbage Project personnel with an assortment of wire mesh screens and saw horses.

Within seconds of the bucket's removal from the ground, the operator maneuvered it directly over the sampling board, and released the contents. The pile was attacked first by Phillip Zack, a civil engineering student from the University of Wisconsin, who, as the temperature was being recorded, directed portions of the material into a variety of airtight conveyances. Then other members of the team moved in—the people who would shovel the steaming refuse atop the wire mesh; the people who would sort and bag whatever didn't go through the mesh; the people who would pour into bags or cannisters or jars whatever did go through the mesh; the people who would label everything for the trip either back to Tucson and the Garbage Project's holding bins or to the laboratories of the various microbiologists. (The shortest trip was to the trailer-laboratory that Procter & Gamble scientists had driven from Cincinnati and parked at the edge of the landfill.) The whole sample-collection process, from dumping to sorting to storing, took no more than twelve minutes. During the Fresh Kills dig it was repeated forty- four times at various places and various depths.

As morning edged toward afternoon the bucket auger began to near the limits of its

reach in one of the wells. Down through the first thirty-five feet, a depth that in this well would date back to around 1984, the landfill had been relatively dry. Food waste and yard waste—hot dogs, bread, and grass clippings, for example—were fairly well preserved. Newspapers remained intact and easy to read, their lurid headlines ("Woman Butchered-Ex-Hubby Held") calling to mind a handful of yesterday's tragedies. Beyond thirty-five feet, however, the landfill became increasingly wet, the garbage increasingly unidentifiable. At sixty feet, a stratum in this well containing garbage from the 1940s and 1950s, the bucket grabbed a sample and pulled it toward the surface. The Garbage Project team ran forward with their equipment, positioning themselves underneath. The bucket rose majestically as the operator sat at the controls, shouting something over the noise. As near as anyone can reconstruct it now, he was saying, "You boys might want to back off some, 'cause if this wind hits that bucket...." The operator broke off because the wind did hit that bucket, and the material inside—a gray slime, redolent of putrefaction—thoroughly showered the crew. It would be an exaggeration to suggest that the victims were elated by this development, but their curiosity was certainly piqued, because on only one previous excavation had slime like this turned up in a landfill. What was the stuff made of? How had it come to be? What did its existence mean? The crew members doggedly collected all the usual samples, plus a few extra bottles of slime for special study. Then they cleaned themselves off.

It would be a blessing if it were possible to study garbage in the abstract, to study garbage without having to handle it physically.[*] But that is not possible. Garbage is not mathematics. To understand garbage you have to touch it, to feel it, to sort it, to smell it. You have to pick through hundreds of tons of it, counting and weighing all the daily newspapers, the telephone books; the soiled diapers, the foam clamshells that once briefly held hamburgers, the lipstick cylinders coated with grease, the medicine vials still encasing brightly colored pills, the empty bottles of scotch, the half-full cans of paint and muddy turpentine, the forsaken toys, the cigarette butts. You have to sort and weigh and measure the volume of all the organic matter, the discards from thousands of plates: the noodles and the Cheerios and the tortillas; the pieces of pet food that have made their own gravy; the hardened jelly doughnuts, bleeding from their side wounds; the half-eaten bananas, mostly still within their peels, black and incomparably sweet in the embrace of final decay. You have to confront sticky green mountains of yard waste, and slippery brown hills of potato peels, and brittle ossuaries of chicken bones and T-bones. And then, finally, there are the "fines," the vast connecting mixture of tiny bits of paper, metal, glass, plastic, dirt, grit, and former nutrients that suffuses every landfill like a kind of grainy lymph. To understand garbage you need thick gloves and a mask and some booster shots. But the yield in knowledge—about people and their behavior as well as about garbage itself—offsets the grim working conditions.

To an archaeologist, ancient garbage pits or garbage mounds, which can usually be located within a short distance from any ruin, are always among the happiest of finds, for they contain in concentrated form the artifacts and comestibles and remnants of behavior of the people who used them. While every archaeologist dreams of discovering spectacular objects, the bread-and-butter work of archaeology involves the most common and routine kinds of discards. It is not entirely fanciful to define archaeology as the discipline that tries to understand old garbage, and to learn from that garbage something about ancient societies and ancient behaviors. The eminent archaeologist Emil Haury once wrote of the aboriginal garbage heaps of the American Southwest: "Whichever way one views the mounds—as garbage piles to avoid, or as symbols of a way of life—they nevertheless are features more productive of information than any others." When the British archaeologist Sir Leonard Woolley, in 1916, first climbed to the top of the ancient city of Carchemish, on the Euphrates River near the modern-day Turkish-Syrian border, he moistened his index finger and held it in the air. Satisfied, he scanned the region due south of the city—that is, downwind—pausing to draw on his map the location of any mounds he saw. A trench dug through the largest of these mounds revealed it to be the garbage dump Woolley was certain it was, and the exposed strata helped establish the chronological sequence for the Carchemish site as a whole. Archaeologists have been picking through ancient garbage ever since archaeology became a profession, more than a century ago, and they will no doubt go on doing so as long as garbage is produced.

Several basic points about garbage need to be emphasized at the outset. First, the creation of garbage is an unequivocal sign of a human presence. From Styrofoam cups along a roadway and urine bags on the moon there is an uninterrupted chain of garbage that reaches back more than two million years to the first "waste flake" knocked off in the knapping of the first stone tool. That the distant past often seems misty and dim is precisely because our earliest ancestors left so little garbage behind. An appreciation of the accomplishments of the first hominids became possible only after they began making stone tools, the debris from the production of which, along with the discarded tools themselves, are now probed for their secrets with electron microscopes and displayed in museums not as garbage but as "artifacts." These artifacts serve as markers—increasingly frequent and informative markers—of how our forebears coped with the evolving physical and social world. Human beings are mere placeholders in time, like zeros in a long number; their garbage seems to have more staying power, and a power to inform across the millennia that complements (and often substitutes for) that of the written word. The profligate habits of our own country and our own time—the sheer volume of the garbage that we create and must dispose of—will make our society an open book. The question is: Would we ourselves recognize our story when it is told, or will our garbage tell tales about us that we as yet do not suspect?

That brings up a second matter: If our garbage, in the eyes of the future, is destined to hold a key to the past, then surely it already holds a key to the present. This may be an obvious point, but it is one whose implications were not pursued by scholars until relatively recently. Each of us throws away dozens of items every day. All of these items are relics of specific human activities—relics no different in their inherent nature from many of those that traditional archaeologists work with (though they are, to be sure, a bit fresher). Taken as a whole the garbage of the United States, from its 93 million households and 1.5 million retail outlets and from all of its schools, hospitals, government offices, and other public facilities, is a mirror of American society. Of course, the problem with the mirror garbage offers is that, when encountered in a garbage can, dump, or landfill, it is a broken one: our civilization is reflected in billions of fragments that may reveal little in and of themselves. Fitting some of the pieces back together requires painstaking effort—effort that a small number of archaeologists and natural scientists have only just begun to apply.

A third point about garbage is that it is not an assertion but a physical fact—and thus may sometimes serve as a useful corrective. Human beings have over the centuries left many accounts describing their lives and civilizations. Many of these are little more than self-aggrandizing advertisements. The remains of the tombs, temples, and palaces of the elite are filled with personal histories as recorded by admiring relatives and fawning retainers. More such information is carved into obelisks and stelae, gouged into clay tablets, painted or printed on papyrus and paper. Historians are understandably drawn to written evidence of this kind, but garbage has often served as a kind of tattle-tale, setting the record straight.

It had long been known, for example, that French as well as Spanish forts had been erected along the coast of South Carolina during the sixteenth century, and various mounds and depressions have survived into our own time to testify to their whereabouts. Ever since the mid-nineteenth century a site on the tip of Parris Island, South Carolina, has been familiarly known as the site of a French outpost, built in 1562, that is spelled variously in old documents as Charlesfort, Charlesforte, and Charles Forte. In 1925, the Huguenot Society of South Carolina successfully lobbied Congress to erect a monument commemorating the building of Charlesfort. Subsequently, people in nearby Beaufort took up the Charlesfort theme, giving French names to streets, restaurants, and housing developments. Gift shops sold kitschy touristiana with a distinctly Gallic flavor. Those restaurants and gift shops found themselves in an awkward position when, in 1957, as a result of an analysis of discarded matter discovered at Charlesfort, a National Park Service historian, Albert Manucy, suggested that the site was of Spanish origin. Excavations begun in 1979 by the archaeologist Stanley South, which turned up such items as discarded Spanish olive jars and broken majolica pottery from Seville, confirmed Manucy's view: "Charlesfort," South established, was actually Fort San Marcos, a Spanish installation built in 1577 to protect a Spanish town named Santa Elena. (Both the fort and the town had been abandoned after only a few years.)

Garbage, then, represents physical fact, not mythology. It underscores a point that can not be too greatly emphasized: Our private worlds consist essentially of two realities—mental reality, which encompasses beliefs, attitudes, and ideas, and material reality, which is the picture embodied in the physical record. The study of garbage reminds us that it is a rare person in whom mental and material realities completely coincide. Indeed, for the most part, the pair exist in a state of tension, if not open conflict.

Americans have always wondered, sometimes with buoyant playfulness, what their countrymen in the far future will make of Americans "now." In 1952, in a monograph he first circulated privately among colleagues and eventually published in *The Journal of Irreproducible Results,* the eminent anthropologist and linguist Joseph H. Greenberg—the man who would one day sort the roughly one thousand known Native American languages into three broad language families—imagined the unearthing of the so-called "violence texts" during an excavation of the Brooklyn Dodgers' Ebbets Field in the year A.D. 2026; what interpretation, he wondered, would be given to such newspaper reports as "Yanks Slaughter Indians" and "Reese made a sacrifice in the infield"? In 1979 the artist and writer David Macaulay published *Motel of the Mysteries,* an archaeological site-report setting forth the conclusions reached by a team of excavators in the year A.D. 4022 who have unearthed a motel dating back to 1985 (the year, Macaulay wrote, in which "an accidental reduction in postal rates on a substance called third- and fourth-class mail literally buried the North Americans under tons of brochures, fliers, and small containers called FREE"). Included in the report are illustrations of an archaeologist modeling a toilet seat, toothbrushes, and a drain stopper (or, as Macaulay describes them, "the Sacred Collar … the magnificent 'plasticus' ear ornaments, and the exquisite silver chain and pendant"), all assumed to be items of ritual or personal regalia. In 1982 an exhibit was mounted in New York City called "Splendors of the Sohites"—a vast display of artifacts, including "funerary vessels" (faded, dusky soda bottles) and "hermaphrodite amulets" (discarded pop-top rings), found in the SoHo section of Manhattan and dating from the Archaic Period (A.D. 1950–1961), the Classical Period (1962–1975), and the Decadent Period (1976–c.1980).

Greenberg, Macaulay, and the organizers of the Sohites exhibition all meant to have some fun, but there is an uneasy undercurrent to their work, and it is embodied in the question: What are we to make of ourselves? The Garbage Project, conceived in 1971, and officially established at the University of Arizona in 1973, was an attempt to come up with a new way of providing serious answers. It aimed to apply *real* archaeology to this very question; to see if it would be possible to investigate human behavior "from the back end," as it were. This scholarly endeavor has come to be known as garbology, and practitioners of garbology are known as garbologists. The printed citation (dated 1975) in the *Oxford English Dictionary* for the meaning of "garbology" as used here associates the term with the Garbage Project.

In the years since its founding the Garbage Project's staff members have processed more than 250,000 pounds of garbage, some of it from landfills but most of it fresh out of garbage cans in selected neighborhoods. All of this garbage has been sorted, coded, and catalogued—every piece, from bottles of furniture polish and egg-shaped pantyhose packaging to worn and shredded clothing, crumpled bubble-gum wrappers, and the full range of kitchen waste. A unique database has been built up from these cast-offs, covering virtually every aspect of American life: drinking habits, attitudes toward red meat, trends in the use of convenience foods, the strange ways in which consumers respond to shortages, the use of contraceptives, and hundreds of other matters.*

The antecedents of the Garbage Project in the world of scholarship and elsewhere are few but various. Some are undeniably dubious. The examination of fresh refuse is, of course, as old as the human species— just watch anyone who happens upon an old campsite, or a neighbor scavenging at a dump for spare parts or furniture. The first systematic study of the components of America's garbage dates to the early 1900s and the work of the civil engineers Rudolph Hering (in New York) and Samuel A. Greeley (in Chicago), who by 1921 had gathered enough information from enough cities to compile *Collection and Disposal of Municipal Refuse,* the first textbook on urban trash management. In academe, not much happened after that for quite some time. Out in the field, however, civil engineers and solid-waste managers did now and again sort and weigh fresh garbage as it stood in transit between its source and destination, but their categories were usually simple: paper, glass, metal. No one sorted garbage into detailed categories relating to particular consumer discard patterns. No one, for example, kept track of phenomena as specific as the number of beer cans thrown away versus the number of beer bottles, or the number of orange-juice cans thrown away versus the number of pounds of freshly squeezed oranges, or the amount of candy thrown away in the week after Halloween versus the amount thrown away in the week after Valentine's Day. And no one ever dug into the final resting places of most of America's garbage: dumps (where garbage is left in the open) and sanitary landfills (where fresh garbage is covered every night with six to eight inches of soil).

Even as America's city managers over the years oversaw—and sometimes desperately attempted to cope with—the disposal of ever-increasing amounts of garbage, the study of garbage itself took several odd detours—one into the world of the military, another into the world of celebrity-watching, and a third into the world of law enforcement.

The military's foray into garbology occurred in 1941, when two enlisted men, Horace Schwerin and Phalen Golden, were forced to discontinue a survey they were conducting among new recruits about which aspects of Army life the recruits most disliked. (Conducting polls of military personnel was, they had learned, against regulations.) Schwerin and Golden had already discovered, however, that the low quality of the food was the most frequently heard complaint, and they resolved to look into this one matter with an investigation that could not be considered a poll. What Schwerin and Golden did was to station observers in mess halls to record the types of food that were most commonly wasted and the volume of waste by type of food. The result, after 2.4 million man-meals had been observed, was a textbook example of how garbage studies can produce not only behavioral insights but also practical benefits. Schwerin and Golden discovered that 20 percent of the food prepared for Army mess halls was eventually thrown away, and that one reason for this was simply excess preparation. Here are some more of their findings, as summarized in a wartime article that appeared in the *The Saturday Evening Post:*

Soldiers ate more if they were allowed to smoke in the mess hall. They ate more if they went promptly to table instead of waiting on line outside—perhaps because the food became cold. They ate more if they fell to on their own initiative instead of by command. They cared little for soups, and 65 percent of the kale and nearly as much of the spinach went into the garbage can. Favorite desserts were cakes and cookies, canned fruit, fruit salad, and gelatin. They ate ice cream in almost any amount that was served to them.

"That, sergeant, is an excellent piece of work," General George C. Marshall, the Army chief of staff, told Horace Schwerin after hearing a report by Schwerin on the research findings. The Army adopted many of Schwerin and Golden's recommendations, and began saving some 2.5 million pounds of food a day. It is perhaps not surprising to learn that until joining the Army Horace Schwerin had been in market research, and, among other things, had helped CBS to perfect a device for measuring audience reaction to radio shows.

The origins of an ephemeral branch of garbage studies focused on celebrities—"peeping-Tom" garbology, one might call it—seem to lie in the work of A. J. Weberman. Weberman was a gonzo journalist and yippie whose interest in the songs of Bob Dylan, and obsession with their interpretation, in 1970 prompted him to begin stealing the garbage from the cans left out in front of Dylan's Greenwich Village brownstone on MacDougal Street. Weberman didn't find much—some soiled Pampers, some old newspapers, some fast-food packaging from a nearby Blimpie Base, a shopping list with the word vanilla spelled "vanilla." He did, however, stumble into a brief but highly publicized career. This self-proclaimed "garbage guerrilla" quickly moved on to Neil Simon's garbage (it included a half-eaten bagel, scraps of lox, the Sunday Times), Muhammad Ali's (an empty can of Luck's collard greens, and empty roach bomb), and Abbie Hoffman's (a summons for hitchhiking, an unused can of deodorant, an estimate of the cost for the printing of *Steal This Book,* and the telephone numbers of Jack Anderson and Kate Millet). Weberman revealed many of his findings in an article in *Esquire* in 1971. It was antics such as his that inspired a prior meaning of the term "garbology," one very different from the definition established today.

Weberman's work inspired other garbage guerrillas. In January of 1975, the *Detroit Free Press* Sunday magazine reported on the findings from its raids on the garbage of several city notables, including the mayor, the head of the city council, the leader of a right-wing group, a food columnist, a disk jockey, and a prominent psychiatrist. Nothing much was discovered that might be deemed out of the ordinary, save for some of the contents of the garbage taken from a local Hare Krishna temple: a price tag from an Oleg Cassini garment, for example, and four ticket stubs from the Bel-Aire Drive-In Theater, which at the time was showing *Horrible House on the Hill* and *The Night God Screamed.* Six months after the *Free Press* exposé, a reporter for the *National Enquirer,* Jay Gourley, drove up to 3018 Dumbarton Avenue, N.W., in Washington, D.C., and threw the five garbage bags in front of Secretary of State Henry A. Kissinger's house into the trunk of his car. Secret Service agents swiftly blocked Gourley's departure, but after a day of questioning allowed him to proceed, the garbage still in the trunk. Among Gourley's finds: a crumpled piece of paper with a dog's teeth marks on it, upon which was written the work schedules of the Secret Service agents assigned to guard the Secretary; empty bottles of Seconal and Maalox; and a shopping list, calling for a case of Jack Daniel's, a case of Ezra Brooks bourbon, and a case of Cabin Still bourbon. Gourley later returned most of the garbage to the Kissingers—minus, he told reporters, "several dozen interesting things."

After the Kissinger episode curiosity about the garbage of celebrities seems to have abated. In 1977 the *National Enquirer* sent a reporter to poke through the garbage of President Jimmy Carter's press secretary, Jody Powell. The reporter found so little of interest that the tabloid decided not to publish a story. In 1980 Secret Service agents apprehended A. J. Weberman as he attempted to abduct former President Richard Nixon's garbage from behind an apartment building in Manhattan. Weberman was released, without the garbage.

The third detour taken by garbage studies involves police work. Over the years, law enforcement agents looking for evidence in criminal cases have also been more-than-occasional students of garbage; the Federal Bureau of Investigation in particular has spent considerable time poring over the household trash of people in whom it maintains a professional interest. ("We take it on a case-by-case basis," an FBI spokesman says.) One of the biggest criminal cases involving garbage began in 1975 and involved Joseph "Joe Bananas" Bonanno, Sr., a resident of Tucson at the time and a man with alleged ties to organized crime that were believed to date back to the days of Al Capone. For a period of three years officers of the Arizona Drug Control District collected Bonanno's trash just before the regular pickup, replacing it with "fake" Bonanno garbage. (Local garbagemen were not employed in the operation because some of them had received anonymous threats after assisting law enforcement agencies in an earlier venture.) The haul in evidence was beyond anyone's expectations: Bonanno had apparently kept detailed records of his various transactions, mostly in Sicilian. Although Bonanno had torn up each sheet of paper into tiny pieces, forensic specialists with the Drug Control District, like archaeologists reconstructing ceramic bowls from potsherds, managed to reassemble many of the documents and with the help of the FBI got them translated. In 1980 Bonanno was found guilty of having interfered with a federal grand jury investigation into the business operations of his two sons and a nephew. He was eventually sent to jail.

Unlike law-enforcement officers or garbage guerrillas, the archaeologists of the Garbage Project are not interested in the contents of any particular individual's garbage can. Indeed, it is almost always the case that a given person's garbage is at once largely anonymous and unimaginably humdrum. Garbage most usefully comes alive when it can be viewed in the context of broad patterns, for it is mainly in patterns that the links between artifacts and behaviors can be discerned.

The seed from which the Garbage Project grew was an anthropology class conducted at the University of Arizona in 1971 that was designed to teach principles of archaeological methodology. The University of Arizona has long occupied a venerable place in the annals of American archaeology and, not surprisingly, the pursuit of archaeology there to this day is carried on in serious and innovative ways. The class in question was one in which students undertook independent projects aimed precisely at showing links between various kinds of artifacts and various kinds of behavior. For example, one student, Sharon Thomas, decided to look into the relationship between a familiar motor function ("the diffusion pattern of ketchup over hamburgers") and a person's appearance, as manifested in clothing. Thomas took up a position at "seven different hamburger dispensaries" and, as people came in to eat, labeled them "neat" or "sloppy" according to a set of criteria relating to the way they dressed. Then she recorded how each of the fifty-seven patrons she studied—the ones who ordered hamburgers—

poured ketchup over their food. She discovered that sloppy people were far more likely than neat people to put ketchup on in blobs, sometimes even stirring it with their fingers. Neat people, in contrast, tended to apply the ketchup in patterns: circles, spirals, and crisscrosses. One person (a young male neatly dressed in a body shirt, flared pants, and patent-leather Oxfords) wrote with ketchup what appeared to be initials.

Two of the student investigations, conducted independently by Frank Ariza and Kelly Allen, led directly to the Garbage Project. Ariza and Allen, wanting to explore the divergence between (or correlation of) mental stereotypes and physical realities, collected garbage from two households in an affluent part of Tucson and compared it to garbage from two households in a poor and, as it happens, Mexican-American part of town. The rich and poor families, each student found, ate about the same amount of steak and hamburger, and drank about the same amount of milk. But the poor families, they learned, bought more expensive child-education items. They also bought more household cleansers. What did such findings mean? Obviously the sample—involving only four households in all—was too small for the results even to be acknowledged as representative, let alone to provide hints as to what lay behind them. However, the general nature of the research effort itself—comparing garbage samples in order to gauge behavior (and, what is more, gauging behavior unobtrusively, thereby avoiding one of the great biases inherent in much social science)—seemed to hold great promise.

A year later, in 1972, university students, under professorial direction, began borrowing samples of household garbage from different areas of Tucson, and sorting it in a lot behind a dormitory. The Garbage Project was under way. In 1973, the Garbage Project entered into an arrangement with the City of Tucson, whereby the Sanitation Division, four days a week, delivered five to eight randomly selected household pickups from designated census tracts to an analysis site that the Division set aside for the Project's sorters at a maintenance yard. (Wilson Hughes, who as mentioned earlier is the Garbage Project's co-director, was one of the first undergraduate garbage sorters.) In 1984 operations were moved to an enclosure where many of the university's dumpsters are parked, across the street from Arizona Stadium.

The excavation of landfills would come much later in the Garbage Project's history,

when to its focus on issues of garbage and human behavior it added a focus on issues of garbage management. The advantage in the initial years of sorting fresh garbage over excavating landfills was a basic but important one: In landfills it is often quite difficult and in many cases impossible to get some idea, demographically speaking, of the kind of neighborhood from which any particular piece of garbage has come. The value of landfill studies is therefore limited to advancing our understanding of garbage in the aggregate. With fresh garbage, on the other hand, one can have demographic precision down to the level of a few city blocks, by directing pickups to specific census districts and cross-tabulating the findings with census data.

Needless to say, deciding just which characteristics of the collected garbage to pay attention to posed a conceptual challenge, one that was met by Wilson Hughes, who devised the "protocol" that is used by the Garbage Project to this day. Items found in garbage are sorted into one of 150 specific coded categories that can in turn be clustered into larger categories representing food (fresh food versus prepared, health food versus junk food), drugs, personal and household sanitation products, amusement-related or educational materials, communications-related materials, pet-related materials, yard-related materials, and hazardous materials. For each item the following information is recorded on a standardized form: the date on which it was collected; the census tract from which it came; the item code (for example, 001, which would be the code for "Beef"); the item's type (for example, "chuck"); its original weight or volume (in this case, derived from the packaging); its cost (also from the packaging); material composition of container; brand (if applicable); and the weight of any discarded food (if applicable). The information garnered over the years from many thousands of such forms, filled out in pursuit of a wide variety of research objectives, constitutes the Garbage Project's database. It has all been computerized and amounts to some two million lines of data drawn from some fifteen thousand household-refuse samples. The aim here has been not only to approach garbage with specific questions to answer or hypotheses to prove but also to amass sufficient quantities of information, in a systematic and open-minded way, so that with the data on hand Garbage Project researchers would be able to answer any future questions or evaluate any future hypotheses that might arise. In 1972 gar-

bage was, after all, still terra incognita, and the first job to be done was akin to that undertaken by the explorers Lewis and Clark.

From the outset the Garbage Project has had to confront the legal and ethical issues its research involves: Was collecting and sorting someone's household garbage an unjustifiable invasion of privacy? This very question has over the years been argued repeatedly in the courts. The Fourth Amendment unequivocally guarantees Americans protection from unreasonable search and seizure. Joseph Bonanno, Sr., tried to invoke the Fourth Amendment to prevent his garbage from being used as evidence. But garbage placed in a garbage can in a public thoroughfare, where it awaits removal by impersonal refuse collectors, and where it may be picked over by scavengers looking for aluminum cans, by curious children or neighbors, and by the refuse collectors themselves (some of whom do a thriving trade in old appliances, large and small), is usually considered by the courts to have been abandoned. Therefore, the examination of the garbage by outside parties cannot be a violation of a constitutional right. In the Bonanno case, U.S. District Court Judge William Ingram ruled that investigating garbage for evidence of a crime may carry a "stench," but was not illegal. In 1988, in *California v. Greenwood,* the U.S. Supreme Court ruled by a margin of six to two that the police were entitled to conduct a warrantless search of a suspected drug dealer's garbage—a search that led to drug paraphernalia, which led in turn to warrants, arrests, and convictions. As Justice Byron White has written, "The police cannot reasonably be expected to avert their eyes from evidence of criminal activity that could have been observed by any member of the public."

Legal issues aside, the Garbage Project has taken pains to ensure that those whose garbage comes under scrutiny remain anonymous. Before obtaining garbage for study, the Project provides guarantees to communities and their garbage collectors that nothing of a personal nature will be examined and that no names or addresses or other personal information will be recorded. The Project also stipulates that all of the garbage collected (except aluminum cans, which are recycled) will be returned to the community for normal disposal.

As noted, the Garbage Project has now been sorting and evaluating garbage, with scientific rigor, for two decades. The Project has proved durable because its findings have supplied a fresh perspective on what we know—and what we think we know—about certain aspects of our lives. Medical researchers, for example, have long made it their business to question people about their eating habits in order to uncover relationships between patterns of diet and patterns of disease. These researchers have also long suspected that people—honest, well-meaning people—may often be providing information about quantities and types and even brands of food and drink consumed that is not entirely accurate. People can't readily say whether they trimmed 3.3 ounces or 5.4 ounces of fat off the last steak they ate, and they probably don't remember whether they had four, five, or seven beers in the previous week, or two eggs or three. The average person just isn't paying attention. Are there certain patterns in the way in which people wrongly "self-report" their dietary habits? Yes, there are, and Garbage Project studies have identified many of them.

Garbage archaeologists also know how much edible food is thrown away; what percentage of newspapers, cans, bottles, and other items aren't recycled; how loyal we are to brandname products and which have earned the greatest loyalty; and how much household hazardous waste is carted off to landfills and incinerators. From several truckloads of garbage and a few pieces of ancillary data—most importantly, the length of time over which the garbage was collected—the Garbage Project staff can reconstruct the community from which it came with a degree of accuracy that the Census Bureau might in some neighborhoods be unable to match.

Garbage also exposes the routine perversity of human ways. Garbage archaeologists have learned, for example, that the volume of garbage that Americans produce expands to fill the number of receptacles that are available to put it in. They have learned that we waste more of what is in short supply than of what is plentiful; that attempts by individuals to restrict consumption of certain foodstuffs are often counterbalanced by extra and inadvertent consumption of those same foodstuffs in hidden form; and that while a person's memory of what he has eaten and drunk in a given week is inevitably wide of the mark, his guess as to what a family member or even neighbor has eaten and drunk usually turns out to be more perceptive.

Some of the Garbage Project's research has prompted unusual forays into arcane aspects of popular culture. Consider the matter of those "amulets" worn by the So-hites—that is, the once-familiar detachable pop-top pull tab. Pull tabs first became important to the Garbage Project during a study of household recycling practices, conducted on behalf of the federal Environmental Protection Agency during the mid-1970s. The question arose: If a bag of household garbage contained no aluminum cans, did that mean that the household didn't dispose of any cans or that it had recycled its cans? Finding a way to answer that question was essential if a neighborhood's recycling rate was to be accurately determined. Pull tabs turned out to hold the key. A quick study revealed that most people did not drop pull tabs into the cans from which they had been wrenched; rather, the vast majority of people threw the tabs into the trash. If empty cans were stored separately for recycling, the pull tabs still went out to the curb with the rest of the garbage. A garbage sample that contained several pull tabs but no aluminum cans was a good bet to have come from a household that recycled.

All this counting of pull tabs prompted a surprising discovery one day by a student: Pull tabs were not all alike. Their configuration and even color depended on what kind of beverage they were associated with and where the beverage had been canned. Armed with this knowledge, Garbage Project researchers constructed an elaborate typology of pull tabs, enabling investigators to tease out data about beverage consumption—say, beer versus soda, Michelob versus Schlitz—even from samples of garbage that contained not a single can. Detachable pull tabs are no longer widely used in beverage cans, but the pull-tab typology remains useful even now. Among other things, in the absence of such evidence of chronology as a newspaper's dateline, pull tabs can reliably help to fix the dates of strata in a landfill. In archaeological parlance objects like these that have been widely diffused over a short period of time, and then abruptly disappear, are known as horizon markers.

The unique "punch-top" on Coors beer cans, for example, was used only between March of 1974 and June of 1977. (It was abandoned because some customers complained that they cut their thumbs pushing the holes open.) In landfills around the country, wherever Coors beer cans were discarded, punch-top cans not only identify strata associated with a narrow band of dates but also separate two epochs one from another. One might think of punch-tops playfully as the garbage equivalent of the famous iridium layer found in sediment toward the end of the Cretaceous Era, marking the moment (proponents of the theory believe) when a giant meteor crashed into the planet Earth, exterminating the dinosaurs.

All told, the Garbage Project has conducted nine full-scale excavations of municipal landfills in the United States and two smaller excavations associated with special projects. In the fall of 1991 it also excavated four sites in Canada, the data from which remains largely unanalyzed (and is not reflected in this book). The logistics of the landfill excavations are complex, and they have been overseen in all cases by Wilson Hughes. What is involved? Permission must be obtained from a raft of local officials and union leaders; indemnification notices must be provided to assure local authorities that the Garbage Project carries sufficient insurance against injury; local universities must be scoured for a supply of students to supplement the Garbage Project team; in many cases construction permits, of all things, must be obtained in advance of digging. There is also the whole matter of transportation, not only of personnel but also of large amounts of equipment. And there is the matter of personal accommodation and equipment storage. The time available for excavation is always limited, sometimes extremely so; the research program must be compressed to fit it, and the staff must be "tasked" accordingly. When the excavation has been completed the samples need to be packed and shipped—frequently on ice—back to headquarters or to specialized laboratories. All archaeologists will tell you that field work is mostly laborious, not glamorous; a landfill excavation is archaeology of the laborious kind.

For all the difficulties they present, the Garbage Project's landfill digs have acquired an increasing timeliness and relevance as concerns about solid-waste disposal have grown. Even as the Garbage Project has trained considerable attention on garbage as an analytical tool it has also taken up the problem of garbage itself—garbage as a problem, garbage as symbolized by *Mobro 4000,* the so-called "garbage barge," which sailed from Islip, Long Island, on March 22, 1987, and spent the next fifty-five days plying the seas in search of a place to deposit its 3,168 tons of cargo. Strange though it may seem, although more than 70 percent of America's household and commercial garbage ends up in landfills, very little reliable data existed until recently as to a landfill's contents and biological dynamics. Much of the conventional wisdom about garbage disposal consists of assertions that turn out, upon investigation, to be simplistic or misleading: among them, the assertion that, as trash, plastic, foam, and fast-food packaging are causes for great concern, that biodegradable items are always more desirable than nonbiodegradable ones, that on a per capita basis the nation's households are generating a lot more garbage than they used to, and that we're physically running out of places to put landfills.

This is not to say that garbage isn't a problem in need of serious attention. It is. But if they are to succeed, plans of action must be based on garbage realities. The most critical part of the garbage problem in America is that our notions about the creation and disposal of garbage are often riddled with myth. There are few other subjects of public significance on which popular and official opinion is so consistently misinformed....

Gaps—large gaps—remain in our knowledge of garbage, and of how human behavior relates to it, and of how best to deal with it. But a lighted candle has at least been seized and thrust inside the antechamber.

---

*A note on terminology. Several words for the things we throw away—"garbage," "trash," "refuse," "rubbish"—are used synonymously in casual speech but in fact have different meanings. *Trash* refers specifically to discards that are at least theoretically "dry"—newspapers, boxes, cans, and so on. *Garbage* refers technically to "wet" discards—food remains, yard waste, and offal. *Refuse* is an inclusive term for both the wet discards and the dry. *Rubbish* is even more inclusive: It refers to all refuse plus construction and demolition debris. The distinction between wet and dry garbage was important in the days when cities slopped garbage to pigs, and needed to have the wet material separated from the dry; it eventually became irrelevant, but may see a revival if the idea of composting food and yard waste catches on. We will frequently use "garbage" in this book to refer to the totality of human discards because it is the word used most naturally in ordinary speech. The word is etymo-logically obscure, though it probably derives from Anglo-French, and its earliest associations have to do with working in the kitchen.

*A question that always comes up is: What about garbage disposers? Garbage disposers are obviously capable of skewing the data in certain garbage categories, and Garbage Project researchers can employ a variety of techniques to compensate for the bias that garbage disposers introduce. Studies were conducted at the very outset of the Garbage Project to determine the discard differential between households with and without disposers, and one eventual result was a set of correction factors for various kinds of garbage (primarily food), broken down by subtype. As a general rule of thumb, households with disposers end up discarding in their trash about half the amount of food waste and food debris as households without disposers. It should be noted, however, that the fact that disposers have ground up some portion of a household's garbage often has little relevance to the larger issues the Garbage Project is trying to address. It means, for example, not that the Garbage Project's findings about the extent of food waste are invalid, but merely that its estimates are conservative.

BUSHMEN

John Yellen

I followed Dau, kept his slim brown back directly in front of me, as we broke suddenly free from the dense Kalahari bush and crossed through the low wire fence that separated Botswana from Namibia to the West. For that moment while Dau held the smooth wires apart for me, we were out in the open, in the full hot light of the sun and then we entered the shadows, the tangled thickets of arrow grass and thorn bush and mongongo trees once again. As soon as the bush began to close in around us again, I quickly became disoriented, Dau's back my only reference point.

Even then, in that first month of 1968, while my desert boots retained their luster, I knew enough to walk behind, not next to Dau. I had expected the Kalahari Desert to be bare open sand. I had imagined myself looking out over vast stretches that swept across to the horizon. But to my surprise, I found that the dunes were covered with trees and that during the rains the grasses grew high over my head. The bare sand, where I could see it, was littered with leaves, and over these the living trees and brush threw a dappled pattern of sunlight and shade. To look in the far distance and maintain a sense of direction, to narrow my focus and pick a way between the acacia bushes and their thorns, and then to look down, just in front of my feet to search out menacing shapes, was too much for me. Already, in that first month, the Bushmen had shown me a puff adder coiled motionless by the base of an acacia tree, but not until Cumsa the Hunter came up close to it, ready to strike it with his spear, could I finally see what all those hands were pointing at.

As Dau walked, I tried to follow his lead. To my discomfort I knew that many of these bushes had thorns—the Kalahari cloaks itself in thorns—some hidden close to the ground just high enough to rake across my ankles and draw blood when I pushed through, others long and straight and white so they reflected the sun. That morning, just before the border fence, my concentration had lagged and I found myself entangled in wait-a-bit thorns that curved backwards up the branch. So I stopped and this short, brown-skinned Bushman pushed me gently backwards to release the tension, then worked the branch, thorn by thorn from my shirt and my skin.

In the mid-1960s, the South African government had decided to accurately survey the Botswana border, mark it with five-strand fence, and cut a thin firebreak on either side. At intervals they constructed survey towers, strange skeletal affairs, like oil drilling rigs, their tops poking well above the highest mongongo trees. It was to one of these that Dau led me across the border, through the midday sun. Although he would not climb it himself, since it was a white man's tower, he assumed I would. I followed his finger, his chain of logic as I started rather hesitantly up the rusted rungs. I cleared the arrow grass, the acacia bushes, finally the broad leafy crowns of the mongongo nut trees. Just short of the top I stopped and sat, hooked my feet beneath the rung below, and wrapped my arms around the metal edges of the sides.

For a month now I had copied the maps—the lines and the circles the !Kung tribesmen had drawn with their fingers in the sand. I had listened and tried to transcribe names of those places, so unintelligible with their clicks, their rising and falling tones. I had walked with Dau and the others to some of those places, to small camps near ephemeral water holes, but on the ground it was too confusing, the changes in altitude and vegetation too subtle, the sun too nearly overhead to provide any sense of where I was or from where I had come.

For the first time from the tower, I could see an order to the landscape. From up there on the tower, I could see that long thin border scar, could trace it off to the horizon to both the north and south. But beyond that, no evidence, not the slightest sign of a human hand. The Bushmen camps were too few in number, too small and well-hidden in the grass and bush to be visible from here. Likewise, the camp where we anthropologists lived, off to the east at the Dobe waterhole, that also was too small to see.

As Dau had intended, from my perch on that tower I learned a lot. At least now I could use the dunes, the shallow valleys, to know whether I was walking east and west or north and south.

In those first years with the Dobe Bushmen, I did gain at least a partial understanding of that land. And I

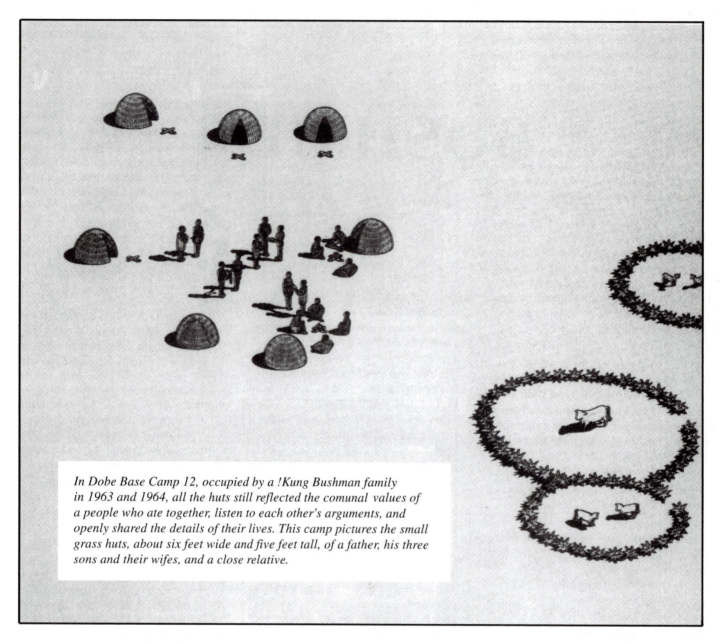

*In Dobe Base Camp 12, occupied by a !Kung Bushman family
in 1963 and 1964, all the huts still reflected the comunal values of
a people who ate together, listen to each other's arguments, and
openly shared the details of their lives. This camp pictures the small
grass huts, about six feet wide and five feet tall, of a father, his three
sons and their wifes, and a close relative.*

learned to recognize many of those places, the ones that rate no name at all but are marked only by events—brief, ephemeral happenings that leave no mark on the land. I learned to walk with the Bushmen back from a hunt or a trip for honey or spear-shaft wood and listen. They talked, chattered almost constantly, decorating the bus, these no-name places as they went, putting ornaments of experience on them: "See that tree there, John? That's where we stopped, my brother and I, long before he was married, when he killed a kudu, a big female. We stopped under that tree, hung the meat up there

and rested in the shade. But the flies were so bad, the biting flies, that we couldn't stay for long."

It took me a long time to realize that this chatter was not chatter at all, to understand that those remarks were gifts, a private map shared only among a few, an overlay crammed with fine, spidery writing on top of the base map with its named waterholes and large valleys, a map for friends to read. Dau would see a porcupine burrow, tiny, hidden in the vastness of the bush. And at night he could sit by the fire and move the others from point to point across the landscape to that small opening in the ground.

But as an archeologist, I had a task to do—to name those places and to discover what life had been like there in the past. "This place has a name now," I told Dau when I went back in 1976. Not the chicken camp, because when I was there I kept 15 chickens, or the cobra camp, for the cobra we killed one morning among the nesting hens, but Dobe Base Camp 18. Eighteen because it's the eighteenth of these old abandoned camps I've followed you to in the last three days. See? That's what goes into this ledger, this fat bound book in waterproof ballpoint ink. We could get a reflector in here—a big piece of tin like some

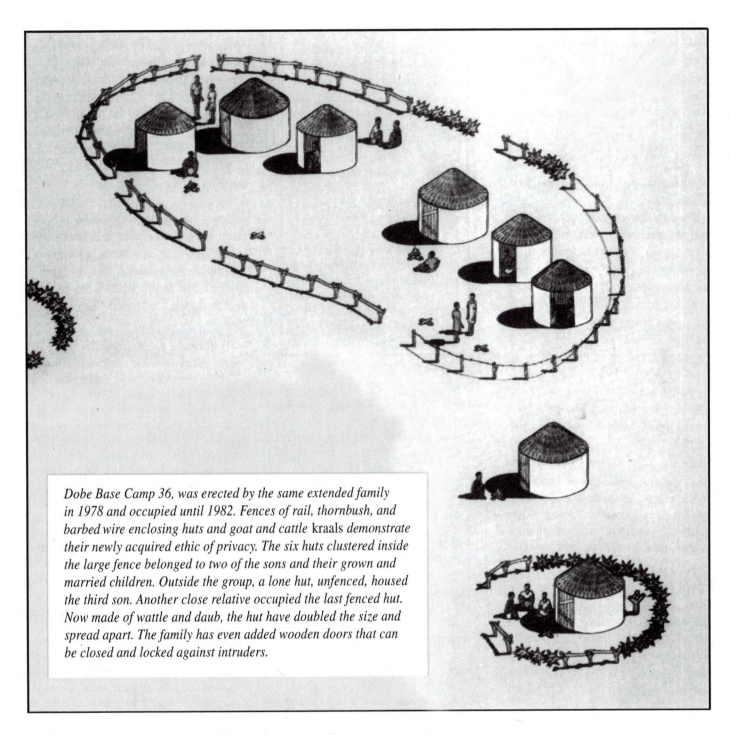

Dobe Base Camp 36, was erected by the same extended family in 1978 and occupied until 1982. Fences of rail, thornbush, and barbed wire enclosing huts and goat and cattle kraals demonstrate their newly acquired ethic of privacy. The six huts clustered inside the large fence belonged to two of the sons and their grown and married children. Outside the group, a lone hut, unfenced, housed the third son. Another close relative occupied the last fenced hut. Now made of wattle and daub, the hut have doubled the size and spread apart. The family has even added wooden doors that can be closed and locked against intruders.

metal off a roof and get some satellite or a plane to photograph it. We could tell just where it is then, could mark it on one of those large aerial maps down to the nearest meter if we wanted.

We came back to these camps, these abandoned places on the ground, not once but month after month for the better part of a year. Not just Dau and myself but a whole crew of us, eight Bushmen and I, to dig, to look down into the ground. We started before the sun was too high up in the sky, and later Dau and I sat in the shade sipping thick, rich tea. I asked questions and he talked.

"One day when I was living here, I shot a kudu: an adult female. Hit it with one arrow in the flank. But it went too far and we never found it. Then another day my brother hit a wildebeest, another adult female and that one we got. We carried it back to camp here and ate it."

"What other meat did you eat here, Dau?"

"One, no two, steenbok, it was."

1948: 28 years ago by my counting was when Dau, his brothers, his family were here. How could he remember the detail? This man sat in the shade and recalled trivial events that have repeated themselves in more or less the

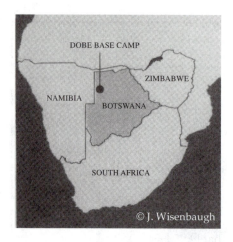

© J. Wisenbaugh

same way at so many places over the last three decades.

We dug day after day in the old camps —and found what Dau said we should. Bones, decomposing, but still identifiable: bones of wildebeest and steenbok among the charcoal and mongongo nut shells.

We dug our squares, sifting through the sand for bones. And when I dumped the bones, the odd ostrich eggshell bead, the other bits and pieces out onto the bridge table to sort, so much of what my eyes and ears told me was confirmed in this most tangible form. If excavation in one square revealed the bones of a wildebeest or kudi or other large antelope, then the others would contain them as well. In an environment as unpredictable as the Kalahari, where the game was hard to find and the probability of failure high, survival depended on sharing, on spreading the risk. And the bones, distributed almost evenly around the individual family hearths confirmed that. What also impressed me was how little else other than the bones there was. Most archeological sites contain a broad range of debris. But in those years the Bushmen owned so little. Two spears or wooden digging sticks or strings of ostrich eggshell beads were of no more use than one. Better to share, to give away meat or extra belongings and through such gifts create a web of debts, of obligations that some day would be repaid. In 1948, even in 1965, to accumulate material goods made no sense.

When it was hot, which was most of the year, I arranged the bridge table and two chairs in a patch of nearby shade. We sat there with the bound black and red ledger and dumped the bones in a heap in the center of the table, then sorted them out. I did the easy stuff, separated out the turtle shells, the bird bones, set each in a small pile around the table's edge. Dau did the harder part, separated the steenbok from the duiker, the wildebeest from kudu, held small splintered bone fragments and turned them over and over in his hands. We went through the piles then, one by one, moved each in its turn to the center of the table, sorted them into finer categories, body part by body part, bone by bone. Cryptic notes, bits of data that accumulated page by page. The bones with their sand and grit were transformed into numbers in rows and columns, classes and subclasses which would, I hoped, emerge from some computer to reveal a grander order, a design, an underlying truth.

Taphonomy: That's the proper term for it. The study of burial and preservation. Archeologists dig lots of bones out of the ground, not just from recent places such as these but from sites that span the millions of years of mankind's existence. On the basis of the bones, we try to learn about those ancient people. We try to reconstruct their diet, figure out how the animals were hunted, how they were killed, butchered, and shared.

What appealed to me about the Dobe situation, why I followed Dau, walked out his youth and his early manhood back and forth around the waterhole was the neat, almost laboratory situation Dobe offered. A natural experiment. I could go to a modern camp, collect those discarded food bones even before the jackals and hyenas had gotten to them, examine and count them, watch the pattern emerge. What happened then to the bones after they'd been trampled, picked over, rained on, lain in the ground for five years? Five years ago? Dobe Base Camp 21, 1971. I could go there, dig up a sample and find out.

What went on farther and farther back in time? Is there a pattern? Try eight years ago. 1968, DBC 18. We could go there to the cobra camp and see. Thirty-four years ago? The camp where Tsaa with the beautiful wife was born. One can watch, can see how things fall apart, can make graphs, curves, shoot them back, watch them arc backwards beyond Dau, beyond Dau's father, back into the true archeological past.

We dug our way through the DBCs, back into the early 1940s, listening day after day to the South African soap operas on the short-wave radio, and our consumption of plastic bags went down and down. Slim pickings in the bone department. And the bones we did find tended to be rotten: They fragmented, fell apart in the sieve.

So we left the 1940s, collapsed the bridge table and the folding chairs and went to that site that played such a crucial role for anthropologists: DBC 12, the 1963 camp where those old myths about hunters and gatherers came up against the hard rock of truth.

They built this camp just after Richard Lee, the pioneer, arrived. They lived there through the winter and hunted warthog with spears and a pack of dogs so good they remember each by name to this day. Richard lived there with them. He watched them—what they did, what they ate, weighed food on his small scale slung with a rope from an acacia tree. He weighed people, sat in camp day after day with his notebook and his wristwatch and scale. He recorded times: when each person left camp in the morning, when each returned for the day.

In this small remnant group, one of the last in the world still living by hunting and gathering, it should be possible, he believed, to see a reflection, a faint glimmer of the distant universal past of all humanity, a common condition that had continued for millions and millions of years. He went there because of that and for that reason, later on, the rest of us followed him.

What he found in that desert camp, that dry, hard land, set the anthropological world back on its collective ear. What his scale and his wristwatch and his systematic scribbles showed was that we were fooled, that we had it all wrong. To be a hunter and gatherer wasn't that bad after all. They didn't work that hard, even in this land of thorns: For an adult, it came to less time than a nine-to-five office worker puts in on the job. They lived a long time, too, didn't wear out and die young but old-looking, as we had always thought. Even in this camp, the camp with the good hunting dogs, it was plants, not meat, which provided the staff of life. Women walked through the nut groves and collected nuts with their toes, dug in the mola-pos and sang to each other through the bush. Unlike the game, which spooked so easily and followed the unpredictable rains, the nuts, roots, and berries were dependable, there in plenty, there for the picking. Another distinguished anthropologist, Marshall Sahlins, termed those DBC 12 people "the original affluent society"—something quite different from the traditional conception of hunting and gathering as a mean, hard existence half a step ahead of starvation and doom.

Over the years that name has held—but life in the Kalahari has changed. That kind of camp, with all the bones and mongongo nuts and dogs, is no more.

By the mid-1970s, things were different at Dobe. Diane Gelburd, another of the anthropologists out there then, only needed to look around her to see how the Bushman lifestyle had changed from the way Richard recorded it, from how Sahlins described it. But what had changed the people at DBC 12 who believed that property should be commonly held and shared? What had altered their system of values? That same winter Diane decided to find out.

She devised a simple measure of acculturation that used pictures cut from magazines: an airplane, a sewing machine, a gold mine in South Africa. (Almost no one got the gold mine right.) That was the most enjoyable part of the study. They all liked to look at pictures, to guess.

Then she turned from what people knew to what they believed. She wanted to rank them along a scale, from traditional to acculturated. So again she asked questions:

"Will your children be tattooed?"

To women: "If you were having a difficult childbirth and a white doctor were there, would you ask for assistance?"

To men: "If someone asked you for permission to marry your daughter would you demand (the traditional) bride service?"

Another question so stereotyped that in our own society one would be too embarrassed to ask it: "Would you let your child marry someone from another tribe—a Tswana or a Herero—a white person?"

First knowledge, then belief, and finally material culture. She did the less sensitive questions first. "Do you have a field?" What do you grow? What kind of animals do you have? How many of what?" Then came the hard part: She needed to see what people actually owned. I tagged along with her one day and remember the whispers inside one dark mud hut. Trunks were unlocked and hurriedly unpacked away from the entrance to shield them from sight. A blanket spread out on a trunk revealed the secret wealth that belied their statements: "Me? I have nothing." In the semidarkness she made her inventory. Then the trunks were hastily repacked and relocked with relief.

She went through the data, looked at those lists of belongings, itemized them in computer printouts. Here's a man who still hunts. The printout shows it. He has a bow and quiver and arrows on which the poison is kept fresh. He has a spear and snares for birds. He has a small steenbok skin bag, a traditional carryall that rests neatly under his arm.

He also has 19 goats and two donkeys, bought from the Herero or Tswana, who now get Dobe Bushmen to help plant their fields and herd their cows. They pay in livestock, hand-me-down clothing, blankets, and sometimes cash. He has three large metal trunks crammed full: One is packed to the top with shoes, shirts, and pants, most well-worn. He has two large linen mosquito nets, 10 tin cups, and a metal file. He has ropes of beads: strand upon strand—over 200 in all, pounds of small colored glass beads made in Czechoslovakia that I had bought in Johannesburg years earlier. He has four large iron pots and a five-gallon plastic jerry can. He has a plow, a gift from the anthropologists. He has a bridle and bit, light blankets, a large

tin basin. He has six pieces of silverware, a mirror and hairbrush, two billycans. His wife and his children together couldn't carry all that. The trunks are too heavy and too large for one person to carry so you would have to have two people for each. What about the plow, those heavy iron pots? Quite a job to carry those through bush, through the thick thorns.

But here is the surprising part. Talk to that man. Read the printout. See what he knows, what he believes. It isn't surprising that he speaks the Herero language and Setswana fluently or that he has worked for the Herero, the anthropologists. Nothing startling there. A budding Dobe capitalist. But then comes the shock: He espouses the traditional values.

"Bushmen share things, John. We share things and depend on each other, help each other out. That's what makes us different from the black people."

But the same person, his back to the door, opens his trunks, unlocks them one by one, lays out the blankets, the beads, then quickly closes each before he opens the next.

Multiply that. Make a whole village of people like that, and you can see the cumulative effect: You can actually measure it. As time goes on, as people come to own more possessions; the huts move farther and farther apart.

In the old days a camp was cosy, intimate and close. You could sit there by one fire and look into the other grass huts, see what the other people were doing, what they were making or eating. You heard the conversations, the arguments and banter.

We ask them why the new pattern?

Says Dau: "It's because of the livestock that we put our huts this way. They can eat the grass from the roofs and the sides of our houses. So we have to build fences to keep them away and to do that, you must have room between the huts."

I look up from the fire, glance around the camp, say nothing. No fences there. Not a single one around any of the huts, although I concede that one day they probably will build them. But why construct a lot of separate small fences, one around each hut? Why not clump the huts together the way they did in the old days and make a single large fence around the lot? Certainly a more efficient approach. Why worry about fences now in any case? The only exposed grass is on the roofs, protected by straight mud walls and nothing short of an elephant or giraffe could eat it.

Xashe's answer is different. Another brief reply. An attempt to dispose of the subject politely but quickly. "It's fire, John. That's what we're worried about. If we put our houses too close together, if one catches fire, the others will burn as well. We don't want one fire to burn all our houses down. That's why we build them so far apart."

But why worry about fire now? What about in the old days when the huts were so close, cheek by jowl? Why is it that when the huts were really vulnerable, when they were built entirely of dried grass, you didn't worry about fires then?

You read Diane's interviews and look at those lists of how much people own. You see those shielded mud huts with doors spaced, so far apart. You also listen to the people you like and trust. People who always have been honest with you. You hear their explanations and realize the evasions are not for you but for themselves. You see things they can't. But nothing can be done. It would be ludicrous to tell these brothers: "Don't you see, my friends, the lack of concordance between your values and the changing reality of your world?"

Now, years after the DBC study, I sit with data spread out before me and it is so clear. Richard's camp in 1963: just grass huts, a hearth in front of each. Huts and hearths in a circle, nothing more. 1968: more of the same. The following year though the first *kraal* appears, just a small thorn enclosure, some acacia bushes cut and dragged haphazardly together for their first few goats. It's set apart way out behind the circle of huts. On one goes, from plot to plot, following the pattern from year to year. The huts change from grass to mud. They become larger, more solidly built. Goats, a few at first, then more of them. So you build a fence around your house to keep them away from the grass

roofs. The *kraals* grow larger, move in closer to be incorporated finally into the circle of huts itself. The huts become spaced farther and farther apart, seemingly repelled over time, one from the next. People, families move farther apart.

The bones tell the same story. 1947: All the bones from wild animals, game caught in snares or shot with poisoned arrows—game taken from the bush. By 1964 a few goat bones, a cow bone or two, but not many. Less than 20 percent of the total. Look then at the early 1970s and watch the line on the graph climb slowly upwards—by 1976 over 80 percent from domesticated stock.

But what explains the shattering of this society? Why is this hunting and gathering way of life, so resilient in the face of uncertainty, falling apart? It hasn't been a direct force—a war, the ravages of disease. It is the internal conflicts, the tensions, the inconsistencies, the impossibility of reconciling such different views of the world.

At Dobe it is happening to them all together. All of the huts have moved farther apart in lockstep, which makes it harder for them to see how incompatible the old system is with the new. But Rakudu, a Bushman who lived at the Mahopa waterhole eight miles down the valley from Dobe, was a step ahead of the rest. He experienced, before the rest of them, their collective fate.

When I was at the Cobra Camp in 1969, Rakudu lived down near Mahopa, off on his own, a mile or so away from the pastoral Herero villages. He had two hats and a very deep bass voice, both so strange, so out of place in a Bushman. He was a comical sort of man with the hats and that voice and a large Adam's apple that bobbed up and down.

The one hat must have been a leftover from the German-Herero wars because no one in Botswana wore a hat like that—a real pith helmet with a solid top and rounded brim. It had been cared for over the years because, although soiled and faded, it still retained the original strap that tucks beneath the chin. The second hat was also unique—a World War I aviator's hat, one of those leather sacks that fits tightly over the head and buckles un-

der the chin. Only the goggles were missing.

I should have seen then how out of place the ownership of two hats was in that hunter-gatherer world. Give two hats like that to any of the others and one would have been given away on the spot. A month or two later, the other would become a gift as well. Moving goods as gifts and favors along that chain of human ties. That was the way to maintain those links, to keep them strong.

When I went to Rakudu's village and realized what he was up to, I could see that he was one of a kind. The mud-walled huts in his village made it look like a Herero village—not a grass hut in sight. And when I came, Rakudu pulled out a hand-carved wood and leather chair and set it in the shade. This village was different from any of the Bushman camps I had seen. Mud huts set out in a circle, real clay storage bins to hold the corn—not platforms in a tree—and *kraals* for lots of goats and donkeys. He had a large field, too, several years before the first one appeared at Dobe.

Why shouldn't Bushmen do it—build their own villages, model their subsistence after the Herero? To plant a field, to tend goats, to build mud-walled houses like that was not hard to do. Work for the Herero a while and get an axe, accumulate the nucleus of a herd, buy or borrow the seeds. That year the rains were long and heavy. The sand held the water and the crickets and the birds didn't come. So the harvest was good, and I could sit there in the carved chair and look at Rakudu's herd of goats and their young ones and admire him for his industry, for what he had done.

Only a year later I saw him and his eldest son just outside the Cobra Camp. I went over and sat in the sand and listened to the negotiations for the marriage Rakudu was trying to arrange. His son's most recent wife had run away, and Rakudu was discussing a union between his son and Dau the Elder's oldest daughter who was just approaching marriageable age. They talked about names and Dau the Elder explained why the marriage couldn't take place. It was clear that the objection was trivial, that he was making an excuse. Even I could see that his explanation was a face-saving gesture to make the refusal easier for all of them.

Later I asked Dau the Elder why he did it. It seemed like a good deal to me. "Rakudu has all that wealth, those goats and field. I'd think that you would be anxious to be linked with a family like that. Look at all you have to gain. Is the son difficult? Did he beat his last wife?"

"She left because she was embarrassed. The wife before her ran away for the same reason and so did the younger brother's wife," he said. "Both brothers treated their wives well. The problem wasn't that. It was when the wives' relatives came. That's when it became so hard for the women because Rakudu and his sons are such stingy men. They wouldn't give anything away, wouldn't share anything with them. Rakudu has a big herd just like the Herero, and he wouldn't kill goats for them to eat."

Not the way Bushmen should act toward relatives, not by the traditional value system at least. Sharing, the most deeply held Bushman belief, and that man with the two hats wouldn't go along. Herero are different. You can't expect them to act properly, to show what is only common decency; you must take them as they are. But someone like Rakudu, a Bushman, should know better than that. So the wives walked out and left for good.

But Rakudu understood what was happening, how he was trapped—and he tried to respond. If you can't kill too many goats from the herd that has become essential to you, perhaps you can find something else of value to give away. Rakudu thought he had an answer.

He raised tobacco in one section of his field. Tobacco, a plant not really adapted to a place like the northern Kalahari, has to be weeded, watered by hand, and paid special care. Rakudu did that and for one year at least harvested a tobacco crop.

Bushmen crave tobacco and Rakudu hoped he had found a solution—that they would accept tobacco in place of goats, in place of mealie meal. A good try. Perhaps the only one open to him. But, as it turned out, not good enough. Rakudu's son could not find a wife.

Ironic that a culture can die yet not a single person perish. A sense of identity, of a shared set of rules, of participation in a single destiny binds individuals together into a tribe or cultural group. Let that survive long enough, let the participants pass this sense through enough generations, one to the next, create enough debris, and they will find their way into the archeological record, into the study of cultures remembered only by their traces left on the land.

Rakudu bought out. He, his wife, and his two sons sold their goats for cash, took the money and walked west, across the border scar that the South Africans had cut, through the smooth fence wire and down the hard calcrete road beyond. They became wards of the Afrikaaners, were lost to their own culture, let their fate pass into hands other than their own. At Chum kwe, the mission station across the border 34 miles to the west, they were given numbers and the right to stand in line with the others and have mealie meal and other of life's physical essentials handed out to them. As wards of the state, that became their right. When the problems, the contradictions of your life are insoluble, a paternalistic hand provides one easy out.

Dau stayed at Dobe. Drive there today and you can find his mud-walled hut just by the waterhole. But he understands: He has married off his daughter, his first-born girl to a wealthy Chum kwe man who drives a tractor—an old man, more than twice her age, and by traditional Bushmen standards not an appropriate match. Given the chance, one by one, the others will do the same.

John Yellen, director of the anthropology program at the National Science Foundation, has returned to the Kalahari four times since 1968.

The Maya Collapses

Mysteries of lost cities ■ The Maya environment ■ Maya agriculture ■ Maya history ■ Copán ■ Complexities of collapses ■ Wars and droughts ■ Collapse in the southern lowlands ■ The Maya message ■

Jared Diamond

By now, millions of modern tourists have visited ruins of the ancient Maya civilization that collapsed over a thousand years ago in Mexico's Yucatán Peninsula and adjacent parts of Central America. All of us love a romantic mystery, and the Maya offer us one at our doorstep, almost as close for Americans as the Anasazi ruins. To visit a former Maya city, we need only board a direct flight from the U.S. to the modern Mexican state capital city of Mérida, jump into a rental car or minibus, and drive an hour on a paved highway [map, p. 161, omitted].

Today, many Maya ruins, with their great temples and monuments, still lie surrounded by jungle, far from current human settlement [Plate 12, omitted]. Yet they were once the sites of the New World's most advanced Native American civilization before European arrival, and the only one with extensive deciphered written texts. How could ancient peoples have supported urban societies in areas where few farmers eke out a living today? The Maya cities impress us not only with that mystery and with their beauty, but also because they are "pure" archaeological sites. That is, their locations became depopulated, so they were not covered up by later buildings as were so many other ancient cities, like the Aztec capital of Tenochtitlan (now buried under modern Mexico City) and Rome.

Maya cities remained deserted, hidden by trees, and virtually unknown to the outside world until rediscovered in 1839 by a rich American lawyer named John Stephens, together with the English draftsman Frederick Catherwood. Having heard rumors of ruins in the jungle, Stephens got President Martin Van Buren to appoint him ambassador to the Confederation of Central American Republics, an amorphous political entity then extending from modern Guatemala to Nicaragua, as a front for his archaeological explorations. Stephens and Catherwood ended up exploring 44 sites and cities. From the extraordinary quality of the buildings and the art, they realized that these were not the work of savages (in their words) but of a vanished high civilization. They recognized that some of the carvings on the stone monuments constituted writing, and they correctly guessed that it related historical events and the names of people. On his return, Stephens wrote two travel books, illustrated by Catherwood and describing the ruins, that became best sellers.

A few quotes from Stephens's writings will give a sense of the romantic appeal of the Maya: "The city was desolate. No remnant of this race hangs round the ruins, with traditions handed down from father to son and from generation to generation. It lay before us like a shattered bark in the midst of the ocean, her mast gone, her name effaced, her crew perished, and none to tell whence she came, to whom she belonged, how long on her journey, or what caused her destruction. ... Architecture, sculpture, and painting, all the arts which embellish life, had flourished in this overgrown forest; orators, warriors, and statesmen, beauty, ambition, and glory had lived and passed away, and none knew that such things had been, or could tell of their past existence. ... Here were the remains of a cultivated, polished, and peculiar people, who had passed through all the stages incident to the rise and fall of nations; reached their golden age, and perished. ... We went up to their desolate temples and fallen altars; and wherever we moved we saw the evidence of their taste, their skill in arts. ... We called back into life the strange people who gazed in sadness from the wall; pictured them, in fanciful costumes and adorned with plumes of feather, ascending the terraces of the palace and the steps leading to the temples. ... In the romance of the world's history nothing ever impressed me more forcibly than the spectacle of this once great and lovely city, overturned, desolate, and lost, ... overgrown with trees for miles around, and without even a name to distinguish it." Those sensations are what tourists drawn to Maya ruins still feel today, and why we find the Maya collapse so fascinating.

The Maya story has several advantages for all of us interested in prehistoric collapses. First, the Maya written records that have survived, although frustratingly incomplete, are still useful for reconstructing Maya history in much greater detail than we can reconstruct Easter Island, or even Anasazi history with its tree rings and packrat middens. The great art and architecture of Maya cities have resulted in far more archaeologists studying the Maya than would have been the case if they had just been illiterate hunter-gatherers living in archaeologically invisible hovels. Climatologists and paleoecologists have recently been able to recognize several signals of ancient climate and environmental changes that contributed to the Maya collapse.

Finally, today there are still Maya people living in their ancient homeland and speaking Maya languages. Because much ancient Maya culture survived the collapse, early European visitors to the homeland recorded information about contemporary Maya society that played a vital role in our understanding ancient Maya society. The first Maya contact with Europeans came already in 1502, just 10 years after Christopher Columbus's "discovery" of the New World, when Columbus on the last of his four voyages captured a trading canoe that may have been Maya. In 1527 the Spanish began in earnest to conquer the Maya, but it was not until 1697 that they subdued the last principality. Thus, the Spanish had opportunities to observe independent Maya societies for a period of nearly two centuries. Especially important, both for bad and for good, was the bishop Diego de Landa, who resided in the Yucatán Peninsula for most of the years from 1549 to 1578. On the one hand, in one of history's worst acts of cultural vandalism, he burned all Maya manuscripts that he could locate in his effort to eliminate "pa-

ganism," so that only four survive today. On the other hand, he wrote a detailed account of Maya society, and he obtained from an informant a garbled explanation of Maya writing that eventually, nearly four centuries later, turned out to offer clues to its decipherment.

A further reason for our devoting a chapter to the Maya is to provide an antidote to our other chapters on past societies, which consist disproportionately of small societies in somewhat fragile and geographically isolated environments, and behind the cutting edge of contemporary technology and culture. The Maya were none of those things. Instead, they were culturally the most advanced society (or among the most advanced ones) in the pre-Columbian New World, the only one with extensive preserved writing, and located within one of the two heartlands of New World civilization (Mesoamerica). While their environment did present some problems associated with its karst terrain and unpredictably fluctuating rainfall, it does not rank as notably fragile by world standards, and it was certainly less fragile than the environments of ancient Easter Island, the Anasazi area, Greenland, or modern Australia. Lest one be misled into thinking that crashes are a risk only for small peripheral societies in fragile areas, the Maya warn us that crashes can also befall the most advanced and creative societies.

From the perspective of our five-point framework for understanding societal collapses, the Maya illustrate four of our points. They did damage their environment, especially by deforestation and erosion. Climate changes (droughts) did contribute to the Maya collapse, probably repeatedly. Hostilities among the Maya themselves did play a large role. Finally, political/cultural factors, especially the competition among kings and nobles that led to a chronic emphasis on war and erecting monuments rather than on solving underlying problems, also contributed. The remaining item on our five-point list, trade or cessation of trade with external friendly societies, does not appear to have been essential in sustaining the Maya or in causing their downfall. While obsidian (their preferred raw material for making into stone tools), jade, gold, and shells were imported into the Maya area, the latter three items were non-essential luxuries. Obsidian tools remained widely distributed in the Maya area long after the political collapse, so obsidian was evidently never in short supply.

To understand the Maya, let's begin by considering their environment, which we think of as "jungle" or "tropical rainforest." That's not true, and the reason why not proves to be important. Properly speaking, tropical rainforests grow in high-rainfall equatorial areas that remain wet or humid all year round. But the Maya homeland lies more than a thousand miles from the equator, at latitudes 17° to 22°N, in a habitat termed a "seasonal tropical forest." That is, while there does tend to be a rainy season from May to October, there is also a dry season from January through April. If one focuses on the wet months, one calls the Maya homeland a "seasonal tropical forest"; if one focuses on the dry months, one could instead describe it as a "seasonal desert."

From north to south in the Yucatán Peninsula, rainfall increases from 18 to 100 inches per year, and the soils become thicker, so that the southern peninsula was agriculturally more productive and supported denser populations. But rainfall in the Maya homeland is unpredictably variable between years; some recent years have had three or four times more rain than other years. Also, the timing of rainfall within the year is somewhat unpredictable, so it can easily happen that farmers plant their crops in anticipation of rain and then the rains do not come when expected. As a result, modern farmers attempting to grow corn in the ancient Maya homelands have faced frequent crop failures, especially in the north. The ancient Maya were presumably more experienced and did better, but nevertheless they too must have faced risks of crop failures from droughts and hurricanes.

Although southern Maya areas received more rainfall than northern areas, problems of water were paradoxically more severe in the wet south. While that made things hard for ancient Maya living in the south, it has also made things hard for modern archaeologists who have difficulty understanding why ancient droughts would have caused bigger problems in the wet south than in the dry north. The likely explanation is that a lens of fresh-water underlies the Yucatán Peninsula, but surface elevation increases from north to south, so that as one moves south the land surface lies increasingly higher above the water table. In the northern peninsula the elevation is sufficiently low that the ancient Maya were able to reach the water table at deep sinkholes called cenotes, or at deep caves; all tourists who have visited the Maya city of Chichén Itzá will remember the great cenotes there. In low-elevation north coastal areas without sinkholes, the Maya may have been able to get down to the water table by digging wells up to 75 feet deep. Water is readily available in many parts of Belize that have rivers, along the Usumacinta River in the west, and around a few lakes in the Petén area of the south. But much of the south lies too high above the water table for cenotes or wells to reach down to it. Making matters worse, most of the Yucatán Peninsula consists of karst, a porous sponge-like limestone terrain where rain runs straight into the ground and where little or no surface water remains available.

How did those dense southern Maya populations deal with their resulting water problem? It initially surprises us that many of their cities were not built next to the few rivers but instead on promontories in rolling uplands. The explanation is that the Maya excavated depressions, modified natural depressions, and then plugged up leaks in the karst by plastering the bottoms of the depressions in order to create cisterns and reservoirs, which collected rain from large plastered catchment basins and stored it for use in the dry season. For example, reservoirs at the Maya city of

Tikal held enough water to meet the drinking water needs of about 10,000 people for a period of 18 months. At the city of Coba the Maya built dikes around a lake in order to raise its level and make their water supply more reliable. But the inhabitants of Tikal and other cities dependent on reservoirs for drinking water would still have been in deep trouble if 18 months passed without rain in a prolonged drought. A shorter drought in which they exhausted their stored food supplies might already have gotten them in deep trouble through starvation, because growing crops required rain rather than reservoirs.

Of particular importance for our purposes are the details of Maya agriculture, which was based on crops domesticated in Mexico—especially corn with beans being second in importance. For the elite as well as commoners, corn constituted at least 70% of the Maya diet, as deduced from isotope analyses of ancient Maya skeletons. Their sole domestic animals were the dog, turkey, Muscovy duck, and a stingless bee yielding honey, while their most important wild meat source was deer that they hunted, plus fish at some sites. However, the few animal bones at Maya archaeological sites suggest that the quantity of meat available to the Maya was low. Venison was mainly a luxury food for the elite.

It was formerly believed that Maya farming was based on slash-and-burn agriculture (so-called swidden agriculture) in which forest is cleared and burned, crops are grown in the resulting field for a year or a few years until the soil is exhausted, and then the field is abandoned for a long fallow period of 15 or 20 years until regrowth of wild vegetation restores fertility to the soil. Because most of the landscape under a swidden agricultural system is fallow at any given time, it can support only modest population densities. Thus, it was a surprise for archaeologists to discover that ancient Maya population densities, estimated from numbers of stone foundations of farmhouses, were often far higher than what swidden agriculture could support. The actual values are the subject of much dispute and evidently varied among areas, but frequently cited estimates reach 250 to 750, possibly even 1,500, people per square mile. (For comparison, even today the two most densely populated countries in Africa, Rwanda and Burundi, have population densities of only about 750 and 540 people per square mile, respectively.) Hence the ancient Maya must have had some means of increasing agricultural production beyond what was possible through swidden alone.

Many Maya areas do show remains of agricultural structures designed to increase production, such as terracing of hill slopes to retain soil and moisture, irrigation systems, and arrays of canals and drained or raised fields. The latter systems, which are well attested elsewhere in the world and which require a lot of labor to construct, but which reward the labor with increased food production, involve digging canals to drain a waterlogged area, fertilizing and raising the level of the fields between the canals by dumping muck and water hyacinths dredged out of canals onto the fields, and thereby keeping the fields themselves from being inundated. Besides harvesting crops grown over the fields, farmers with raised fields also "grow" wild fish and turtles in the canals (actually, let them grow themselves) as an additional food source. However, other Maya areas, such as the well-studied cities of Copán and Tikal, show little archaeological evidence of terracing, irrigation, or raised- or drained-field systems. Instead, their inhabitants must have used archaeologically invisible means to increase food production, by mulching, floodwater farming, shortening the time that a field is left fallow, and tilling the soil to restore soil fertility, or in the extreme omitting the fallow period entirely and growing crops every year, or in especially moist areas growing two crops per year.

Socially stratified societies, including modern American and European society, consist of farmers who produce food, plus non-farmers such as bureaucrats and soldiers who do not produce food but merely consume the food grown by the farmers and are in effect parasites on farmers. Hence in any stratified society the farmers must grow enough surplus food to meet not only their own needs but also those of the other consumers. The number of non-producing consumers that can be supported depends on the society's agricultural productivity. In the United States today, with its highly efficient agriculture, farmers make up only 2% of our population, and each farmer can feed on the average 125 other people (American non-farmers plus people in export markets overseas). Ancient Egyptian agriculture, although much less efficient than modern mechanized agriculture, was still efficient enough for an Egyptian peasant to produce five times the food required for himself and his family. But a Maya peasant could produce only twice the needs of himself and his family. At least 70% of Maya society consisted of peasants. That's because Maya agriculture suffered from several limitations.

First, it yielded little protein. Corn, by far the dominant crop, has a lower protein content than the Old World staples of wheat and barley. The few edible domestic animals already mentioned included no large ones and yielded much less meat than did Old World cows, sheep, pigs, and goats. The Maya depended on a narrower range of crops than did Andean farmers (who in addition to corn also had potatoes, high-protein quinoa, and many other plants, plus llamas for meat), and much narrower again than the variety of crops in China and in western Eurasia.

Another limitation was that Maya corn agriculture was less intensive and productive than the Aztecs' chinampas (a very productive type of raised-field agriculture), the raised fields of the Tiwanaku civilization of the Andes, Moche irrigation on the coast of Peru, or fields tilled by animal-drawn plows over much of Eurasia.

Still a further limitation arose from the humid climate of the Maya area, which made it difficult to store corn beyond a year, whereas the Anasazi living in the dry climate of the U.S. Southwest could store it for three years.

Finally, unlike Andean Indians with their llamas, and unlike Old World peoples with their horses, oxen, donkeys, and camels, the Maya had no animal-powered transport or plows. All overland transport for the Maya went on the backs of human porters. But if you send out a porter carrying a load of corn to accompany an army into the field, some of that load of corn is required to feed the porter himself on the trip out, and some more to feed him on the trip back, leaving only a fraction of the load available to feed the army. The longer the trip, the less of the load is left over from the porter's own requirements. Beyond a march of a few days to a week, it becomes uneconomical to send porters carrying corn to provision armies or markets. Thus, the modest productivity of Maya agriculture, and their lack of draft animals, severely limited the duration and distance possible for their military campaigns.

We are accustomed to thinking of military success as determined by quality of weaponry, rather than by food supply. But a clear example of how improvements in food supply may decisively increase military success comes from the history of Maori New Zealand. The Maori are the Polynesian people who were the first to settle New Zealand. Traditionally, they fought frequent fierce wars against each other, but only against closely neighboring tribes. Those wars were limited by the modest productivity of their agriculture, whose staple crop was sweet potatoes. It was not possible to grow enough sweet potatoes to feed an army in the field for a long time or on distant marches. When Europeans arrived in New Zealand, they brought potatoes, which beginning around 1815 considerably increased Maori crop yields. Maori could now grow enough food to supply armies in the field for many weeks. The result was a 15-year period in Maori history, from 1818 until 1833, when Maori tribes that had acquired potatoes and guns from the English sent armies out on raids to attack tribes hundreds of miles away that had not yet acquired potatoes and guns. Thus, the potato's productivity relieved previous limitations on Maori warfare, similar to the limitations that low-productivity corn agriculture imposed on Maya warfare.

Those food supply considerations may contribute to explaining why Maya society remained politically divided among small kingdoms that were perpetually at war with each other, and that never became unified into large empires like the Aztec Empire of the Valley of Mexico (fed with the help of their chinampa agriculture and other forms of intensification) or the Inca Empire of the Andes (fed by more diverse crops carried by llamas over well-built roads). Maya armies and bureaucracies remained small and unable to mount lengthy campaigns over long distances. (Even much later, in 1848, when the Maya revolted against their Mexican overlords and a Maya army seemed to be on the verge of victory, the army had to break off fighting and go home to harvest another crop of corn.) Many Maya kingdoms held populations of only up to 25,000 to 50,000 people, none over half a million, within a radius of two or three days' walk from the king's palace. (The actual numbers are again highly controversial among archaeologists.) From the tops of the temples of some Maya kingdoms, it was possible to see the temples of the nearest kingdom. Maya cities remained small (mostly less than one square mile in area), without the large populations and big markets of Teotihuacán and Tenochtitlán in the Valley of Mexico, or of Chan-Chan and Cuzco in Peru, and without archaeological evidence of the royally managed food storage and trade that characterized ancient Greece and Mesopotamia.

Now for a quick crash-course in Maya history. The Maya area is part of the larger ancient Native American cultural region known as Mesoamerica, which extended approximately from Central Mexico to Honduras and constituted (along with the Andes of South America) one of the two New World centers of innovation before European arrival. The Maya shared much in common with other Mesoamerican societies not only in what they possessed, but also in what they lacked. For example, surprisingly to modern Westerners with expectations based on Old World civilizations, Mesoamerican societies lacked metal tools, pulleys and other machines, wheels (except locally as toys), boats with sails, and domestic animals large enough to carry loads or pull a plow. All of those great Maya temples were constructed by stone and wooden tools and by human muscle power alone.

Of the ingredients of Maya civilization, many were acquired by the Maya from elsewhere in Mesoamerica. For instance, Mesoamerican agriculture, cities, and writing first arose outside the Maya area itself, in valleys and coastal lowlands to the west and southwest, where corn and beans and squash were domesticated and became important dietary components by 3000 B.C., pottery arose around 2500 B.C., villages by 1500 B.C., cities among the Olmecs by 1200 B.C., writing appeared among the Zapotecs in Oaxaca around or after 600 B.C., and the first states arose around 300 B.C. Two complementary calendars, a solar calendar of 365 days and a ritual calendar of 260 days, also arose outside the Maya area. Other elements of Maya civilization were either invented, perfected, or modified by the Maya themselves.

Within the Maya area, villages and pottery appeared around or after 1000 B.C., substantial buildings around 500 B.C., and writing around 400 B.C. All preserved ancient Maya writing, constituting a total of about 15,000 inscriptions, is on stone and pottery and deals only with kings, nobles, and their conquests [Plate 13, omitted]. There is not a single mention of commoners. When Spaniards arrived, the Maya were still using bark paper coated with plaster to write books, of which the sole four that escaped Bishop Landa's fires turned out to be treatises on astronomy and the calendar. The ancient Maya also had had such bark-paper books, often depicted on their pottery, but only decayed remains of them have survived in tombs.

The famous Maya Long Count calendar begins on August 11, 3114 B.C.—just as our own calendar begins on January 1 of the first year of the Christian era. We know the significance to us of that day-zero of our calendar: it's the supposed beginning of the year in which Christ was born. Presumably the Maya also attached some significance to their own day zero, but we don't know what it was. The first preserved Long Count date is only A.D. 197 for a monument in the Maya area and 36 B.C. outside the Maya area, indicating that the Long Count calendar's day-zero was backdated to August 11, 3114 B.C. long after the facts; there was no writing anywhere in the New World then, nor would there be for 2,500 years after that date.

Our calendar is divided into units of days, weeks, months, years, decades, centuries, and millennia: for example, the date of February 19, 2003, on which I wrote the first draft of this paragraph, means the 19th day of the second month in the third year of the first decade of the first century of the third millennium beginning with the birth of Christ. Similarly, the Maya Long Count calendar named dates in units of days (*kin*), 20 days (*uinal*), 360 days (*tun*), 7,200 days or approximately 20 years (*katunn*), and 144,000 days or approximately 400 years (*baktun*). All of Maya history falls into baktuns 8, 9, and 10.

The so-called Classic period of Maya civilization begins in baktun 8, around A.D. 250, when evidence for the first kings and dynasties appears. Among the glyphs (written signs) on Maya monuments, students of Maya writing recognized a few dozen, each of which was concentrated in its own geographic area, and which are now considered to have had the approximate meaning of dynasties or kingdoms. In addition to Maya kings having their own name glyphs and palaces, many nobles also had their own inscriptions and palaces. In Maya society the king also functioned as high priest carrying the responsibility to attend to astronomical and calendrical rituals, and thereby to bring rain and prosperity, which the king claimed to have the supernatural power to deliver because of his asserted family relationship to the gods. That is, there was a tacitly understood quid pro quo: the reason why the peasants supported the luxurious lifestyle of the king and his court, fed him corn and venison, and built his palaces was because he had made implicit big promises to the peasants. As we shall see, kings got into trouble with their peasants if a drought came, because that was tantamount to the breaking of a royal promise.

From A.D. 250 onwards, the Maya population (as judged from the number of archaeologically attested house sites), the number of monuments and buildings, and the number of Long Count dates on monuments and pottery increased almost exponentially, to reach peak numbers in the 8th century A.D. The largest monuments were erected towards the end of that Classic period. Numbers of all three of those indicators of a complex society declined throughout the 9th century, until the last known Long Count date on any monument fell in baktun 10, in the year A.D. 909. That decline of Maya population, architecture, and the Long Count calendar constitutes what is known as the Classic Maya collapse.

As an example of the collapse, let's consider in more detail a small but densely built city whose ruins now lie in western Honduras at a site known as Copán, and described in two recent books by archaeologist David Webster. For agricultural purposes the best land in the Copán area consists of five pockets of flat land with fertile alluvial soil along a river valley, with a tiny total area of only 10 square miles; the largest of those five pockets, known as the Copán pocket, has an area of only 5 square miles. Much of the land around Copán consists of steep hills, and nearly half of the hill area has a slope above 16% (approximately double the slope of the steepest grade that you are likely to encounter on an American highway). Soil in the hills is less fertile, more acidic, and poorer in phosphate than valley soil. Today, corn yields from valley-bottom fields are two or three times those of fields on hill slopes, which suffer rapid erosion and lose three-quarters of their productivity within a decade of farming.

As judged by numbers of house sites, population growth in the Copán Valley rose steeply from the 5th century up to a peak estimated at around 27,000 people at A.D. 750–900. Maya written history at Copán begins in the year with a Long Count date corresponding to A.D. 426, when later monuments record retrospectively that some person related to nobles at Tikal and Teotihuacán arrived. Construction of royal monuments glorifying kings was especially massive between A.D. 650 and 750. After A.D. 700, nobles other than kings also got into the act and began erecting their own palaces, of which there were about twenty by the year A.D. 800, when one of those palaces is known to have consisted of 50 buildings with room for about 250 people. All of those nobles and their courts would have increased the burden that the king and his own court imposed on the peasants. The last big buildings at Copán were put up around A.D. 800, and the last Long Count date on an incomplete altar possibly bearing a king's name has the date of A.D. 822.

Archaeological surveys of different types of habitats in the Copán Valley show that they were occupied in a regular sequence. The first area farmed was the large Copán pocket of valley bottomland, followed by occupation of the other four bottomland pockets. During that time the human population was growing, but there was not yet occupation of the hills. Hence that increased population must have been accommodated by intensifying production in the bottomland pockets by some combination of shorter fallow periods, double-cropping, and possibly some irrigation.

By the year A.D. 650, people started to occupy the hill slopes, but those hill sites were cultivated only for about a century. The percentage of Copán's total population that was in the hills, rather than in the valleys, reached a maximum of 41%, then declined until the population again became concentrated in the valley pockets. What caused that pullback of population from the hills? Excavation of the foundations of buildings in the valley floor showed that they became covered with sediment during the 8th century, meaning that the hill slopes were getting eroded and probably also leached of nutrients. Those acidic infertile hill soils were being carried down into the valley and blanketing the more fertile valley soils, where they would have reduced agricultural yields. This ancient quick abandonment of hillsides coincides with modern Maya experience that fields in the hills have low fertility and that their soils become rapidly exhausted.

The reason for that erosion of the hillsides is clear: the forests that formerly covered them and protected their soils were being cut down. Dated pollen samples show that the pine forests originally covering the upper elevations of the hill slopes were eventually all cleared. Calculation suggests that most of those felled pine trees were being burned for fuel, while the rest were used for construction or for making plaster. At other Maya sites from the pre-Classic era, where the Maya went overboard in lavish use of thick plaster on buildings, plaster production may have been a major cause of deforestation. Besides causing sediment accumulation in the valleys and depriving valley inhabitants of wood supplies, that deforestation may have begun to cause a "man-made drought" in the valley bottom because forests play a major role in water cycling, such that massive deforestation tends to result in lowered rainfall.

Hundreds of skeletons recovered from Copán archaeological sites have been studied for signs of disease and malnutrition, such as porous bones and stress lines in the teeth. These skeletal signs show that the health of Copán's inhabitants deteriorated from A.D. 650 to 850, both among the elite and among the commoners, although the health of commoners was worse.

Recall that Copán's population was increasing steeply while the hills were being occupied. The subsequent abandonment of all of those fields in the hills meant that the burden of feeding the extra population formerly dependent on the hills now fell increasingly on the valley floor, and that more and more people were competing for the food grown on those 10 square miles of valley bottomland. That would have led to fighting among the farmers themselves for the best land, or for any land, just as in modern Rwanda (Chapter 10). Because Copán's king was failing to deliver on his promises of rain and prosperity in return for the power and luxuries that he claimed, he would have been the scapegoat for this agricultural failure. That may explain why the last that we hear from any Copán king is A.D. 822 (that last Long Count date at Copán), and why the royal palace was burned around A.D. 850. However, the continued production of some luxury goods suggest that some nobles managed to carry on with their lifestyle after the king's downfall, until around A.D. 975.

To judge from datable pieces of obsidian, Copán's total population decreased more gradually than did its signs of kings and nobles. The estimated population in the year A.D. 950 was still around 15,000, or 54% of the peak population of 27,000. That population continued to dwindle, until there are no more signs of anyone in the Copán Valley by around A.D. 1250. The reappearance of pollen from forest trees thereafter provides independent evidence that the valley became virtually empty of people, and that the forests could at last begin to recover.

The general outline of Maya history that I have just related, and the example of Copán's history in particular, illustrates why we talk about "the Maya collapse." But the story grows more complicated, for at least five reasons.

First, there was not only that enormous Classic collapse, but at least two previous smaller collapses at some sites, one around the year A.D. 150 when El Mirador and some other Maya cities collapsed (the so-called pre-Classic collapse), the other (the so-called Maya hiatus) in the late 6th century and early 7th century, a period when no monuments were erected at the well-studied site of Tikal. There were also some post-Classic collapses in areas whose populations survived the Classic collapse or increased after it—such as the fall of Chichén Itzá around 1250 and of Mayapán around 1450.

Second, the Classic collapse was obviously not complete, because there were hundreds of thousands of Maya who met and fought the Spaniards—far fewer Maya than during the Classic peak, but still far more people than in the other ancient societies discussed in detail in this book. Those survivors were concentrated in areas with stable water supplies, especially in the north with its cenotes, the coastal lowlands with their wells, near a southern lake, and along rivers and lagoons at lower elevations. However, population otherwise disappeared almost completely in what previously had been the Maya heartland in the south.

Third, the collapse of population (as gauged by numbers of house sites and of obsidian tools) was in some cases much slower than the decline in numbers of Long Count dates, as I already mentioned for Copán. What collapsed quickly during the Classic collapse was the institution of kingship and the Long Count calendar.

Fourth, many apparent collapses of cities were really nothing more than "power cycling": i.e., particular cities becoming more powerful, then declining or getting conquered, and then rising again and conquering their neighbors, without changes in the whole population. For example, in the year 562 Tikal was defeated by its rivals Caracol and Calakmul, and its king was captured and killed. However, Tikal then gradually gained strength again and finally conquered its rivals in 695, long before Tikal

joined many other Maya cities in the Classic collapse (last dated Tikal monuments A.D. 869). Similarly, Copán grew in power until the year 738, when its king Waxaklahuun Ub'aah K'awil (a name better known to Maya enthusiasts today by its unforgettable translation of "18 Rabbit") was captured and put to death by the rival city of Quirigua, but then Copán thrived during the following half-century under more fortunate kings.

Finally, cities in different parts of the Maya area rose and fell on different trajectories. For example, the Puuc region in the northwest Yucatán Peninsula, after being almost empty of people in the year 700, exploded in population after 750 while the southern cities were collapsing, peaked in population between 900 and 925, and then collapsed in turn between 950 and 1000. El Mirador, a huge site in the center of the Maya area with one of the world's largest pyramids, was settled in 200 B.C. and abandoned around A.D. 150, long before the rise of Copán. Chichén Itzá in the northern peninsula grew after A.D. 850 and was the main northern center around 1000, only to be destroyed in a civil war around 1250.

Some archaeologists focus on these five types of complications and don't want to recognize a Classic Maya collapse at all. But this overlooks the obvious facts that cry out for explanation: the disappearance of between 90 and 99% of the Maya population after A.D. 800, especially in the formerly most densely populated area of the southern lowlands, and the disappearance of kings, Long Count calendars, and other complex political and cultural institutions. That's why we talk about a Classic Maya collapse, a collapse both of population and of culture that needs explaining.

Two other phenomena that I have mentioned briefly as contributing to Maya collapses require more discussion: the roles of warfare and of drought.

Archaeologists for a long time believed the ancient Maya to be gentle and peaceful people. We now know that Maya warfare was intense, chronic, and unresolvable, because limitations of food supply and transportation made it impossible for any Maya principality to unite the whole region in an empire, in the way that the Aztecs and Incas united Central Mexico and the Andes, respectively. The archaeological record shows that wars became more intense and frequent towards the time of the Classic collapse. That evidence comes from discoveries of several types over the last 55 years: archaeological excavations of massive fortifications surrounding many Maya sites; vivid depictions of warfare and captives on stone monuments, vases [Plate 14, omitted], and on the famous painted murals discovered in 1946 at Bonampak; and the decipherment of Maya writing, much of which proved to consist of royal inscriptions boasting of conquests. Maya kings fought to take one another captive, one of the unfortunate losers being Copán's King 18 Rabbit. Captives were tortured in unpleasant ways depicted dearly on the monuments and murals (such as yanking fingers out of sockets, pulling out teeth, cutting off the lower jaw, trimming off the lips and fingertips, pulling out the fingernails, and driving a pin through the lips), culminating (sometimes several years later) in the sacrifice of the captive in other equally unpleasant ways (such as tying the captive up into a ball by binding the arms and legs together, then rolling the balled-up captive down the steep stone staircase of a temple).

Maya warfare involved several well-documented types of violence: wars between separate kingdoms; attempts of cities within a kingdom to secede by revolting against the capital; and civil wars resulting from frequent violent attempts by would-be kings to usurp the throne. All of these types were described or depicted on monuments, because they involved kings and nobles. Not considered worthy of description, but probably even more frequent, were fights between commoners over land, as overpopulation became excessive and as land became scarce.

The other phenomenon important to understanding Maya collapses is the repeated occurrence of droughts, studied especially by Mark Brenner, David Hodell, the late Edward Deevey, and their colleagues at the University of Florida, and discussed in a recent book by Richardson Gill. Cores bored into layers of sediments at the bottoms of Maya lakes yield many measurements that let us infer droughts and environmental changes. For example, gypsum (a.k.a. calcium sulfate) precipitates out of solution in a lake into sediments when lake water becomes concentrated by evaporation during a drought. Water containing the heavy form of oxygen known as the isotope oxygen-18 also becomes concentrated during droughts, while water containing the lighter isotope oxygen-16 evaporates away. Molluscs and crustacea living in the lake take up oxygen to lay down in their shells, which remain preserved in the lake sediments, waiting for climatologists to analyze for those oxygen isotopes long after the little animals have died. Radiocarbon dating of a sediment layer identifies the approximate year when the drought or rainfall conditions inferred from those gypsum and oxygen isotope measurements were prevailing. The same lake sediment cores provide palynologists with information about deforestation (which shows up as a decrease in pollen from forest trees at the expense of an increase in grass pollen), and also soil erosion (which shows up as a thick clay deposit and minerals from the washed-down soil).

Based on these studies of radiocarbon-dated layers from lake sediment cores, climatologists and paleoecologists conclude that the Maya area was relatively wet from about 5500 B.C. until 500 B.C. The following period from 475 to 250 B.C., just before the rise of pre-Classic Maya civilization, was dry. The pre-Classic rise may have been facilitated by the return of wetter conditions after 250 B.C., but then a drought from A.D. 125 until A.D. 250 was associated with the pre-Classic collapse at El Mirador and other sites. That collapse was followed by the resumption of wetter conditions and of the buildup of Classic Maya cities, temporarily interrupted by a drought around A.D. 600 corresponding to a decline at Tikal and some other sites. Finally, around A.D. 760 there began the worst drought in the last 7,000 years, peaking around the year A.D. 800, and suspiciously associated with the Classic collapse.

Careful analysis of the frequency of droughts in the Maya area shows a tendency for them to recur at intervals of about 208 years. Those drought cycles may result from small variations in the sun's radiation, possibly made more severe in the Maya area as a result of the rainfall gradient in the Yucatán (drier in the north, wetter in the south) shifting southwards. One might expect those changes in the sun's radiation to affect not just the Maya region but, to varying degrees, the whole world. In fact, climatologists have noted that some other famous collapses of prehistoric civilizations far from the Maya realm appear to coincide with the peaks of those drought cycles, such as the collapse of the world's first empire (the Akkadian Empire of Mesopotamia) around 2170 B.C., the collapse of Moche IV civilization on the Peruvian coast around A.D. 600, and the collapse of Tiwanaku civilization in the Andes around A.D. 1100.

In the most naïve form of the hypothesis that drought contributed to causing the Classic collapse, one could imagine a single drought around A.D. 800 uniformly affecting the whole realm and triggering the fall of all Maya centers simultaneously. Actually, as we have seen, the Classic collapse hit different centers at slightly different times in the period A.D. 760–910, while sparing other centers. That fact makes many Maya specialists skeptical of a role of drought.

But a properly cautious climatologist would not state the drought hypothesis in that implausibly oversimplied form. Finer-resolution variation in rainfall from one year to the next can be calculated from annually banded sediments that rivers wash into ocean basins near the coast. These yield the conclusion that "The Drought" around A.D. 800 actually had four peaks, the first of them less severe: two dry years around A.D. 760, then an even drier decade around A.D. 810–820, three drier years around A.D. 860, and six drier years around A.D. 910. Interestingly, Richardson Gill concluded, from the latest dates on stone monuments at various large Maya centers, that collapse dates vary among sites and fall into three clusters: around A.D. 810, 860, and 910, in agreement with the dates for the three most severe droughts. It would not be at all surprising if a drought in any given year varied locally in its severity, hence if a series of droughts caused different Maya centers to collapse in different years, while sparing centers with reliable water supplies such as cenotes, wells, and lakes.

■ ■ ■

The area most affected by the Classic collapse was the southern lowlands, probably for the two reasons already mentioned: it was the area with the densest population, and it may also have had the most severe water problems because it lay too high above the water table for water to be obtained from cenotes or wells when the rains failed. The southern lowlands lost more than 99% of their population in the course of the Classic collapse. For example, the population of the Central Petén at the peak of the Classic Maya period is variously estimated at between 3,000,000 and 14,000,000 people, but there were only about 30,000 people there at the time that the Spanish arrived. When Cortés and his Spanish army passed through the Central Petén in 1524 and 1525, they nearly starved because they encountered so few villages from which to acquire corn. Cortés passed within a few miles of the ruins of the great Classic cities of Tikal and Palenque, but he heard or saw nothing of them because they were covered by jungle and almost nobody was living in the vicinity.

How did such a huge population of millions of people disappear? By analogy with the cases of the Anasazi and of subsequent Pueblo Indian societies during droughts in the U.S. Southwest, we infer that some people from the southern Maya lowlands survived by fleeing to areas of the northern Yucatán endowed with cenotes or wells, where a rapid population increase took place around the time of the Maya collapse. But there is no sign of all those millions of southern lowland inhabitants surviving to be accommodated as immigrants in the north, just as there is no sign of thousands of Anasazi refugees being received as immigrants into surviving pueblos. As in the U.S. Southwest during droughts, some of that Maya population decrease surely involved people dying of starvation or thirst, or killing each other in struggles over increasingly scarce resources. The other part of the decrease may reflect a slower decrease in the birthrate or child survival rate over the course of many decades. That is, depopulation probably involved both a higher death rate and a lower birth rate.

In the Maya area as elsewhere, the past is a lesson for the present. From the time of Spanish arrival, the Central Petén's population declined further to about 3,000 in A.D. 1714, as a result of deaths from diseases and other causes associated with Spanish occupation. By the 1960s, the Central Petén's population had risen back only to 25,000, still less than 1% of what it had been at the Classic Maya peak. Thereafter, however, immigrants flooded into the Central Petén, building up its population to about 300,000 in the 1980s, and ushering in a new era of deforestation and erosion. Today, half of the Petén is once again deforested and ecologically degraded. One-quarter of all the forests of Honduras were destroyed between 1964 and 1989.

To summarize the Classic Maya collapse, we can tentatively identify five strands. I acknowledge, however, that Maya archaeologists still disagree vigorously among themselves—in part, because the different strands evidently varied in importance among different parts of the Maya realm; because detailed archaeological studies are available for only some Maya sites; and because it remains puzzling why most of the Maya heartland remained nearly empty of population and failed to recover after the collapse and after regrowth of forests.

With those caveats, it appears to me that one strand consisted of population growth outstripping available resources. As the archaeologist David Webster succinctly puts it, "Too many farmers grew too many crops on too much of the landscape." Compounding that mismatch between population and resources was the second strand: the effects of deforestation and hillside erosion, which caused a decrease in the amount of useable farmland at a time when more rather than less farmland was needed, and possibly exacerbated by an anthropogenic drought resulting from deforestation, by soil nutrient depletion and other soil problems, and by the struggle to prevent bracken ferns from overrunning the fields.

The third strand consisted of increased fighting, as more and more people fought over fewer resources. Maya warfare, already endemic, peaked just before the collapse. That is not surprising when one reflects that at least 5,000,000 people, perhaps many more, were crammed into an area smaller than the state of Colorado (104,000 square miles). That warfare would have decreased further the amount of land available for agriculture, by creating no-man's lands between principalities where it was now unsafe to farm. Bringing matters to a head was the strand of climate change. The drought at the time of the Classic collapse was not the first drought that the Maya had lived through, but it was the most severe. At the time of previous droughts, there were still uninhabited parts of the Maya landscape, and people at a site affected by drought could save themselves by moving to another site. However, by the time of the Classic collapse the landscape was now full, there was no useful unoccupied land in the vicinity on which to begin anew, and the whole population could not be accommodated in the few areas that continued to have reliable water supplies.

As our fifth strand, we have to wonder why the kings and nobles failed to recognize and solve these seemingly obvious problems undermining their society. Their attention was evidently focused on their short-term concerns of enriching themselves, waging wars, erecting monuments, competing with each other, and extracting enough food from the peasants to support all those activities. Like most leaders throughout human history, the Maya kings and nobles did not heed long-term problems, insofar as they perceived them.

Finally, while we still have some other past societies to consider in this book before we switch our attention to the modern world, we must already be struck by some parallels between the Maya and the past societies discussed in Chapters 2–4. As on Easter Island, Mangareva, and among the Anasazi, Maya environmental and population problems led to increasing warfare and civil strife. As on Easter Island and at Chaco Canyon, Maya peak population numbers were followed swiftly by political and social collapse. Paralleling the eventual extension of agriculture from Easter Island's coastal lowlands to its uplands, and from the Mimbres floodplain to the hills, Copán's inhabitants also expanded from the floodplain to the more fragile hill slopes, leaving them with a larger population to feed when the agricultural boom in the hills went bust. Like Easter Island chiefs erecting ever larger statues, eventually crowned by pukao, and like Anasazi elite treating themselves to necklaces of 2,000 turquoise beads, Maya kings sought to outdo each other with more and more impressive temples, covered with thicker and thicker plaster—reminiscent in turn of the extravagant conspicuous consumption by modern American CEOs. The passivity of Easter chiefs and Maya kings in the face of the real big threats to their societies completes our list of disquieting parallels.

UNIT 3
Techniques in Archaeology

Unit Selections

Key Points to Consider

- How has modern technology been combined with folklore to locate archaeological sites in rural Iceland?

- What kind of advances have been made in techniques to date archaeological sites in the last 50 years or so? Discuss the use of laser technology, nuclear physics, and computers.

- How has DNA been used to help date archaeological materials? Please explain.

- How can a wasp's nest possibly be used to date archaeological sites? Explain the technique of "optical luminescence." How is it that this technique can go back in time about 17,000 years?

- What have archaeologists been able to borrow from physical anthropologists in terms of dating techniques? Give examples.

- How is forensics used in archaeology?

- How has computer modeling helped to unravel the archaeological mysteries of the American Southwest?

- How can techniques such as a gas chromatograph/mass spectrometer be used to identify and date archaeological materials? Give an example of this using a prehistoric unglazed piece of pottery.

Student Website
www.mhcls.com/online

Internet References
Further information regarding these websites may be found in this book's preface or online.

American Anthropologist
   http://www.aaanet.org
NOVA Online/Pyramids—The Inside Story
   http://www.pbs.org/wgbh/nova/pyramid/

Archaeology has evolved significantly from being an exercise in separating the remains of past human behavior from the "dirt." And as such, archaeology in turn employs a diversified group of highly sophisticated techniques. Digging in itself has gone through its own evolution of techniques ranging from the wild thrashings of Heinrich Schielmann to the obsessive military precision of Sir Mortimer Wheeler.

Archaeology continues to expand the use of a multidisciplinary approach and is therefore incorporating more techniques that will prove to enlighten us about our human past.

The most well-known technique to be developed in archaeology was radiocarbon dating. This provides archaeologists with one of their most valuable means of establishing the age of archaeological materials. This technique was developed by W. F. Libby at UCLA in 1949. This new technique was a major revolu-tion. It has enabled archaeologists for the first time (in all of history and prehistory!) to have an empirical means of determining the age of archaeological sites in terms of absolute years. This dating technique is based on the principle of radioactive decay in which unstable radioactive isotopes transform into stable elements at a constant rate. In order to fine-tune accuracy, dates are presented with a standard statistical margin of error. Great care is taken with respect to any factors that may skew the results of materials being dated. Radiocarbon dating is limited to the dating of organic materials and is not able to date such things as stone tools. It can date materials as far back as 100,000 years or more. As the technique is perfected, it will be able to date organic matter of even earlier times. The word "present" was designated to be 1950 A.D. Now of course, we can add another 53 years to this date.

The state of preservation of archaeological materials is dependent upon many variables. These include the original material of the artifact and the conditions of the site in which it is preserved. For example, a nineteenth-century adobe mission in the Mojave Desert in California may be so weathered as to be unrecognizable. This is due to the fact that extreme temperatures, varying from very hot to very cold, typical of a low desert climate, tend to rapidly destroy any kind of matter. On the other hand, consistently wet or consistently dry conditions tend to preserve organic matter in a relatively pristine state for long periods of time. The preservation of human remains is therefore very good in bogs, such as in Denmark, or in coastal deserts of Peru. In the coastal deserts of Peru the conditions remain dry. Therefore archaeological material may be preserved for many thousands of years.

Since the discovery of radiocarbon dating, numerous other techniques have been invented that have their applications to archaeology to further clarify dates, preservation, and in general, add to the ability of archaeologists to do cultural historical reconstruction.

Discussed in this section are some of the extraordinary applications of such varied hard sciences as nuclear physics, laser technology, and computers. We can now describe sites in terms of time-space systemics and virtual reality in a way that exceeds recent science-fiction fantasies.

Remote sensing devices from outer space allow sites to be reconstructed without invasive excavation. New, cleverly devised radiometric techniques are being developed to suit specific conditions to date archaeological remains by association. The use of wasp's nests is one such example.

Archaeologists sometimes rely on the use of forensic specialists to present images of the past that we could never before see. Used in conjunction with the exponential knowledge rapidly developing from DNA analysis, our images from the past are focused into a detail comparable to a digital camera.

Unglazed cooking pots have been tested to yield information on prehistoric diets through molecular analysis.

Yet, the simple time-tested technique of archaeological surveying still helps reconstruct sites, again without invasive excavation. The future of archaeology will increasingly depend on techniques to maximize preservation of sites and minimize archaeological excavation. Archaeological excavation, for all its good intents and purposes, destroys archaeological sites as fully as pot hunting or parking lots.

Through Dirt to the Past

Archaeology in Rural Iceland

E. Paul Durrenberger

The first settlers came to Iceland little more than a thousand years ago. Eventually, more than thirty chieftains from Norway, with their followers and slaves, occupied the island. During the twelfth century, their descendants started to write down everything known about the settlement and the events of the tenth, eleventh, and twelfth centuries. During the thirteenth century, the competition among the chieftains became fierce, and soon only five remained. By 1262 there was only one. He then became a subject of the king of Norway. This effectively ended Icelandic self-government until 1944, when the modern country gained independence.

During the struggle for independence, Iceland followed the rest of Europe in its attempt to build a national culture. As in Scandinavia and Europe, there was great interest in collecting and preserving folklore from the countryside. In this period, the manuscripts of the famous Icelandic sagas were found being used as shirt patterns and recycled in other ways. Scholars rescued and collected them. These scholars began to study the manuscripts, standardize the spellings and versions, and prepare and publish standard editions.

Along with these efforts there was a drive to purify the Icelandic language of the influences of Danish and other languages. The independence movement developed the idea of a pure Icelandic language preserved in the countryside, a folk wisdom preserved in the folklore, and a continuous oral tradition going back to the first settlement. Many Icelanders even have names that are the same as those of the famous characters of the saga times.

Icelandic archaeologists also respect the power of oral tradition. They believe they can locate sites by talking to people who live in places that still bear the names used in the sagas. Farms are a potentially rich source of information. Some are known to have been in use for most of the thousand years of Iceland's settlement. Farmhouses and barns are generally built on a rise overlooking a hayfield below. Ask the farmer and he'll likely tell you that the original settlement farm is close to where his house stands today, up on the rise.

There haven't been many excavations of settlement-period farms in such places, but the basic business of farms may have changed little over the centuries. It's too cold in Iceland to grow anything outdoors except grass, so farmers specialize in livestock husbandry. Sheep and cattle predominate. The animals have to be kept indoors over the winter. Each spring, people shovel out the stable areas and piles of refuse build up beside barns. Imagine what that means. Farms may literally sit on top of thousand-year-old dung heaps, potential records of history, continuously deposited since the era of the sagas.

See Through the Soil

It has been notoriously difficult for foreign archaeologists to work in Iceland. One American archaeologist wanted to study the diet of the early settlers and farmers. What better way to find out, he thought, than to recover the remains of their food in those deep barn-door deposits. He located deposits that were washing into the sea, but his research encountered significant opposition. Some Icelanders thought it was the height of heresy to let this foreigner take historic treasures such as fish and animal bones from the eroding dung heap.

Those attitudes are gradually changing. Today, Icelandic archaeologists are more welcoming of the technical expertise of their foreign colleagues. For example, in 1998, Icelandic archaeologist Gudmundur Olafsson was excavating the homestead of Erik the Red (the discoverer of Greenland and father of Leif Eriksson) in the Westfjords. He invited John Steinberg, an archaeologist from the University of California in Los Angeles, to use electronic sensing gear to search an area approximately 150 by 150 feet, adjoining the site. Olafsson believed that an outbuilding must have stood somewhere in the space. Sure enough, Steinberg located it, right where Olafsson thought it would be.

Nevertheless, Olafsson remained unconvinced that the technology the American was using would be of significant

Unearthing History

One day, Steinberg sent me and Nilka, one of the female Icelandic archaeologists, to a farm named Torfgardur. He wanted us to dig a test pit where remote sensing suggested another, more recent, house had been located. "I just need the date for the house," he said. "The historical records suggest this farm was split off from a larger one in the fourteenth century."

Nilka located the site with the GPS receiver, and we marked the corners of a square about a yard in each direction. Then we started digging straight down through one and then another ash layer, turf walls, a midden deposit full of animal and fish bones, and more turf walls. We broke for lunch and got a bucket, as we could no longer heave the dirt out of the narrow pit. After lunch we continued downward until we hit the 1001 ash layer.

Steinberg arrived, and we walked the site with him. We could see the remains of old turf houses, wind-eroded banks, and the bank of a drainage ditch that showed where people had taken turf for hundreds of years, stripping the soil down nearly to the glacial gravels. "That must be why it's called turf farm," said Steinberg.

We walked through the rain-wet grass to the pit at the top of the ridge. Steinberg jumped in and exclaimed in surprise at the extraordinary preservation of the ash layer. I managed the bucket on a rope as he continued to dig through the ash and into another midden deposit. "This means people were here before 1100," he said. "What's going on here? We need to learn more about this place. Look at this." He handed up a piece of metal.

"What is it?" I asked.

"Probably a ship's rivet," he said. Elizabeth Ward confirmed his theory later when I handed it to her.

Cold and covered with mud, we piled into the vehicle, satisfied with another day of unearthing Icelandic history. These experiences don't always go by the books, but that's one of the exciting prospects of archaeology in Iceland, filling in the gaps that the books leave.

—E.P.D.

use in helping find early Icelandic sites. Because preservation has been poor, the orthodox view has been that we know little about medieval Iceland's archaeology. But American archaeologists often confront such difficulties. The first settlers came to the Americas at least twelve thousand years ago and spread across the continent in a series of changing economic, political, and ethnic systems. They left no written records and underwent such complex changes that the Native Americans Europeans encountered were not necessarily related to the peoples who had lived in the same regions earlier.

American archaeologists see themselves as anthropologists, extending our understanding of the human condition into the distant past. Whereas cultural anthropologists talk to and observe living people, archaeologists have to use the evidence they can recover from the ground. They care less about finding swords or boats or the skulls of specific individuals than about understanding the economic conditions of the period. "I want to know how big the buildings were and when they were occupied," says Steinberg. "I only need to dig enough to find out those things. Then it's time to move to the next site."

Steinberg chose to do his research here because he knew that medieval Iceland had not yet developed the complex bureaucratic organization of a state. He knew of similar systems from the archaeology of Africa, the Pacific, and the Americas. Only the Icelanders had preserved any written records to supplement the archaeological remains. He consulted with Olafsson and others to find the place where he could best find the data he needed. They suggested Skagafjördur in the north. The area was appropriate because of its deposits of volcanic ash.

Iceland is a volcanic island. Volcanoes can be deadly, but they offer one advantage for archaeologists: they cover whole areas with distinctive tephra (ash). Geologists can use various kinds of evidence to date ashfalls to the year. Identifying and dating tephra is its own science. "Listen," Steinberg says as he scrapes a thin layer of ash in the sidewall of a trench. "You can hear the sound of it. You can even taste the difference." He puts a pinch of the ash on his tongue and spits it out with the concentration of a wine-tasting connoisseur. Though he will take a stab at identifying the ash, he defers any final judgment until he's spoken with Magnus Sigurgeirsson, the tephra guru of Iceland.

"This layer," Steinberg explains, pointing to a white ash below the level of the grass roots, "is from 1104, from the volcano Hekla." He moves his trowel down a bit and says: "Here's the 1000 layer; and down here is the Landnam layer," referring to ash fall from the time of the first settlement of Iceland. The volcanic ash allows even more precise dating of structures than carbon 14 or other methods of dating do.

How can we determine the size of buildings without excavating them to find all of their walls? See through the soil that covers them. Geophysicist Brian Dimiata does just that with devices that measure the electronic resistivity (capacity for resistance) and conductivity of soil. He sends an electric current through the soil and records how much it resists electricity. Differences in resistivity indicate anomalies such as water, stones, and turf walls. "If I knew what was down here, I wouldn't be digging this hole," says Steinberg. "The only way to find out just what is causing the changes in resistivity that Brian's computer has stored is to dig far enough down to see what is causing them."

Steinberg and Dimiata can use this system to locate the remains of structures and date them by studying the volcanic ash. Once they have the measure of a place, they're done. That's the information they came to get. They move on to the next field or designated area.

The technical expertise amounts to complex bookkeeping tasks. Everything is in a place, and it is imperative to remember just where that is, even when you dig things up. To do that, Steinberg has his crew locate fields with a geographical positioning system receiver, or GPS. When he has found a precise point, he uses long tape measures to lay out the whole area in sections about a yard square. He marks these with small colored plastic flags on wire pins. Then Dimiata's helper, Hans, can walk each line going from north to south and east to west as the computer records the resistivity data.

The long Arctic summer nights find Dimiata and Hans working through their matrices of data and notebooks to prepare pictures to show what is under the soil of the field. They share their findings with Steinberg in the evening. The next day he assigns a crew of two or three people to start removing sod—from a strip maybe fifteen feet long and a yard wide—to see what is causing the blips in the diagrams. Then the expertise is more in how to handle a shovel, a trowel, and a brush and to know when to use each one.

Where It's Not Supposed to Be

In the summer of 2002, three years after his experiment with Erik the Red's house, and funded with a grant from the National Science Foundation, Steinberg and his crew returned to Iceland for a second season. (They had done some preparatory work the year before.) He invited me to join the crew because of my interest in archaeology and medieval Iceland. Also, he thought we could learn something if a cultural anthropologist and archaeologists worked together. I agreed.

I soon found myself in a trench with a shovel and trowel. I had given away my archaeologist's toolkit a long time ago, but I can move dirt. That may seem to require no skill at all, but that isn't true on a dig. I had to learn expert shovel techniques from Steinberg's well-trained crew. Though it began to come back after a while, I'd never excavated sites like this.

Olafsson joined us, giving up a week of his vacation from his job as the chief archaeologist at the National Museum. The entire crew was eager to know whether this new technique of remote sensing could really locate sites from Iceland's first settlement. With Olafsson's arrival, it became time to put up or shut up. The Icelander is an expert at excavating Viking-age longhouses. He's done that in Greenland, Iceland, and sites in Scandinavia. But Steinberg had been finding potential sites where accepted wisdom said he should not—in the pastures below the contemporary farms, not in the bluffs where the farms are now. Could he convince Olafsson that the blips he had marked on paper might really indicate old long houses, buildings located where they were not "supposed" to be?

It was a Tuesday afternoon, and I was working to help remove the dirt Steinberg's crew had put into one of their trenches when they left the previous year. (When you leave a site, you have to return it to its original condition as closely as possible, otherwise it could be dangerous to livestock.) Olafsson came onto the site and grabbed a short-handled spade. He started digging a trench. "I'll do that," I offered, practicing my Icelandic. "You take care of my back dirt," he said, meaning I should remove the soil he was digging up. He kept me busy. Soon we were both sweating. Finally he turned the trench over to two Icelandic women archaeologists who were working with our crew. "Take it down another ten centimeters," he said, setting off to examine the other trenches with Steinberg.

I was too busy moving dirt to pay close attention, but out of the corner of my eye I saw him striding between trenches,

jumping in, jumping out, and consulting Steinberg's diagrams. "He's a good shovel man," one of my companions said to the other. "Yes," the second grunted as we moved dirt.

In a few minutes Olafsson was back to check on what we'd uncovered. He told us to take it down again. Down the trench went. Eventually he found the wall he was looking for, but then he was clearly puzzled.

The next day Steinberg asked me to help open a new trench. This wasn't one of his neatly oriented north-south-east-west satellite-oriented trenches. This went at an angle to the others, tracing through the middle of what Olafsson thought would be a Viking-age longhouse—if there was one. Steinberg, Olafsson, and I all started cutting and moving sod and soil, exposing the earth underneath. Then Steinberg called other members of the crew to join us. Soon, six or so of us were working on the project. The grass was gone, and the trench was slowly and carefully going down. "Here it is," said Olafsson, pointing to the exposed turf wall. "Just where it should be," smiled Steinberg. A second wall was soon visible. The two walls connected in a corner that we were now uncovering.

Olafsson was openly more convinced of the benefits of the technology. He and I paced off lines to connect all the dots of wall the trenches had uncovered and marked them with plastic flags. The outline of a Viking longhouse became evident. That night at supper I asked Olafsson how certain he was of our discovery: 20 percent? 80 percent? He didn't want to be pinned down. I changed the question: "What would convince you?"

"Finding the hearth," he said. Longhouses had characteristic hearths at their centers. If we could find that, he would be convinced. But he didn't need any more trenches. We had uncovered enough of the walls. It would take a slow and painstaking excavation to uncover the details of this house. Steinberg and Dimiata were ready to move to the next site, but we were all pleased with the results of our efforts. American and Icelandic archaeologists and a cultural anthropologist had worked successfully together to uncover salient facts that might well lead to a greater understanding of the fragile and transitory social organization that characterized the early years of Iceland's settlement.

New Mysteries Uncovered

The next day, Olafsson and Sigurgeirsson went to the site with us to examine the tephra and walls in the trenches we'd dug. Whenever one of them would grab a shovel, we'd pitch in and help dig so they could see more. The trench went from a neat, one-level affair to a multilevel thing. At the end of that cold and rainy day we all huddled around Olafsson as he interpreted the evidence for us. "Here," he pointed with his trowel, "there was a settlement period pithouse. Then comes the A.D. 1000 ash layer, and we see a turf house. After the 1100 ashfall, we see a third turf house. This wasn't the simple longhouse I thought it was."

Elizabeth Ward, the Smithsonian Institution's curator of Viking artifacts, was in her trench sketching charcoal that she'd uncovered. "Could this be the hearth?" she asked. "Yes," said Olafsson. "It could be. We'd have to extend the trench to see." We went from trench to trench as he connected the dots, but at best there was still a confusing picture. "What we know for sure is this," he said. "There was a farm here at the time of the settlement. Then after 1000 there was a turf house. There was another turf house after 1100. This much we know for sure. The rest? That we can't know unless we excavate the whole site, and that would be a major long-term undertaking."

"And I can't even dig off the grid," Steinberg grumbled, jokingly.

"But your crew can," Olafsson retorted, in that laconic way that typifies the Icelanders' reputation for stark humor. The conversation went on. Ignoring the rain, we stood up and reviewed all the evidence one more time.

Even from this day's work we could begin to speculate on possible conclusions to our study. The long-term objective of the research was to survey the whole valley. Then we could begin to understand the relationships of all the farms. In particular we hoped to answer certain key questions: When did the smaller ones get started? Was it circa the year 1000?

The sagas suggest that about then the larger farmers began freeing their slaves and allowing them to settle on small plots around the perimeter of the big estates. The freed slaves then had enough land to support themselves but not for the whole year. To make up the difference, they had to be available to the large landowners for the labor-intensive periods of making hay and rounding up sheep. This move gave large landowners access to labor that was much cheaper than slaves. No longer did the landowners have to support slaves the whole year round. A slave generally could barely produce enough to support one person in a year.

With such cheap labor available, landowners could actually control more land. The problem was that all of it was occupied. That may be the reason for the intensive conflicts that followed.

But to know this, we had to know more. We had to learn the dates and sizes of the houses. So the survey continued through the end of the summer. The process was essentially repetitive. First, locate a farm that was in the historical records. Then make a 150-foot-square grid. Take soil cores every 150 feet, north to south and east to west. Is there any evidence of charcoal? Of midden deposits? If so, bring in the remote sensing team and see what's under the soil. Does that evidence suggest turf walls? When walls appear to have been located, send someone out with a shovel to see if he can find the turf under the soil. If he finds it, dig a standard one-yard pit to investigate the date of the structure from the tephra.

We Must Return

Throughout the summer, Steinberg's crew was dispersed across several sites. Some laid out grids, some helped the remote sensing crew, some took soil cores, some dug test pits, and others did the more painstaking excavations when something interesting turned up in one of the pits. One find was a pile of nine sheep horns inside a turf wall. What was the purpose of that? There were lots of guesses, all of them about equally good without more facts.

So, one farm, soil core, test pit, and house after another, the data accumulated. Record keeping also became more complex, but we began to see patterns in the complexity. The small farms were established after the large ones. Significantly, we could determine that—contrary to accepted lore—the early houses were built on the lower plain, the later ones on the bluff.

Why? Maybe defense. Up on the bluff you can see for great distances. A landowner could see anyone coming who might present a threat or be trying to take his land away. To be sure of our conclusions, we still need to uncover more information.

For example, one day Steinberg sent Ward and myself to a midden deposit up on a bluff. He gave us instructions to get to the bottom of it. We set up a screen to sift the soil, so we would be sure we missed nothing, and started digging. Sheep bones. Nineteenth-century ceramics. More sheep bones. Eighteenth-century ceramics. One meter down. Fish bones and sheep bones. Slag from making iron. Farther down. A piece of cloth. Ward jumps into the pit to excavate that, as I'm not sure what to do with cloth. Later she called an Icelandic expert for instructions on how to preserve it. Two meters down and I asked for a ladder; I was having trouble getting out of the pit. Three meters down and we got to the 1104 tephra. The deposit gave out shortly after that.

So, we can conclude that about 1100 people moved to the bluff. What prompted the move? That's the question we closed the summer with. One possible explanation concerns freeing slaves, expanding land, fighting, and defense. There are others.

How will we know? We have to return to survey more sites and excavate those we've located. But Steinberg isn't prepared for long-term excavation; his forte is survey work. The Icelandic archaeologists are great excavators, and we have discussed the prospects with them. They will oversee excavations, and we will continue the survey. That way, in time, we will be able to put the pieces of the puzzle together.

These are plans for the future. In the meantime, there are the holes to be filled in before everyone returns to California, Pennsylvania, or Washington, D.C. Our next task will require a different kind of digging. We must write proposals, outline the questions we hope to answer and the methods we're using, and see if we can dig up some grant money to continue our work.

E. Paul Durrenberger is professor of anthropology at Penn State University.

High-Tech "Digging"

Fifty years of technological innovation has revolutionized the practice of archaeology.

by Chris Scarre

Archaeology is the study of people, of past human societies. For many, this simple and obvious fact makes the subject a humanity or social science and distinguishes it sharply from hard sciences such as physics or chemistry. Yet modern archaeology uses a wide range of scientific aids, and a great deal of what we discover about the past comes directly from the application of technology. Here as much as anywhere, the last 50 years have seen enormous changes. Archaeology has benefited from the growing computerization of society; advances in nuclear physics, like electron microscopes and particle accelerators; and the development of laser technology used in sophisticated and highly accurate surveying equipment. Meanwhile, DNA analysis is opening up possibilities for studying relationships among people buried in ancient cemeteries, detecting the arrival of immigrant groups, and more. This, in turn, links directly with ideas of ethnicity and identity, among the hottest topics in politics today. It is all part of the great transformation of archaeology from an amateur pursuit with relatively few salaried full-timers to a highly professional discipline employing thousands of university-trained specialists. Men and women in white coats, toiling away in their laboratories, have become as

important as rugged fieldworkers slogging away under the hot sun.

Today's rugged fieldworkers, however, slog away rather differently than did their predecessors 50 years ago. At my own excavation of a Neolithic burial mound at Prissé-la-Charrière in western France, the picks, shovels, and trowels haven't changed much. We still cart earth away in wheelbarrows and pile it neatly beyond the edges of the site. But when we lay out the trenches, we use an electronic distance meter (EDM), which automatically records distances, directions, and heights by laser beam and then sends them to a computer. Before deciding where to dig, we carry a fluxgate gradiometer (a type of magnetometer) over the site to detect tiny variations in the magnetic sensitivity of deposits. The results are downloaded onto an onsite computer to produce a diagram of what is below ground. It picks up quarry ditches cut into the limestone bedrock on either side of our burial mound and even detects walls and other features within the mound itself. Last year, we also used radar sounding to see if we could locate burial chambers within the mound. One day we may be able to "excavate" a site by remote sensing alone, without ever setting spade to earth.

Remote sensing in its more sophisticated forms isn't limited to individual sites: airborne remote sensing has already led to the detection of entire buried landscapes in some regions of the world. One such technique is radar, used to detect Maya field systems in Guatemala, another is its close cousin sonar, which led to the discovery of the armed schooners *Hamilton* and *Scourge,* sunk in Lake Ontario in the War of 1812. Radar imagery employing a long wavelength that can penetrate forest canopy has recently been used to locate and map new sites around Angkor in Cambodia, throwing light on the development of the early Khmer state. Satellite imagery from the U.S. LANDSAT and French SPOT satellites has extended this technology into space. Meanwhile, space-imaging radar (SIR) deployed from the shuttle *Columbia* in 1991 has traced former river courses in China's hyperarid Taklamakan desert.

When it comes to mapping our site, the new technology takes over again. Gone are the tape measures and drawing boards; the new technology uses a video camera mounted on a long raised arm to take overlapping pictures looking straight down at the site, feeding them directly into a computer. The resulting computer-generated plans take a fraction of the time required to make a hand-drafted map and allow us to record exactly the positions of the thousands of stones that make up our burial mound.

Other innovations involve not so much sophisticated technology as new approaches and priorities. No competent archaeologist today would ignore the wealth of evidence to be obtained by sieving the soil. Excavators who chose to sieve their material a half-century ago (and not many did) would have used a ¼-inch mesh screen, whereas today, fine meshes measuring down to 500 microns (½ of a millimeter) or less are regularly used to permit a more comprehensive recovery of faunal remains, including those of small animals, like mice, voles, and shrews. Though such animals were presumably not eaten, they live in particular habitats, so the presence of their remains can be an important indicator of environmental conditions at a site. This technique is slow, but essential in cases where a single bone can be crucial. Also standard on many sites is a flotation machine, which uses a liquid (usually water) to dissolve sediments, allowing recovery of organic remains from insect parts to plant fragments. We don't only want to know what pottery people made, what houses they lived in, and what livestock they kept, but also what plants they cultivated and ate. Almost all of our knowledge about the origins of wheat and barley cultivation has come to us by careful excavation and sieving or flotation of deposits at key Near Eastern sites such as Jericho and Abu Hureyra.

Some ancient seeds can easily be identified by eye, but to study them properly (and to classify the less obvious fragments) requires a microscope and a laboratory. Seeds now go to the lab to be studied along with pollen, which has been analyzed for more than 80 years, and newer interests such as phytoliths, the microscopic silica structures that give plants their stiffness. Like pollen, phytoliths are durable and survive after all other parts of the

plant have decayed. Whereas pollen, because it is airborne, tells us what plants grew in the vicinity of a site, phytoliths show us what plants the ancient occupants actually brought to it. They can also tell us what parts of a plant were present, like grain for eating or stalks for thatching or animal bedding.

Alongside seeds, pollen, and other plant remains, we find laboratory technicians specializing in dendrochronology, dating based on patterns of growth variation in tree rings, or palaeoclimatology, the study of ancient climates and climatic change. Many of these draw on techniques developed with no archaeological application in mind. One of the most important techniques in modern palaeoclimatology, for example, is oxygen-isotope analysis. This relies on the discovery that oxygen exists in two stable forms with different numbers of neutrons and hence different atomic mass. The proportions of the two forms, oxygen-16 and oxygen-18, vary according to global temperature (warmer means higher ^{16}O, colder means higher ^{18}O). Marine organisms incorporate both forms of oxygen in their shells, recording the $^{16}O/^{18}O$ proportion. After the organism dies, its shell falls to the sea floor and is preserved in the sediments. By determining the $^{16}O/^{18}O$ proportion in shells from sediment cores extracted from the sea floor, it is possible to trace changes in global temperature.

This technique has revolutionized our understanding of world climate, and in particular of the famous Ice Ages. Fifty years ago the best interpretation of the Ice Ages was still one published by German geologists Albrecht Penck and Eduard Brückner in 1909. They believed that there had been not just one Ice Age but a series of four, which they named Günz, Mindel, Riss, and Würm after rivers in the Alps (the most recent being the Würm; the North American equivalents were Nebraskan, Kansan, Illinoian, and Wisconsin). Since then better techniques for coring in ocean

floors (an innovation of oil exploration) and advances in nuclear physics made oxygen isotope analysis possible. We now know that there were not four successive Ice Ages, but actually around 20 such cold periods spanning more than two million years. We can also chart exactly how the average global temperature changed, period by period and degree by degree, during that enormous expanse of time. Ice cores in Greenland and Antarctica have given similar results, oxygen being a major component of water. They show how frighteningly rapid—an increase in the mean annual temperature of 7°C, or 12.6°F, in 50 years— was the change in the fluctuating climate at the end of the last Ice Age some 11,600 years ago.

While palaeoclimatology and pollen analysis tell us what was going on in the environment, microstratigraphy (microscopic study of the nature and composition of minute sequences of soils and surfaces) can tell us in detail what was happening in a particular rock-shelter or room, such as which areas of a building were for living or sleeping, which were open courtyards, and what fuel was being burned on the fire. To do this, a section of sediment has to be consolidated in situ by applying resin, then removed as a block to a laboratory where a thin section of it can be examined under a microscope. In northern Syria, microstratigraphy at several early city sites has detected a layer of dust, suggesting widespread fallout and burning around 2350 B.C. This was initially interpreted as a volcanic event, but a more recent, tentative suggestion is that a meteor impact might have been the cause.

So far, we haven't said much about artifacts, but they are as much the focus of attention as they ever were. A whole battery of techniques—including optical emission spectrometry (OES), X-ray fluorescence spectrometry (XRF), neutron activation analysis

(NAA), and atomic absorption spectrometry (AAS)—is now available to tell archaeologists what their artifacts are made of and, in some cases, where they come from. Each technique has its own range of applications, whether it be to metals, stone, amber, or shell. One early and still important example of this kind of study was the analysis of obsidian from sites in the Near East and Mediterranean. Obsidian was used like flint in many prehistoric societies, but it comes from only a limited number of sources. Hence analysis (by XRF, NAA, and AAS, among others) made it possible in many cases to match obsidian from archaeological sites to sources. This revealed far-flung trade patterns, connecting sites in southern Iran to sources in eastern Turkey, and demonstrated beyond question that by the end of the Upper Palaeolithic, 10,000 years ago, Aegean sailors were already crossing from mainland Greece to the obsidian-rich island of Melos.

Without doubt the greatest advance in archaeological technology over the past 50 years has been in dating. Today it is hard to imagine archaeology without the huge battery of scientific dating techniques, from reliable workhorses such as radiocarbon, to uranium-series, fission-track, potassium-argon (K-A), thermoluminescence (TL), optically-stimulated luminescence (OSL), and electron-spin resonance (ESR) dating, to various experimental methods (such as cation ratio or chlorine-36) that researchers are using in trying to crack the problem of dating rock art.

Radiocarbon overturned many chronological schemes painstakingly assembled by prehistorians over the previous 100 years.

In 1949, Willard F. Libby published the first radiocarbon dates, and announced to the world the discovery of his new method. A chemist, Libby had spent the war years researching cosmic radiation, and established that cosmic rays hitting the atmosphere created radioactive carbon (^{14}C) at a constant and predictable rate. Carbon (both "ordinary" ^{12}C and radioactive ^{14}C) is present in all living things; plants take up carbon dioxide during photosynthesis, herbivores eat plants, and carnivores eat herbivores. Carbon-14, however, is unstable and decays at a steady rate. After an organism dies, the ^{14}C in its tissues is no longer replenished and the clock begins ticking. Libby realized that the age of organic materials could be determined from the amount of residual ^{14}C they contained. The discovery revolutionized prehistoric archaeology, and in 1960 Libby was awarded a Nobel Prize for his work, the only time anyone has been so honored for an archaeological achievement.

Yet the introduction of radiocarbon dating didn't go smoothly. When it was used to date Egyptian historical material, such as samples of wood thought to be contemporary with the pyramids, the radiocarbon dates were too recent. Was the method at fault, or was the Egyptian chronology in need of radical revision? The answer came when tree rings from the bristlecone pine, which grows at high altitude in the White Mountains of California, were radiocarbon dated. The annual rings in the trees could be counted, giving an exact calendar year. Comparisons of tree-ring and ^{14}C dates from the same samples showed that, yes, radiocarbon dating yielded dates that were too recent, but also gave the means to correct or "calibrate" them. Tree-ring sequences are now used to calibrate radiocarbon dates back to 6000 B.C. and similar pairs of radiocarbon and uranium-series dates, from samples of ancient coral reef near Barbados, have now provided an even longer calibration curve going back to around 40,000 years before the present.

Radiocarbon overturned many chronological schemes painstak-ingly assembled by prehistorians over the previous 100 years. In Europe, for example, archaeologists such as V. Gordon Childe in the 1920s to 1940s had built up a chronology that relied on the assumption that most innovations (such as metallurgy) had arisen in the Near East and only later had spread to Europe. Childe and others used comparisons with Near Eastern sites and artifacts to date European prehistory. Where there are actual imports—Mycenaean pottery from the Greek mainland found in Egyptian tombs, for example—these schemes can be made to work, but in most cases the supposed links to the Near East were only the vaguest of stylistic parallels. For as long as this climate of thought existed, it was difficult to believe that western Europeans had ever invented anything. With radiocarbon dating, all that changed. Specious links, such as that claimed for northwestern European megaliths and monumental structures in the eastern Mediterranean, were broken. It was soon shown, for example, that Stonehenge was older than the Bronze Age citadel of Mycenae, not a dim reflection of it in a barbarous, distant land. For the first time it became possible to date layers and artifacts on their own terms, to place the chronology of Australia or North America alongside that of historic Egypt or Mesopotamia; and to delve far back into prehistory, to date the end of the last Ice Age and the beginnings of agriculture in the Near East. Refinements have recently allowed radiocarbon dating to be applied to thorny questions such as the authenticity of the Turin shroud, now widely believed to be a thirteenth-century fabrication. Today, only a tiny fragment of carbonbearing material is needed, making it possible to radiocarbon date French Palaeolithic cave paintings, such as those of the Chauvet Cave in southern France, now known to be 32,000 years old. Initial estimates on stylistic grounds had suggested the Chauvet paintings were less than two-thirds that age.

However spectacular the technological successes of the past half-century, archaeology, as in the 1950s, is primarily about people and past societies. Thus it is with great excitement that archaeologists have been watching developments in one of the newest of all scientific pursuits: the study of human DNA. One of the big questions in archaeology has always been relatedness: to understand whether a group of people buried in adjacent graves in a cemetery might be members of a single family; to know whether two contemporary peoples making differently patterned pots were in fact entirely different in origin; to discover whether agriculture was brought to Europe by farmers from the Near East; and to determine whether the Americas were colonized across the Bering Strait only once or on many occasions.

For archaeology, two types of DNA analysis have been employed. First, attempts have been made to extract DNA from ancient human remains. Archaeologists sat up and took notice when Swedish scientist Svante Pääbo announced in 1985 that he had succeeded in extracting 2,400-year-old DNA from an Egyptian mummy. The expectations this early success generated died away to some extent as problems of contamination became more and more apparent. The method has been given a recent fillip, however, by the announcement that Pääbo and his colleagues have succeeded in extracting DNA from Neandertal remains and found it to be significantly different from that of modern humans. If this is shown beyond question, then one of the longest-running enigmas in human evolution—whether Neandertals were a separate species or figure in our ancestry—will have been finally resolved.

Second, DNA has been studied through sampling modern populations of "indigenous" peoples (those known not to be recent immigrants). Biological anthropologist Robert Williams has sampled blood from thousands of American Indians and found they divide into two groups, with a third group formed by Eskimo-Aleut. Williams argues from this that America was settled by three separate incoming groups. Not everyone accepts these conclusions—and it is still early days for the study of ancient populations through DNA analysis—but here we see new techniques answering the age-old questions that lie behind so much archaeology: where are we from, and how did we come to be here?

The introduction of new techniques of many and varied kinds is perhaps archaeology's greatest success of the past 50 years. The discipline remains at heart a humanity or social science, but the new techniques allow archaeologists to ask new questions and to get new answers to old ones, squeezing ever more information out of a dwindling number of sites, as growing numbers of them are lost to development, looting, and natural processes such as erosion. But this technology doesn't come cheap. As archaeology becomes more and more sophisticated and better tooled, it also becomes more expensive, and as the quest for adequate funding becomes more intense, so does the need to convince the world at large that it is worth the cost.

CHRIS SCARRE is Deputy Director of the McDonald Institute for Archaeological Research at the University of Cambridge and editor of the Cambridge Archaeological Journal. _A specialist in French prehistory, he has written widely on archaeology and ancient history. This is the last in a series of articles documenting 50 years of archaeological achievement._

A Wasp's-Nest Clock

With a highly unusual dating technique, two Australian researchers have
identified what may be the world's oldest portrait of a human.

By Rachel F. Preiser

The rock outcroppings of the Kimberley region of northwestern Australia are painted, pecked, and engraved with vestiges of aboriginal art. Unfortunately, except for the odd charcoal sketch, most aboriginal rock art is nearly impossible to date—it is often colored with ocher, a mineral pigment that lacks the organic carbon compounds required by radioactive-dating techniques. Without an absolute scale, archeologists have had to rely on informed guesswork to date most aboriginal art. But that may soon change. Some Australian researchers have found a way to use fossilized wasps' nests to determine the age of ancient art.

Grahame Walsh, a rock-art specialist at the Takarakka Rock Art Research Center at Carnarvon Gorge, was studying the Kimberley paintings when he noticed that a nearby wasp's nest he had assumed to be of recent origin was in fact fossilized. Wasps' nests—made of a loosely packed fabric of sand, silt, and pollen grains—are not generally durable. But Walsh found that silica carried by water apparently seeped through the sandstone overlying the rock shelters and filled in the pores in the nest, reinforcing it to withstand the ravages of time.

Walsh realized that the sand grains worked into the nest would make it possible to date the nest. He contacted Richard Roberts, a geologist at La Trobe University in Melbourne who specializes in reading these grainy timepieces using a method known as optical luminescence dating. Radiation from radioactive trace elements in the sand bombards the grains. The radiation causes atoms in the grains to spit out electrons that become trapped in imperfections in the grains' crystalline structure. Here the displaced electrons remain until ultraviolet radiation in sunlight frees them from their crystal prisons. As the electrons return to more stable positions, each emits a photon of light. By exposing sand grains to light and measuring the intensity of the light emitted by the grains, geologists can estimate how long ago they were last exposed to sunlight.

Two years ago Roberts joined Walsh on an expedition to Kimberley in search of petrified wasps' nests built on top of rock art. While clambering around the rocky outcroppings, the researchers came across two fossilized nests overlying a mulberry-colored painting of a human figure whose elongated body, narrow head, and semicircular headdress suggested it belonged to a style believed by most archeologists to date back some 5,000 years. The researchers pried the fossilized nests free and extracted sand grains from their cores.

Using luminescence dating, Roberts discovered that the nests were more than 17,000 years old. That makes the underlying aboriginal rock painting the oldest depiction of a human figure in the world. Roberts believes the figure may actually be much older than the nest, since the Ice Age had reached its height at that time and the Kimberley region would thus have been arid and inhospitable to humans.

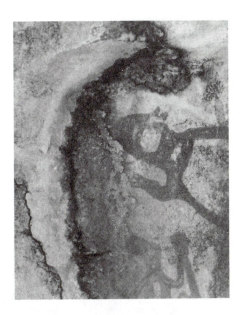

A fossilized wasp's nest lies just to the left of the painted figures. (Photo © Richard Roberts)

"Presumably the paintings were made during a previous, wetter period," says Roberts, "perhaps 25,000 to 30,000 years ago or even earlier, before the peak of the last glacial maximum." If he's right, the mulberry-colored figure may rival the oldest known paintings of animals—from the Chauvet cave in France—thought to be about 30,000 years old.

Although too sparse to date, the pollen found in the petrified nests can be used to identify the plants the wasps visited while building their homes many thousands of years ago. The nests Walsh and Roberts found contain mostly eucalyptus pollen and smatterings of pollen from an array of flowering plants and grasses. For Roberts, that makes the nests a still more important record, enabling a detailed reconstruction of the environment in which the ancient artists lived. "My feeling is that the greatest global application of the approach will be to examine past vegetation histories and infer past climate from preserved nests," says Roberts. "That wasn't the main aim of our project—the presence of pollen was pure luck but the combination of being able to date the rock art and reconstruct past environments makes wasp nests extremely versatile time capsules.".

From *Discover*, November 1997, p. 42. © 1997 by Rachel F. Preiser. Reprinted with permission of *the author*.

Profile of an Anthropologist

No Bone Unturned

Patrick Huyghe

The research of some physical anthropologists and archaeologists involves the discovery and analysis of old bones (as well as artifacts and other remains). Most often these bones represent only part of a skeleton or maybe the mixture of parts of several skeletons. Often these remains are smashed, burned, or partially destroyed. Over the years, physical anthropologists have developed a remarkable repertoire of skills and techniques for teasing the greatest possible amount of information out of sparse material remains.

Although originally developed for basic research, the methods of physical anthropology can be directly applied to contemporary human problems.... In this profile, we look briefly at the career of Clyde C. Snow, a physical anthropologist who has put these skills to work in a number of different settings....

As you read this selection, ask yourself the following questions:

- Given what you know of physical anthropology, what sort of work would a physical anthropologist do for the Federal Aviation Administration?
- What is anthropometry? *How might anthropometric surveys of pilots and passengers help in the design of aircraft equipment?*
- What is forensic anthropology? *How can a biological anthropologist be an expert witness in legal proceedings?*

Clyde Snow is never in a hurry. He knows he's late. He's always late. For Snow, being late is part of the job. In fact, he doesn't usually begin to work until death has stripped some poor individual to the bone, and no one—neither the local homicide detectives nor the pathologists—can figure out who once gave identity to the skeletonized remains. No one, that is, except a shrewd, laconic, 60-year-old forensic anthropologist.

Snow strolls into the Cook County Medical Examiner's Office in Chicago on this brisk October morning wearing a pair of Lucchese cowboy boots and a three-piece pin-striped suit. Waiting for him in autopsy room 160 are a bunch of naked skeletons found in Illinois, Wisconsin, and Minnesota since his last visit. Snow, a native Texan who now lives in rural Oklahoma, makes the trip up to Chicago some six times a year. The first case on his agenda is a pale brown skull found in the garbage of an abandoned building once occupied by a Chicago cosmetics company.

Snow turns the skull over slowly in his hands, a cigarette dangling from his fingers. One often does. Snow does not seem overly concerned about mortality, though its tragedy surrounds him daily.

"There's some trauma here," he says, examining a rough edge at the lower back of the skull. He points out the area to Jim Elliott, a homicide detective with the Chicago police. "This looks like a chopping blow by a heavy bladed instrument. Almost like a decapitation." In a place where the whining of bone saws drifts through hallways and the sweet-sour smell of death hangs in the air, the word surprises no one.

Snow begins thinking aloud. "I think what we're looking at here is a female, or maybe a small male, about thirty to forty years old. Probably Asian." He turns the skull upside down, pointing out the degree of wear on the teeth. "This was somebody who lived on a really rough diet. We don't normally find this kind of dental wear in a modern Western population."

"How long has it been around?" Elliott asks.

Snow raises the skull up to his nose. "It doesn't have any decompositional odors," he says. He pokes a finger in the skull's nooks and crannies. "There's no soft tissue left. It's good and dry. And it doesn't show signs of having been buried. I would say that this has been lying around in an attic or a box for years. It feels like a souvenir skull," says Snow.

Souvenir skulls, usually those of Japanese soldiers, were popular with U.S. troops serving in the Pacific during World War II; there was also a trade in skulls during the Vietnam War years. On closer inspection, though, Snow begins to wonder about the skull's Asian origins—the broad nasal aperture and the jutting forth of the upper-tooth-bearing part of the face suggest Melanesian features. Sifting through the objects found in the abandoned building with the skull, he finds several loose-leaf albums of 35-millimeter transparencies documenting life among the highland tribes of New Guinea. The slides, shot by an anthropologist, include graphic scenes of ritual warfare. The skull, Snow concludes, is more likely to be a trophy from one of these tribal battles than the result of a local Chicago homicide.

"So you'd treat it like found property?" Elliott asks finally. "Like somebody's garage-sale property?"

"Exactly," says Snow.

Clyde Snow is perhaps the world's most sought-after forensic anthropologist. People have been calling upon him to identify skeletons for more than a quarter of a century. Every year he's involved in some 75 cases of identification, most of them without fanfare. "He's an old scudder who doesn't have to blow his own whistle," says Walter Birkby, a forensic anthropologist at the University of Arizona. "He know's he's good."

Yet over the years Snow's work has turned him into something of an unlikely celebrity. He has been called upon to identify the remains of the Nazi war criminal Josef Mengele, reconstruct the face of the Egyptian boy-king Tutankhamen, confirm the authenticity of the body autopsied as that of President John F. Kennedy, and examine the skeletal remains of General Custer's men at the battlefield of the Little Bighorn. He has also been involved in the grim task of identifying the bodies in some of the United States' worst airline accidents.

Such is his legend that cases are sometimes attributed to him in which he played no part. He did not, as the *New York Times* reported, identify the remains of the crew of the *Challenger* disaster. But the man is often the equal of his myth. For the past four years, setting his personal safety aside, Snow has spent much of his time in Argentina, searching for the graves and identities of some of the thousands who "disappeared" between 1976 and 1983, during Argentina's military regime.

Snow did not set out to rescue the dead from oblivion. For almost two decades, until 1979, he was a physical anthropologist at the Civil Aeromedical Institute, part of the Federal Aviation Administration in Oklahoma City. Snow's job was to help engineers improve aircraft design and safety features by providing them with data on the human frame.

One study, he recalls, was initiated in response to complaints from a flight attendants' organization. An analysis of accident patterns had revealed that inadequate restraints on flight attendants'

jump seats were leading to deaths and injuries and that aircraft doors weighing several hundred pounds were impeding evacuation efforts. Snow points out that ensuring the survival of passengers in emergencies is largely the flight attendants' responsibility. "If they are injured or killed in a crash, you're going to find a lot of dead passengers."

Reasoning that equipment might be improved if engineers had more data on the size and strength of those who use it, Snow undertook a study that required meticulous measurement. When his report was issued in 1975, Senator William Proxmire was outraged that $57,800 of the taxpayers' money had been spent to caliper 423 airline stewardesses from head to toe. Yet the study, which received one of the senator's dubious Golden Fleece Awards, was firmly supported by both the FAA and the Association of Flight Attendants. "I can't imagine," says Snow with obvious delight, "how much coffee Proxmire got spilled on him in the next few months."

It was during his tenure at the FAA that he developed an interest in forensic work. Over the years the Oklahoma police frequently consulted the physical anthropologist for help in identifying crime victims. "The FAA figured it was a kind of community service to let me work on these cases," he says.

The experience also helped to prepare him for the grim task of identifying the victims of air disasters. In December 1972, when a United Airlines plane crashed outside Chicago, killing 43 of the 61 people aboard (including the wife of Watergate conspirator Howard Hunt, who was found with $10,000 in her purse), Snow was brought in to help examine the bodies. That same year, with Snow's help, forensic anthropology was recognized as a specialty by the American Academy of Forensic Sciences. "It got a lot of anthropologists interested in forensics," he says, "and it made a lot of pathologists out there aware that there were anthropologists who could help them."

Each nameless skeleton poses a unique mystery for Snow. But some, like the second case awaiting him back in the autopsy room at the Cook County morgue, are more challenging than oth-

ers. This one is a real chiller. In a large cardboard box lies a jumble of bones along with a tattered leg from a pair of blue jeans, a sock shrunk tightly around the bones of a foot, a pair of Nike running shoes without shoelaces, and, inside the hood of a blue windbreaker, a mass of stringy, blood-caked hair. The remains were discovered frozen in ice about 20 miles outside Milwaukee. A rusted bicycle was found lying close by. Paul Hibbard, chief deputy medical examiner for Waukesha County, who brought the skeleton to Chicago, says no one has been reported missing.

Snow lifts the bones out of the box and begins reconstructing the skeleton on an autopsy table. "There are two hundred six bones and thirty-two teeth in the human body," he says, "and each has a story to tell." Because bone is dynamic, living tissue, many of life's significant events—injuries, illness, childbearing—leave their mark on the body's internal framework. Put together the stories told by these bones, he says, and what you have is a person's "osteobiography."

Snow begins by determining the sex of the skeleton, which is not always obvious. He tells the story of a skeleton that was brought to his FAA office in the late 1970s. It had been found along with some women's clothes and a purse in a local back lot, and the police had assumed that it was female. But when Snow examined the bones, he realized that "at six foot three, she would have probably have been the tallest female in Oklahoma."

Then Snow recalled that six months earlier the custodian in his building had suddenly not shown up for work. The man's supervisor later mentioned to Snow, "You know, one of these days when they find Ronnie, he's going to be dressed as a woman." Ronnie, it turned out, was a weekend transvestite. A copy of his dental records later confirmed that the skeleton in women's clothing was indeed Snow's janitor.

The Wisconsin bike rider is also male. Snow picks out two large bones that look something like twisted oysters—the innominates, or hipbones, which along with the sacrum, or lower backbone, form the pelvis. This pelvis is narrow and steep-walled like a male's, not broad and shallow like a female's. And the sciatic notch (the V-shaped space where the sciatic nerve passes through the hipbone) is narrow, as is normal in a male. Snow can also determine a skeleton's sex by checking the size of the mastoid processes (the bony knobs at the base of the skull) and the prominence of the brow ridge, or by measuring the head of an available limb bone, which is typically broader in males.

From an examination of the skull he concludes that the bike rider is "predominantly Caucasoid." A score of bony traits help the forensic anthropologist assign a skeleton to one of the three major racial groups: Negroid, Caucasoid, or Mongoloid. Snow notes that the ridge of the boy's nose is high and salient, as it is in whites. In Negroids and Mongoloids (which include American Indians as well as most Asians) the nose tends to be broad in relation to its height. However, the boy's nasal margins are somewhat smoothed down, usually a Mongoloid feature. "Possibly a bit of American Indian admixture," says Snow. "Do you have Indians in your area?" Hibbard nods.

Age is next. Snow takes the skull and turns it upside down, pointing out the basilar joint, the junction between the two major bones that form the underside of the skull. In a child the joint would still be open to allow room for growth, but here the joint has fused—something that usually happens in the late teen years. On the other hand, he says, pointing to the zigzagging lines on the dome of the skull, the cranial sutures are open. The cranial sutures, which join the bones of the braincase, begin to fuse and disappear in the mid-twenties.

Next Snow picks up a femur and looks for signs of growth at the point where the shaft meets the knobbed end. The thin plates of cartilage—areas of incomplete calcification—that are visible at this point suggest that the boy hadn't yet attained his full height. Snow double-checks with an examination of the pubic symphysis, the joint where the two hipbones meet. The ridges in this area, which fill in and smooth over in adulthood, are still clearly marked. He concludes that the skeleton is that of a boy between 15 and 20 years old.

"One of the things you learn is to be pretty conservative," says Snow. "It's very impressive when you tell the police, 'This person is eighteen years old,' and he turns out to be eighteen. The problem is, if the person is fifteen you've blown it—you probably won't find him. Looking for a missing person is like trying to catch fish. Better get a big net and do your own sorting."

Snow then picks up a leg bone, measures it with a set of calipers, and enters the data into a portable computer. Using the known correlation between the height and length of the long limb bones, he quickly estimates the boy's height. "He's five foot six and a half to five foot eleven," says Snow. "Medium build, not excessively muscular, judging from the muscle attachments that we see." He points to the grainy ridges that appear where muscle attaches itself to the bone. The most prominent attachments show up on the teenager's right arm bone, indicating right-handedness.

Then Snow examines the ribs one by one for signs of injury. He finds no stab wounds, cuts, or bullet holes, here or elsewhere on the skeleton. He picks up the hyoid bone from the boy's throat and looks for the tell-tale fracture signs that would suggest the boy was strangled. But, to Snow's frustration, he can find no obvious cause of death. In hopes of identifying the missing teenager, he suggests sending the skull, hair, and boy's description to Betty Pat Gatliff, a medical illustrator and sculptor in Oklahoma who does facial reconstructions.

Six weeks later photographs of the boy's likeness appear in the *Milwaukee Sentinel*. "If you persist long enough," says Snow, "eighty-five to ninety percent of the cases eventually get positively identified, but it can take anywhere from a few weeks to a few years."

Snow and Gatliff have collaborated many times, but never with more glitz than in 1983, when Snow was commissioned by Patrick Barry, a Miami orthopedic surgeon and amateur Egyptologist, to reconstruct the face of the Egyptian boy-king Tutankhamen. Normally a facial reconstruction begins with a skull, but since Tutankhamen's 3,000-year-old remains were in Egypt, Snow had to

make do with the skull measurements from a 1925 postmortem and X-rays taken in 1975. A plaster model of the skull was made, and on the basis on Snow's report—"his skull is Caucasoid with some Negroid admixtures"—Gatliff put a face on it. What did Tutankhamen look like? Very much like the gold mask on his sarcophagus, says Snow, confirming that it was, indeed, his portrait.

Many cite Snow's use of facial reconstructions as one of his most important contributions to the field. Snow, typically self-effacing, says that Gatliff "does all the work." The identification of skeletal remains, he stresses, is often a collaboration between pathologists, odontologists, radiologists, and medical artists using a variety of forensic techniques.

One of Snow's last tasks at the FAA was to help identify the dead from the worst airline accident in U.S. history. On May 25, 1979, a DC-10 crashed shortly after takeoff from Chicago's O'Hare Airport, killing 273 people. The task facing Snow and more than a dozen forensic specialists was horrific. "No one ever sat down and counted," says Snow, "but we estimated ten thousand to twelve thousand pieces or parts of bodies." Nearly 80 percent of the victims were identified on the basis of dental evidence and fingerprints. Snow and forensic radiologist John Fitzpatrick later managed to identify two dozen others by comparing postmortem X-rays with X-rays taken during the victim's lifetime.

Next to dental records, such X-ray comparisons are the most common way of obtaining positive identifications. In 1978, when a congressional committee reviewed the evidence on John F. Kennedy's assassination, Snow used X-rays to show that the body autopsied at Bethesda Naval Hospital was indeed that of the late president and had not—as some conspiracy theorists believed—been switched.

The issue was resolved on the evidence of Kennedy's "sinus print," the scalloplike pattern on the upper margins of the sinuses that is visible in X-rays of the forehead. So characteristic is a person's sinus print that courts throughout the world accept the matching of antemortem and postmortem X-rays of the sinuses as positive identification.

Yet another technique in the forensic specialist's repertoire is photo superposition. Snow used it in 1977 to help identify the mummy of a famous Oklahoma outlaw named Elmer J. McCurdy, who was killed by a posse after holding up a train in 1911. For years the mummy had been exhibited as a "dummy" in a California funhouse—until it was found to have a real human skeleton inside it. Ownership of the mummy was eventually traced back to a funeral parlor in Oklahoma, where McCurdy had been embalmed and exhibited as "the bandit who wouldn't give up."

Using two video cameras and an image processor, Snow superposed the mummy's profile on a photograph of McCurdy that was taken shortly after his death. When displayed on a single monitor, the two coincided to a remarkable degree. Convinced by the evidence, Thomas Noguchi, then Los Angeles County corner, signed McCurdy's death certificate ("Last known occupation: Train robber") and allowed the outlaw's bones to be returned to Oklahoma for a decent burial.

It was this technique that also allowed forensic scientists to identify the remains of the Nazi "Angel of Death," Josef Mengele, in the summer of 1985. A team of investigators, including Snow and West German forensic anthropologist Richard Helmer, flew to Brazil after an Austrian couple claimed that Mengele lay buried in a grave on a São Paulo hillside. Tests revealed that the stature, age, and hair color of the unearthed skeleton were consistent with information in Mengele's SS files; yet without X-rays or dental records, the scientists still lacked conclusive evidence. When an image of the reconstructed skull was superposed on 1930s photographs of Mengele, however, the match was eerily compelling. All doubts were removed a few months later when Mengele's dental X-rays were tracked down.

In 1979 Snow retired from the FAA to the rolling hills of Norman, Oklahoma, where he and his wife, Jerry, live in a sprawling, early-1960s ranch house. Unlike his 50 or so fellow forensic anthropologists, most of whom are tied to academic positions, Snow is free to pursue his consultancy work full-time. Judging from the number of miles that he logs in the average month, Snow is clearly not ready to retire for good.

His recent projects include a reexamination of the skeletal remains found at the site of the Battle of the Little Bighorn, where more than a century ago Custer and his 210 men were killed by Sioux and Cheyenne warriors. Although most of the enlisted men's remains were moved to a mass grave in 1881, an excavation of the battlefield in the past few years uncovered an additional 375 bones and 36 teeth. Snow, teaming up again with Fitzpatrick, determined that these remains belonged to 34 individuals.

The historical accounts of Custer's desperate last stand are vividly confirmed by their findings. Snow identified one skeleton as that of a soldier between the ages of 19 and 23 who weighed around 150 pounds and stood about five foot eight. He'd sustained gunshot wounds to his chest and left forearm. Heavy blows to his head had fractured his skull and sheared off his teeth. Gashed thigh bones indicated that his body was later dismembered with an ax or hatchet.

Given the condition and number of the bodies, Snow seriously questions the accuracy of the identifications made by the original nineteenth-century burial crews. He doubts, for example, that the skeleton buried at West Point is General Custer's.

For the last four years Snow has devoted much of his time to helping two countries come to terms with the horrors of a much more recent past. As part of a group sponsored by the American Association for the Advancement of Science, he has been helping the Argentinian National Commission on Disappeared Persons to determine the fate of some of those who vanished during their country's harsh military rule: between 1976 and 1983 at least 10,000 people were systematically swept off the streets by roving death squads to be tortured, killed, and buried in unmarked graves. In December 1986, at the invitation of the Aquino government's Human Rights Commission, Snow also spent several weeks training Philippine scientists to investigate the disappearances that occurred under the Marcos regime.

But it is in Argentina where Snow has done the bulk of his human-rights work. He has spent more than 27 months in and around Buenos Aires, first training a small group of local medical and anthropology students in the techniques of forensic investigation, and later helping them carefully exhume and examine scores of the *desaparecidos*, or disappeared ones.

Only 25 victims have so far been positively identified. But the evidence has helped convict seven junta members and other high-ranking military and police officers. The idea is not necessarily to identify all 10,000 of the missing, says Snow. "If you have a colonel who ran a detention center where maybe five hundred people were killed, you don't have to nail them with five hundred deaths. Just one or two should be sufficient to get him convicted." Forensic evidence from Snow's team may be used to prosecute several other military officers, including General Suarez Mason. Mason is the former commander of the I Army Corps in Buenos Aires and is believed to be responsible for thousands of disappearances. He was recently extradited from San Francisco back to Argentina, where he is expected to stand trial this winter [1988].

The investigations have been hampered by a frustrating lack of antemortem information. In 1984, when commission lawyers took depositions from relatives and friends of the disappeared, they often failed to obtain such basic information as the victim's height, weight, or hair color. Nor did they ask for the missing person's X-rays (which in Argentina are given to the patient) or the address of the victim's dentist. The problem was compounded by the inexperience of those who carried out the first mass exhumations prior to Snow's arrival. Many of the skeletons were inadvertently destroyed by bulldozers as they were brought up.

Every unearthed skeleton that shows signs of gunfire, however, helps to erode the claim once made by many in the Argentinian military that most of the *desaparecidos* are alive and well and living in Mexico City, Madrid, or Paris. Snow recalls the case of a 17-year-old boy named Gabriel Dunayavich, who disappeared in the summer of 1976. He was walking home from a movie with his girlfriend when a Ford Falcon with no license plates snatched him off the street. The police later found his body and that of another boy and girl dumped by the roadside on the outskirts of Buenos Aires. The police went through the motions of an investigation, taking photographs and doing an autopsy, then buried the three teenagers in an unmarked grave.

A decade later Snow, with the help of the boy's family, traced the autopsy reports, the police photographs, and the grave of the three youngsters. Each of them had four or five closely spaced bullet wounds in the upper chest—the signature, says Snow, of an automatic weapon. Two also had wounds on their arms from bullets that had entered behind the elbow and exited from the forearm.

"That means they were conscious when they were shot," says Snow. "When a gun was pointed at them, they naturally raised their arm." It's details like these that help to authenticate the last moments of the victims and bring a dimension of reality to the judges and jury.

Each time Snow returns from Argentina he says that this will be the last time. A few months later he is back in Buenos Aires. "There's always more work to do," he says. It is, he admits quietly, "terrible work."

"These were such brutal, cold-blooded crimes," he says. "The people who committed them not only murdered; they had a system to eliminate all trace that their victims even existed."

Snow will not let them obliterate their crimes so conveniently. "There are human-rights violations going on all around the world," he says. "But to me murder is murder, regardless of the motive. I hope that we are sending a message to governments who murder in the name of politics that they can be held to account."

From *Discover* magazine, December 1988, pp. 51–56. © 1988 by Patrick Huyghe. Reprinted with permission of the author.

SIMULATING ANCIENT SOCIETIES

Computer modeling is helping unravel the archaeological mysteries of the American Southwest

Timothy A. Kohler
George J. Gumerman and
Robert G. Reynolds

Only a small fraction of human history is known through texts. For the rest, archaeology is the main source. By examining ruins, artifacts and remains, archaeologists have painstakingly constructed a series of pictures showing human societies as they existed thousands and even millions of years ago. It is much more difficult, however, to determine the processes that produced and changed these societies. Researchers are still struggling to understand the long chain of cause-and-effect (and chance events) stretching from our hominid ancestors of four million years ago—small bands of upright-walking primates with no stone tools and scarcely any conversation—to the communities and cultures we see around the world today.

With the advent of computers, archaeologists began to experiment with simulation as an aid to exploring human prehistory. The logic is simple: you program the computer to mimic processes such as population growth and resource usage, then see how well the software's predictions coincide with the archaeological record. An early example is the well-known attempt in the late 1970s to examine the collapse of the Classic Maya civilization, which dominated a vast swath of Mexico and Central America from A.D. 300 to 900. Led by researchers at the Massachusetts Institute of Technology, this effort looked at the relations between variables such as total population and the rate of construction of Mayan monuments. Because the study considered the variables in aggregate form, however, it could not provide information on spatial relations—for instance, which areas of the Mayan territory had the highest agricultural production.

This research promises to shed some light on the calamities that engulfed Puebloan society.

In recent years, though, a new style of computer language has encouraged the development of more detailed simulations of ancient societies. Object-oriented programming languages such as Java allow researchers to create models containing many interacting agents, which can represent individual households distributed across a landscape. The interactions between the agents can simulate the formation of alliances or the exchange of resources or information. Programmers give the agents built-in rules to specify their actions, but the agents can learn to acquire new behaviors as well.

Our own simulations have focused on the prehistory of the North American Southwest, particularly the Four Corners area where the states of Arizona, New Mexico, Colorado and Utah meet. This region, home to the ancient Puebloan peoples (also called the Anasazi), has one of the best-known archaeological records in the world, especially for the 1,000 years before the Spaniards arrived in the 16th century. Puebloan culture in this area reached its apex between A.D. 1000 and 1300 with the construction of elaborate towns and cliff dwellings, but by the end of this period the Puebloans had abruptly abandoned their settlements and migrated south to central and eastern Arizona, western New Mexico and the northern Rio Grande Valley.

By comparing the cut timber at Puebloan sites with the tree-ring records for the area, archaeologists can often date the occupation of the settlements quite precisely. Also, paleoclimatologists can use data from tree rings, pollen analysis and the local geology to determine the temperatures and precipitation at the time. Currently we have two agent-based modeling projects that employ this information to reconstruct Puebloan settlement and land-use patterns in the Long House Valley in Arizona and the Central Mesa Verde region in Colorado. This research promises to enhance our understanding of the ancient Puebloans and perhaps shed some light on the mysterious calamities that engulfed their society about 700 years ago.

A Virtual Prehistory

LONG HOUSE VALLEY is a 180-square-kilometer landform in northeastern Arizona that was inhabited by Puebloans from about 1800 B.C. to about A.D. 1300. The valley has been the subject of intensive archaeological investigation for a century, and over the past 25 years multidisciplinary teams led by Jeffrey S. Dean of the University of Arizona's Laboratory of Tree-Ring Research have reconstructed its past environment in great detail. Basing their analysis on precipitation patterns, watertable fluctuations, and cycles of erosion and deposition, Dean and one of us (Gumerman) estimated the maize-growing potential for each hectare in the valley for every year from A.D. 400 to 1450.

Our simulations for the Long House Valley derived from an agent-based computer program developed by Joshua M. Epstein and Robert L. Axtell of the Brookings Institution and the Santa Fe Institute. We began by entering the environmental data on a digitized map of the valley, then placed the agents—simulated households—randomly on the map. The characteristics of the modeled households, such as their nutritional requirements, were based on archaeological data as well as ethnographic studies of contemporary Pueblo groups and other subsistence farmers. In our original model

we assumed that each household consisted of five individuals, each individual consumed 160 kilograms of maize per year, only 64 percent of the potential maize yield could be eaten (to account for losses from rodents, insects and so on), and up to 1,600 kilograms of corn could be stored.

The program implemented simple rules to model settlement patterns. A household would move to a different location in the valley if the expected yield from its farm plot, combined with the amount of grain in storage, fell below what was necessary to sustain the family. Also, a new household would be created whenever a daughter reached the age of 15 (when she would presumably marry and move out). A household's residence had to be located within one kilometer of its farm plot and as close as possible to water sources. The program allowed researchers to adjust certain variables, such as fertility and life expectancy.

Overview/Virtual Archaeology

- With the help of new agent-based software, archaeologists have created computer models showing how environmental conditions could have shaped the history of the Puebloan peoples of the U.S. Southwest.
- The simulations suggest that the mysterious disappearance of the Puebloans from Mesa Verde and adjacent areas cannot be entirely explained by the severe drought that occurred in the late 1200s.
- To examine other factors that may have influenced the Puebloans, researchers are building new models that simulate the effects of hunting, fuelwood collection, and cultural processes such as trade and gift giving.

The simulations indicated that environmental conditions largely determined the placement and size of the residences as well as the ebb and flow of population density over time (see box above). The locations of the virtual residences turned out to be quite

near the actual house sites discovered and dated by archaeologists working in the Long House Valley. The original model had one significant discrepancy from reality: the program predicted a population about six times as large as that estimated from archaeological evidence. But when we readjusted the farm production levels to those expected for prehistoric varieties of maize and varied the fertility and longevity of the households, the predicted populations tracked the actual numbers much more closely.

The studies also showed the dramatic effects of the deteriorating environment during the late 1200s, when a long drought coincided with falling groundwater levels. The number of virtual households dropped from more than 200 in 1250 to about 80 half a century later. According to the archaeological evidence, however, Long House Valley was completely empty by the 1300s. Although the environmental conditions could have supported a small population, all the Puebloans in the valley either died or moved away. We can only conclude that sociopolitical, ideological or environmental factors not included in our model must have contributed to the total depopulation of the valley. Perhaps the dearth of food made the Puebloans more susceptible to epidemic diseases. Or perhaps the devastated population could no longer maintain their cultural or religious institutions, leading to a collective decision to leave the valley.

Pit Houses to Great Houses

AN ALLIED SERIES of experiments begun at the Santa Fe Institute uses agent-based modeling to study the prehistory of southwestern Colorado. This area, most of which was originally covered with sagebrush parklands or sparse forests of piñon and juniper, was colonized by farmers around A.D. 600 during the period archaeologists call Basketmaker III. Households lived in pit houses, semisubterranean dwellings where the earthen sides of a shallow pit formed the lower parts of the walls. Pit houses were grouped in hamlets, which were in turn organized in small neighborhoods or communities. Hunting was almost as important as agriculture in their diet. The pioneers were very successful, and aided by additional immigration, their numbers increased markedly. Villages of hundreds of people—a dramatic change in settlement form—appeared in the area in the late 700s, and some became considerably larger by the late 800s. Two of us (Kohler and Reynolds) are investigating why these villages formed where and when they did: Was it perhaps a response to the economic advantages of those locations? Or was it for protection?

These villages were abandoned around 900 when most of the Puebloan peoples left the area. The reasons for this depopulation are under debate. Two possible causes may be deforestation near the villages and a series of cool, dry summers. (The normal climatic variation in this area is from warm, dry weather to cool, wet conditions; cool, dry weather presents special problems for local farmers who depend on rainfall rather than irrigation.) During the 900s and 1000s the conditions for farming improved, both here and throughout the northern Southwest, and local populations slowly rebounded. The raising of domesticated turkey became increasingly important in this period. Once again, most people lived in small hamlets grouped in loose communities. By the late 1000s the villages that acted as centers for these dispersed communities became larger and more numerous. Many appear to have been influenced by the complex Puebloan settlements in Chaco Canyon to the south, in what is now northwestern New Mexico. Some of the Colorado villages have "great houses"—multistory buildings containing many rooms—that resemble structures at Chaco more than they do local architectural styles. The presence of some stockaded sites in our study area in the mid-1000s may represent resistance, ultimately futile, to a Chacoan expansion.

Chaco-style great houses ceased to be built around 1135 at the beginning of a severe 45-year-long drought, a transition marked by episodes of extreme violence, including possible cannibalism. Population growth slowed in the Central Mesa Verde region, but the pattern of larger community centers and smaller surrounding hamlets persisted. By the mid-1200s most community centers shifted to more defensible canyon-head locations or alcoves such as the famous cliff dwellings in Mesa Verde National Park. As elsewhere in the northern Southwest, the occupation of this area terminated in the late 1200s as the remaining population fled to the south and east from the large canyon-head villages amid unfavorable climatic conditions and violence. Explaining this dramatic de-

population remains one of the classic problems of archaeology.

Our simulations cover an 1,800 square-kilometer area northwest of Mesa Verde National Park. We divided the virtual landscape into 45,400 square cells, each 200 meters on a side, with the potential maize productivity for each cell based on its soil type and elevation as well as the yearly precipitation. (Carla R. Van West, now at Statistical Research in Tucson, Ariz., constructed our original annual productivity landscapes as part of her Ph.D. project at Washington State University.) Our early research examined only the period from 900 to 1300. As with the Long House Valley simulation, we generated a random distribution of households and endowed them with rules specifying that they should locate on or near the highest-productivity farming areas not already in use.

The settlement patterns produced by these agents roughly matched the real patterns known from archaeological research in the region. When we also required that the agents take into account the distribution of water in their decisions about where to live—a reasonable assumption given the semiarid landscape—the results were better approximations of the real patterns. Finally, when we adjusted the program to account for the slow degradation of soil under subsistence farming, which would cause households to periodically seek out new plots, the settlement patterns fit the known record better still.

Once again, however, none of our simulations terminated with a population decline as dramatic as what actually happened in the Mesa Verde region in the late 1200s. What other factors could have contributed to the catastrophe? One factor that we didn't model is the distribution of surface water in the area, which probably changed as the climate shifted. During the late 1200s, the Puebloan villages clustered around springs, and any cessation of their flow could have been disastrous. Furthermore, the depopulation of our study area (and the rest of the northern Southwest) took place near the onset of the Little Ice Age, a generally cold period from about 1300 to 1850 whose effects in the Southwest remain controversial. Because our area is both high in elevation and near the local northern limit for maize farming at this time in prehistory, even a slight decline in growing-season temperatures or in the length of the growing season could have had perilous consequences.

One thing that is becoming apparent from work now being conducted by Washington State University graduate students C. David Johnson and Jason A. Cowan is that the Puebloan peoples depleted the fuelwood in the Mesa Verde region. Johnson and Cowan assumed that Puebloan households burned 1.1 metric tons of wood per person every year, similar to the rates observed for societies in Pakistan at roughly similar elevations and latitudes. Simulations showed that 700 years of fuel use would have denuded large tracts around the settlements. We are now creating similar programs to model the long-term effects of hunting on the major game in the region (deer, rabbits and jackrabbits). Our initial studies strongly suggest that hunting would have wiped out most of the deer in the area, which may explain why domesticated turkey became so important to the Puebloan diet after 900.

One of the great benefits of computer simulation is that it allows researchers to conduct experiments, a luxury that is otherwise impossible in an historical science such as archaeology. Scientists can incrementally add detail to their models, testing new environmental and social factors to see if they bring the virtual prehistory closer to the archaeological record. As we extend our research back to 600, we are now using simulations to study the dramatic growth and decline of the early Pueblo villages. The Crow Canyon Archaeological Center in Cortez, Colo., has recently completed new field surveys and an extensive program to redate the more than 3,300 residential sites found in our study area. This work has significantly increased our knowledge of the distribution of Puebloan households over time, providing more precise maps to compare with the simulated household behavior.

Meanwhile Kenneth E. Kolm, a hydrologist at Washington State University and BBL, Inc., and Schaun Smith, a graduate student at the Colorado School of Mines, are developing a model that estimates how much the swings in temperature and precipitation in the study area affected the local springs and streams. When this model is coupled with our settlement simulation, we will be able to see whether changing distributions of water resources could have influenced the decisions of the Puebloan peoples about where to live and farm. We are also incorporating the effects of temperature on farm productivity. Finally, and perhaps most intriguingly, we are making attempts to simulate some of the social and cultural factors that shaped Puebloan societies.

TIMOTHY A. KOHLER, GEORGE J. GUMERMAN AND ROBERT G. REYNOLDS have applied their various talents and expertise to the problem of simulating ancient societies. Kohler is a professor in the department of anthropology at Washington State University and a research associate at the Crow Canyon Archaeological Center in Cortez, Colo. He has worked in the U.S. Southwest for more than 20 years, primarily in southwestern Colorado and the northern Rio Grande Valley in New Mexico. Gumerman, the interim president of the School of American Research in Santa Fe, has done archaeology in the Southwest for more than 30 years and published more than 20 volumes on the topic. (Both Kohler and Gumerman are also external faculty members at the Santa Fe Institute.) Reynolds is a professor of computer science at Wayne State University and an associate research scientist in the Museum of Anthropology at the University of Michigan at Ann Arbor. He has written two books and numerous articles on cultural algorithms. *The authors would like to acknowledge the support of the National Science Foundation.*

What Did They Eat?

Eleanora Reber (Harvard)

Most archaeologists know that visible food residues can appear on potsherds, offering a possibility of dietary reconstruction. Visible residues are not, however, the only means of identifying the contents of pots. When an unglazed pottery vessel is used for cooking, lipids and water-soluble compounds from the contents absorb into the vessel walls. These absorbed residues, which are protected by the unyielding clay matrix from chemical degradation, can be extracted and identified.

MAKINGS OF PREHISTORIC STEW

As a meal is cooked in an unglazed vessel, the prehistoric cook may have added a variety of foods into a stew. From the cook's point of view, she was boiling food until properly cooked, serving, then rinsing the vessel for its next use. On the molecular level, as the foods were added to the stew, heat and the circulation of water caused fats, vitamins, starches, proteins and other substances to circulate through the water, and to be absorbed by the walls of the pot. Bacteria may have begun to work on the foods even before they were added to the pot; if the vessel was not washed for several hours following cooking, even more spoilage could occur. Water-soluble chemicals—such as most vitamins—absorbed into the pot are easily washed out by groundwater following archaeological deposition of the pot. Less water-soluble chemicals, however, once safely absorbed into the walls of the pot become a fixture until polluted by modern

solvents or chemicals, or removed for study.

EXTRACTION TO RECONSTRUCTION

The procedure for residue identification involves extraction of preserved residue from the walls of a vessel. Because these residues are held in the walls of the vessel by weak chemical bonds, their recovery involves powdering 1–3 grams of the sherd, and then extracting the powder with solvent. This destructive procedure is painful for both the archaeologist and analyst, and is not undertaken lightly.

The precious residue-impregnated solvent is then evaporated to produce a tiny amount of unimpressive grease, which is injected into a chemical instrument called a gas chromatograph/mass spectrometer. This instrument separates the residue into its component compounds, and identifies each compound through its molecular fragments.

With the habits of our prehistoric cook in mind, however, it is clear that identifying diet from a residue is not a simple task. Many pottery vessels were used for more than one type of food. If a vessel was used for cooking, we need to consider the effect of heat on the foods. Furthermore, even when absorbed into a pot, some degradation of the chemicals can slowly occur. Polyunsaturated fats tend to degrade first, then monounsaturated fats, leaving the saturated fats behind. Bacterial action complicates matters further. So, the analyst looks for marker compounds—compounds that are unique to a particular food or group

of foods, such as cholesterol in meat, theobromine in cocoa, or leaf waxes in turnips or cabbage. Ratios of lipids can also tell the analyst something about the basic classes of foods. If a high ratio of unsaturates to saturates survives, it suggests the presence of vegetables or grain.

IDENTIFYING MAIZE

Although analysis of absorbed residues is not infallible, and cannot identify everything cooked in a pot, the technique is already useful. Stable isotopic data give a snapshot of the residue. The presence of meat or vegetable can be determined with a fairly high degree of certainty. In an ambiguous pot it is also possible to tell whether or not food in a pot has been cooked, thereby answering questions about vessel function. If marker compounds are present, the corresponding food can be identified. Many, or perhaps even most foods may have marker compounds, but to discover this, each food must be carefully investigated. This is a worthy goal, and one that attracts students to the field, but progress is, of necessity, slow.

One archaeological application of residue is my own research, in which I am developing a technique using stable isotope and lipid analysis to identify maize residues. When established I will apply the technique to Mississippian pottery from a variety of temporal and geographical locations. The appearance of maize in residues should correspond to the change in cooking vessel thickness and temper, which has generally been attributed to the appearance of maize in the region. Thus, residue analysis can answer a variety of archaeological and anthropological questions by any researcher with questions about diet and pottery.

SAVE YOUR RESIDUES!

Once an absorbed residue is safely preserved inside the matrix of the clay, few things can remove or damage it. One of these culprits, unfortunately, is post-excavation washing or treatment of a sherd. Acid-washing and varnish-ing both damage absorbed residues irretrievably. Labeling a sherd with a nail polish and white-out will also contaminate residues, though they may be salvageable. Touching a sherd during excavation or storing it in a plastic bag can result in modern residues which may make the analysis of older remains difficult. A sherd submitted for residue study should not be washed, it should be touched as little as possible and stored and sent to the lab in tin foil or acid-free paper.

Eleanora Reber is presently in the doctoral program at Harvard U, Department of Anthropology. Following an undergraduate career at Beloit College as a chemistry/anthropology major, she spent time digging for contract firms. She is presently working on a preliminary study involving the identification of maize residues in pottery from around the world. One hundred sherds are needed, and analysis will be free of charge. If you have a sherd which you believe has been used to cook maize, please send samples and inquires, by March 1, to: Eleanora Reber, Dept of Anthropology, Harvard, 11 Divinity Ave, Cambridge, MA 02138; 617/495-4388, reber@fas.harvard.edu.

UNIT 4

Historical Archaeology

Unit Selections

Key Points to Consider

- What is historical archaeology? Give some examples.

- What do excavations at Hierakonpolis tell us about the economic underpinnings of pharaonic civilization?

- What evidence is there that early Israel was polytheistic?

- Recent historical data on the Aztec provinces give a different view of the distribution of wealth and services in that empire. What are these revised views?

- What has the excavation of the Medici tombs revealed about the lives and deaths of Florence's first family?

- How is the Donner Pass story an example of cultural/historical reconstruction, even though it is not strictly archaeology?

Student Website

www.mhcls.com/online

Internet References

Further information regarding these websites may be found in this book's preface or online.

GIS and Remote Sensing for Archaeology: Burgundy, France
   http://www.informatics.org/france/france.html

Petra Great Temple/Technology
   http://www.brown.edu/Departments/Anthropology/Petra/excavations/technology.html

Radiocarbon Dating for Archaeology
   http://www.rlaha.ox.ac.uk/orau/index.html

Zeno's Forensic Page
   http://forensic.to/forensic.html

How many times have you misplaced your car keys? Locked yourself out of the house? Lost your wallet? Your address book? Eyeglasses? Sometimes these artifacts are recovered and brought back into the historical present. Sometimes they are lost forever, becoming part of the garbage of an extinct culture. Have you ever noticed that lost things, when found, are always in the last place you look? Is this a law of science? Be skeptical.

Here is an opportunity to practice historical archaeology. You may wish to try this puzzler in order to practice thinking like an archaeologist. (Do not forget to apply the basics discussed in unit 1.) The incident recounted here is true. Only the names, dates, and places were changed to protect the privacy of the famous personages involved in this highly-charged mystery.

Problem: Dr. Wheeler, a British archaeologist at a large university left his office on December 17, 2003, around 10 P.M. on a cold Friday evening. This was his last night to be at the university because he would not be back again until after the holidays. Right before he left his office, he placed a thin, reddish, three-ring notebook in an unlocked cupboard in his office.

Dr. Wheeler then proceeded to go directly to his designated campus parking space, got into his Mini Cooper S, and drove directly to his flat in Marshalltown Goldens. When he arrived at home he went straightaway to his study. He remained at his flat with his family and never left his flat during the entire holiday.

Dr. Wheeler and family had a jolly good holiday and Dr. Wheeler thought nothing more of his notebook until the university resumed its session on Wednesday, January 5, 2004 at the beginning of the New Year.

Upon returning to his office, Dr. Wheeler could not find his notebook in the cupboard, and he became very agitated. He chased his assistant, Miss Mortimer, around the office, wielding a wicked looking Acheulean hand ax. Poor Miss Mortimer claimed she had no knowledge of the whereabouts of the notebook. But Dr. Wheeler had always suspected that Miss Mortimer pinched pens and pencils from his desk, so, naturally.... But Miss Mortimer protested so earnestly that Dr. Wheeler eventually settled in, had a cup of tea, and decided that perhaps he had absentmindedly taken the notebook home after all.

However, a thorough search of his flat indicated that the notebook was clearly not there. It was lost! Dr. Wheeler was almost lost himself when his wife, Sophia, caught him excavating her rose garden in the vain hope that Tut, the family dog, had buried the lost article there. It was a professor's nightmare, since the notebook contained the only copy of all his class records for the entire term. What could he do? He knew he was in danger of being fired for incompetence.

So, Dr. Wheeler approached the problem in the manner of a proper, eccentric archaeologist. He had another cup of tea and generated several hypotheses about where his notebook might have gone. He tested several hypotheses, but to no avail! His notebook still remained missing. However, being the good archaeologist he is, he kept on generating hypotheses. But his notebook was still not found. Then he began to wonder if maybe the post-processualists weren't right after all!

Dr. Wheeler was at his wit's ends when, sometimes as it happens, pure luck intervened as it often does in archaeology. You just get lucky sometimes. Everyone does. His faithful assistant Miss Mortimer received a phone call on January 9, 2004, from a woman who had found the missing notebook on the evening of December 31, 2003. The helpful lady found his notebook in a gutter! To be precise, she found it in a family neighborhood located on the corner of Olduvai Drive and East Turkana Avenue in Hadar Heights, about 1 mile away from the university. Please note that this area is in the opposite direction from Dr. Wheeler's flat in Marshalltown Goldens. The notebook was wet and muddy, and furthermore, it was wedged down into a gutter grill in the street.

Greatly relieved, the next day, January 10, 2004, Dr. Wheeler has Miss Mortimer run over to the kind woman's flat. So it was in this mysterious way that he recouped his class records. Dr. Wheeler was so delighted that when Miss Mortimer returned with the notebook, he invited her to sit and join him for a spot of tea (which was not his habit, being misogynist). Yet, Dr. Wheeler was not satisfied with merely recovering his notebook. He was curious to know what had happened to it and why! He continued to generate more sophisticated hypotheses to solve the mystery.

Challenge to the Student:

Try to place yourself in Dr. Wheeler's position. Attempt to generate your own hypotheses as to the whereabouts of the lost three-ring notebook from the night of Friday, December 17, 2003, to the time of its return to Dr. Wheeler on January 10, 2004.

How do you go about doing this? First, review everything you "believe" to be true. Be very careful and skeptical about what is true and what is not. Then convert this into your original database. From that point again set up even more hypotheses and/or make alternative hypotheses until you arrive at the simplest possible explanation. The simplest possible explanation is most likely to be the correct answer. Support your answer with your database.

Pretend that you are doing historical archaeology. Ask your living informant(s) for information first. What could you ask Dr. Wheeler? You could ask, "Did you go back to the lavatory before you left the building on December 17, 2003? Are you sure of where your motorcar was parked or could you be mistaken? What was the weather like? Was it raining? Is it possible that you in fact stopped and talked to someone on your way to your motorcar? Are you sure you were at home on December 31, 2003 and you did not go out to celebrate the New Year?" Be very precise with your questioning. Also, let your imagination run wild with possibilities. Brainstorm. Sometimes this is when you are most likely to get the answer. Creativity is the essence of all science.

Hints:

Dr. Wheeler's university office was never broken into. Poor Miss Mortimer and the kind lady who found the notebook had nothing to do with the disappearance of the notebook. Dr. Wheeler's dog Tut did not bury his notebook. So what did happen? There is in fact a correct answer that will explain the mystery. Try to find that answer! If you do this, you will have to think like an archaeologist. It is a lot of fun, and it will reward you well!

City *of the* Hawk

From ancient breweries to the earliest mummies, excavations
at Hierakonpolis are rewriting the origins of Egyptian civilization.

Renée Friedman

IN EARLY 1897, THE ANTIQUITIES MARKETS of Luxor were awash with objects dating from the Predynastic period (4000 –3100 B.C.). It was suspected that the source of these artifacts was Hierakonpolis, sixty miles to the south. British archaeologist James Quibell rushed to the site to investigate and within a week discovered a gold-headed cult statue of a falcon god. His colleague Frederick Green soon joined him, and together they found a finely carved gray stone palette depicting a king named Narmer, on which our understanding of the rise of Egyptian civilization would be based for the next hundred years.

The Greek name Hierakonpolis (*hierakon* means "of the hawk") comes from the falcon-headed god Horus of the city Nekhen, the site's ancient Egyptian name. Pharaohs were considered the earthly incarnation of this all-seeing celestial bird, who was the patron deity of kingship. And the first pharaoh? On either side of the palette, Narmer is shown engaged in battle and its aftermath wearing the traditional crowns of the two culturally and politically distinct regions of Egypt: the white crown of the Nile Valley and the red crown of the Delta. The palette was thought to celebrate the unification of the two lands after a bloody battle won by Narmer, who marched forth from his capital of Hierakonpolis in about 3100 B.C. and, with his victory over the Delta people, inaugurated Egypt's 1st Dynasty.

Today, Hierakonpolis is a sandy, desolate landscape with mounds and craters left by farmers who mine its organic-rich middens to fertilize their fields. It is difficult to envision the site in Narmer's time, or even five hundred years before that, when it was a vibrant, bustling city—perhaps the largest in all of Egypt—stretching for almost three miles along the edge of the Nile floodplain. From ongoing excavations here, begun some thirty years ago by the late Michael Hoffman of the University of South Carolina, we now know that the rise of Egypt did not happen suddenly with Narmer's victory but was a gradual, if not necessarily peaceful, process and that unification was only the end

point of social and technological developments that began at least five centuries before Narmer was born.

Egypt would be barren without the Nile and its annual flood, but the life-giving river was not always predictable. One of every five inundations would be too high, destroying settlements on the edge of the floodplain, or too low, resulting in famine. Such disasters were known to the Egyptians as "chaos." In the face of such possibilities, control of the food supply must have been a key step in the concentration of power in a small number of hands and, ultimately, in pharaonic rule. Among the discoveries was an industrial facility with huge ceramic vats showing that the brewing of beer was already a big business at Hierakonpolis by 3500 B.C. The eight vats found so far could churn out more than 300 gallons of beer a day, and only a small part of this precinct has been explored. From the same time period, more than thirteen kilns have now been tentatively identified throughout the site, some having produced rough domestic cooking wares, others fine red polished and black-topped vessels that are among the finest pottery Egypt ever produced. These discoveries show that the basic economic infrastructure that later supported pharaonic civilization—large-scale production and specialization—was already developing at this early date.

Dominating the Predynastic town was an impressive ceremonial center, one of Egypt's earliest temple complexes, with a 130-foot-long oval courtyard in front of a monumental shrine. The shrine's facade was marked by four immense wooden pillars, possibly cedar logs imported from Lebanon. It is a prototype of temple facades characteristic of Egypt for millennia after. During excavation of this sacred precinct in 1985, I joined the Hierakonpolis team, cataloging sherds from hundreds of fine vessels manufactured specifically for use in temple rites in which wild and dangerous animals—crocodile, hippopotamus, gazelle, and barbary sheep—were sacrificed as symbols of the natural chaos the temple was built to control. The temple proclaimed the authority of the king, but this was not the only

Deciphering the Narmer Palette

THE MOST STRIKING ASPECT of the Narmer Palette is the king's headgear—this is the first document on which a king is shown wearing both the red and white crowns. On one side he wears the white crown of Upper Egypt in the regal stance of smiting an enemy, who is identified by hieroglyphs as possibly coming from the domain of the "Harpoon," a place in the Nile Delta. This act takes place in the presence of the falcon god Horus, who presents the king with the people and land of the papyrus plant as captives, symbolized by a man held by a hook through his nose and papyrus reeds on his back. Below, the sprawled dead of still unidentified cities or realms underscore the king's triumph. The meaning is clear: The king has defeated the Delta enemy, and Horus, the patron god of Narmer's kingship, takes them prisoner. The king's name, written with a catfish (*nar*) and a chisel (*mer*), appears at the top in a panel that represents the gates of the royal palace, or *serekh*. On either side of his name, the cow goddess Bat offers her personal protection.

Narmer's smiting stance, destined to be an icon of royal power for the next 3,500 years, and the presence of a servant bearing sandals and a ewer with which to wash the king's feet have suggested to some that the action depicted is ritualistic rather than historic. But the recent discovery of a similar scene—with the king as a catfish smiting an enemy out of whose head sprout papyrus reeds—on a carved bone tag used to date an oil shipment suggests that this was a real event that occurred in a certain year. Whether this event is the decisive battle that wiped out the final pocket of resistance, a minor skirmish, a battle beyond Egypt's borders (a fortress of Narmer has recently been found in Gaza), or a ceremonial occasion remains unknown.

On the other side, Narmer, now wearing the red crown of Lower Egypt, marches in a victory procession to view decapitated prisoners. Accompanying him are his sandal bearer and his vizier or eldest son, who wears an animal skin and carries some as yet unidentified piece of regalia. Before them are carried four standards on high poles that may represent the royal ancestors or portray certain aspects of kingship. The identity of the enemy laid out in two rows is also debated. Whoever they are, they have been dealt with harshly: their arms are trussed, and between their feet lay their severed heads upon which have been placed their severed genitals in a display meant to humiliate completely and strike fear. Below, the serpentine necks of two captive lions frame the dish in which cosmetics were ground. These animals symbolize unity and portray the control and balance of the powerful, but opposing forces vested in the king. The lowest register indicates that when necessary the king, as a raging bull, can trample town walls and gore inhabitants to maintain order, cosmic or otherwise.

—R.F.

have so far uncovered the remains of more than four hundred individuals interred here from about 3600 to 3400 B.C., with very few, if any, grave goods. The pitlike graves were dug into hot, dry sand that has preserved mats and baskets as well as hair, bone, body tissue, and foods.

As at other Predynastic cemeteries in Upper Egypt, the body was usually placed on a mat in a crouched position on the left side facing toward the west and the setting sun. Covered with a linen shroud, the corpse was protected by more mats. More than ten different mats had been laid over one intact burial. We have been able to distinguish two basic types that came in two standard sizes, suggesting that a specialized mat-making industry was already in existence at this time. One type was for everyday use, but the other was apparently produced for the grave, as it is too flimsy for daily use and none show signs of wear.

Study of the bones shows that these people were generally healthy and well-nourished but died around twenty-five to thirty-five years of age. The examination has also revealed cut marks on the front of the upper neck vertebrae of thirteen men and women. The high location of the lacerations suggests the cuts were not the cause of death—there are easier ways to kill someone. In some cases the cut marks indicate decapitation, but curiously, where the burial is intact, the head is always found in place on the body. It would appear that this treatment is part of a funerary ritual of dismemberment followed by the reassembling of the body. We also have three examples of what may be another part of this ritual—the removal of internal organs that were wrapped in resin-soaked textiles and then returned to the body.

Altogether, these practices indicate the beginning of that hallmark of Egyptian civilization—mummification. Ours was an unexpected discovery in a working-class cemetery from about 3500 B.C., because the next evidence of mummification we have is five centuries later and from a king's tomb. Despite the early date, one can link such practices with the myth of the god Osiris, who was killed and dismembered by his brother, Seth, reassembled by his wife, Isis, and then wrapped and mummified by the embalming god Anubis before attaining the afterlife as king of the underworld. For later periods, when there are texts to guide us, we know that in death all Egyptians became Osiris, and the mummification of the body was viewed as a reenactment of the events in Osiris' death. Here at Hierakonpolis we may have the very first manifestations of this belief.

Rich burials at Hierakonpolis contemporary with the working-class cemetery were explored from 1997 to 2000 by the late Barbara Adams of the University College London. The contrast between the two could not be more stark. The wealth of the elites is evident in the objects still to be found within their plundered graves—flint figurines, beautiful pottery, and funerary masks. Made of fired clay, these expressive masks—with cut-out eyes and mouth and finely modeled ears and nose—are curved to fit over the human head and attached by means of a thong passed through holes behind the ears. As Egypt's earliest funerary masks,

way the established social order expressed itself, as our work in the site's cemeteries has shown.

Of the hundreds of known Predynastic sites, Hierakonpolis is one of the few at which distinct cemeteries for the different segments of society have been found. On the southern edge of town was the burial ground for the working class, while the elite were interred in the large wadi, or dry valley, that runs through the center of the site. We began digging in the working-class cemetery in 1996 and they stand at the beginning of a tradition whose origins had long been a matter of conjecture.

The size and complexity of the graves also distinguishes the two cemeteries. One elite tomb was surrounded by a rectangular wooden post enclosure at least thirty feet wide and probably sixty-five feet long, while stout timbers along the edge of the grave itself suggest a substantial super structure over it. This is the earliest example of above-ground funerary architecture in Egypt and it is clearly the forerunner of complexes constructed in stone centuries later, as at the Step Pyramid at Saqqara.

During her excavation of this funerary complex, Adams observed animal bones on the surface nearby. Investigating there last year, we found a large grave with a posthole at each corner suggesting that it, too, had a superstructure above it. This was not, however, a tomb constructed for more of Hierakonpolis' great ones but for an elephant. On the tomb floor we found the creature's massive pelvis, tail, and fore leg still in place, proving the beast had been laid on its left side and covered both above and below with what must have been a vast quantity of fine fabric. A thick layer of blackened elephant skin and a substance that looked like bone but felt like soap, later identified as blubber, confirms that the elephant had gone to its grave fully fleshed. No expense was spared: this elephant was buried with grave goods including decorated and imported pottery, red ocher and green malachite cosmetics, a stone macehead, alabaster jars, a slate palette, an amethyst bead, and an ivory bracelet.

Study of the bones revealed the tomb owner to be a male African elephant ten or eleven years old, the age at which males are expelled from the maternal herd and go off to live with other young bulls. Young and inexperienced, they can be captured and trained. Other burials in the same cemetery provide evidence for a royal menagerie, with smaller animals like baboons and even a wildcat captured and kept to accompany their owners to the next life. The effort and expense involved in the burial of this elephant, however, suggests that this mighty beast was not simply a trophy or an exotic pet but a very special animal, perhaps the spiritual manifestation of the strength and power of a ruler—what later Egyptians called the *ka*.

In ancient Egypt, everyone had a *ka*, a creative life force that came into existence in the womb as a spiritual double of the person that lived on after the body died. The *ka* of the king was a special entity, and *ka* statues, the focus of lavish funerary offerings, were sometimes buried with kings in special shrines. Although the *ka* was shown in human form later on, an animal form seems likely in the Predynastic period. We know the earliest kings all had animal names and derived their spiritual might from the power of the animal whose name they bore. King Scorpion and King Catfish (Narmer) are the best-known examples, but there were earlier kings who wrote their names with signs including bulls, elephants, and other powerful creatures. If the elephant is the *ka* or animal manifestation of an early ruler, this may help to explain discovery elsewhere in the elite cemetery of remains of a wild bull, or aurochs, buried on a funerary bed with grave goods. With time it may be possible to reconstruct from animal burials at Hierakonpolis a dynasty of early kings stretching farther back into pre history than ever imagined.

Taken together, the evidence of industrial production, temples, masks, mummies, and funerary architecture as early as 3500 B.C. is placing Hierakonpolis at the forefront of traditions and practices that would come to typify Egyptian culture centuries later. These discoveries may have knocked Narmer and his palette off their historical pedestal, but they confirm the central role the city played in the long development of Egyptian civilization. It is little wonder that for millennia the deified early kings of Hierakonpolis, called the Souls of Nekhen, were honored guests at the coronations and funerals of all pharaohs.

RENÉE FRIEDMAN *directs excavations at Hierakonpolis, made possible by permission of Egypt's Supreme Council of Antiquities and its secretary general Zahi Hawass with funds from the National Science Foundation, University of Arkansas, Tom and Linda Heagy, and the Friends of Nekhen. For more information see www.hierakonpolis.org and www.archaeology.org.*

The Lost Goddess of Israel

Sandra Scham

And [the king] set a graven image of Asherah, that he had made, in the house of which the Lord said to David and Solomon his son, "In this House, and in Jerusalem, which I have chosen out of all tribes of Israel, will I put my name for ever."

—II KINGS 21:7

ASHERAH IS ARGUABLY most important goddess in the Canaanite pantheon. The prototypical mother of gods and humans and consort of the chief god, El, she is also the mistress of the sea and the land, and protector of all living things. We have long known Asherah from the immense library of thirteenth-century cuneiform tablets found in Syria at the site of Ugarit. But there are also more than 40 references to Asherah in the Old Testament. What could she have meant to the people of monotheistic ancient Israel?

A bit too much, apparently, at least according to the authors of the biblical texts, who attack her relentlessly. They praise Asa, king of Judah (911–870 B.C.), for removing his mother Ma'acah from official duties after "she had an abominable image made for Asherah" (I Kings 15.13, II Chronicles 15.6). They condemn the long-reigning Manas'seh of Judah (698–642) for doing "what was evil in the sight of the Lord" in "making an Asherah" (II Kings 21.7). And they trumpet the achievements of Josiah (639–609), including the destruction of offerings made to Asherah at the temple in Jerusalem, the abolition of "the Asherah from the house of the Lord," and demolition of a shrine there in which women "did weaving for Asherah" (II Kings 23). These passages reflect both the worship of Asherah and efforts to stamp out her cult during in the Iron Age. But it was only in the succeeding Persian period, after the fall of Judah in 586 B.C. and the exile in Babylon, that Asherah virtually disappeared.

Ultimately, the campaign to eliminate the goddess has failed. "Asherah was buried long ago by the Establishment," declares respected biblical scholar William H. Dever. "Now, archaeology has excavated her." Dever is quite certain that he knows who the Asherah of ancient Israel and of the biblical texts is—she is the wife or consort of Yahweh, the one god of Israel. Many of his colleagues would agree.

The origin of Yahweh, the god of Israel, has been a matter of speculation among archaeologists and biblical scholars for generations. The biblical narrative of the covenant of the one god with the descendants of Abraham and later Jacob, the Exodus from Egypt, and the subsequent conquest of the "Holy Land" is now viewed as legend by most scholars—albeit one that has some basis in fact. Those facts, most scholars would concur, have a lot to do with a basic culture change that can be detected in the archaeology of the region in the early Iron Age, around 1100 B.C. In the central hill country of Palestine, in what is now considered the heartland of Israelite settlement, we suddenly find numerous small rural settlements and simple houses of sheep and goat herders, who seemed to reject the raising of pigs.

What we do *not* find is any conclusive evidence that this change was in any way rooted in a religious movement. Rather, what we see is a rural resettlement of people who may have formerly dwelt on the margins of urban Canaanite society. When these people "took to the hills," for whatever reason, they seemed to have brought many of the old Canaanite gods with them. One of those gods may have been Yahweh. There is certainly an argument as to whether Yahweh is simply a version of the Canaanite great god El or a new god incorporating some traits of several different gods. Regardless of his origin, it does seem that he came to the hills replete with that most important accoutrement of Canaanite deities—a consort.

Even a cursory reading of the Books of I and II Samuel and I and II Kings demonstrates that the worship of Yahweh's wife, Asherah, did not die out but remained a part of ritual and cult throughout the monarchies and until the conquest of Judah, that is, from circa 1000 to 586 B.C. The writers of the Bible, many living in the period after the exile and in the midst of a religious reform movement, sought to give monotheism greater authority by ascribing it to the period of the kings. They then had to determine what to do with God's wife. There was nothing unusual in their desire to subordinate or eradicate the influence of goddesses—it was a process that had occurred in many different places. As a result, Asherah was relegated to the status of the wife of the reviled Ba'al—the god of the evil Queen Jezebel and other villainous biblical figures, because, as Dever says, the writers wanted to discredit her. The Hebrew and Aramaic texts preserve the word "Asherah," but there is nothing to suggest that she was once the queen of the gods of Canaan and, later, Israel.

Only the numerous artifacts found in biblical contexts all over Israel indicate her importance, and Dever's new book, provocatively titled *Did God Have a Wife?*, details these finds. Yahweh and Asherah are directly associated on artifacts known from sites such as Khirbet El-Kôm, Ta'anach, and Kuntillet Ajrud (Horvat Teman in Hebrew). The last, in particular, is famous for both the number of its images that link Yahweh and Asherah as well as the clarity with which their association is depicted. In the 1970s, excavations at Ajrud in the northern Sinai revealed what most scholars now believe was a fort, one of many such ninth-to-eighth-century B.C. structures built on the edges of the small kingdoms that had arisen in the region a century or more previously. Some of the rooms within the fort contained fragments of plaster walls, and it was this surface upon which the first of the famous inscriptions was found, invoking the blessing of "Yahweh by his Asherah." Other inscriptions on the walls speak of blessings by the gods Ba'al and El.

Biblical scholars were at first reluctant to accept the pairing of Yahweh and Asherah. Those who were wont to take the biblical narrative at face value were incensed by the image of a polytheistic Israel that worshiped a divine couple. Other scholars were slow to accept artifacts as a refutation of the Bible because they looked upon archaeological evidence as secondary when it was in conflict with the text. Any number of people disputed the find, the translation, and the interpretation of the translation. But after two large storage jars with similar inscriptions, and what may be a depiction of Asherah on one, were found at the site, mainstream scholars began to "pay attention," according to Dever. As he recalls in his book, Dever himself was originally "stunned, both by the scene and by the Hebrew inscription above it." He then remembered finding a similar inscription at Khirbet El-Kôm in 1969, which read "Yahweh by his Asherah." Only after the Ajrud discoveries, however, did he fully believe that this interpretation of his earlier find was not only correct but signaled a significant and hitherto unrecognized cult.

That the storage jars have both words and pictures illuminates the relationship between the male and female deities far better than do a host of other unillustrated inscriptions or illustrations with no text. The expression "Yahweh and his Asherah" is unmistakable. Equally unambiguous are the painted scenes on the jars of stylized animals and trees, by then age-old Near Eastern fertility imagery, and an unusual frontal depiction of two possibly male figures (one resembling the Egyptian dwarf-god Bes, who protected women in childbirth) and a curious seated female figure playing a lyre. Dever and others believe that the last, based upon her attire, headgear, and

seated position, is none other than the goddess Asherah, since most Near Eastern goddesses of this and earlier periods are shown seated. But some biblical scholars, like Diana Edelman of the University of Sheffield, dispute this identification of the figure, though they agree with the interpretation of the inscription.

What we have with these inscriptions, according to Dever, is evidence of the worship of Asherah as part of what he calls popular religion. "We don't know about popular religion in ancient times," he says. "What was the ultimate concern of most people in the ancient world? To get the theological formula correct? I don't think so. I think it was reproduction. The graffiti don't discuss rituals. The texts are all about blessings and they don't prescribe any actual worship." For his interpretation, Dever relies heavily upon the traditional anthropological distinction between "folk" and "official" religion, a distraction, it should be added, not upheld by many cultural anthropologists today.

Edelman, along with Dartmouth's Susan Ackerman and Duke's Carol Meyers, takes issue with the characterization of Asherah worship by Dever as "folk tradition" or "little tradition" in contrast to the "official religion" of monotheistic worship. They see it as widespread and including the highest ranks of society. "When we have queen mothers who are making images of Asherah, you just can't make that distinction," says Edelman. "It's ridiculous to go against the inscriptional evidence to say 'It's not the official cult, it's just the people messing up and doing the wrong thing.'" Ackerman adds, "The biblical texts speak of an Asherah in Jerusalem and in the temple of Jerusalem—now, that's not a little tradition."

Meyers rejects the entire concept of official versus unofficial religion. "I don't like the term 'popular religion,'" she says. "If the kings themselves have Asherah in the Temple, then what is more official than that?"

Despite their differences, all question whether Israelite monotheism ever truly existed in the pre-Exile period. These days, says Dever, "It's hard to find a mainstream scholar who believes that early Israel was monotheistic." As Edelman notes, "When God said, 'You shall have no other gods before me,' what do people think he meant—that there weren't any other gods? Then why bother to mention them?" And there is no shortage of polytheistic ritual artifacts from sites in the Holy Land. Although the ritual symbolism from many of these finds is a matter of interpretation, it is difficult to ignore the great similarities between archaeological finds from the Holy Land to those found elsewhere in the ancient Near East.

There is, for example, virtually no evidence of a monotheistic religious cult at Shiloh, the biblical location of the resting place of the Ark, site of the early Israelite sanctuary, and seat of the judges and prophets Eli and Samuel. But levels at the site from the time of the Israelite settlement have produced a cult stand showing a lioness, a ram's head, and a leopard attacking a deer. And artifacts depicting bulls, rams, and ibex, as well as ibex flanking trees, have been found at surrounding sites. Individually, none of these images necessarily indicates a polytheistic cultic practice, but all of them are repeated, sometimes even duplicated, in clear cultic associations elsewhere in the region.

Other important Israelite cult centers, Shechem and Ta'anach, have yielded cult stands featuring lions and winged sphinxes, ibex with trees, and a rare human image of a youth strangling a serpent. These sites have Canaanite occupations followed by Israelite ones, but not so the "Bull Site" near Dothan with its statuettes of bulls and standing stones, and a site on Mt. Ebal, which the excavator dubbed "Joshua's altar." Scholars were skeptical regarding the interpretation of the rectangular open-air altar on Mt. Ebal, but agree today that the site was certainly cultic, although an association with Joshua cannot be demonstrated. Cult sites coinciding with the emergence of Israel without Canaanite antecedents may provide important evidence for the origins of Israelite religion. At neither the Bull Site nor Mt. Ebal, however, do we detect any traces of developing monotheism.

In the later Iron Age, from 900 to 586 B.C., the archaeological evidence suggests even more strongly that the people worshiped many gods. Jerusalem and its environs—center of state and cult, site of the Temple, and seat of the divinely ordained king—has yielded cultic stands, inscribed animal bones used in divination, seals bearing the symbols of Mesopotamian and Egyptian gods, and hundreds of figurines of large-breasted women that many people associate with either Asherah herself or the Asherah cult. These finds, mainly from Judean households, depict only upper bodies, with the lower bodies encased in a "pillar." The pillar has been interpreted as exemplifying a tree, but it may be just a stylized way of representing the goddess.

It has been several decades since most archaeologists have come to accept that the Israelites of the Iron Age were no less "pagan" than their Canaanite neighbors. In doing so, they have slowly brought biblical scholars toward the same conclusion. It is, in fact, despite any desire to adhere to the monotheistic spirit of the Bible, difficult to interpret many of the prophetic messages without postulating the worship of other gods among the Israelites. The real question, and one that is far from resolved, is whether this worship resulted from "backsliding" into the ways of the other peoples of the region or simply was a stubborn, established, and often officially sanctioned cultic practice.

Archaeologists have also brought the religious practices of the Canaanites into the sphere of biblical studies and have opened up the field for the exploration of the origins of the god of Israel. Philologist Mark Smith, author of *The Early History of God*, has tried to determine why the Israelites turned away from the Canaanite gods. He believes that all of the Canaanite practices that the biblical writers condemned were part and parcel of the native Israelite cult—including child sacrifice. The last is a provocative thought, since many theologians maintain that Isaac was saved from being sacrificed in order to precisely make the point that child sacrifice was disapproved of as part of the Yahwistic cult.

This is the dark side of Canaanite religion and one more associated with Ba'al than Asherah. Meyers argues that such sacrifices are not of the kind demanded by a cult focusing on life and the life-giving properties of the female deities. Whether or not the cult of Asherah was a women's cult or a popular cult for both sexes is a matter of conjecture. Dever seems to suggest that it is a cult of particular interest to women, but Edelman, Ackerman, and Meyers disagree. Ackerman says plainly that Asherah was "equally as appealing to men as to women" and that "even if we see Asherah as a goddess associated with women's reproduction there is no reason to suppose that it isn't as crucially a men's issue as it is a women's issue."

All of this begs the question of what happened to the cult, which does not seem to have lasted as long as that of Ba'al, the violent sacrificial rites of which were practiced even into Roman times. If the cult satisfied needs of both men and women and did not threaten—and even enhanced—the status of the main deity, why did it disappear? Archaeology offers a clue. Edelman notes that the Asherah household figurines, if indeed that's what they are, become "severely limited in number and virtually disappear by the Persian period." She speculates that in the elite circles, toward the end of the monarchy, there may already have been recognition of the usefulness of monotheism in the Amun in Egypt during the New Kingdom (circa 1540–1070 B.C.) and Marduk in Babylon during the Neo-Babylonian Empire (circa 629–539 B.C.) arose. That is, it enabled the development of a powerful priesthood in support of a state religion and divinely inspired monarchy. Then came the fall of Judah and exile in Babylonia from 586 to 538 B.C. "Priests didn't want to be out of a job," she proposes. "It was easier during the exile to say 'Our god has defeated us, he is punishing us.'"

Dever agrees that the Exile was critical in the ascendancy of monotheism. He writes in *Did God Have a Wife?* that the Bible is revisionist history, revised according to the lessons that the authors "presumed to have drawn from their own stormy history. The fundamental lesson for them was that Yahweh was indeed a 'jealous god,' punishing those who flirted with other gods. The conclusion? Don't do this again! And many of the exiles in Babylon, as well as the remnant left back in Judah, learned that lesson."

Sandra Scham, the editor of Near Eastern Archaeology and a contributing editor to ARCHAEOLOGY, teaches biblical archaeology at the Catholic University of America in Washington, D. C.

From *Archaeology*, March/April 2005, pp. 36–40. Copyright © 2005 by Archaeological Institute of America. Reprinted by permission.

Secrets of the Medici

Excavation of Florence's first family reveals clues to the lifestyles of the Renaissance rich, solves a murder mystery, and turns up a lost treasure.

Gino Fornaciari, Bob Brier and Antonio Fornaciari

THE MEDICI WERE AMONG the most powerful families in the world. Beginning in the fourteenth century, they built a fortune bankrolling popes and kings. Through their wealth and their political abilities, they went from being one of many patrician clans in Florence to the city's hereditary rulers. They married into the royal houses of Austria and France, and two of their number were made pope. Scholars and lovers of art, the Medici were patrons of Leonardo, Raphael, Botticelli, Galileo, Michelangelo, and Cellini. And under their rule, Florence became the intellectual hub of the Western world.

The Medici were also legendary for their adeptness at intrigue and murder. In 1537, for example, Cosimo I came to power when the reigning duke, Alessandro Medici, was assassinated by a cousin. The 18-year-old Cosimo—son of Giovanni Medici, the family's greatest military captain, but from a junior branch—was not accepted by many of the leading families of Florence. They took up arms against him, but Cosimo was victorious on the battlefield. And those of his opponents who survived, including Alessandro's murderer, met with "unfortunate accidents" shortly thereafter.

Many of the leading Medici were buried in the Chapel of San Lorenzo in Florence, which long enjoyed the family's patronage. In 2004, we obtained Superintendent Antonio Paolucci's permission to examine 47 of the Medici interred there, including Cosimo. The multiyear project is a unique opportunity to study the health of the Medici (a rare look at a single family over a long period) and might settle allegations of murder to be found in legends about the dynasty.

We had no idea what we would find. In 1857, after it was discovered that the Medici tombs, then above ground in the chapel, had been plundered, their remains were buried below its floor for protection. Brass plaques set into the floor indicate where they were buried, but there were no precise records of how they were buried. Moreover, in 1947 researchers intent primarily on examining the skulls exhumed several Medici but left virtually no record of what they found or how they reburied them.

A final uncertainty was what effect the disastrous 1966 flood of the Arno River, which inundated the chapel, might have had on the remains.

Our first subjects were Cosimo I; his wife, Eleonora of Toledo; and two of their sons, Giovanni and Garzia. Cosimo married Eleonora, daughter of the Spanish viceroy of Naples, in 1540 when she was 16 years old. She was young, charming, well educated, and very rich. She shared her husband's love of the arts and she financed the family's purchase of the Pitti Palace so their children would have more room to play. It was a politically smart marriage for Cosimo, but all indications are that it was also a happy marriage.

We started with Cosimo and his family because they were buried together in an area of the chapel that could easily be screened from the thousands of tourists that visit San Lorenzo daily. We would examine the remains in a field lab set up in the chapel's New Sacristy, with its beautiful Michelangelo sculptures commissioned by the Medici.

We lifted the marble flooring where a plaque indicated Eleonora was buried, and found a layer of rubble—plaster, brick fragments, and small stones—with some human bones, mostly small bones of the hands and feet. Apparently this was the work of the 1940s excavators, who had exhumed several bodies at once, then examined and reburied them. (Their research, relating skull shapes to intelligence and personality, is now discredited.) Then they apparently discovered a few small bones left over and threw them in the rubble before replacing the floor. Beneath this we found three stone slabs sealing a rectangular chamber lined with bricks and then plastered. We were surprised to see two metal boxes within, but Eleonora and her husband, Cosimo, had been reburied together, each in a zinc ossuary, in 1947. So we had two Medici for the price of one.

The bottom of the chamber was covered with dried-out mud left by the Amo flood, and we were concerned that water might have penetrated the ossuaries and led to the decay of the remains. But when we opened Eleonora's box, we found that although no soft tissue was preserved, the bones were in good condition.

We know quite a bit about Eleonora, and it was interesting to compare her skeleton with the historical record. In their 24 years of marriage, Eleonora gave birth 11 times in 14 years, when she was 18, 19, 20, 21, 23, 24, 25, 26, 27, 31, and 32. She was pregnant for most of her adult life, and her skeleton showed it. Every birth is a trauma to the mother's pelvis and leaves its mark. In Eleonora's case, the bones that come together at the front of the pelvis were extremely rough and irregular. She was a small woman, and every time she had a child there was damage to the bones, followed by regrowth and remodeling of them. And the back of her pelvis, which is normally somewhat angular, was flattened by the many children coming down the birth canal.

All those pregnancies, during which calcium is leached from the mother for the bone development of the fetus, had had a serious effect on Eleonora's teeth. She had lost several, and others were abscessed. Even today in Italy there is the expression "For each baby a tooth." Eleonora was one of the richest women in the world, but her wealth didn't protect her from dental distress or an early death from malaria at the age of 40.

Cosimo's life, too, is mirrored in his bones. He was a sportsman who lifted weights, rode, and hunted regularly. Strenuous physical activity causes muscle size to increase, and this, in turn, causes bone to thicken and strengthen. Not surprisingly, his skeleton is what anthropologists call "robust." His upper leg bones have marked protuberances where the thigh muscles used to grip a horse during riding attached to them. His shoulder blades were asymmetrical, the right considerably larger than the left. Cosimo was a righty. But he did not sail into old age smoothly. Three of his vertebrae were fused, the result of a metabolic disorder, which would have caused him difficulty bending in old age. His teeth also gave him problems. Many were fractured from a lifetime of eating hard foods such as nuts and raw vegetables. The dentist on our team said it looked as if Cosimo had had a diet of wood.

What was unexpected was that someone had rather crudely sawed off the top of Cosimo's skull, probably to remove the brain. They knew that to preserve the body you must remove the brain or else it will putrefy. Perhaps a family physician who had never done anything like that before was given the job of preserving the great Cosimo for posterity.

WITH COSIMO AND ELEONORA'S sons Giovanni and Garzia, we moved into the darker side of the Medicis. Archival evidence suggests that the boys succumbed to malaria a few days apart in 1562. But there is also a legend, preserved in histories of the family, that Giovanni, then aged 19, and Garzia, then 16, quarreled during a hunting trip and that Garzia stabbed and killed his brother. When their father, Cosimo, learned of the murder of his favorite

son, in a fit of rage he ran Garzia through with his sword. Their mother, Eleonora, died six days later, supposedly of a broken heart. Which was the real story? Would the brothers' remains show evidence of violence or preserve clues that point to malaria? Giovanni's tomb proved to be covered by a single large limestone slab. On the lid of the zinc box in the chamber was a lead plaque from his original burial that read: *Ossa Iohanuis Cardinalls Cosimo 1 Filli*—the bones of Cardinal Giovanni, son of Cosimo I. (That he had been made a cardinal at the age of 17 attests the power of the Medici.)

Skeletal age markers—his molars, long bones, and pelvis—indicated that Giovanni had indeed died at around 19. While his lower teeth were perfect, one of the uppers had a terrible abscess. And the evidence for murder? Often the truth is less sensational than the legend, and that seems to be the case with Giovanni. His skeleton showed no signs of violence, no cut marks to the breastbone, ribs, or vertebrae. But we still had his brother Garzia's remains to examine. Supposedly he died by his father's sword. Perhaps we would find evidence of fatal trauma there.

Garzia's tomb proved similar to his brother's and parents'. He was about three years younger than his brother, and his skeleton confirmed his age. At Corregi Hospital, the team's radiologist did a full study of Garzia's bones. Medici biographers mention that the child was chronically ill, and the x-ray images of his leg bones revealed horizontal "growth-arrest" lines indicating serious illness at around two years old and at least four more times before he was 10. But as with Giovanni, the skeleton showed no signs of violence. Both brothers died within weeks of each other. So what killed them?

Our team's historian, Donatella Lippi of the University of Florence, knows as much about the Medici as anyone and is familiar with Italy's National Archives. Several letters in the archives revealed a probable cause of death. One from the family physician warns Cosimo not to take the boys on a hunting trip to the Marema, an area infested with malaria southwest of Florence. Cosimo didn't listen to the doctor, and on November 20, 1562, wrote to another son, "on the 15th Giovanni suffered from a high fever but became worse and died." Soon after his brother's death, Garzia also died. It is possible that Cosimo's letter was a cover-up for his violent rage, but our examination of the bones showed no evidence of violence. Malaria probably was the cause of their deaths, and also of their mother, Eleonora, who nursed them through their illnesses. Our team's pathologists are now trying to find clinical evidence of malaria in small bone samples from Giovanni, Garzia, and Eleonora. They are looking for the DNA of the parasite that causes malaria, but it is pioneering work and will be difficult, as the Arno flood waters might have washed away the evidence.

WE HAD EXAMINED THE bodies of four Medici, revealing aspects of their health unknown in the archival record and confirming other conditions that were. And we showed that, at least with Giovanni and Garzia, the Medici were not murderers. Our first season was coming to a close, and we had time for just one more Medici: Gian Gastone, the last Medici to rule Florence, who died in 1737. Renowned as an eccentric, Gian Gastone had an interest in botany and led a dissipated life. He spent the last five years of his life in bed—he wasn't sick, he just liked it there—and reportedly never bathed.

The 1857 commission that reburied the Medici recorded the funerary equipment that accompanied each corpse, and this gave us an idea of what we might find with Gian Gastone:

> In a cypress coffin, which was very well preserved, covered with black velvet and a small golden braid, there was another lead coffin, that had on its lid a cross on three mountains. After having opened it, a corpse was found, enveloped in a black silky sheet. Unrolled, it was clear that this corpse belonged to a Grand Duke because he wore the Grand-Ducal crown of golden metal on his head and he was dressed with a silky Great Cape, the sign of the Grand Master of Saint Steven. There were two gold medals, the first near the head, the other on the breast…

The researchers who exhumed the Medici in 1947 did not examine Gian Gastone, so there was some hope that we might find him just as he was described.

We thought that exhuming him would be simple, but when we raised the brass plaque and removed the floor tiles, we found a solid brick-and-stone masonry floor. We removed more floor tiles but still encountered the same masonry. Almost all the flooring stones were rectangular, but one was a perfect circle set inside a square. I asked several chapel employees what was beneath it, but they had no idea. One suggested a sewer. We decided to lift the stone and see if it led to Gian Gastone.

Inserting a thin file between the circle and the rectangle it was set into, one of our workmen removed the cement between the two. Then with the aid of suction cups, we lifted the marble circle, revealing a layer of sand. Beneath this was another circular stone, with an iron ring in its center, and below it we found stairs going down to a crypt. Peering in, I could see that a layer of undisturbed mud covered all the stairs: no one had been down since the 1966 flood. I could see several coffins, perhaps a dozen, many for children. They had clearly been disturbed. Some had the lids off and some lay smashed on the floor, which was littered with human bones. In addition to Gian Gastone's coffin, the crypt held the remains of a man and seven children, and a skull lacking the rest of its skeleton. (We do not yet know who these individuals are.) What caused this chaos? Gian Gastone's gold crown and medallions would have been a tempting treasure for tomb robbers.

Once we photographed and recorded the state of the tomb, various team members came down to have a look. Donatella Lippi peered into the lead coffin of Gian Gastone and surveyed the mass of wood fragments inside it but found no sign of his bones or crown or gold medals. She asked, "What happened to the gold?" We concluded that it had probably been melted down by thieves long ago.

Photographing and recording the crypt took weeks, and only after that was completed did we focus on Gastone. When we cleared the wood debris from inside his lead coffin, we found that the lid had in fact fallen into it. And beneath the lid, there was Gian Gastone, with his crown and medals! Our guess that robbers had rifled the tomb was wrong; the flood was the culprit. As a result of these finds, our next year will be spent conserving the artifacts from Gian Gastone's tomb and preparing publications on the findings. When that is done, we have several dozen more Medici buried in the chapel, waiting to be studied, including Cosimo's father, the great general Giovanni Medici. Historical accounts say that Giovanni had captured Milan on behalf of Pope Leo X (another Medici), but at the siege of Pavia in 1525, was hit in the leg by a bullet. In 1526 he was shot again in the same leg, which had to be amputated. He is said to have survived the operation, but died a week later. Certainly Giovanni's bones, and likely those of his relatives, have tales to tell.

Gino Fornaciari is professor of the history of medicine and pathology at the University of Pisa.

Bob Brier is senior research fellow at the C.W. Post Campus of Long Island University and a contributing editor of ARCHAEOLOGY.

Antonio Fornaciari is an archaeologist with the Medici project

From *Archaeology*, July/August 2005, pp. 36–41. Copyright © 2005 by Archaeological Institute of America. Reprinted by permission.

Living Through the Donner Party

The nineteenth-century survivors of the infamous Donner Party told cautionary tales of starvation and cannibalism, greed and self-sacrifice. But not until now are we learning why the survivors survived.

Jared Diamond

Jared Diamond is a contributing editor of DISCOVER, a professor of physiology at UCLA School of Medicine, a recipient of a MacArthur genius award, and the author of The Third Chimpanzee.

> *"Mrs. Fosdick and Mrs. Foster, after eating, returned to the body of [Mr.] Fosdick. There, in spite of the widow's entreaties, Mrs. Foster took out the liver and heart from the body and removed the arms and legs.... [Mrs. Fosdick] was forced to see her husband's heart broiled over the fire." "He eat her body and found her flesh the best he had ever tasted! He further stated that he obtained from her body at least four pounds of fat." "Eat baby raw, stewed some of Jake and roasted his head, not good meat, taste like sheep with the rot."*
>
> —GEORGE STEWART,
> *Ordeal by Hunger: The Story
> of the Donner Party*

Nearly a century and a half after it happened, the story of the Donner Party remains one of the most riveting tragedies in U.S. history. Partly that's because of its lurid elements: almost half the party died, and many of their bodies were defiled in an orgy of cannibalism. Partly, too, it's because of the human drama of noble self-sacrifice and base murder juxtaposed. The Donner Party began as just another nameless pioneer trek to California, but it came to symbolize the Great American Dream gone awry.

By now the tale of that disastrous journey has been told so often that seemingly nothing else remains to be said—or so I thought, until my friend Donald Grayson at the University of Washington sent me an analysis that he had published in the *Journal of Anthropological Research*. By comparing the fates of all Donner Party members, Grayson identified striking differences between those who came through the ordeal alive and those who were not so lucky. In doing so he has made the lessons of the Donner Party universal. Under more mundane life-threatening situations, who among us too will be "lucky"?

Grayson's insights did not depend on new discoveries about the ill-fated pioneers nor on new analytical techniques, but on that most elusive ingredient of great science: a new idea about an old problem. Given the same information, any of you could extract the same conclusions. In fact, on page 163 you'll find the roster of the Donner Party members along with a few personal details about each of them and their fate. If you like, you can try to figure out for yourself some general rules about who is most likely to die when the going gets tough.

The Lewis and Clark Expedition of 1804 to 1806 was the first to cross the continent, but they didn't take along ox-drawn wagons, which were a requirement for pioneer settlement. Clearing a wagon route through the West's unmapped deserts and mountains proved far more difficult than finding a footpath. Not until 1841 was the first attempt made to haul wagons and settlers overland to California, and only in 1844 did the effort succeed. Until the Gold Rush of 1848 unleashed a flood of emigrants, wagon traffic to California remained a trickle.

As of 1846, when the Donner Party set out, the usual wagon route headed west from St. Louis to Fort Bridger in Wyoming, then northwest into Idaho before turning southwest through Nevada and on to California. However, at that time a popular guidebook author named Lansford Hastings was touting a shortcut that purported to cut many miles from the long trek. Hastings's route continued west from Fort Bridger through the Wasatch mountain range, then south of

Utah's Great Salt Lake across the Salt Lake Desert, and finally rejoined the usual California Trail in Nevada.

In the summer of 1846 a number of wagon parties set out for California from Fort Bridger. One, which left shortly before the Donner Party, was guided by Hastings himself. Using his shortcut, the party would eventually make it to California, albeit with great difficulty.

The pioneers who would become the members of the Donner Party were in fact all headed for Fort Bridger to join the Hastings expedition, but they arrived too late. With Hastings thus unavailable to serve as a guide, some of these California-bound emigrants opted for the usual route instead. Others, however, decided to try the Hastings Cutoff anyway. In all, 87 people in 23 wagons chose the cutoff. They consisted of 10 unrelated families and 16 lone individuals, most of them well-to-do midwestern farmers and townspeople who had met by chance and joined forces for protection. None had had any real experience of the western mountains or Indians. They became known as the Donner Party because they elected an elderly Illinois farmer named George Donner as their captain. They left Fort Bridger on July 31, one of the last parties of that summer to begin the long haul to California.

Within a fortnight the Donner Party suffered their first crushing setback, when they reached Utah's steep, brush-covered Wasatch Mountains. The terrain was so wild that, in order to cross, the men had first to build a wagon road. It took 16 backbreaking days to cover just 36 miles, and afterward the people and draft animals were worn out. A second blow followed almost immediately thereafter, west of the Great Salt Lake, when the party ran into an 80-mile stretch of desert. To save themselves from death by thirst, some of the pioneers were forced to unhitch their wagons, rush ahead with their precious animals to the next spring, and return to retrieve the wagons. The rush became a disorganized panic, and many of the animals died, wandered off, or were killed by Indians. Four wagons and large quantities of supplies had to be abandoned.

Not until September 30—two full months after leaving Fort Bridger—did the Donner Party emerge from their fatal shortcut to rejoin the California Trail.

By November 1 they had struggled up to Truckee Lake—later renamed Donner Lake—at an elevation of 6,000 feet on the eastern flank of the Sierra Nevada, west of the present-day California-Nevada border. Snow had already begun to fall during the last days of October, and now a fierce snowstorm defeated the exhausted party as they attempted to cross a 7,200-foot pass just west of the lake. With that storm, a trap snapped shut around them: they had set out just a little too late and proceeded just a little too slowly. They now faced a long winter at the lake, with very little food.

Death had come to the Donner Party even before it reached the lake. There were five casualties: on August 29 Luke Halloran died of "consumption" (presumably tuberculosis); on October 5 James Reed knifed John Snyder in self-defense, during a fight that broke out when two teams of oxen became entangled; three days later Lewis Keseberg abandoned an old man named Hardkoop who had been riding in Keseberg's wagon, and most of the party refused to stop and search for him; sometime after October 13 two German emigrants, Joseph Reinhardt and Augustus Spitzer, murdered a rich German named Wolfinger while ostensibly helping him to cache his property; and on October 20 William Pike was shot as he and his brother-in-law were cleaning a pistol.

They cut off and roasted flesh from the corpses, restrained only by the rule that no one partook of his or her relative's body.

In addition, four party members had decided earlier to walk out ahead to Sutter's Fort (now Sacramento) to bring back supplies and help. One of those four, Charles Stanton, rejoined the party on October 19, bringing food and two In-

dians sent by Sutter. Thus, of the 87 original members of the Donner Party, 79—plus the two Indians—were pinned down in the winter camp at Donner Lake.

The trapped pioneers lay freezing inside crude tents and cabins. They quickly exhausted their little remaining food, then killed and ate their pack animals. Then they ate their dogs. Finally they boiled hides and blankets to make a glue-like soup. Gross selfishness became rampant, as families with food refused to share it with destitute families or demanded exorbitant payment. On December 16 the first death came to the winter camp when 24-year-old Baylis Williams succumbed to starvation. On that same day 15 of the strongest people—5 women and 10 men, including Charles Stanton and the two Indians—set out across the pass on homemade snowshoes, virtually without food and in appallingly cold and stormy weather, in the hope of reaching outside help. Four of the men left behind their families; three of the women left behind their children.

On the sixth morning an exhausted Stanton let the others go on ahead of him; he remained behind to die. On the ninth day the remaining 14 for the first time openly broached the subject of cannibalism which had already been on their minds. They debated drawing lots as to who should be eaten, or letting two people shoot it out until one was killed and could be eaten. Both proposals were rejected in favor of waiting for someone to die naturally.

Such opportunities soon arose. On Christmas Eve, as a 23-year-old man named Antoine, a bachelor, slept in a heavy stupor, he stretched out his arm such that his hand fell into the fire. A companion pulled it out at once. When it fell in a second time, however, no one intervened—they simply let it burn. Antoine died, then Franklin Graves, then Patrick Dolan, then Lemuel Murphy. The others cut off and roasted flesh from the corpses, restrained only by the rule that no one would partake of his or her own relative's body. When the corpses were consumed, the survivors began eating old shoes.

On January 5, 23-year-old Jay Fosdick died, only to be cut up and boiled by Mrs. Foster over the protests of Mrs. Fosdick. Soon after, the frenzied Mr. Foster chased down, shot, and killed the two Indians to eat them. That left 7 of the original 15 snowshoers to stagger into the first white settlement in California, after a midwinter trek of 33 days through the snow.

On January 31 the first rescue team set out from the settlement for Donner Lake. It would take three more teams and two and a half months before the ordeal was all over. During that time many more people died, either in the winter camp or while fighting their way out with the rescue teams. There was never enough food, and by the end of February, cannibalism had established itself at the lake.

When William Eddy and William Foster, who had gotten out with the snowshoers, reached the lake with the third rescue team on March 13, they found that Keseberg had eaten their sons. The Foster child's grandmother accused the starving Keseberg of having taken the child to bed with him one night, strangling him, and hanging the corpse on the wall before eating it. Keseberg, in his defense, claimed the children had died naturally. When the rescuers left the lake the next day to return to California, they left Keseberg behind with just four others: the elderly Lavina Murphy, the badly injured George Donner, his 4-year-old nephew Samuel and his healthy wife Tamsen, who could have traveled but insisted on staying with her dying husband.

The fourth and last rescue team reached the lake on April 17 to find Keseberg alone, surrounded by indescribable filth and mutilated corpses. George Donner's body lay with his skull split open to permit the extraction of his brains. Three frozen ox legs lay in plain view almost uneaten beside a kettle of cut-up human flesh. Near Keseberg sat two kettles of blood and a large pan full of fresh human liver and lungs. He alleged that his four companions had died natural deaths, but he was frank about having eaten them. As to why he had not eaten ox leg instead, he explained that it was too dry: human liver and lungs

tasted better, and human brains made a good soup. As for Tamsen Donner, Keseberg noted that she tasted the best, being well endowed with fat. In a bundle held by Keseberg the rescuers found silk, jewelry, pistols, and money that had belonged to George Donner.

After returning to Sutter's Fort, one of the rescuers accused Keseberg of having murdered his companions, prompting Keseberg to sue for defamation of character. In the absence of legal proof of murder the court verdict was equivocal, and the issue of Keseberg's guilt remains disputed to this day. However, Tamsen Donner's death is especially suspicious since she had been in strong physical condition when last seen by the third rescue team.

Experience has taught us that the youngest and oldest people are the most vulnerable even under normal conditions, and their vulnerability increases under stress.

Thus, out of 87 Donner Party members, 40 died: 5 before reaching Donner Lake, 22 in their winter camp at the lake, and 13 (plus the two Indians) during or just after efforts to leave the lake. Why those particular 40? From the facts given in the roster, can you draw conclusions, as Grayson did, as to who was in fact the most likely to die?

As a simple first test, compare the fates of Donner Party males and females irrespective of age. Most of the males (30 out of 53) died; most of the females (24 out of 34) survived. The 57 percent death rate among males was nearly double the 29 percent death rate among females.

Next, consider the effect of age irrespective of sex. The worst toll was among the young and the old. Without exception, everyone over the age of 50 died, as did most of the children below the age of 5. Surprisingly, children and teenagers between the ages of 5 and 19 fared better than did adults in their prime

(age 20 to 39): half the latter, but less than one-fifth of the former, died.

By looking at the effects of age and sex simultaneously, the advantage the women had over the men becomes even more striking. Most of the female deaths were among the youngest and oldest, who were already doomed by their age. Among those party members aged 5 to 39—the ones whose ages left them some reasonable chance of survival—half the men but only 5 percent of the women died.

The dates of death provide deeper insight. Of the 35 unfortunates who died after reaching the lake, 14 men but not a single woman had died by the end of January. Only in February did women begin to buckle under. From February onward the death toll was essentially equal by sex—11 men, 10 women. The differences in dates of death simply underscore the lesson of the death rates themselves: the Donner Party women were far hardier than the men.

Thus, sex and age considered together account for much of the luck of the survivors. Most of those who died (39 of the 40 victims) had the misfortune to be of the wrong sex, or the wrong age, or both.

Experience has taught us that the youngest and oldest people are the most vulnerable even under normal conditions, and their vulnerability increases under stress. In many natural disasters, those under 10 or over 50 suffered the highest mortality. For instance, children under 10 accounted for over half the 240,000 deaths in the 1970 Bangladesh cyclone, though they constituted only one-third of the exposed population.

Much of the vulnerability of the old and young under stress is simply a matter of insufficient physical strength: these people are less able to walk out through deep snow (in the case of the Donner Party) or to cling to trees above the height of flood waters (in the case of the Bangladesh cyclone). Babies have special problems. Per pound of body weight a baby has twice an adult's surface area, which means double the area across which body heat can escape. To maintain body temperature, babies have to in-

Manifest of a Tragic Journey

DONNER FAMILY

Jacob Donner	M	65	died in Nov. in winter camp
George Donner	M	62	died in Apr. in winter camp
Elizabeth Donner	F	45	died in Mar. in winter camp
Tamsen Donner	F	45	died in Apr. in winter camp
Elitha Donner	F	14	
Solomon Hook	M	14	
William Hook	M	12	died Feb. 28 with first rescue team
Leanna Donner	F	12	
George Donner	M	9	
Mary Donner	F	7	
Frances Donner	F	6	
Isaac Donner	M	5	died Mar. 7 with second rescue team
Georgia Donner	F	4	
Samuel Donner	M	4	died in Apr. in winter camp
Lewis Donner	M	3	died Mar. 7 or 8 in winter camp
Eliza Donner	F	3	

MURPHY-FOSTER-PIKE FAMILY

Lavina Murphy	F	50	died around Mar. 19 in winter camp
William Foster	M	28	
William Pike	M	25	died Oct. 20 by gunshot
Sara Foster	F	23	
Harriet Pike	F	21	
John Landrum Murphy	M	15	died Jan. 31 in winter camp
Mary Murphy	F	13	
Lemuel Murphy	M	12	died Dec. 27 with snowshoers
William Murphy	M	11	
Simon Murphy	M	10	
George Foster	M	4	died in early Mar. in winter camp
Naomi Pike	F	3	
Catherine Pike	F	1	died Feb. 20 in winter camp

GRAVES-FOSDICK FAMILY

Franklin Graves	M	57	died Dec 24. with snowshoers
Elizabeth Graves	F	47	died Mar. 8 with second rescue team
Jay Fosdick	M	23	died Jan. 5 with snowshoers
Sarah Fosdick	F	22	
William Graves	M	18	
Eleanor Graves	F	15	
Lavina Graves	F	13	
Nancy Graves	F	9	
Jonathan Graves	M	7	
Franklin Graves Jr.	M	5	died Mar. 8 with second rescue team
Elizabeth Graves	F	1	died soon after rescue by second team

BREEN FAMILY

Patrick Breen	M	40	
Mary Breen	F	40	
John Breen	M	14	
Edward Breen	M	13	
Patrick Breen Jr.	M	11	
Simon Breen	M	9	
Peter Breen	M	7	
James Bren	M	4	

Isabella	F	1	

REED FAMILY

James Reed	M	46	
Margaret Reed	F	32	
Virginia Reed	F	12	
Patty Reed	F	8	
James Reed Jr.	M	5	
Thomas Reed	M	3	

EDDY FAMILY

William Eddy	M	28	
Eleanor Eddy	F	25	died Feb. 7 in winter camp
James Eddy	M	3	died in early Mar. in winter camp
Margaret Eddy	F	1	died Feb. 4 in winter camp

KESEBERG FAMILY

Lewis Keseberg	M	32	
Phillipine Keseberg	F	32	
Ada Keseberg	F	3	died Feb. 24 with first rescue team
Lewis Keseberg Jr.	M	1	died Jan. 24 in winter camp

MCCUTCHEN FAMILY

William McCutchen	M	30	
Amanda McCutchen	F	24	
Harriet McCutchen	F	1	died Feb. 2 in winter camp

WILLIAMS FAMILY

Eliza Williams	F	25	
Baylis Williams	M	24	died Dec. 16 in winter camp

WOLFINGER FAMILY

Mr. Wolfinter	M	?	killed around Oct. 13 by Reinhardt and Spitzer
Mrs. Wolfinger	F	?	

UNRELATED INDIVIDUALS

Mr. Hardkoop	M	60	died around Oct. 8, abandoned by Lewis Keseberg
Patrick Dolan	M	40	died Dec. 25 with snowshoers
Charles Stanton	M	35	died around Dec. 21 with snowshoers
Charles Burger	M	30	died Dec. 29 in winter camp
Joseph Reinhardt	M	30	died in Nov. or early Dec. in winter camp
Augustus Spitzer	M	30	died Feb.7 in winter camp
John Denton	M	28	died Feb. 24 with first rescue team
Milton Elliot	M	28	died Feb. 9 in winter camp
Luke Halloran	M	25	died Aug. 29 of consumption
William Herron	M	25	
Samuel Shoemaker	M	25	died in Nov. or early Dec. in winter camp
James Smith	M	25	died in Nov. or early Dec. in winter camp
James Smith	M	25	died in Nov. or early Dec. in winter camp
John Snyder	M	25	killed Oct. 5 by James Reed
Jean Baptiste Trubode	M	23	
Antoine	M	23	died Dec. 24 with snowshoers
Noah James	M	20	

crease their metabolic rate when air temperature drops only a few degrees below body temperature, whereas adults don't have to do so until a drop of 20 to 35 degrees. At cold temperatures the factor by which babies must increase their metabolism to stay warm is several times that for adults. These considerations place even well-fed babies at risk under cold conditions. And the Donner Party babies were at a crippling further disadvantage because they had so little food to fuel their metabolism. They literally froze to death.

But what gave the women such an edge over the men? Were the pioneers practicing the noble motto "women and children first" when it came to dividing food? Unfortunately, "women and children last" is a more accurate description of how most men behave under stress. As the *Titanic* sank, male crew members took many places in lifeboats while leaving women and children of steerage class below decks to drown. Much grosser male behavior emerged when the steamship *Atlantic* sank in 1879: the death toll included 294 of the 295 women and children on board, but only 187 of the 636 men. In the Biafran famine of the late 1960s, when relief agencies tried to distribute food to youngsters under 10 and to pregnant and nursing women, Biafran men gave a brutally frank response: "Stop all this rubbish, it is we men who shall have the food, let the children die, we will make new children after the war." Similarly, accounts by Donner Party members yield no evidence of hungry men deferring to women, and babies fared especially poorly.

Instead, we must seek some cause other than male self-sacrifice to account for the survival of Donner Party women. One contributing factor is that the men were busy killing each other. Four of the five deaths before the pioneers reached the lake, plus the deaths of the two Indians, involved male victims of male violence, a pattern that fits widespread human experience.

However, invoking male violence still leaves 26 of 30 Donner Party male deaths unexplained. It also fails to explain why men began starving and freezing to death nearly two months before women did. Evidently the women had a

big physiological advantage. This could be an extreme expression of the fact that, at every age and for all leading causes of death—from cancer and car accidents to heart disease and suicide—the death rate is far higher for men than for women. While the reasons for this ubiquitous male vulnerability remain debated, there are several compelling reasons why men are more likely than women to die under the extreme conditions the Donner Party faced.

The Donner Party records make it vividly clear that family members stuck together and helped one another at the expense of the others.

First, men are bigger than women. Typical body weights for the world as a whole are about 140 pounds for men and only 120 pounds for women. Hence, even while lying down and doing nothing, men need more food to support their basal metabolism. They also need more energy than women do for equivalent physical activity. Even for sedentary people, the typical metabolic rate for an average-size woman is 25 percent lower than an average-size man's. Under conditions of cold temperatures and heavy physical activity, such as were faced by the Donner Party men when doing the backbreaking work of cutting the wagon road or hunting for food, men's metabolic rates can be double those of women.

To top it all off, women have more fat reserves than men: fat makes up 22 percent of the body weight of an average nonobese, well-nourished woman, but only 16 percent of a similar man. More of the man's weight is instead made up of muscle, which gets burned up much more quickly than does fat. Thus, when there simply was no more food left, the Donner Party men burned up their body reserves much faster than did the women. Furthermore, much of women's fat is distributed under the skin and acts as heat insulation, so that they can withstand cold temperatures better than men can. Women don't

have to raise their metabolic rate to stay warm as soon as men do.

These physiological factors easily surpass male murderousness in accounting for all those extra male deaths in the Donner Party. Indeed, a microcosm of the whole disaster was the escape attempt by 15 people on snowshoes, lasting 33 days in midwinter. Of the ten men who set out, two were murdered by another man, six starved or froze to death, and only two survived. Not a single one of the five women with them died.

Even with all these explanations, there is still one puzzling finding to consider: the unexpectedly high death toll of people in their prime, age 20 to 39. That toll proves to be almost entirely of the men: 67 percent of the men in that age range (14 out of 21) died, a much higher proportion than among the teenage boys (only 20 percent). Closer scrutiny shows why most of those men were so unlucky.

Most of the Donner Party consisted of large families, but there were also 16 individuals traveling without any relatives. All those 16 happened to be men, and all but two were between 20 and 39. Those 16 unfortunates bore the brunt of the prime-age mortality. Thirteen of them died, and most of them died long before any of the women. Of the survivors, one—William Herron—reached California in October, so in reality only 2 survived the winter at the lake.

Of the 7 men in their prime who survived, 4 were family men. Only 3 of the 14 dead were. The prime-age women fared similarly: the 8 survivors belonged to families with an average size of 12 people, while Eleanor Eddy, the only woman to die in this age group, had no adult support. Her husband had escaped with the snowshoers, leaving her alone with their two small children.

The Donner Party records make it vividly clear that family members stuck together and helped one another at the expense of the others. A notorious example was the Breen family of nine, every one of whom (even two small children) survived through the luck of retaining their wagons and some pack animals much longer than the others, and through their considerable selfishness toward others. Compare this with the old bachelor Hardkoop, who was ordered out of the Keseberg family wagon and abandoned to die, or the fate of the young bachelor Antoine, whom none of the hungry snowshoers bothered to awaken when his hand fell into the fire.

Family ties can be a matter of life and death even under normal conditions. Married people, it turns out, have lower death rates than single, widowed, or divorced people. And marriage's life-promoting benefits have been found to be shared by all sorts of social ties, such as friendships and membership in social groups. Regardless of age or sex or initial health status, socially isolated individuals have well over twice the death rate of socially connected people.

For reasons about which we can only speculate, the lethal effects of social isolation are more marked for men than for women. It's clear, though, why social contacts are important for both sexes. They provide concrete help in case of need. They're our source of advice and shared information. They provide a sense of belonging and self-worth, and the courage to face tomorrow. They make stress more bearable.

All those benefits of social contact applied as well to the Donner Party members, who differed only in that their risk of death was much greater and their likely circumstances of death more grotesque than yours and mine. In that sense too, the harrowing story of the Donner Party grips us because it was ordinary life writ large.

From *Discover* magazine, March 1992, pp. 100-107. © 1992 by Jared Diamond. Reproduced with permission of the author.

Israel's Mysterious Stone

Researchers battle over the authenticity of an ancient inscription

BY HAIM WATZMAN

JERUSALEM When Edward L. Greenstein, professor of biblical studies at Tel Aviv University, opened his newspaper one Tuesday in January, he was surprised to find front-page news from his field. Three scientists from the Geological Survey of Israel, a government research institute, had reported a major discovery: a black sandstone tablet engraved with ancient Hebrew letters.

According to the scientists, the stone and its inscription date to the ninth century BC and are apparently a remnant of the Holy Temple that, according to the Bible, King Solomon constructed in Jerusalem. That would make it the first material evidence ever found of the existence of the Temple. The discovery, Mr. Greenstein realized, would challenge the theories of "minimalist" scholars, who contend that Solomon's reign and other parts of biblical history might never have happened.

Far from just an academic dispute, the issue has profound religious and political implications. The hill in Jerusalem where Solomon is said to have built his temple has become a flashpoint in the Israeli-Palestinian conflict. Jews regard the site, which they call the Temple Mount, as sacred, and some fundamentalists want to rebuild the Holy Temple there. But the spot, now the site of the Dome of the Rock and the Al Aqsa mosque, is the third holiest in the Islamic world. The Muslim religious authorities who control it deny that a Jewish temple ever stood there.

Mr. Greenstein took a closer look at the photograph in the paper. "I had some time, and ancient Semitic texts is one of my areas of expertise, so I copied out the letters on a pad. And certain things struck me wrong," he said.

Fact or faked? An apparently ancient stone tablet, slightly larger than a sheet of office paper, describes repairs made to Solomon's Temple.

Mr. Greenstein was among several scholars here who took their concerns to the press. Around the world, other textual scholars have also detected problems with the inscription, ones that lead many to call the tablet a forgery. In fact, *Biblical Archaeology Review* has offered a $10,000 reward for someone who can duplicate the chemical signature of the "ancient" tablet. But the geologists who studied the stone stand by their conclusions, leading to a showdown between humanities researchers and scientists about who can best judge the authenticity of ancient material.

ANONYMOUS SOURCE

Rumors of the discovery first started circulating more than a year ago, yet details of the inscription emerged only in January, when the geological-survey scientists published their finding in their institute's journal, *Current Research*. The tablet had been delivered to the institute for analysis by agents of an anonymous antiquities collector.

The scientists analyzed the chemical composition of the tablet's surface, looking in particular at the patina that had formed on top of the sandstone. Such coatings often develop on ancient materials as their surface reacts with the air or with the ground in which they are buried. Among other tests, they sent samples of the patina to a laboratory in Miami for radiocarbon dating. This technique can measure the age of organic material, such as the carbon in the patina, and it indicated that the patina is more than 2,000 years old. The geologists concluded that "artificial production ... in recent years is not impossible, but seems to us not very probable.... [W]e propose that stages ... of the formation of the tablet predate 2,250 years BP [before present]." In other words, according to the scientists, the inscription is most likely genuine.

But the government survey geologists were not the only ones to be contacted by agents of the mysterious collector. According to press reports, scholars specializing in the vocabulary and syntax of ancient texts, and others whose expertise is paleography (the study of the physical forms of ancient writing) were shown the tablet at clandestine meetings in hotel rooms in Israel. Even then some suspected a forgery. It was not until the geologists' report was published, though, that the textual scholars could examine the inscription, with the help of the photograph in the institute's journal.

The text of the inscription commemorates repairs to the Temple. While the name of the king who had the inscription carved does not appear—it would most likely have been on a corner of the tablet that had broken off—from the context it is clear that the biblical king in question is Jehoash, whose reign of Judah is generally dated by historians to 836-798 BC. It closely parallels the account of these repairs given in the biblical Book of II Kings, Chapter 12, described also in II Chronicles, Chapter 24.

TOO GOOD TO BE TRUE

It was that closeness to the biblical text that aroused the suspicion of Nadav Neeman, a historian of the biblical period at Tel Aviv University. The find seemed too good to be true. In 1998, he had published an article in a Dutch biblical-studies journal, *Vetus Testamentum,* about the sources that the author of the Book of Kings had used in composing his work. Relying on differences of vocabulary and syntax in sections of Kings, Mr. Neeman theorized that the author of those sections had based his work on various texts available at the time. In particular, Mr. Neeman surmised that King Jehoash had placed a plaque in the area of the Temple to commemorate his renovation project and that the author of Kings had borrowed from that inscription. Royal inscriptions marking the important works of kings are a well-known genre of the ancient Middle East, though at that point none from the kingdom of Judah had ever been found.

Mr. Greenstein also found the inscription's similarity to the biblical text suspicious. But several other textual anomalies jumped out at him as he transcribed the text from the newspaper photograph onto a legal pad. By the time he had gone through the text, six major problems and a number of minor ones emerged, he says.

For example, one is the use of the phrase *bedeq habayit.* In modern Hebrew, this phrase has come to mean "renovations" or "home repairs." But the literal meaning is "breach in the house"—that is, cracks in the Temple walls. The Book of Kings thus uses the verb "to strengthen" in association with this phrase, meaning "to repair the breach in the house." But the verb used in the Jehoash inscription is "to do"—to do the breach in the house. That only makes sense, says Mr. Greenstein, if the person who wrote the text is using the phrase in the modern way, meaning "to do the renovations." Mr. Greenstein sees such evidence as a sign of a forger who knew enough chemistry to fool the geologists but not enough biblical Hebrew to fool the textual scholars.

Another problem he found was in the use of the word *edut.* The Jehoash inscription uses this word in the sense of "testimony," its meaning in modern Hebrew. But in parts of the Bible thought to date from the First Temple period, says, Mr. Greenstein, "*edut* means 'covenant,' while 'testimony' is signified by a related but distinct word, *ed.*"

The inscription has also been criticized by paleographers, who argue that the form of the ancient Hebrew letters is not appropriate to the time and place of King Jehoash. Frank Moore Cross, an emeritus professor of Hebrew at Harvard Divinity School, is publishing his paleographic analysis of the stone in a forthcoming issue of *Israel Exploration Journal.* In an e-mail message to *The Chronicle,* he says that "the script of the Plaque is not ninth-century Hebrew script (which we know well) but a mixture of ninth-century Phoenician, Moabite, and Old Aramaic scripts, [and] that the spelling does not follow in two cases the spelling rules used in pre-Exilic Hebrew texts...."

"Any one of these howlers would demonstrate the spurious character of the inscription on the sandstone plaque," he writes.

Both Mr. Greenstein and Mr. Cross have told the Israeli press that the chemical and geological results cannot, by themselves, validate the find. If the text does not match what humanities scholars know about the ancient Hebrew language and alphabet, the results obtained by the "hard sciences" must be mistaken, they say. Both suggest that the Israeli geological-survey scientists did not perform sufficiently rigorous tests. The geological survey's analysis has been criticized in detail by the chairman of Tel Aviv University's department of archaeology and ancient Near Eastern cultures, Yuval Goren, in an article posted on a site called the Bible and Interpretation (http://www.bibleinterp.com/articles/alternative_interpretation.htm).

Mr. Goren points out that royal inscriptions are generally engraved on basalt. He says that the choice of sandstone in this instance is no coincidence. It is much easier to apply a fake patina to sandstone, Mr. Goren argues in his paper. He offers a step-by-step process by which, he says, the patina could have been applied, weathered, and aged.

The authors of the Israeli geological-survey paper, Shimon Hani, Amnon Rosenfeld, and Michael Dvorachek, are government employees and are not permitted to speak to journalists directly. But a scientist close to them says that the geologists stand by their results and that Mr. Goren's critique is "garbage."

$10,000 PRIZE

The scientist supports the geologists' claim that some of the chemical characteristics of the patina would be nearly impossible to fake. Even the doubters accept the geologists' dating of the patina to the ancient period, though they say that patina from some other object could have been applied to the inscription.

Beyond that, the geologists also reported that the patina contains minute globules of pure gold, measuring from one to a few microns in size. Formation of such globules of gold, the geologists write in their paper, requires temperatures of more than 1,800 degrees Fahrenheit, and their distribution in the patina indicates a natural rather than an artificial process. The geologists suggest that the globules may have formed, and adhered to the inscription, when the Temple, which contained gold objects and decorations, was burned by the Babylonians, according to the Bible.

The scholars in the humanities simply don't know enough chemistry to judge the scientists' results, the scientist close to the Israeli geologists suggests. But Mr. Cross says that he has an undergraduate degree in chemistry, did postgraduate work in the field, and knows it quite well.

Hershel Shanks, editor of the magazine *Biblical Archaeology Review,* published in Washington, says that he finds the textual evidence of a forgery compelling. He also points out, though, that he knows of no other cases in which an ancient patina of this type has been successfully faked. In the current issue of the magazine he is announcing a $10,000 prize for anyone who can convincingly fake a patina of the type found on the Jehoash inscription.

> Microscopic globs of gold embedded in the tablet's surface could have come from the burning of gold objects when the Temple was destroyed. But skeptics say that the gold bits reflect the process used to fake the stone's patina.

Everyone involved agrees that the find is especially problematic because it was not excavated in a methodical archaeological dig where scientists could record its context and surroundings. Such context is important for dating and authenticating ancient objects. Still, antiquities are valuable, and as a result there is a thriving black market in them, and that market has always been a source of both important finds (such as the Dead Sea Scrolls) and forgeries. It is little surprise that the tablet's provenance remains obscure: According to Israeli law, all antiquities are public property. Private excavations and the sale of antiquities are felonies. The law is so strict that even the marketing of forgeries and replicas can land you in jail.

TESTING THE STONE

When rumors of the existence of the Jehoash inscription began circulating, the Israel Antiquities Authority, the statutory body charged with protection of archaeological objects, began an investigation that eventually led to an antiquities collector, Oded Golan, who acknowledged having the inscription in his possession, although he denied being its owner. Mr. Golan is now under investigation, and the sandstone plaque has been turned over to the antiquities authority, which has established two committees to study the object. One will be responsible for chemical and geological analysis, and the other will examine the textual and paleographical issues the inscription raises. The stone may be sent overseas for further chemical tests. While the committees have no deadline for submitting their report, Osnat Goaz, the spokesman for the authority, says that the process will probably take a number of weeks.

That will provide time for tempers to cool and egos to calm, says Gabriel Barkay, an archaeologist from Bar-Ilan University. Mr. Barkay says that the textual and paleographic arguments made against the tablet's authenticity so far are weak. None of them is unambiguous, and, he adds, a forger could have opened any modern Hebrew dictionary to find out the biblical sense of *bedeq habayit.* He views the chemical analysis as compelling.

Yet the field of archaeology has known many forgeries, he acknowledges, and it will take time and study to reveal the truth about the Jehoash inscription.

For now, Mr. Barkay remains undecided. Despite his skepticism about the textual and paleographic arguments made to date, he does think that such research is more important than the work of chemists and geologists.

"An inscription is made by man, not by nature," he points out, "and so the natural sciences have to take second place to the humanities."

Legacy *of the* Crusades

The ruins of castles on hillsides throughout the Middle East are mute
reminders of a bloody chapter in medieval history.

by Sandra Scham

A STORY IS TOLD IN KERAK, a small city in Jordan dominated by a well-preserved crusader castle, about the fortress'
most notorious denizen, Reynauld of Chatillon. According to
this tale, the Hajj route to Mecca during Reynauld's time, the
late twelfth century A.D., passed beneath his castle walls. At-
tracted by the richness of one caravan, Reynauld swooped down
on the unfortunate pilgrims, capturing all and relieving them of
their worldly goods. At the end of his foray, he found, to his immense glee, that one of his hostages was the sister of the legendary Islamic leader Saladin. Reynauld's fellow crusaders
were appalled by his brazen violation of a rather tenuous truce.
Baldwin IV, king of Jerusalem, sent a message forthwith, demanding that Reynauld release his distinguished prisoner. Reynauld's answer reflects his customary bravado: "You are king
of Jerusalem," he wrote, "but I am king in Kerak."

Kerak, though, never had a king, a fact well known to both
Reynauld and the local guides who repeat this story. Nevertheless, although it was within the boundaries of the crusader
kingdom of Jerusalem, Kerak was also far enough away from
the center of power to enable its ruler to do pretty much as he
pleased—that is, summarily executing prisoners, whether they
were men, women, or children, in the most brutal manner imag-
inable. Reynauld eventually got his just desserts, and has the dubious distinction of being the only important crusader to have
been personally executed by Saladin.

The castle of Kerak is built on a spur to take advantage of the
natural defense accorded by this topography. The town of Kerak
has grown all around the spur and it is usually a lively tourist
destination. I visited the site, familiar to me from previous so-
journs in Jordan, on a beautiful day this past summer, when one
would normally expect to see tour buses and guides hustling
large groups through the castle gates. The streets were empty.
Abdul Hamied, one of Kerak's more knowledgeable local
guides, explained, "Tourism in Jordan is down by 70 percent-I

worked only seven days this year." Jordan is feeling the effects
of the prolonged Israeli-Palestinian struggle, despite the fact
that it has been relatively free from conflict itself.

The castle of Kerak in Jordan was once
home to notorious crusader knight
Reynauld of Chatillon, who preyed on
pilgrims traveling to Mecca. A popular
tourist destination in modern times, the
castle has recently seen a drop in visitors
because of the ongoing Israeli-
Palestinian conflict.

Reflecting on battles both past and present, and the physical
legacy of these conflicts ever-present in the landscape, I asked
Hamied what he learned about crusader history growing up in
Kerak in the shadow of this looming medieval structure. "We
were taught that they came from Pharaoh's Island [off the coast
of the Sinai Peninsula] and built this line of castles here [from
Aqaba to Turkey] to control the trading business," he replied.
"When these crusaders came, they came as invaders—killing
thousands. And they were not coming for religion or 'holy war.'
It was an economic war that used religion."

Aziz Azayzeh, another guide at Kerak, agrees with this assessment. "As a Jordanian, I learned in school that the crusaders
came and took our lands just because of greed and gave us
nothing in return." Both men, however, true to their professions,
say similar things about the crusader sites. Azayzeh continues,
"Later, when I studied more about them, I think they did give us
something—they were good architects. You know Saladin was

smart. He asked the best architects and artists from the crusaders to stay and work." Hamied is more philosophical: "The crusaders—they came as invaders, the Romans came as invaders, in Hellenistic times also. The big powers everywhere—they look to their own interests, but they left something behind for us at these places."

Listening to these remarks, as I stood at the summit of Kerak, I recalled a conversation I had with a colleague before leaving the United States. Salman Elbedour, an American psychology professor who is also an Israeli Bedouin, told me that there is a "Crusader Complex" in the Middle East. Consequently, it was no surprise to him that President Bush's rather bizarre juxtaposition of ideas, promising to rid the world of the perpetrators of violence in the name of religion, while at the same time labeling the American incursion in Afghanistan a "crusade," was perceived as a major affront by the Arab world. Elbedour and other Muslims, whose ancestors lived in the very heart of crusader territory, see the crusaders as the ultimate vicious usurpers. Archaeologist Adel Yahyeh, who lives in Ramallah on the West Bank, adds, "When we were children in Palestine, our nightmares were about monsters coming after us, wearing crosses on their chests. We even started to see Israeli soldiers that way—strange as it seems."

> "*Y*ou go to Lebanon, Syria, Jordan today...you can see that many of the crusaders stayed and married, and that today we are a mixture of people."

Crusader sites, like the crusader tradition, inspire a variety of emotions and thoughts. The castles are what most people think of when they envision the crusader period (1097-1291), and many Arabs, says Yahyeh, take a measure of pride in them, since it was the Arabs who liberated the castles from their Christian enemy. But there are other effects of the period to be considered, as well. "You go to Lebanon, Syria, Jordan today...you can see that many of the crusaders stayed and married, and that today we are a mixture of people," says Azayzeh. This casual statement actually reflects the focus of a great deal of new archaeological activity relating to crusader sites in the region. Although it was long believed that European culture did not penetrate rural areas in the Levant, excavations of villages and farmsteads with crusader architecture, sugar refining equipment (a fairly new industry in the medieval period), and a general increase in pig bones at rural sites now indicate otherwise.

Of course, Muslims are not the only ones to have suffered at the hands of the crusaders. Eastern Orthodox Christians and Jews have their own perspectives on this period. As Jörg Bremer, a German historian and journalist who is now living in Jerusalem, says, "Today, we talk of special [collective] memories of the Crusades." Jews see the Crusades, he continues, "as having started in Germany with killing of Jews." Then, there is "the tradition of the Eastern Church relating to the sack of Byzantium" (by crusaders in 1204—when it was an entirely Christian city). Finally, he speaks of the revival of crusader consciousness among Muslims who see "the state of Israel today as neo-crusader."

Bremer is a latter-day member of the Order of the Knights of St. John (the Hospitallers), as were his ancestors, and explains, "The Hospitallers were in the Holy Land long before the Crusades and were not called 'knights' until the real crusaders came." Hospitaller tradition, he says, avers that "we were the only European group that was allowed to stay [after the crusaders were defeated]." Bremer laments the fact that the Hospitallers, originally a peaceful group, were forced by the coming of the Templars to bear arms. The Templars were founded in 1119 for the purpose of defending Christian pilgrims in the Holy Land, while the Hospitallers, so-called because their principal mission was to care for the sick, did not become a military order until 1130, some 60 years after having been founded in Jerusalem.

The historical and cultural legacy of the Crusades is accompanied by a concrete, or rather stone, legacy, dotting hillsides throughout the Middle East. Less obvious than the isolated castles like Kerak are the crusader remains in the cities, many of which were built upon in subsequent eras. Jerusalem and Akko (Acre), the two most important cities of medieval times, are replete with varied examples of crusader architecture. In Jerusalem, the centerpiece of the crusader kingdom, many sites were modified by the crusaders, but they built from the ground up as well. Not surprisingly, most of these activities centered on churches; the complete rebuilding of the Church of the Holy Sepulchre was a major project. The church was consecrated in 1149, a half-century after the crusaders first seized Jerusalem, and stands today largely in its crusader form.

> *A*kko's harbor served as the primary port of entry for pilgrims to the Holy Land. Today, local residents take a plunge into the Mediterranean from the city's crusader fortifications.

Despite this fact, many members of Eastern Orthodox denominations think of the Church of the Holy Sepulchre as Byzantine. "It was first built in the fourth century, and there are still Byzantine structures," explains Ardin Sisserian, an Eastern Orthodox gatekeeper and guide at the Church. The reason for his de-emphasis on crusader architecture here may have something to do with tensions between the Catholics, "whose ancestors came with the sword and the Cross," says Sisserian, and the other four faiths that have access to the Church—all Eastern Christian.

Bremer encountered similar tensions when he and other modern Hospitallers asked to pray at Jerusalem's twelfth-century Church of St. John the Baptist, patron saint of their order. Although the Greek Orthodox Church now owns the structure, it was once so important to the Hospitallers that they maintained guards there after the expulsion of other crusaders and the re-taking of Jerusalem by Saladin in 1244. The Hospitallers were denied permission to pray there until 2001, when, Bremer says, they went to Greek Orthodox officials to open what he calls a "diplomatic channel," with the formal admission that "this part of our history is horrible" and that they wanted to go "on the record as recognizing special ties with the Eastern Church." As a result, Bremer says, they "could pray in the church for the first time in 800 years."

These days, most visitors to the Church of the Holy Sepulchre appear to be Israelis rather than Christian pilgrims—who, like many others, are leery of coming to what they perceive to be a war zone. Among the groups speaking Hebrew and touring the church on one Shabbat (Jewish Sabbath) afternoon were several people wearing yarmulkes, as well as seemingly secular Jews. A nonreligious member of a group of mixed religious and secular students, Hagai Dror, explained, "Christians today seem closer to Jews than Muslims do. We see these sites as European, and many of us who have a European background are interested in them." His friend, Gal Ariely, added, "The main reason we are here is because we live here. This is my city, and it's my duty to know about it." This last statement reflects the sense of ownership that many young Israelis feel about Jerusalem. Yossi is an ultra-orthodox Jewish resident of the Mt. Zion's Diaspora Yeshiva, which is housed in a building that was at one time a fourteenth-century crusader monastery. Yossi, who had a strictly religious education in Jerusalem, says that he knows nothing about crusaders except that "I live in a crusader house."

THE CITY OF AKKO was the last major crusader foothold in Palestine—finally falling to the Muslim forces in 1291, after 100 years of renewed crusader rule. Akko's crusader remains can now be seen below the city's current street level in the northern part of today's walled Old Town. It's a fascinating labyrinth of underground structures unearthed by excavations that began in the late 1950s and continue today. There are barracks for the knights, a hall of the crusader palace, an underground sewage system with a number of public toilets, and portions of crusader streets and walls—all visible beneath the bustling Ottoman city above.

Akko's Ottoman structures, largely built on top of the crusader ruins, represent the Arab character of the city, past and present. The people who live in most of the houses in the Old City, however, were moved there from the Galilee after 1948 (the year of the establishment of the state of Israel), when Akko's older indigenous Arab population fled the city. Ron Be'eri, an archaeologist from the University of Haifa who works at Akko, says that the people who live there today "feel little connection with the city's history" and generally view the historical character of their own houses as an annoyance. Considered abandoned property owned by the State of Israel, these places are occupied mostly by Arab renters who are not permitted, even if they have the funds, to buy them. They are also not permitted, because these are historic structures, to alter them in any way. Consequently, most of the Old City's residences are in great disrepair.

Nevertheless, Erica Gal of the Akko Development Corporation insists that Akko's locals take an interest in the heritage of their city. "Schools visit the subterranean [crusader] site all the time and, from the fifth grade, local students take a course called 'Akko, My Town' in which they learn all of the local history." She does suggest that visits by local people to Akko underground may be limited by the fact that they must buy tickets to gain access to it. Be'eri believes that "very few" of the Old City's residents have ever visited the crusader site, but this may reflect their hostility toward "heritage sites" in general, given their experience with them, rather than any residual resentment of crusaders.

Although the schools of Akko may take an interest in crusader sites as part of the local history, education in most of Israel, as distinct from Jordan, glosses over the crusader occupation. "We learn nothing about this period in school," says Salman Elbedour, who received an Israeli education. According to Israeli archaeologist Adrian Boas, the crusader period, which is his area of specialization, is not a favored subject for Israeli historians and archaeologists, although he points out that a recent crusader exhibit at the Israel Museum in Jerusalem drew large crowds. As to the historical antagonism, "If you asked the average Jew here about this," he says, "they wouldn't have a clue what you were talking about." Attitudes toward crusader sites in Israel are a reflection of cultural ties to, or antipathies toward, the Crusades as well as individually held beliefs. Boas, originally from Australia, says that his interest in the Crusades and crusader sites comes "from basically having grown up in an Anglo-Saxon country. As a child, I was always interested in the medieval period." Elbedour says that he has no interest in visiting crusader sites. Bremer, who has visited the sites, says that many of the castles look "so militant—like tank posts on top of a hill."

While Boas admires the "tactical advantages" of Kerak and other spur castles, he says that he is most impressed with Belvoir, a Hospitaller castle overlooking the Jordan River and the Damascus to Jerusalem Road. In this case, the strategical importance of Belvoir's location in the past is repeated in the present as today, it overlooks the boundaries between Israel and the West Bank, and Israel and Jordan. One of the earliest examples of the "concentric castle" or castrum, a building with one fortification wall entirely enclosing another, Belvoir remains one of the most remarkable buildings of this type.

On the coast south of Akko is probably one of the few crusader sites in the Middle East that is regularly visited by people who live there. Elbedour admits to having been to only one crusader site, Caesarea, but only "because it's on the [Mediterranean] Sea." Although the town witnessed few historical events in the past, some crusader buildings at Caesarea have an interesting modern history. One of them, the citadel, became a mosque after the defeat of the crusaders. With the founding of the state of Israel and subsequent displacement of the local population of Muslims, the mosque became a restaurant and bar, a state of affairs that was bound to offend those Muslims remaining in the region. The restaurant, called "The Castle," is now closed.

Caesarea's crusader—and Roman-era ruins were restored to attract foreign tourists. Its location on a stretch of sandy Mediterranean beach makes it popular with Israeli visitors.

Caesarea, according to Pennsylvania State University archaeologist Ann Killebrew, was among those sites that the Israel Antiquities Authority decided early on to develop. Crusader remains and Roman ruins, although they do not precisely reflect the ethnic or religious character of the country today, were restored specifically to attract foreign tourists, she says. In the 1990s, Caesarea was further embellished as a result of the government's efforts to provide employment to workers from the nearby town of Or Akiva. As a result, says Killebrew, the site has been "completely uncovered, and has become unattractive to tourists."

Some writers who have recently looked at the legacy of the Crusades, such as Karen Armstrong (*Holy War*) and, to a lesser extent, Bernard Lewis (*What Went Wrong?*) believe they are the source of the troubles afflicting the Middle East today. Whether or not the Crusades were responsible for bringing West and East together or, conversely, the origin of the struggles now taking place in the region, it seems certain that a crusader legacy, lasting almost 1,000 years, is not a media fantasy. In few places in the world is ancient history given such immediacy as in the Middle East. The founding of the state of Israel in 1948 was partially predicated on the biblical history of the region during the Iron Age—a period some 3,000 years in the past. A trauma that is only 900 years old is relatively recent in a place where history is marked by millennia rather than centuries.

SANDRA SCHAM, *a contributing editor for* ARCHAEOLOGY, *is an archaeologist who has been living and working in Israel since 1996. A former curator of the Pontifical Biblical Institute Museum in Jerusalem, she is currently affiliated with the department of anthropology at the University of Maryland at College Park.*

UNIT 5

Contemporary Archaeology

Unit Selections

Key Points to Consider

- What are the differences between "creationism," "alternative archaeology," and the science of archaeology? What needs do each seem to satisfy and why can they not be reconciled?
- Why do both ethnographers and archaeologists go into the field to gather the same data? How do these approaches differ? What is their impact on native people?
- What is the latest word on the controversial skull known as "Kennewick Man?" Does "Kennewick Man" belong to archeologists or to "the American Indians?" How old is the skull?
- In the absence of government funding, should archaeological fieldwork be financed with private business deals if it means getting there before the looters?
- Should a badly needed highway be allowed to cover a World War I battlefield or should the area be preserved as a memorial?
- What happens if archaeologists themselves lie about their findings to suit their own purposes? Give an example of this based on the findings at the Nazi death camps.
- Did Brazil's rain forest once support an ancient civilization or not? Support your position.
- What evidence is there that modern humans replaced the Neandertals? Why were the Neandertals unable to resist the encroachment?
- How have the new methods of "virtual paleoanthropology" revised our views on the Neandertal?
- Should historical landmarks and artifacts accumulating on the Moon and on Mars be protected from profiteers and souvenir hunters?

Student Website

www.mhcls.com/online

Internet References

Further information regarding these websites may be found in this book's preface or online.

Archaeology and Anthropology: The Australian National University
http://online.anu.edu.au/AandA/

WWW: Classical Archaeology
http://www.archaeology.org/wwwarky/classical.html

Al Mashriq-Archaeology in Beirut
http://almashriq.hiof.no/base/archaeology.html

American Indian Ritual Object Repatriation Foundation
http://www.repatriationfoundation.org/

ArchNet—WWW Virtual Library
http://archnet.asu.edu/archnet/

Current Archaeology
http://www.archaeology.co.uk

National Archeological DataBase
http://www.cast.uark.edu/other/nps/nagpra/nagpra.html

Society for Archaeological Sciences
http://www.socarchsci.org/

The origins of contemporary archaeology may be traced back to the nineteenth century. Several currents of thought and beliefs coalesced in that unique century. Some say it started with a Frenchman named Boucher de Perthes who found odd-shaped stones on his property, stones that could comfortably be held by a human hand. Undoubtedly, thousands of other people made such finds throughout history. But to Monsieur de Perthes, these stones suggested a novel meaning. He wondered if these odd rocks might not be tools, made by humans long lost in the mists before history.

Other exciting changes were occurring in the epistemology of the nineteenth century that would soon lend credibility to this hypothesis. In 1859 there was the publication of *On the Origin of Species* by Charles Darwin. In this book, (which, by the way, never mentioned humans or any implied relationship they might have to apes) Darwin suggested a general process that became known as natural selection. The theory suggested that a species could change gradually through time in response to the environment. This was an idea counterintuitive to scientific thought. Even biologists believed that species were immutable. But it changed forever the nature of the way human beings regarded their place in nature. If species could change, then the implication was so could humans. And that idea knocked humankind down from its loft and into the archaeological record.

There was the concurrent emergence of the idea of uniformitarianism, which implied that Earth was old, very old, perhaps hundreds of thousands of years old. (It is, in fact, about 5 billion years old.) But with this idea, the revolutionary possibility that hu-

man beings could have existed before history became more plausible. Such a serious challenge to the established wisdom that Earth was only about 6,000 years old additionally contributed to this new age of speculation on the meaning of being human.

The newly emerging science of paleontology and the discovery and recognition of extinct fossil species seriously challenged the traditional elevated status of human beings. Nineteenth-century philosophers were forced to reexamine the nature of humanity. Among the intellectuals of the Western world, the essential anthropocentrism of the Christian view gradually shifted to a more secular view of humankind as part and parcel of nature. Therefore humans became subject to the rules of nature and natural events, without reference to a theology.

So it was then, within this new nineteenth-century enlightenment, that Boucher de Perthes suggested his hypothesis regarding the antiquity of his stone tools. The time had come, and others answered that they too had found these same odd-shaped stones and had thought similar thoughts. The study of archaeology had begun.

As a science evolves, it naturally diversifies. There is now worry that archaeologists will specialize themselves right out of the mainstream of anthropology. But the shared cultural concept and holistic approach tend to maintain this traditional relationship. That is not to deny that mainstream archaeology is now being pulled in many different directions.

The saving grace in contemporary archaeology may be found in the current trend of moving toward a more public archaeology. There is awareness that archaeologists should tell more stories or talk about their own digs and portray a larger picture that says something more than the sum of tedious detail. And above all, archaeologists should stop talking inbred lingo to each other. Now is the time to start a give-and-take dialogue with the public.

Article selections deal with the interest in the preservation, conservation, reconstruction, and transformation of archaeological sites into the present for the educational and aesthetic value of the sites themselves. This is the direction of contemporary archaeology. More attention must be directed toward the financing of archaeological endeavors as well as the incorporation of alternate sources of labor in these new political times.

Ethical questions must be faced. An archaeological site should be viewed as nonrenewable resource. What of the needs of developers? It is their livelihood to do this work even if it means destroying archaeological sites. What of the rights of landowners versus persons with a perceived historical ownership of the same land? Archaeological excavation itself is the systematic destruction of sites and their ecological context. Anything overlooked, mislaid, not measured, or in some way not observed is a lost piece of the past. If the information is never shared with an audience, it is a complete loss.

Archaeology from the Dark Side

Creationists and New Agers have formed a common front to undermine mainstream archaeology and its scientific view of the human past. Are they winning?

Andrew O'Hehir

In February of 1961, three amateur gem collectors dug a mechanical gizmo encased in fossil-encrusted rock out of a mountainside in the Southern California desert. They didn't know what it was, and began showing it to friends and associates. Within a few years this thin gummy, which became known as the Coso artifact, had assumed an almost mythic importance.

It consisted of a cylinder of what seemed to be porcelain with a 2-millimeter shaft of bright metal in its center, enclosed by a hexagonal sheath composed of copper and another substance they couldn't identify. Yet its discoverers at first believed it had been found in a geode, a hardened mineral nodule at least 500,000 years old. If the Coso artifact was real—that is, if it was really an example of unknown technology from many millennia before the accepted emergence of Homo sapiens, let alone the dawn of human history—it would turn everything scientists thought they knew about the past of our species upside down.

Critics of mainstream science from all over the ideological and theological spectrum seized on the object. Some were followers of "alternative archaeology," especially believers in a lost Atlantis-type civilization deep in antiquity that gave birth to all the known civilizations of early human history. Others were followers of Erich von Däniken's hypothesis that human civilization has its roots in outer space. Still others were "young-earth" Biblical creationists, who thought the artifact might be a fragment of

the forgotten world that existed before the great Flood described in the Book of Genesis. (Of course, they didn't buy the idea that it might be hundreds of thousands of years old, since most creationists believe that God created the heavens and the earth somewhere between 6,000 and 10,000 years ago.)

The Coso artifact was featured in publications of the Charles Fort Society, which propounds all kinds of quirky pseudoscience. It appeared prominently in "Secrets of the Ancient Races," a 1977 collection of alternative-archaeology evidence by journalist Rene Noorbergen. As recently as 1999, it was a staple of lectures by chemist Donald Chittick, a leading "creation science" evangelist. Its fans had various theories about what it might be: a transmitter, a superconductor, a spark plug or a capacitor, or simply an unknown instrument "as old as legendary Mu or Atlantis," as one of its discoverers mused. If they didn't agree on much, they shared a common enemy. They all longed for a discovery that would destroy the accepted chronologies of archaeology, paleontology and history.

Very few of these people actually saw the artifact itself, which seems to have been lost sometime after 1969. Photographs and X-ray images of it can easily be found on the Internet, and in 1999, when skeptic Paul Heinrich sent those to four different spark-plug collectors, who had never seen the pictures or heard about the find, they unanimously and independently agreed: It was an old plug, all right, but not exactly a wonder of ancient Mu.

The Coso artifact, they reported, looked an awful lot like a standard Champion spark plug from the 1920s, which had most likely powered the engine of a Model T or Model A Ford. Furthermore, the object wasn't sealed in a geode after all, but just a sun-baked lump of clay, pebbles and shells. It had been on that mountain no longer than 40 years. Case closed, or pretty much so.

About the only thing that distinguishes the Coso artifact from the rest of the murky realm of fringe archaeology is the fact that no one—or almost no one—is still prepared to defend it as an ancient mystery. In every other way, it's a classic example: an odd discovery or "out-of-place artifact" ("oopart," in alternative-archaeology jargon) that lends itself to unorthodox and highly speculative notions about the origins of human civilization. The Internet, with its unique ability to elevate bogosity and cheapen fact, is awash with this stuff: video footage of underwater Atlantean "roads" near Bimini; engineering diagrams of Noah's ark; evidence linking the "face on Mars" to the Pyramids of Giza and the Old Testament.

As the Coso story demonstrates, over the last several decades, a loose and sometimes uncomfortable common front has been forged between fundamentalist Christian creationists and New Age-flavored practitioners of alternative archaeology. Although the two sides' philosophies are sharply different in some areas, they've both launched forceful attacks against the authority and guiding ideology of modern science. (In general, these movements rely on reinterpreting existing data, although some prominent alternative-archaeology researchers fund their own expeditions and research, and there are creationists involved in biblical archaeology.)

In a society sharply divided by politics, culture and religion, there's ample hostility—on both the disaffected right and disaffected left—toward what many perceive as the dogmatic pronouncements of a scientific elite. In the case of archaeology, these movements have channeled that hostility into alternative visions of the human past that engage surprisingly large sectors of the public. Although both creationism and alternative archaeology have adopted some scientific trappings, they seek ultimate answers to the riddles of human existence on the spiritual or supernatural plane, where scientists cannot and should not venture.

"If you examine the methodologies of pseudoarchaeology and creationism—the way they construct their arguments—you'll find that they're almost identical," says Garrett Fagan, a professor of classics and ancient Mediterranean studies at Penn State who has devoted much of his career to battling alternative archaeology. "These are essentially not intellectual arguments; they are political arguments. It looks like science, but it's not. They blame science and evolution for any number of social ills, and they regard undermining and destroying science as a primary goal."

Fagan's notion that the conflict between the archaeological establishment and the barbarians at its gates is politics masquerading as science is about the only thing all sides can agree on. Complaints that the other side has abandoned science for ideology flow liberally in both directions. "I don't think archaeology is a scientific enterprise," says British journalist Graham Hancock, the author of several books on the search for a quasi-Atlantean lost civilization.

While archaeology "takes shelter behind a scientific facade and uses some scientific tools," Hancock says by telephone from his home in England, "it really involves the interpretation of some limited evidence, done in the normally limited human way." (Some archaeologists would generally agree with this.) "Those who control knowledge about the past control a great deal," he goes on. "All of us are involved in a relationship with the past, and I think it's extremely unhealthy that a small group of like-minded specialists should be given a blank sheet to interpret it."

Hancock, a former East Africa bureau chief for the Economist, is a talented writer and one of the most reasonable exponents in a field full of wild guesses and conspiracy theories. But his claims about the past, like most of alternative archaeology, are generally unsupported by hard evidence. His view of mainstream archaeology as a closed-minded cabal of experts, which is also typical of the field, is overly simplistic. Despite the troubled past of their discipline—19th century archaeology could fairly be described as imperialist plundering, with overtones of racism—and the all too human limitations Hancock cites, archaeologists have pieced together a compelling picture of the human past, which necessarily remains incomplete and full of genuine controversy.

It would be easy to cast this as a matter of rational scientists under siege from religious fanatics and zoned-out goofballs. But that doesn't help us understand what the long-running conflict over archaeology is really about. It's certainly about the rejuvenation of the search for Atlantis, and about the ambiguous intellectual flowering of the creationist movement. More fundamentally, it's another front in our society's intractable cultural and religious wars, a collision between people whose sincerely held beliefs about human origins and human culture are not just different but epistemologically opposed. In some sense they don't inhabit the same universe, but in the United States they are trying to share the same nation.

There isn't exactly a smoking gun linking creationism to alternative archaeology; there was no secret 1970s summit meeting between evangelists in Sears Roebuck suits and tie-dyed New Agers from the New Mexico mountains. But there are numerous points of contact, some of them surprising, and one can detect a pattern of common interests and common approaches stretching back at least as far as Ignatius Donnelly, the 19th century Minnesota politician who launched the modern Atlantis craze.

Donnelly suggested that the story of Noah's Flood was one of the many global legends that authenticated Plato's account of a lost continent (found in the Socratic dialogues "Timaeus" and "Critias"). Fundamentalists saw (and still see) the same equation in reverse: Plato's story about a proud civilization doomed by the gods was one of many heathen distortions of the true account given in the Hebrew Bible. The two sides have basically been mirroring each other's arguments and cribbing from each other's textual readings ever since.

American archaeologists have been aware of this pincer movement against their discipline for decades. Books and magazine articles speculating on the historicity of Atlantis and similar foremother civilizations have flowed virtually uninterrupted since the publication of Donnelly's "Atlantis: The Antediluvian World" in 1882. Not surprisingly, the 1960s and '70s marked a golden age for this genre. Erich von Däniken claims to have sold more than 60 million copies of his various books on the ancient-astronaut hypothesis, which could be called an outer-space version of the Atlantis story. Other alternative archaeology titles became cult classics, including some by genuine if eccentric scholars like historians Charles Hapgood and Giorgio de Santillana. Most remain in print today.

More recently, Hancock's "Fingerprints of the Gods," a summary of many converging currents in the Atlantean quest, was an international bestseller in the mid-'90s; he reports more than 5 million sales for all his titles. Other influential alternative-archaeology exponents, most associated with Hancock in some way, include amateur Egyptologist John Anthony West ("Serpent in the Sky"), engineer Robert Bauval ("The Orion Mystery"), the Canadian couple Rand and Rose Flem-Ath ("When the Sky Fell: In Search of Atlantis") and archaeological/historical researchers Michael Cremo and Richard Thompson ("Forbidden Archeology [sic]: The Hidden History of the Human Race").

That same period saw a resurgence of evangelical Christianity and the founding of the Institute for Creation Research and numerous other "creation science" organizations. By the '80s it was clear that creationism—which most scientists viewed as an irrelevant cult belief—had never died out in the United States and was in fact becoming increasingly popular and influential. Polls consistently suggest that 40 to 50 percent of Americans believe that the Genesis account of Creation is literally true, although the depth of that conviction is impossible to measure.

Alternative archaeology and creation science converged spectacularly in a notorious television special called "The Mysterious Origins of Man," which aired on NBC in February 1996. Hosted by Charlton Heston, the show presented an incoherent farrago of mutually contradictory

hypotheses from "a new generation of scientific researchers," as Heston soberly intoned.

Hancock appeared to announce that the pre-Incan archaeological site of Tiwanaku in the Bolivian Andes might be 12,000 years old and a remnant of his lost civilization; creationist Carl Baugh held up molds of egregiously phony human footprints found alongside dinosaur footprints in a Texas riverbed. Pseudoscience researcher David Hatcher Childress discussed the alleged plesiosaur dredged up by a Japanese fishing boat in 1977 (probably a rotten shark carcass). Cremo and Thompson explained that archaeologists have ignored or suppressed evidence that the human race has been on this planet for millions, perhaps billions, of years. Nowhere was it mentioned that these people have vastly different ideas about the age of the earth and the origins of human civilization. The only thing they shared—and the program's only plausible goal—was a desire to damage the credibility of science with a mass audience.

If there were a smoking gun linking creationism to alternative archaeology, Michael Cremo would be holding it. A soft-spoken man who radiates calm and measured intellect, Cremo is a singular figure on the scientific fringe. He is friendly with mainstream archaeologists and with Graham Hancock. He has delivered papers at the World Archaeological Congress and been cited as a "fellow-traveler" by creation evangelists. His 1993 "Forbidden Archeology," written with mathematician Thompson, has become a canonical text for both New Agers and fundamentalists.

This is especially remarkable when you consider that virtually all those people would agree that Cremo's central contention—that anatomically modern humans have existed for billions of years—is ludicrous. His genuine intellectual achievement in "Forbidden Archeology," a dense 900-page discussion of "ooparts" and other anomalous findings, is the development of a meme that's now ubiquitous in creationism and alternative archaeology. Mainstream science, he argues, has become a "knowledge filter" designed to keep the most challenging ideas out of the discourse. His explorations of this question—how scientific consensus can become a kind of groupthink, and how contradictory evidence then becomes unacceptable—have gained him the grudging respect of at least some scholars.

"I've had some degree of recognition from mainstream academic circles that what I'm doing makes a contribution," Cremo says from his Los Angeles office. "I think I've gotten a fair hearing; it's not like on one side you have Michael Cremo and on the other side you've got mainstream science."

This is true, but only up to a point. "Forbidden Archeology" was favorably reviewed in a few specialized academic journals. But even Cremo hastens to explain that those reviewers don't agree with his underlying belief system. His entire posture as an almost respectable historian or sociologist of science (he doesn't claim any scientific credentials) and a bridge between fundamentalist Christians and New Agers is only possible because no one agrees with him.

Cremo is a follower of the Western Hindu sect founded by the late Bhaktivedanta Swami—in layman's terms, he's a Hare Krishna. According to the Vedas of ancient India, Lord Krishna created the human race at the dawn of time, roughly 2 billion years ago. (Which is pretty close to the accepted emergence of life on earth, as it happens.) Cremo's research, as he freely admits, is an effort to buttress this faith with hard evidence. Like Christian creationists, he believes that humans were divinely created in our present form and did not evolve from lower life forms; like the alternative-archaeology crowd, he accepts scientific arguments that the earth is billions of years old, but believes ancient humans may have possessed wisdom and technology beyond our understanding.

Creation evangelists Ken Ham, Jonathan Sarfati and Carl Wieland, the co-founders of Answers in Genesis, probably the creation-science movement's most articulate and aggressive organization, cite "Forbidden Archeology" approvingly in "The Revised and Expanded Answers Book" (2000), a key popular text of current creationism.

"We're interested in their work and supportive of their lines of inquiry," Ham says during a break in an Alabama creation-science conference. "When they present evidence that humans coexisted with dinosaurs, or that human artifacts are present in what mainstream geology would describe as very old strata, that certainly supports our view. Now, clearly we disagree with their underlying philosophy."

Creationists also sympathize, Ham says, with Cremo's view of science as a "knowledge filter," especially when it comes to evidence contradicting Darwinian theory. "People ask us why creationists don't publish articles in mainstream scientific journals. Well, primarily it's because we're not allowed to. Once they find out you believe in the Bible, you believe in Creation, you believe in a young earth, they say, 'Well, you're not doing science.'"

It's not entirely fair to say that creationism and alternative archaeology are two sides of the same coin. For one thing, archaeologists view one of them as a much greater threat—you can probably guess which. "You're never going to see the Atlantis people being given equal time in social studies class," says Kenneth Feder, an archaeologist at Central Connecticut State and author of "Frauds, Myths, and Mysteries," a college textbook on pseudoarchaeology.

Professionals have long presumed that support for alternative archaeology is fairly broad but not very deep. Alternative archaeology has "very few true believers," suggests Garrett Fagan of Penn State, but also "very few true skeptics. There are a lot of people somewhere in the middle who cannot distinguish absolute drivel from the real thing."

He may be understating the case. Over the course of 20 years, Feder has periodically surveyed college students in different parts of the country to determine their belief in various staples of alternative archaeology. In 2000, he found that 45 percent of students surveyed believed in the Lost Continent of Atlantis (an all-time high), while 36 percent believed that a curse on the pharaoh Tutankhamun's tomb had actually killed people, and 23 percent believed that aliens had visited earth in prehistoric times.

It seems clear that alternative archaeology is a multimillion-dollar publishing business based on Hancock and von Däniken's sales figures alone. In recent years several pseudoarchaeological expeditions have been mounted at a cost of further millions, although whether any of that money would have otherwise gone to reputable scientists is doubtful. Explorers associated with various New Age institutions have claimed the discovery of submerged pyramids off Japan, Atlantean ruins near Cyprus, and an entire sunken city near Cuba (under 2,000 feet of water!).

If anything, Atlantis lust seems to be enjoying a new golden age. In July, an international conference on "The Atlantis Hypothesis" took place on the Greek island of Milos. It was a hodgepodge event, drawing a variety of genuine scholars interested in the historical, geological, volcanological and psychological roots of the legend, as well as "independent researchers" (read: alt-archaeology buffs) hoping to prove pet theories: Atlantis was Malta, Atlantis was Crete, Atlantis was Gibraltar, Atlantis was in Serbia (!).

Although alternative archaeology wanders all over the place, and regularly intersects with creationism on the topic of Noah's ark and some of the loopier material in the Book of Genesis (Google the word "Nephilim" if you're curious), it has two principal, semi-overlapping currents. These are belief in an Atlantean mother civilization and a belief that Old World people—Celts, Hebrews, Romans, Phoenicians, Africans, you name it—came to America long before Columbus or the Vikings. (Archaeologists call this "hyper-diffusionism" or "extreme diffusionism.")

These propositions are at different levels of plausibility. Graham Hancock postulates a lost civilization—perhaps in an ice-free Antarctica, or disseminated around the continental fringes and now underwater—at the time of the last Ice Age, 10,000 to 12,000 years ago. This flies in the face of most available evidence, which suggests that our ancestors that far back belonged to hunter-gatherer cultures, just beginning to settle down and practice agriculture. On the other hand, the premise that some Phoenician navigator, way back when, got blown off course in a gale and wound up in South Carolina isn't inherently implausible at all (that's pretty much how the Vikings got to Canada).

But as archaeologists will tell you till they're blue in the face, in neither case is there any physical evidence that these things happened. "There are, literally, tens of thousands of sites being dug around the world," Fagan writes in an e-mail message. "Hundreds of thousands of sites have been identified, and millions of archaeological strata unearthed and stratified. And guess what? In all of that, not a sausage from Atlantis. Nothing. Nada. Not a town, a house, a burial, a pot, a potshard, not a bone hairpin. Nothing."

For his part, Hancock says he has tried to point scientists in the directions that might prove or disprove his case, but they're not interested. "I've done my best to deliver material evidence where I think it's most likely to be found, which is underwater," he says. "There are 10 million square miles of land that went underwater at the end of the last Ice Age, and they've hardly been looked at by archaeologists."

To the discomfort of the professional establishment, Hancock has been proven partly right at least once. He has written about local legends suggesting that there might be a sunken city off Mahabalipuram, in India—and last December's tsunami exposed impressive ruins at exactly that spot. It's an important discovery, but it does little to confirm Hancock's proposed chronology: No professional archaeologist believes the site to be more than 2,000 years old.

Fagan admits that archaeologists can never say Hancock's hypotheses are impossible. "But we don't alter our views on the basis of conceivable snippets of possibility. We operate on the basis of tested methodologies."

Kenneth Feder believes that the trouble with the hyper-diffusionist argument is similar—the total absence of stuff, as he puts it. "Archaeologists are experts at identifying people's stuff," he says. "People's stuff is unique. It's diagnostic; it identifies people's cultures. When you don't find stuff, you've got a problem."

Mainstream scientists like Fagan and Feder have a litany of other criticisms to offer: Alternative-archaeology researchers proceed from conclusions rather than from evidence. (Wouldn't it be cool if the Chinese discovered America? Let's see what we can find to support that idea!) They cherry-pick puzzling nuggets of evidence and rely on grand and bogus parallels, arguing, for instance, that since the Egyptians and the Maya both built pyramids, their cultures must be related. Never mind that they're separated by 10,000 miles and 2,000 years, and that their architecture and mythology are totally dissimilar.

Diffusionist theories are often advanced to explain how nonwhite peoples of the Americas and the Third World could have built such impressive monuments. Obviously the Egyptians or Maya or Aztecs or Incas or Zimbabweans or Moundbuilders of the American Midwest couldn't have developed sophisticated cultures on their own; they must have had help from Irish monks or Atlanteans or spacemen! For archaeologists, this has unfortunate echoes of their own profession's avowedly racist past.

"There's a terrific anathema [in alternative archaeology] to the idea that different people in different places have arrived at similar solutions to the same problems," Fagan says. "One particular development can only have taken place once, and its true source is invariably white people. I'm not proposing that Graham Hancock etc. are racists, but they are purveyors of dangerous ideas that should be left in the past."

Critiques like these have done little to squelch the popularity of mythic speculation, which is precisely what alternative archaeology has to offer. Some scholars even wonder whether such speculation, unfounded and reckless as it may often be, should be understood as an unruly cousin of the profession, rather than its direct competitor. Accepting myths and legends as at least potentially accurate enabled Heinrich Schliemann to find the ruins of Troy, and enabled Helge Ingstad to find L'Anse aux Meadows, the Newfoundland site that authenticated the idea that the Norse had visited America 500 years before Columbus. Given the intensity of archaeological activity over the last century, it's not very likely anything similar will happen again. But as spiritual or imaginative inquiry into the past and the nature of humanity, alternative archaeology may be said to possess its own kind of legitimacy.

"Archaeologists do not serve as a special state police force dedicated to eradicate interpretations that are considered false or inappropriate by a self-selected jury," writes Cornelius Holtorf, an archaeologist at the University of Lund in Sweden and something of a professional maverick. "Neither students nor other audiences should be indoctrinated with a particular version of the past or an exclusive approach to its proper study."

Not many American archaeologists share Holtorf's views, but most would admit that belief in Atlantis, or in even the dopiest of diffusionist claims (King Arthur, after leaving Camelot, apparently retired to Kentucky), causes no obvious harm. Creationism is another matter. What's at stake isn't religious belief per se, although archaeologists have the reputation of being a secular bunch, but rather a particular doctrine that has aligned itself with right-wing politics and declared war against modern science.

While Atlantis-hunters and diffusionists have attacked mainstream archaeology throughout the 70 or 80 years it has existed, creationists have mainly targeted biology, geology and astronomy, areas of science that most obviously contradict the Genesis account. They have brushed against archaeology every so often, while hunting for Noah's ark in Turkey, claiming Mesopotamian sites for the Garden of Eden and the Tower of Babel, or trumpeting "oopart" discoveries, like the Coso artifact, that struck them as potential relics of the pre-Flood world.

But as archaeology and its close cousin, paleoanthropology (the study of early man), have pushed ever deeper into the human past—and as creation-science evangelism has grown more sophisticated and recruited more people with academic credentials—conflict became inevitable. Creationists have gone to war over the fossil skulls of early hominids, arguing that they are either clearly apes or clearly humans, but never an intermediate evolutionary stage (although they have yet to formulate a consistent case about which bones fall into which category). They have labored mightily to make Middle Eastern archaeological evidence fit the chronology of the Old Testament—impressive scholarly powers have been devoted to proving that the walls of Jericho did indeed come tumbling down.

The creationist movement has also become much more cautious about looking foolish. Answers in Genesis, which acts as a clearinghouse for the most coherent presentations of creation science, has pretty much backed away from the Garden of Eden, the quest for Noah's ark and the Ark of the Covenant, and those long-cherished human footprints that Carl Baugh found among dinosaur prints in Texas. Its basic position on the Genesis Flood is that it was such a devastating catastrophe, and altered the globe so thoroughly, that real evidence of the pre-Flood world is very difficult to find. If you can suspend disbelief about creationism's starting point, this might be described as a sensible view.

Ken Ham, AIG's U.S. president and himself a former science teacher from Australia, says the organization's aim is "a reasoned and logical defense of the faith," in the classic tradition of Christian apologetics. Rejecting spurious or easily disproven claims, he says, "is an evangelical tool, to be honest. Our mission is to bring people to Jesus Christ, and we want them to understand that science, properly considered, should be no impediment to that."

Ham claims no archaeological expertise, but AIG refers callers to Bryant G. Wood, a professional archaeologist who edits a Christian journal called Bible and Spade. Wood's main work involves authenticating biblical proper names and dates—if Ashdod and Belshazzar and the Hittites were real, the argument goes, the Bible becomes more plausible—and he declines to speculate about any archaeological evidence on Atlantis or the pre-Flood world.

While mainstream archaeologists would say they seek to learn the truth about the past, Wood makes no secret of his mission to bring the past, as it were, to the Truth. "The discoveries of archaeology can be helpful in removing doubts that a person might have about the historical trustworthiness of the Bible," Wood writes in an online article.

As Ham and Wood are clearly aware, archaeology and paleanthropology pose a larger challenge than the question of how tall Goliath really was and whether slings like David's are well attested. Leaving aside Cremo's litany of anomalous findings, there's plenty of physical evidence of human culture many thousands of years before any date creationists could possibly accept. In North America alone, the long-accepted date of 12,000 years ago for the first Paleoindian arrivals has pretty much been dumped. Most archaeologists would say there is decent evidence for a human population arriving here 30,000 to 50,000 years ago. On a global scale, the fully modern form of Homo sapiens appeared at least 160,000 years ago, and the archaeological record of human or hominid tools and weapons goes back roughly 2.5 million years.

Creationists don't seem ready or eager to take on this challenge, beyond their customary protestations that the radiometric dating methods used by scientists are unreliable. Their intellectual energy is largely devoted to battling evolutionary theory and developing elegant solutions to astrophysical problems. (Given a 10,000-year-old universe, how can we see the stars?) One could speculate that they're grateful to see people like Cremo and Hancock attacking archaeology on their behalf.

In an influential 1987 essay, historian William H. Stiebing Jr. wrote that alternative archaeology "functions in the way myth does in primitive cultures. It resolves psychological dilemmas and provides answers for the unknown or unknowable." The "strong emotional attachment" some people feel for such explanations, he went on, seemed directly related to "the unscientific, quasi-religious, anti-Establishment nature of the theories."

Many archaeologists remain disturbed about widespread belief in these modern mythologies, but its consequences aren't clear. "Science requires public funding to survive, and it should be public property," says Fagan. "When the public isn't sure about what's valid science and what isn't, that's not a good situation."

Michael Cremo, who more than anyone else connects creationism to alternative archaeology, offers a key to understanding this whole conflict. He says it's "a fair characterization" for Answers in Genesis to call him a "fellow-traveler," but explains that he isn't exactly like the Christians: "I don't claim to have a monopoly on truth, which might distinguish me from other kinds of creationists. I'm part of the larger spiritual family of alternatives to Darwinism."

Alternative archaeology and creationism offer "alternatives to Darwinism," and in so doing they respond to an inchoate need that characterizes our era. Alt-archaeologists engage in outrageous speculation but make no claim to absolute truth. Creationists make absolute truth their first principle, shining the Word of God into the darkness and chaos of science. Both seek to provide a picture of the past that is more orderly—and certainly more meaningful—than the bloody chronicles offered by science and history.

Fairly or not, archaeology's assailants see this rich and contentious field as part of a great scientific machine of meaninglessness. Graham Hancock sees archaeology as subscribing to "a materialist ideology which states as a fact that there is no meaning to life, simply an accidental combination of molecules evolving into the situation we find today. I think huge numbers of people find that extremely unpromising, extremely dark."

As archaeology has become more rigorous and more scientific, it has formed a picture of the human past generally compatible with that developed by evolutionary biology and paleoanthropology. Our ancestors were not perfect beings, molded from the clay of Eden by the hands of God, nor were they the ultra-enlightened citizens of the Hancock's lost civilization, casting our age of greed and technology into the shadows. They were tool-using apes who got surprisingly good at it and began to accomplish strange, even shocking things around 50,000 years ago. They started painting animals on cave walls, burying their dead in ceremonies, and piling rocks one atop the other, in tribute to their developing sense of the sacredness of life—their own and the life they saw around them.

One could argue that human history from that point forward has involved the development of parallel capacities, for technology and science on one hand, for myth and spirituality on the other. It's only a dark story if you choose to see it that way; it's certainly a rich and ambiguous one. Arguably we need both myth and science to think about the world and our place in it; perhaps their uneasy coexistence is what makes us human.

As somebody who writes about culture for a living, I want to insist on the centrality of myth to the human experience. But myth posing as science is quite another matter. If myth, whether in the form of art or religion, can be said to illuminate certain truths about the human condition, they are categorically distinct from the quantifiable and falsifiable truths of science. Maybe this is why we evolved those big brains—we have to balance competing and often contradictory systems of thought, when we can't do without either of them.

The conflict over archaeology forms part of the long-running argument between science and religion, which scientists thought they had won generations ago. The public, at least in this country, has not acknowledged their victory. Various terms for peace have been proposed. Since the time of Augustine, if not Socrates, philosophers, priests and scientists have argued that science and religion ask different kinds of questions and seek different kinds of answers, that they are, in the famous phrase of biologist Stephen Jay Gould, "non-overlapping magisteria."

But that's something of an egghead dodge, isn't it? Gould clearly wanted to consign religion to the role of airy-fairy speculation, but most Tibetan Buddhists don't understand reincarnation, nor most Christians the Resurrection of Jesus, as an interesting metaphor. Creationists are doing us all the favor of challenging our commitment to truth. They know what they believe; do the rest of us?

Cornelius Holtorf and others from the postmodern philosophy of science tradition might remind us that truth is a thorny question about which scientists (and especially archaeologists) should never feel confident. So maybe we should ask ourselves what kind of epistemology we want: a scientific model that claims to be open to doubt, potential reversal and the hypothetical possibility that its opponents might be right; or a rock-solid doctrine of revelation?

Alternative archaeology buffs don't want to choose; Graham Hancock told me in an e-mail that he sees the conflict between science and creationism as that of two competing orthodoxies howling at each other and drowning out everyone else. One can sympathize with that on an abstract intellectual level, but as a practical matter most of us will conclude that we have to pick sides. Holtorf may be comfortable with the idea that the Coso artifact can be a Model T spark plug to some people and a transmitter dropped by one of Noah's drowning cousins to others, or that, depending on context, australopithecine skull fragments can simultaneously signify a hominid ancestor millions of years old and an extinct ape created by Jehovah in 4004 B.C. Most people, I suspect, are content with a simpler conception of historical truth, even if they understand that it is always conditional and always potentially wrong.

If science has sometimes leached into religion in ways it shouldn't, religion—at least of a certain stripe—has devoted immense energy to dressing itself awkwardly in scientific drag. This is where alternative archaeology and creationism show their essential kinship. It isn't just that they call for lost utopias, the interference of powerful supernatural beings, and chains of occurrence that seem impossible to those outside the faith. Those things are legitimate after their fashion. But they claim their view is not just revealed truth but also sound science, and that the so-called science of the infidel universities is a grand conspiracy. You can agree or disagree with these propositions as a matter of faith, but there's no point debating them. They have left the realms of rationality and coherence behind.

Archaeologists, meanwhile, can only hope that there continues to be a public interested in what they have to tell us about the past. Holtorf suggests that the question of "what really happened" in the past is irrelevant. Professional and alternative archaeologists, he argues, "fulfill a similar social demand of providing the present with larger historical perspectives and narratives." Furthermore, the only criteria by which to judge those narratives is their "credibility and appropriateness" in a given context. The profession's future, he writes, lies in an openness to "multiple pasts and alternative archaeologies."

Archaeologists should stop trying to tell people what to think about the past, "because it has not been established that scientifically acceptable accounts of the past benefit society more than mythical, biblical or other accounts."

Kenneth Feder's view of his job is more traditional. He explains that he has just completed a grueling summer dig at a site in rural Connecticut where a nomadic group of Native Americans camped for a few weeks, perhaps 3,000 years ago. "Why the hell would I spend six weeks out in the broiling sun, picking bloodsucking ticks off myself, if it didn't make any fucking difference?" he asks. "If the truth doesn't matter, I can sit at home and make up good stories."

Ownership and Control of Ethnographic Materials

SJOERD R JAARSMA

U of Nijmegen/Papua Heritage Foundation

What has changed most about ethnographic research in the present age of globalization is not the way academic anthropologists deal with the communities they study, but how members of those communities deal with their anthropologists. A few years ago, I met with a group of anthropologists, ethnomusicologists, archivists and librarians to consider the problems relating to the disposition of ethnographic field materials. We concluded that basic questions like "Who owns the information?" and "Should everything be accessible?" should be reconsidered not only by academic anthropologists, but also by the communities being studied.

Ever since fieldwork became the preferred approach to gathering ethnographic information, the quality and quantity of research data being gathered has increased radically. Present-day students have both the training and equipment to make the most of their temporary stay in the field. Yet, the way we relate to the people we study has changed little since the first anthropologists left for the field in colonial days. Most fieldwork still follows the same general pattern. Anthropologists go into the field and gather their material, usually explaining that it will be used to write a book. Having gathered the material needed, they leave, establishing their careers on the merits of the research done. While these days a copy of the thesis written is sent back to local informants, research data will remain under the anthropologists' care and control. Access to raw field materials rarely is granted to others, including members of the study community, during an anthropologist's lifetime.

Indigenous Access and Control

Until recently, people in the field rarely were able to follow up on any of the issues dealt with in the published research results, let alone seek access to the data gathered by the researcher. Equally, they were unable to point out the lack of balance in "services rendered" that surrounds this pattern of research. Even today, with more rules and regulations in place, local grip on field research remains limited. Unless the local community sponsors the research being done, it has few means for managing the flow of research information.

Two issues that academic anthropologists can no longer ignore stand out. First, the flow of information going in and out of any fieldwork location is, as a rule, hugely unbalanced. Second, very little thought has been given so far to control over and access to the data gathered while in the field.

A world growing ever smaller makes it easier for anthropologists to visit the field and keep in contact. Likewise, informants may keep in touch with the anthropologists via phone, email, visits, or communication through family or friends. The Internet allows people to access materials even from the field. The ease with which information can be shared makes the control over data gathered by individual anthropologists an ever more relevant issue.

Value of Information

Ethnographic information, like all information, has a market value, even if anthropologists are not used to thinking in such terms. Although ethnobiologists appreciate the need to establish an equitable tradeoff based on the value placed on indigenous knowledge concerning plants and medicines, the opposite is well-known too. First World musicians still harvest indigenous songs written down by ethnomusicologists to include in their compositions. Sampled compositions sell millions of CDs without revenues flowing to the original indigenous artists or mention being made of their contributions.

Ethnography affects the nature of indigenous knowledge itself. Anthropologists' published materials place indigenous knowledge, previously protected by individual ownership, in the public domain. For example, written records of land ownership differ from "traditional" oral discourse on such matters. Access to the written records by anthropologists shifts the power balance inherent in the use of knowledge. Here, too, the disposition of control over and access to indigenous knowledge is of paramount importance.

Effects on Anthropology

Recently indigenous peoples have become aware that they have a right to exercise control over their own cultural resources. Conferences like the 1993 First International Conference on the Cultural and Intellectual Property Rights of Indigenous Peoples sponsored by the UN provide a forum on these rights. Similarly, the 1991 Native American Graves Protection Act has established indigenous control over ethnographic artifacts in museums and the disposition of burial sites. Such rights will only expand further.

What does this mean for anthropological fieldwork? With anthropologists studying ever more critically aware and emancipated communities, they will be held accountable for their responsibilities concerning the data gathered. Laws will circumscribe rights to the data gathered. Though not written with anthropologists in mind, these laws apply to the anthropologists' research. Similarly, a foreseeable increase in sponsoring of research by indigenous communities themselves will affect the way anthropologists deal with data.

Needed Action

The field data presently in the possession of anthropologists and stored by them in archives and libraries should be made more readily accessible. Implicitly, this means sorting out and protecting ownership rights to knowledge recorded in the field notes, sifting out potentially harmful and damaging information and safeguarding future research interests. This is best done by the original researcher, as archivists and librarians, or even fellow anthropologists, rarely share the knowledge necessary to do this properly.

It is better to plan all this at the start of fieldwork than put it in place afterward. Therefore not only the setup of field-work, but also training for fieldwork, should be reviewed in such a way that safeguarding the informant's interests in the data becomes second nature to anthropologists.

Anthropologists are entrusted to use and work with other people's knowledge, but "ownership" remains limited to what they add as interpretation. They have to acknowledge that the communities being studied have equal if not greater legitimate rights to the ethnographic materials gathered. These rights are only mitigated by an obligation to prevent damage deriving from any access provided to the material. If the academic community does not make itself and the data anthropologists gather accessible and accountable, it may eventually be forced to do so.

Sjoerd R Jaarsma specializes in the history of anthropology and comparative ethnography of New Guinea. He discusses the implications of indigenous rights to ethnographic knowledge and field materials. Also see Jaarsma's edited volume Handle with Care: Ownership and Control of Ethnographic Materials (*2002*).

Last Word on Kennewick Man?

A court ruling on the controversial remains pleases archaeologist James Chatters.

On August 30, Judge John Jelderks of the U.S. District Court of Oregon ruled against the government's 1996 decision that declared the 9,400-year-old skeleton known as Kennewick Man to be Native American, a classification which would require the remains to be turned over to a coalition of tribes for reburial. James Chatters, archaeologist and author of *Ancient Encounters: Kennewick Man and the First Americans* (New York: Simon and Schuster, 2001), identified the remains when they were found on the banks of Washington's Columbia River in 1996. He talked with ARCHAEOLOGY about the recent ruling and the larger issues raised by Kennewick Man.

What was your reaction to Jelderks' ruling?

I experienced a tremendous feeling of relief, followed by a sense of validation that taking a stand for science, and advocacy for Kennewick Man, had been the right things to do. The decision validated all that the plaintiffs [eight scientists who wished to study the remains], attorneys, and I have gone through for the past six years.

What do you think of the media coverage surrounding this issue?

It's been mixed. Some media outlets have shown a clear understanding of the issues and intent of the lawsuit and are consistently accurate in their reporting. Others, particularly tabloids, political talk shows, and many prominent eastern newspapers, fixated on the "Science-versus-Indians" angle and clung to the erroneous idea that Kennewick Man was Caucasian and that we wanted to study him for that reason. Several big papers, including the *New York Times* and *Washington Post*, really attacked us on the red herring of race.

Why do you think race became such a flash point with Kennewick Man?

You really should ask the people for whom that was an issue. To me, the significant point of the discovery is that Kennewick Man and his contemporaries differ greatly from all present-day peoples. It reopens the question of how and by whom the Americas were peopled. Race is an issue of the present that should not be extended into the distant past.

You were investigated by the FBI for possible involvement in the disappearance of some of the Kennewick Man bones, which were later found in the local sheriff's office. Can you tell us something about that experience?

I only learned of the investigation indirectly and was never questioned. Even so, it was very intimidating. At any one time I'm working on collections of bones for half a dozen or more projects, any or all of which agents could have seized in their quest for the missing femur fragments.

What's your position on the Native American Grave Protection and Repatriation Act (NAGPRA)?

We need a law like NAGPRA. We can't silently condone desecration of Indian graves and keep the bones of people's known kin on museum shelves and expect the general populace to see living Native Americans as fellow human beings. But NAGPRA is being misapplied as a license for tribes to take control of any and all early skeletons, and, as we are seeing increasingly, any and all archaeological materials.

When do you think repatriation and reburial are appropriate?

When any fair person would agree that the culture practiced by the dead was directly antecedent to that of a modern tribe, that tribe is most likely to know how the deceased would like to be treated in death. But that connection only rarely goes back beyond a few hundred to a thousand years. For the preceding 6,000 years, when no cultural link exists, the dead could be ancestors of anyone of Indian ancestry, including most Hispanics and a significant proportion of African Americans and Whites.

Where do you see Kennewick Man in another six years?

I'd like to see him securely preserved, like the Cro-Magnon and Neanderthal fossils of Europe, as a national treasure at the Smithsonian, where future generations could learn from him through ever-improving technologies. But if this case is appealed, or if the federal government or tribes attempt to bypass Jelderks' decision by changing regulations or the law, he might remain in limbo, or dissolve underground.

Guardians

of the

Dead

Peru's citizens' brigades patrol a coastal landscape in
an effort to curb a growing national industry—looting.

by ROGER ATWOOD

A LEAN MAN IN HIS 50S with skin-burnished from a life-time working in sugar cane fields, Gregorio Becerra remembers the days when his father used to bring home ancient ceramic pots to their home in the village of Úcupe. Birds, faces, fruits, animals—the whole pantheon of Moche pottery themes stood on their living room shelf, where his father would place the perfectly preserved vessels he and his buddies dug up. "Everyone had a few pots in his house. They were nice decorations," says Becerra.

But sometime around 1990, all that changed. "It became a business," he recalls. "Outsiders came. They came from the city, and you'd see them out in the hills digging up everything they could find. They'd take it all away and sell it."

And so the modern looting industry came to little Úcupe and a hundred villages like it up and down the coast of northern Peru. People who used to excavate pots as a back-lot hobby or family activity at Holy Week, as much a part of local social life as fishing or football, watched first with bafflement and then anger as professional grave robbers descended on their lands to search for pieces to supply the international market for Peruvian antiquities.

Poor, neglected, hurt by the fall of sugar prices, these villages suddenly found themselves living literally on top of a commodity hotter than sugar ever was: Moche ceramics from the first millennium A.D. that, for a time, had collectors in their thrall, fetching prices in New York that for the best pieces could surpass $30,000.

Now Becerra is the leader of his village's *grupo de protección arqueológica,* or *la grupa,* a citizens' patrol armed with binoculars, a dirt bike, one revolver, and one shotgun but whose most important weapon is the eyes and ears of people living in the village's adobe houses. The brigade's mission is to stop people from occupying the land and plundering what lies beneath it. The patrol chases away bands of looters, or surrounds them, seizes their tools—shovels, poles, buckets—and ties up their wrists with rope until the police come.

The Brüning Museum warehouse is filled with Moche and Chimú ceramics excavated by archaeologists, seized by patrols, or donated by guilt-stricken collectors.

Walter Alva, director of the new Museum of the Royal Tombs of the Lord of Sipán in the town of Lambayeque, 30 miles north of Úcupe, organized eight such patrols in the early 1990s in response to the phenomenal growth of commercial looting in the Moche heartland. In doing so, he took a cue from rural Peru's long tradition of ragtag peasant militias known as *rondas campesinas,* which have fought scourges ranging from cattle rustlers to Shining Path Maoist guerrillas. This time the enemy was looters prospecting for ancient art, and it was ironically Alva's own 1987 excavation of the tombs at Sipán that helped inspire the plundering.

On February 6 of that year, looters digging at Sipán's burial mound, or *huaca,* struck a tomb where a Moche lord had been buried around A.D. 300. They carried out about a dozen rice sacks full of gold and silver artifacts, somewhere between 200 and 300 objects in all, and smashed or discarded hundreds more either inadvertently or because they didn't think they were good enough to sell. Police stopped the pillage and notified Alva, who, under constant harassment from townspeople who wanted to ransack the site, began excavating where the looters had left off. He found a dozen more tombs, two as rich in artifacts as the looted one. Alva's excavations brought new insights into the social complexity of the Moche, who ruled the north coast from about A.D. 100 to 700.

Meanwhile the looted artifacts had already hit the market, whetting the appetite of collectors as never before. Once an exotic niche product, Peruvian artifacts became almost overnight one of the hottest items in the international antiquities trade. "It was a gold rush," recalls Alva. "It's been a constant struggle against looters ever since." More has been destroyed in Peru in the past 40 years than in the previous 400, he claims.

I HAD COME TO ÚCUPE because I wanted to see if what Alva and his followers were doing was actually effective in stopping the rampant looting.

Archaeologist Carlos Wester, who helped Alva and Alva's late wife, Susana Meneses, develop the patrols and is now acting director of the Brüning National Archaeological Museum in Lambayeque, led me to the top of an unmolested 1,800-year-old Moche *huaca* less than a mile from Úcupe. As such mounds go it was pretty small, maybe three stories high, overlooking the *algarrobo*·trees, grazing goats, and the village in the distance.

"The patrols have really worked," said Wester. "If you come here to loot, they'll chase you out before the police even get here. People have become aware of the value of preserving the *huacas*. Inside this one, there are probably some good things. Someday we'll excavate it, but until we do it's well protected."

In Úcupe, Wester introduced me to Becerra and another patrol leader, Gilberto Romero. I returned by bus a few days later to see the patrol in action. The road to Úcupe passed through a moonscape of barren hills before reaching the lazy Zaña River where the women of Úcupe were washing clothes while children splashed among water lilies and goats nibbled weeds by the banks. The village itself is a collection of single-story brick and adobe houses along the main road; dirt streets lead away through farms and sand dunes to the Pacific coast a few miles away.

Romero met me at the bus stop. A man with a gravelly voice and a sleepy smile, his manner was so mild that I was surprised to learn he doubled as a security guard for the local sugar cooperative and, as such, was licensed to carry a gun. He is the only member of the patrol who regularly carries a weapon, although he told me that he had never shot directly at looters. "This isn't war," he said.

Becerra, Romero, and I hired a motorcycle fitted with a passenger seat wide enough for the three of us. With a young driver named Julio, we bumped along a rutted dirt road past fields of spicy red pepper plans and sugar cane. Now and then Romero would point out a bare hill and explain that it was not a hill. It was another *huaca,* weathered by many centuries of wind and sun. "We have virgin *huacas,* never been touched and known only to us," said Romero, shouting above the sound of the engine.

A Chavín-era wall, dating from about 200 B.C., was excavated in the 1980s. It was later reburied to protect its priceless murals from the elements. Patrols now guard it from pillagers, who would cut it up and sell the pieces to dealers in Lima.

The Úcupe *grupa* was created in July 1994, Romero told me. "There are about 20 of us active in the *grupa*, but directly or indirectly I would say 90 percent of the people in the town collaborate with us. There are always a few who still want to dig up pots to sell, but we keep an eye on them. If we see somebody looting, we call the [Brüning] museum, and it calls teh police. If the police can't get here fast enough, we hold them ourselves. A month ago we detained three looters and their tools. We let down our guard for an hour and before we knew it hey were digging. It's like that here. You go to lunch and you come back, and there they are, digging. It's always people from outside, mosly from Cayaltí."

The market town of Cayaltí, with a population of about 10,000, lies 12 miles northeast of Úcupe. It is built around a rambling, wooden plantation mansion with peeling yellow paint. In the late 1960s, a left-wing government confiscated the house and the surrounding sugar plantations and turned them over to a workers' cooperative. Thirty years later the cooperative went bankrupt, and residents say the town has been struggling ever since. "No jobs here. Nothing to do," said a young man in the town square.

Cayaltí is known throughout the region as a looting center, a town where plundered antiquities are bought and sold with impunity. It's a busy town of woodworking shops and stands selling pirated videos, where fruit sellers and prostitutes in clingy black pants stand in the street and little cafes sell sandwiches and warm Cokes. One day as Wester and I drove into town, he pointed to two men walking beside a horse-drawn cart. "The older one, he's been arrested several times for looting," he said. "We know who he is."

Social hierarchy in Cayaltí is no longer based on sugar but on loot, with grimy tomb-diggers at the bottom, small-time dealers above them, and at the top, antiquities traders who sell to Peruvian and occasionally European collectors who come to town to buy. Two carpentry shops serve as fronts for the antiquities business. A taxi stand at the edge of town is known as a distribution center.

I wandered alone through Cayaltí, posing as a buyer and asking around for *antiguedades*. It didn't take long before a dealer led me to an alley behind his house, where he offered me point-bottomed Inka pots, a broken Moche portrait vessel, and an exquisite little ceramic jar no bigger than a perfume bottle in the shape of a spondylus seashell. All freshly dug up, he told me. (I bought an Inka pot and the broken portrait vessel for the equivalent of $3 each and took them to Alva at the National Museum in Lima, where he confirmed they were authentic. I donated them to the museum.) The dealer wanted to know if I was a museum director. Like loot sellers everywhere, he boasted that he sold his best pieces to museums. The son of the late owner of Lima's Gold Museum, he told me, occasionally came to town in a big black car to see what he had to offer.

The hills outside Cayaltí are pockmarked with holes left by looters and strewn with human bones, empty water bottles, and worthless bits of ancient textile. *"Aquí todo el pueblo huaquea"* (everybody loots here), the dealer told me, including the former president of Cayaltí's sugar cooperative, who was arrested in 1996 along with four other men for looting.

The people of Úcupe speak with disgust about places like Cayaltí. "No respect for their ancestors," an Úcupe woman told me as we waited for a bus. Archaeologists and the brigade have made the people of Úcupe more aware of their cultural heritage. "When I was a boy, people knew nothing about the importance of these objects we found," said Becerra. "We didn't know what the pre-Columbian cultures were. Moche, Chimú, Chavín, we'd never heard those names. Now everyone knows them. They teach them to the children in school."

Úcupe and Cayaltí are also divided by a bitter land feud. Farmers in tranquil Úcupe fear that Cayaltí people will descend on their lands and then petition a judge for legal title. Whole towns are born this way in Peru. Squatters take over idle private land by the light of the moon, and months or years later they ask that their settlement be incorporated as a town.

"People come from Cayaltí saying they want to work on the farms," said Romero. "Some of them have family members here. But to us, everyone who comes from Cayaltí is a looter." Becerra added, "We have extinguished looting in this area, because after the looters come the cattle rustlers, the thieves, and the land invaders. All the bad elements."

Some 350 people are now actively involved in the brigades. Alva calculates they have seized about 3,200 objects from looters. He also knows their efforts have pushed the problem elsewhere. Partly because of police and *grupa* pressure, and partly because the tastes of international collectors have changed, the professionals are moving south.

IT'S TOUGH WORKING in the north these days. You can get arrested," says 23-year-old Robin. In Italy he would be a *tombarolo,* in Guatemala an *estelero;* in Peru he's a *huaquero,* a professional grave robber who has been digging up tombs almost every night since his early teens. He loves his job and lives in a small brick house with his wife and two daughters in a town north of Lima. He earns a little money on the side driving a taxi.

Robin and his buddies now work mostly in the Cañete area south of Lima, where there are no citizens' patrols, less police interference, and abundant ancient textiles of the kind that bring big bucks on the international art market—$10,000 for good ones, a quarter of a million for the very best. I met Robin and his colleagues through a collector friend. It took some persuading but he finally agreed to take me along on a nighttime raid. I told him I wouldn't buy anything or join in the digging. I just wanted to watch and take notes. They agreed.

We met late in the afternoon and took a bus south. There were four of us: Robin, two other looters named Remi and Harry, and me, a 39-year-old American reporter who drew a lot of stares as we crowded onto the bus with armfuls of shovels and tools. We got out at an empty stretch of highway some 80 miles south of Lima and walked for nearly an hour across cotton fields illuminated by moonlight. A few dogs barked but we encountered no one as we walked. Eventually we came to a tree. Sitting on its gnarled roots, we chewed coca leaves. About 100 feet away rose the Inkaera *huaca* they were about to assault.

The looters drank cane liquor and talked about strange and beautiful things they had found over the years—perfectly preserved pots, color-spangled weavings, piles of human bones and skulls. Robin told of a weaving that bore the image of a huge condor with outstretched wings.

They also talked about the fickle spirits of the dead. The *huaca* was a living force, with jealousies and resentments, moments of generosity, and fits of spite. "If you act greedy, the *huaca* won't give you anything," said Robin. "You take too much, and it will close up and never give you anything again."

"But it warns you," added Remi. "When the coca leaf tastes sweet, the *huaca* is about to give you something."

The looters particularly liked this *huaca;* it was relatively untouched, and they knew, having dug into it before, that the tombs within were not too deep. But, unusual for the south coast, there was some police presence here. Police had chased them away before, and Robin only barely escaped arrest one night at a burial site in the area. They told me the ground rules: no flash pictures (the flash might attract police), make as little noise as possible, and if you must talk, whisper.

I followed them to the *huaca* and sat on the chalky surface as they began their work. Shaped like a kidney, it stood about 40 feet high and stretched a quarter of a mile end to end. First they plunged metal poles into its smooth, bald surface to locate tombs. When they hit nothing but sand, they moved on. If the pole suddenly met no resistance, that meant they had hit an empty pot, probably within a tomb. And if the pole made a certain muffled crack, that meant they had hit human remains. The excruciating crack of metal hitting bone made me recoil.

After an hour of sinking their poles and making mental notes of where they had hit bodies, they began to dig—fast. In 15 minutes, they excavated a hole six feet deep; in half an hour, they had broken into tombs ten feet down. These seemed to belong to Inka commoners, simple graves with gourds containing peanuts or bird bones, woven bags, and coils of string. There were knitting instruments, broken ceramics, a child's tiny bone flute with a string attached. I looked at all this in the moonlight, fascinated, disgusted and saddened. They couldn't sell this stuff, and they were throwing it into heaps of debris.

"We know what people are buying and what they don't want," said Robin. "We leave a lot of stuff because we can't sell it. It's hard to sell ceramics these days. Too much of it is on the market. These days buyers want textiles and more textiles." They often get specific requests relayed from collectors through middlemen—customized looting.

Within a few hours they had ripped into half a dozen tombs and the remains of adults and children who had lain together for 500 years were scattered all over the *huaca.* The looters grasped human skulls by the hair and chucked them out like basketballs. They shoveled out bones, some with bits of desiccated human tissue still attached.

At about 4 A.M. they found what they wanted—an Inka weaving. At the bottom of a hole nine feet deep, using a flashlight, they could see the fabric wrapped around a bundle that surely contained human remains. In the light they could see the deep red and ocher of the fabric. "Look at those colors! We've got a good one," said Robin. "I'm going to dig around the sides, carefully so as not to damage the weaving. If you rip it out, you'll destroy it." Another half-hour of digging and he pulled the weaving free and clambered out of the pit. He held it up to the flashlight and shook it, releasing a cloud of dust. It was indeed a lovely piece, a design of red, yellow, blue, and beige diamonds. It was a shirt, almost perfectly intact, with a hole for the head and two for the arms. It probably belonged to a boy or a young man. The bones of the body it had wrapped lay at the bottom of the pit; a femur, a spine, a skull gazing up at the stars.

"This is the best thing we've found in two weeks," said Robin. They were all the more lucky because the pole had not pierced the fabric. They gathered their tools and put the weaving in a knapsack. As we walked back across the fields, they anxiously discussed how much money the textile might bring them. A thousand dollars, maybe $1,500.

As the sun came up we flagged down a bus making the all-night trip from Cuzco to Lima. Back in the small house where Remi lived, the men spread out the weaving on the dirt floor. They were tired but excited as they made calls with Robin's cell phone to find a buyer. By 9 A.M., they had one, a smuggler they knew only as Lucho, and asked him to come see it. "Believe me, it's a good piece, *una belleza,*" said Robin. "We're not going to bring you all the way down here for something that's not worth it."

That was when I had to leave. I could not be present at the deal because Lucho might not like it. Would he be armed? I asked. No, he does not carry a weapon, but he is an important buyer and might feel uncomfortable having someone he doesn't know present, Robin explained.

The looters told me later that they asked for $1,500, but Lucho bargained them down to $1,000. The weaving would be on a plane out of Peru within days.

I had asked the looters how they felt about digging up bodies. "When you first start doing this, it makes you nervous," Remi said. "Digging up bones, you think you're going to incur a curse. But after a while it becomes easy. You don't even think about it."

"But," I inquired, "doesn't it bother you personally? I mean, how would you like it if someone dug up your grave and stole everything your family had put in it?" They looked at each other nervously, and then at me as if suddenly they wished I weren't there. Then Remi said, "Around here there is no other kind of work."

ROGER ATWOOD *is a journalist writing on the antiquities trade with a fellowship from the Alicia Patterson Foundation. He can be reached at atwoodsy@aol.com*

Thracian Gold Fever

Archaeologist and showman Georgi Kitov's spectacular discoveries raise questions about managing Bulgaria's past

Matthew Brunwasser

ON A SOFT, GRAY FALL AFTERNOON, a crowd of several hundred waited patiently outside the Iskra History Museum in Kazanluk, the unprepossessing main town in central Bulgaria's rose-growing region. The blank concrete facade of the museum, like that of most Communist-era cultural institutions, created a notably joyless impression.

But inside, the 15 visitors allowed at a time into the small exhibition hall were awed by fantastic Thracian gold, silver, bronze, and ceramic objects, 28 in all, recently discovered only eight miles away and on public display for the first time. An ancient amphora housed on a wobbly metal stand rocked ominously as a woman brushed by. The excitement of the visitors washed over the tiny provincial museum as they carefully studied the objects that have been heralded across the world.

"We are filled with history from the land to the sky," remarked Albena Mileva, who is 24 and unemployed. She hitchhiked 20 miles from the neighboring city of Stara Zagora with two friends to see the exhibit. "So long ago the Thracians were

so developed in so many ways. You can touch their spirit and their way of life."

"I have no words," sighed Nadka Nenkova, a 66-year-old retired economist who had just seen the exhibit. "All this time it's been underground, and we didn't even know it was there."

While the sensational finds from a 2,500-year-old necropolis dubbed the "Valley of the Thracian Kings" have fired the imagination of the Bulgarian public and the world beyond, the story behind the discoveries, centered around the controversial methods of the archaeologist who made them—unorthodox excavation practices, shady business deals, allegations of collaborations with looters—raises questions about how this poor former Eastern Bloc nation will manage the future of its past.

It all started on August 19 of last year, when Georgi Kitov of the Bulgarian Academy of Sciences discovered a gold mask in a late fifth-century B.C. burial mound outside the town of Shipka, eight miles from Kazanluk.

The discovery made headlines worldwide ("Putting a New Face on Thrace," November/December 2004), and the 61-year-old Kitov, an archaeologist specializing in Thracian tomb studies who has been in the field for more than 30 years, became a household name in Bulgaria. Photographs of the robust man with the bushy Abraham Lincoln beard cradling the exquisite mask were splashed across national and international newspapers. In different press statements he attributed the mask to two different Thracian kings who lived more than a century apart, although it was later determined to be the death mask of a warrior, and proudly pointed out to journalists that, at 1.5 pounds, the mask was much more impressive than the Mycenaean Mask of Agamemnon, which, he said, was made of only a paltry 2.5 oz. of gold leaf (in fact, it weighs in at 6 oz. of gold).

Although it may seem amusing to outsiders, Kitov's game of artifact one-upmanship played right to the hearts of his countrymen. Today's Bulgarians are not considered direct descendants of the Thracians, powerful but illiterate Indo-European tribes who were commonly described by their Greek neighbors as "barbarians." Rather, Bulgarians are descended from Central Asian proto-Bulgars who came to the area in the seventh century A.D. and mixed with the remains of local Thracian tribes and Slavs. Nonetheless, the Thracians offer an unusually strong common identity of which all Bulgarians can feel proud—not just because they share the same real estate, but because they offer a comforting association in Bulgaria's current period of post-Communist social dislocation. "Bulgarians need to go back before the divisive historical memories of the Turks and the Russians to find an identity they can agree on," says anthropologist Margarita Karamihova of the Bulgarian Ethnological Institute. "We can't even agree on who to hate anymore. We love to have bigger and better things which increase our self-confidence in comparison with our neighbor countries. And we are so proud that our gold mask is bigger than their gold mask!"

Adding to the wellspring of national pride that the discovery engendered, Kitov allowed himself to speculate generously on an elegant gold ring with a depiction of a seated, spear-wielding athlete that was also found in the tomb along with Greek pottery and bronze and iron weapons. Six days into the 2004 Olympic Games in Athens, and the day after he opened the tomb, the archaeologist was quoted telling Reuters that he believed the ring featured an Olympic rower. "We are dedicating this find to our rowers in Athens," said Kitov. "It's a sign that they should win a gold medal." What he failed to mention was that the ancient games had never hosted the sport of rowing.

A month later, on September 21, together with his team of 12 specialists, a crew of workers, and the ever-present crowd of onlookers, Kitov found what many say is the most exquisite object of his career, a 26-pound bronze head that appears to have been crudely severed at the neck from a life-size statue. As if acting as a sentry, it was found buried deep in a stonelined pit some 15 feet in front of the entrance to Golyamata Kosmatka, "The Big Shaggy One," a burial mound more than 60 feet high and 10 times as long, located less than a mile from the tomb of the gold mask. Due to the size of the mound and its location some seven

miles from Seuthopolis, a city built by the late-fourth-century B.C. king Seuthes III, the tomb is believed to be the burial site of the ruler.

Using three large earthmoving machines, Kitov located the entrance to the Golyamata Kosmatka tomb three days after the discovery of the bronze head. Miners on his team spent approximately a week removing dirt from the 40-foot corridor that lay beyond the entrance; scorch marks on stones indicated that a fire had caused the wooden infrastructure of the corridor to collapse, protecting it from looters for millennia. Ninety-nine percent of Thracian tombs were looted during antiquity, and Kitov and other experts say the fire was likely to have been set deliberately to protect the tomb.

While the crowds of locals and reporters buzzed around, limited air and cramped space kept outsiders from entering the tomb. Finally, in the early afternoon of October 4, Kitov stood at the head of his assembled team at the end of the corridor, facing an enormous marble door beyond which, most likely, was something every archaeologist dreams organ unlooted tomb. Could this enormous burial mound be in fact the very resting place of Seuthes III?

The narrow first room, about five feet wide and twice as long, contained the intact skeleton of a sacrificed horse. A blocked-up doorway lay on the opposite side of the chamber. The doorway was cleared to reveal a second room, empty but much larger, with stone walls and a graceful domed ceiling 15 feet high. The "perfect acoustics" led Kitov to believe it had a ritual purpose. And there across the room was yet another doorway, again packed with rocks and dirt.

That night, Kitov and his team entered the third and final chamber, the centerpiece of which was a sarcophagus tall enough to stand in, carved from a single piece of granite and weighing more than 60 tons. Amid thick dust, exactly as they were laid out 2,300 years ago on the bed and the floor, were more than 70 gold, silver, bronze, and ceramic objects fit for a king, including armor, a gold kylix (drinking cup) and wreath, bronze coins depicting Seuthes III, and three human teeth.

But then, as often happens in Bulgarian life, the story of this amazing archaeological discovery took a sharp turn for the absurd. According to Kitov's account in later press reports—as no journalists were present in the tomb—the archaeologist called the Kazanluk police chief and requested a few policemen to help escort the treasure back to expedition headquarters at a Shipka hotel. Kitov reportedly did not consider the private security firm he used to guard the entrance of the tomb up for the job. Witnesses say more than 50 Bulgarian law enforcement officers, ordered by the Interior Ministry, showed up outside the tomb: regular uniformed police, masked special forces armed with Kalashnikov assault rifles, and even a local prosecutor.

Adding to the circus was the presence of Ivan Juchnovski, president of the Bulgarian Academy of Sciences, and Vassil Nikolov, director of the National Archaeological institute and Museum. The police frisked them, as well as everybody else present, for artifacts each time they exited the tomb. Tempers flared all around.

The cops insisted that they would have to take the priceless objects to a Kazanluk police station. Kitov refused, insisting that they be taken to his hotel headquarters. At a standoff, the archaeologist, his team, and his guests instead decided to sit it out in the tomb, where they stayed up all night drinking wine in celebration of their discovery and in defiance of the masked and armed authorities outside. Kitov refused to let any outsiders enter, so the police spent a chilly night camped out in their cars parked outside the tomb. The next morning, team members packed the artifacts into expedition cars and authorities escorted them to the hotel.

When Kitov's latest bonanza made news across the country that day, the government's storm-trooper reaction to the discovery elicited boundless amusement among the press and public. The police justified their response by saying it was suspicious that the team needed to remove precious artifacts in the middle of the night, and that one of Kitov's private security guards had a criminal record. The archaeologist fired back by demanding, in the country's biggest national daily, Trud Daily, the resignation of the Interior Minister.

After the team went home and got some sleep, the anger evaporated. There had never been a better time to be an archaeologist in Bulgaria. A photograph of Kitov smiled from the front page of Trud Daily, sipping from the gold kylix while 39-year-old Diana Dimitrova, his deputy expedition leader and mother of his child, held the gold wreath over his head like a halo. The huge headline announced KITOV wanes IN GOLD. Other papers showed masked policemen guarding the tomb with automatic rifles. Political cartoons ridiculed the Interior Ministry.

A few days later, Kitov, dressed casually in a white T-shirt, welcomed the Foreign Minister at Golyamata Kosmatka and was awarded the Gold Honorary Badge of the Foreign Ministry. The minister said the finds were exceptional significance for the future of cultural tourism and tourism in Bulgaria in general" and announced that the government would give Kitov's expedition 50,000 levs (about $35,000) to continue its work. The Construction Minister even promised to fix the roads in the depressed region around the tombs. "I will be the Bulgarian Schliemann," Kitov had once boasted to colleagues years ago. His lifetime of talk had become reality.

AMONG HIS COLLEAGUES, HOWEVER, Kitov does not receive nearly the same respect as he does from the local media, public, and politicians. The archaeological community in Bulgaria is very small, perhaps only 250 professionals in all, so most agreed to talk only anonymously. Kitov clearly prefers to dig, focusing his energy on discovering objects, and appears to have little interest in documenting or scientifically analyzing his finds. Several specialists noted that he rarely published his dis-

coveries until several years ago, when he was publicly criticized by colleagues. A former colleague, who recalled that Kitov once bragged that he hadn't been to the library of the Bulgarian Archaeological Institute "since 1977," characterizes him as "a typical villager, the worst example of those who succeeded in the late Communist system, not academic at all." Nonetheless, he has recently excavated some of the country's most significant Thracian sites, including the Alexandrovo tomb, which contains elaborate painted depictions of Thracians, and Starosel, perhaps the largest Thracian sanctuary yet discovered.

A maestro of heavy earthmoving equipment—even orchestrating four machines at the same time—Kitov has pioneered what his detractors say is its overuse on archaeological sites in Bulgaria. Many archaeologists are bewildered by his hastiness. While established Bulgarian archaeologists have spent 20 years investigating one site, he excavated six sites this summer alone, and had permission for at least 10. "Ninety percent of us reject his methods," says a colleague.

"If we didn't hurry, [looters] would've entered the grave, and taken out everything. That's why we hurry, and that's why we use machines."

Kitov is unapologetic. "The looters were one step away from the town where the ring and mask were found," said Kitov in a recent telephone conversation (granted only grudgingly on the condition that it be quick). "If we didn't hurry, if we were a week late, for example, they would've entered the grave, and taken out everything that was inside and no one would have ever known what was there in Shipka. That's why we hurry and that's why we work very hard, and that's why we use machines without damaging the archaeological site. We once found 27 beads from a gold necklace in a huge mound, which means that the machines don't stop us from finding objects. Nothing is destroyed, nothing is damaged."

KITOV WAS CENSURED in February 2001 by the Council for Scientific Field Studies at the National Archaeological Institute and Museum (AIM), to which he belonged. The other 13 members voted unanimously to take away his permission to lead expeditions for a year, based on violations that included excavating three sites without permission; "nonprofessional digging" and "covering a site without consideration of conservation"; working 10 sites in one season, including two at the same time; the uncontrolled use of earthmoving equipment and metal detectors despite complex geological deposits; working with a team lacking any sufficiently qualified or experienced members; and not leaving any unstudied sites for future generations. Kitov defended himself by saying he was morally obligated to work the sites without permission because he had seen looters nearby and needed to save them.

Then in September the same year, the institute's Scientific Council voted unanimously to expel Kitov from his leadership post of the Thracian Section of AIM, which he had held for 11 years, as well as to form a commission to investigate all his expedition documentation for the previous five years. Among an even longer series of professional issues such as those featured at the February meeting, Kitov was accused of acting like a "spoiled child," and the council chair protested at his accusing her in the media of "filling orders for the looter's Mafia" and calling her a "moron."

But Kitov still has one very well-placed ally. Vassil Nikolov, who was present for the opening of the Golyamata Kosmatka tomb and as director of AIM is responsible for approving excavation licenses in the country, says he has no concerns about control over archaeological activity in Bulgaria, or about Kitov, although he could not say how many dig permissions Kitov holds. The archaeologist himself believes he had "12 or 15 [permissions in 2004], somewhere around there." Nikolov said the high number is the result of a new and improved system whereby a separate permit is given for each mound, instead of one permission for a whole complex of mounds. And because Nikolov was working in the area and visited Kitov every day, he says, he personally saw that the archaeologist never worked more than one site at a time.

Bulgarian scholars are deeply concerned not only about Kitov and his methods, or the respectability he commands, but also about the broader repercussions for archaeology in their country. The attention he receives risks shifting public and financial focus onto "treasure" and Thracians at the expense of all other archaeological investigations. There is a wealth of heritage in Bulgaria from other cultures as well, including Greek, Roman, Ottoman, Byzantine, and ancient Bulgarian. "Colleagues say it is offensive that the government awards Kitov because he finds gold," says one archaeologist, "but others who don't live with their families for six years because of their work get nothing."

Such attitudes are most likely a result of jealousy, Kitov says. "It's not a matter of finding gold, it's a matter of gathering a lot of facts about the Thracians. We only work four, five months a year like other colleagues and we get results. We work 10, 12 hours a day. While some of the other colleagues might work four, five, six hours and want to have our results, they won't have them."

IT WAS TWO DAYS after the Golyamata Kosmatka finds were put on display for the first time in Kazanluk that I met Kitov. Bulgaria was still buzzing about the Thracians. When I arrived, he was sitting alone at a folding table near the tomb entrance,

doing a newspaper crossword puzzle—the stereotypical pursuit of the bored Communist-era worker. He was wearing a mobile phone promo T-shirt, cheap plastic sunglasses, and a black Speedo. "Should I grab a chair?" I asked. "No," he said, "we'll stand." He clearly did not welcome scrutiny of his work, but perhaps he was fatigued by the insatiable press interest.

The conversation was very strained, but Kitov became animated when the topic steered into what is clearly favorite territory: state neglect and incompetence in archaeological affairs, in particular with regard to the Valley of the Thracian Kings. He complained that the area was awash with looters and that the authorities did nothing to stop them or preserve the sites. "We want to turn this into a tourist site," he said. "Little by little, we hope to have a person stay here, sell tickets, another to take people inside. You need very little money; fortunately, most of these mounds are near the road." Kitov described how, because of tourism at Starosel, more than 20 people "have bread and work thanks to our work." If tourism were to come to Shipka, he argued, he could put more than 50 people to work. "We simply want the local government to not stop us, to look favorably on our work, and turn the tombs into tourist sites."

> ### *"When tourists come and there is no road, no electricity, no lights and water, and nowhere to eat or sleep, they are not going to come back."*

BULGARIA'S INFATUATION WITH ITS self-styled Schliemann got its first dose of reality a few weeks later on October 30, when the cover of the weekly Politika featured a picture of Kitov wearing a T-shirt with the bronze head, shrugging his shoulders with his arms upraised. The two-inch headline exclaimed: GEORGI KITOV—THE CASHIER OF THE THRACIAN GOLD. The accompanying story accused Kitov of illegally trying to develop the concessions for the tomb area, and showed images of an admitted looter in the tomb at the moment he entered the third chamber of Golyamata Kosmatka.

A contract had been signed by Kitov, the director of the Kazanluk Museum, which financed the expedition, and a third party known as the Bulgarian Investment Fund to develop the Golyamata Kosmatka site for tourism. It was not yet a legal contract because the mayor of Kazanluk had not signed (the Kazanluk municipality owns the land beneath the site). But even if he had, the contract would not have been valid because the Culture Ministry is required by law to develop any archaeological site anywhere in the country.

Still, an initiative in developing sites where the state does nothing is somewhat difficult to fault. All Bulgarian archaeologists work for local, regional, or national museums or institutes and all artifacts are property of the state, but the state has little money available for fieldwork, let alone for protection or maintenance of monuments after they are opened. "State administration has no relationship to science," laments one archaeologist. The Culture Ministry also recommended that prosecutors investigate Kitov's nonprofit association TEMP (the Bulgarian acronym for "Thracian Expedition for Tomb Studies") because of clauses in its association's registration that allow for activities which under law only licensed archaeologists or the state can perform.

Of particular concern to the archaeological community was Kitov's association with the Bulgarian. Investment Fund, which provided private security guards for Golyamata Kosmatka and also claims to have supplied a $90,000 "scanner" used to locate sites during Kitov's expeditions. The fund employee who operated the equipment, Mario Shopov, also freely admitted a grave-robbing background. Asked by *Politika* whether he dealt with looting or archaeological expeditions, Shopov replied, "Both. I'm interested in history, and separately I work with the equipment of Mr. Dinov," [co-owner of the Bulgarian Investment Fund]. Shopov is a signatory for the finds in Golyamata Kosmatka, and a Kitov-produced DVD about the excavations confirms his presence in the third chamber just after it was opened—shaking hands with Kitov. Shopov also says he was a responsible party for the finds in the gold-mask burial and another Kitov tomb. Shopov declined to tell ARCHAEOLOGY anything about the scanner used in Kitov's discoveries, citing "commercial secrets." A police source is quoted in the Politika story saying Shopov is "operationally interesting."

Kitov described the admitted looter to ARCHAEOLOGY as someone who was in the tomb "coincidentally" at 2:30 A.M. when the third chamber was opened, although he previously told the magazine that not even the police were allowed to enter the tomb. Nikolov and others confirm the latter version of events.

A police investigator later revealed that the official list of artifacts found at Golyamata Kosmatka was incomplete enough for some objects to have gone unaccounted for—an administrative but not a criminal offense. Konstantin Dimitrov, chief expert of the investigative branch of Crimes Against Cultural Artifacts in the National Police, says the police have never "investigated" Kitov—a formal term for the beginning of a law-enforcement operation on specific charges. He does say that the police were "checking signals" from the Culture Ministry about various possible violations, but would not be more specific.

T HE PRESS ATTENTION GIVEN to Kitov has raised fresh debate on how to protect Bulgaria's cultural heritage. There is currently no law against buying antiquities in Bulgaria, only for digging for them or selling them—and even those laws are rarely enforced, making the country, according to Bozhidar Dimitrov, director of the National History Museum, the largest exporter of illicit antiquities in Europe. The parliament passed a law that went into effect January 1 giving all private collectors one year to register their collections with local museums, without having to establish origins or ownership.

The gold mask and ring, as well as the bronze head, are on display in the National Archaeological Museum in Sofia, while the Golyamata Kosmatka artifacts are in Kazanluk. Some are being restored but others are on display. There are no plans for any of the artifacts to travel abroad before the summer.

Kitov is currently in Sofia, where he says he is writing up his finds for the Bulgarian journal *Archaeologia*. At the end of 2004, readers of the country's second-largest daily named him one of the year's 55 "Most Honorable Bulgarians." Next spring he plans to return to the Valley of the Thracian Kings to continue work on other tombs in the same area, some of which he has worked on before, and some of which he hasn't.

Back in Shipka, people are readying themselves for the tourists they think will come. An unusual example of private initiative is being undertaken by Ali Kachan, a 58-year-old former tractor driver who owns a restaurant 300 yards from the burial mound where the gold mask was found. Within three weeks of the discovery, he had received all the required permissions and already begun building a defensive "house" around the tomb with his own money. "Private people need help," he says. "They are not used to having initiative. The moment the state gives serious money for the infrastructure of the burial mounds, things will happen as they should."

Kachan is not the only one thinking about what the finds might mean in concrete terms for Bulgarians. There is serious talk about basing the national tourism strategy on the Valley of the Thracian Kings. "Gold masks, bronze heads, tombs—all this makes me very happy," says Ivan Kalchev, who rents rooms to tourists in his enormous house in Shipka. He began construction work on a separate hotel just weeks before the first discovery. Most agree the Valley of the Kings is right now more a business strategy than scientific fact, but few fault the idea. "If someone wants to advertise it, that's great," says Vassil Nikolov, who is helping Bulgaria's president develop a strategy for managing the country's cultural heritage. "But first real money needs to be invested to develop the sites. When the foreign tourists come and there is no road, no electricity, no lights and no water, and nowhere to eat or sleep, they are not going to come back." As a start, the government recently allotted 1.2 million levs (about $800,000) to build roads and bring water and electricity to a few of the valley's tombs, including Golyamata Kosmatka.

Driving back toward Kachan's restaurant, a car cuts across the muddy field passing us in the opposite direction, toward the tomb of the golden mask. Kachan shakes his head and clicks his tongue against his teeth with disappointment. "No one will be there to show them anything," he tells me. Sometimes the restaurant owner gives tours himself. He feels each visitor who comes to the valley is a precious opportunity to share his pride and help the impoverished local economy. His vision for the future includes hotels, restaurants, and shops rising in the desolate fields where socialist agricultural cooperatives once raised roses. Kachan expects plenty of problems for at least a few years until the area develops enough infrastructure for feeding and housing foreign tourists. "In Bulgaria, people still aren't adapted to doing things 100 percent privately. When they learn to accept this, things will be different."

Matthew Brunwasser is an investigative journalist based in Sofia, Bulgaria.

In Flanders Fields

Uncovering the carnage of World War I

Neil Asher Silberman

The Belgian City of Ieper—better known by its French name, Ypres—is really two cities. One is a growing center of high-tech entrepreneurship and commerce with light manufacturing, biotechnology laboratories, and software-development firms clustered around the city in office complexes and industrial parks. The other is a place of cemeteries and war monuments: Flanders fields is where "the poppies blow/between the crosses, row on row," according to the poem by World War I Canadian combat surgeon John McCrae. For four hellish years during World War I, huge armies were bogged down here in a bloody stalemate. By the time of the Armistice in November 1918, this once-proud city, with its massive gothic Cloth Hall, step-gabled shop facades, cathedral, and medieval town square, had been pulverized by incessant bombardment. Its surrounding farmlands were transformed into a cratered, treeless wasteland. It was here that brutal trench warfare claimed the lives of nearly half a million British, Irish, Canadian, Australian, Indian, South African, New Zealand, German, French, and Belgian soldiers. Today, battlefield tours of the "Ypres Salient," as the Allied position deep in German-held territory was known during the war, the 144 official war cemeteries, and memorial ceremonies annually attract hundreds of thousands of visitors to Ieper. A new , state-of-the-art museum, In Flanders Fields, offers a sobering multimedia vision of trench warfare for tourists, descendants of World War I veterans, and a steady stream of school groups.

Now archaeologists have been thrust into a new battle for the soul of Ieper that pits the city's physical expansion against the commemoration of its tragic past. A plan for a new major highway, intended to bring economic development to the region, threatens its vast archaeological remains. Just beneath the surface of the fields, farmyards, and roads all around Ieper for at least three miles in every direction are the remains of trenches, fortifications, ammunition dumps, bunkers, and dugouts; unexploded munitions; discarded equipment; and the unrecovered bodies of at least one hundred thousand soldiers who are listed as missing in action on the various memorials erected throughout the battlefield.

The struggle over Ieper's future has highlighted many of the challenges facing battlefield archaeology the world over. What right does a community have to expand and develop land that is the site of a historic battlefield? What are the obligations of the present generation to preserve the integrity of battlefield landscapes as a memorial to the fallen and a reminder of the horrors of the past? And what role can archaeology play in examining the nature of modern warfare and preserving its physical remains?

High-tech Ieper and war-memorial Ieper have always lived in polite coexistence, but in 2002, a new regional transportation plan suddenly brought their conflicting interests into sharp relief. The A19, a major eight-lane highway that currently ends at the edge of the battlefield, was slated to continue its northward extension from France, eventually connecting Ieper to the Belgian coast of the English Channel, with its heavily visited tourist spots and ferry ports. Supporters argued that A19 would be a boon to Ieper's economy and draw off summertime traffic congestion from its narrow secondary roads. The plan for an initial four-and-a-half-mile extension was approved by Ieper's city council and sent for final approval and funding to the regional Flemish government.

Naturally, the farmers whose lands would be expropriated for road building immediately objected. But wider and more pervasive protests soon began to be heard: Historians, veterans' groups, preservation activists, and commemorative organizations were outraged that the new highway would rip through a four-and-a-half-mile swath of Flanders fields, almost certainly obliterating all traces of the bodies, trenchworks, and fortifications.

In response to these complaints, the Flemish ministry of culture ordered the Institute for Archaeological Patrimony (IAP), the public research body responsible for excavation and archaeological preservation in Flanders, to undertake a detailed assessment of the proposed route of the A19 extension. The project would provide an opportunity to learn more about Ieper's World War I artifacts. Archaeology in the region has long been focused on the prehistoric, Roman, and medieval periods. Twentieth-century archaeology, and particularly twentieth-century battlefield archaeology, was something new. "At first, I wasn't particularly enthusiastic about his assignment," says Marc DeWilde, head of the IAP West Flanders regional office and a specialist in the area's medieval period. "But we all now recognize how interesting and important this work is."

Over the years, battlefield archaeology at Ieper has been a sporadic, ad hoc affair. Year after year, a grim harvest of bones, twisted metal, and unexploded ordnance has complicated and sometimes endangered the inhabitants' lives. Even today, more than eighty-five years after the end of fighting, a Belgian army bomb-disposal truck makes weekly rounds of the rural roads around the city collecting bombs, artillery shells, and rusted clumps of ammunition and hand grenades that have turned up in the plowing and tending of fields. On rare occasions local farmers have been injured or killed. At building sites and roadworks on the expanding fringes of Ieper, workers regularly uncover trenches, bunkers, military equipment, and human remains. It is impossible to tell how many finds have been dug up and kept or sold as relics by the area's World War I buffs, working with metal detectors and digging in secrecy. Buried artifacts from World War I are protected by the antiquities laws of Flanders, but in practice they are vulnerable: Because the region is so archaeologically rich, it has been impossible for local IAP archaeologists to effectively patrol the entire area.

In other places along the Western Front, World War I archaeology has been limited to small-scale research projects on select French and Belgian battlefields. But here at Ieper the potential size of the dig was unprecedented. To get a better sense of the nature of the fighting and the places most likely to contain extensive battlefield remains, an enormous cache of contemporaneous documents was studied: military maps, reports, requisition orders, personal snapshots, diaries and letters, and World War I aerial photos.

Assisted by British colleagues from the University of Greenwich, the Imperial War Museum, the National Army Museum, and University College London, De Wilde and his team began work in the spring of 2002. Using the archival maps and documents, first they plotted the recorded locations of trench lines and other fortifications on modern topographical maps of the survey area. They then field walked the entire four-and-a-half-mile strip to spot concentrations of artifacts on the surface and tie them into documented battle sites. This turned up several intense concentrations of material: wire, supplies, tracks, bunkers, dugouts, pipelines, glass bottles with markings, shovels, helmets, concretized sandbags, bullets, cartridges, shells, and indications of trenches. The location of the finds closely matched the documentary record.

Nine areas were selected for excavation on the basis of the surface finds, and digging on two started right away. The IAP archaeologists began with a site identified from the WWI maps and accounts as "The High Command Redoubt," the German front established after the second Battle of Ieper, In April 1915, when the Germans' devastating chemical attack using canisters of acrid, blinding chlorine gas cleared the way to this strategic point. The English war chronicler Edmund Blunden, an Ieper veteran himself, noted that this redoubt was the highest strategic significance to the German forces, as it directly overlooked the Allied frontlines. The excavation revealed a system of trenches and machine-gun positions linked to substantial wooden structures. One of the walls still bore the initials "K.W.," carved by one of the builders or soldiers stationed there. It was eerily empty except for a rusted bayonet blade and a cache of unexploded hand grenades. Luckily, the IAP team had been trained to handle such potentially dangerous finds by the bomb-disposal unit of the Belgian army. "Once we learned how to deal with the grenades, shell cases, and unexploded bombs, we had no problem with these types of finds," says archaeologist Pedro Pype.

Within the shell craters were the shattered remains of five soldiers, two of them still wearing leather webbing, entrenching tools, pistol, bayonet, and ammunition packs.

At the second site, known in war accounts as Turco Farm, the discoveries were much more numerous and grisly. According to historical sources, this was the place where first the French and later the British established their frontlines after 1915. Excavations revealed a network of narrow trenches with "duckboards"—wood planks laid to keep soldiers above the mud—that had been lined with now-rusted sheets of corrugated iron. Within these trenches, the team recovered digging tools, a copper teaspoon, shoes, a water-logged woolen sock, and a shattered skeleton, identified as British from the distinctive uniform buttons found with it. Nearby they discovered the bones of a lower leg, with the foot still intact, inside a well-preserved military boot. The French factory marks stamped into the sole indicated the likely nationality of the fallen soldier.

The discovery of human remains changed everything. Over the years, whenever bones were found in the Ieper area, local police had been called in to determine whether they were those of battle casualties or evidence of a more recent crime. If war related, the bones were taken to a government morgue and eventually given over to the appropriate combatant nation. Often the remains could be linked to a particular army, unit, or even individual by the equipment, uniform buttons, or personal possessions found with them. England's Commonwealth War Graves Commission (CWGC) had been particularly active in identifying the remains of British and Commonwealth soldiers and burying them with full military honors in national cemeteries. Since one of the bodies from Turco Farm was British, it was transferred to the CWGC for proper burial. Though no German archaeologists or scholars have been involved in the excavations, had the bodies of the country's soldiers been recovered, German authorities would have been contacted to repatriate the remains.

The excavation at the next site, Crossroads Farm, was not merely a battlefield recovery operation. The archaeologists were also able to verify the hellish dynamics of trench warfare. The level farmland between the outer ring of the city and the low ridges that surrounded it—through which A19 would run—had been the deadly no man's land between the Allied trenches and those of the besieging German forces on the ridges above. Here, the IAP team traced the complex trench system that the Allies had expanded in preparation for an assault on the German positions during the Third Battle of Ieper in the summer of 1917. A variety of structural details and artifacts were uncovered, including duckboards, a deep concrete bunker, a wooden dugout, and cap badges representing the Royal King's Rifle Corps, the Dorsetshire Regiment, and the East Kent Regiment known as the "Buffs." The archaeologists also examined the clearly defined shell craters that pockmarked the entire area. Within the shell craters were the shattered remains of five soldiers, two of them still wearing leather webbing, entrenching tools, pistol, bayonet, and ammunition packs. British visitors to the excavation created a temporary memorial there, marking the places where the bodies were found with the familiar poppy-decorated wooden crosses used in Ieper's military cemeteries; formal military burials are planned for the coming months. From these remains and the location of the trenches, the archaeologists were able to trace in precise detail how the British had expanded and shifted the orientation of their trenches as they edged closer to the German frontlines.

At the very start of the project, the IAP had convened a panel of military historians and preservation experts from the United Kingdom, France, and Belgium to compile a background report on the historical significance of the threatened section of the Ieper battlefield. Though the panel was cautious in expressing its political opinions about the wisdom of the proposed highway plan, they were unambiguous in their opinion about the site's enormous historical and archaeological value as one of the most important battlefields of World War I. The excavations dramatically confirmed this conclusion.

Yet for the problem of the proposed highway, there are no easy answers. The panel recommended that the area be declared a protected heritage zone, but the supporters of the road project countered that the extent of the battlefield is so vast that any attempt to shift the road's path to skirt the entire area would be too expensive and inefficient to achieve the region's development aims. Alternatively, raising the highway on pillars to protect the human remains and archaeological deposits beneath it would also be costly and, as the preservationists pointed out, would forever destroy the visual context of the open ground and low ridges where the battles of Ieper were fought. Excavating the entire four-and-a-half-mile stretch would be far beyond the capacity of the IAP—or of any similar archaeological organization—considering the hundreds of bodies, dense network of trenches and fortifications, and tons of equipment that would almost certainly be found.

Something will have to be done to prevent the total destruction of the World War I remains, says Marc DeWilde. "I am concerned about any destruction of archaeological deposits. If the highway plan is approved and the archaeological remains are in danger, it's our responsibility to excavate what we must and preserve what we can."

At the time of this writing, no decision on the A19 extension has been made, and the archaeological project goes on. More finds—and more funerals—can be expected. And with elections for the Flemish Parliament in

June, no decision is anticipated soon. As the preservation and development debates continue, only one thing is certain: The pioneering project at Ieper has demonstrated archaeology's essential role in preserving and understanding the great historical trauma of modern warfare, whose gruesome traces lie beneath the surface of this now-peaceful ground.

Neil Asher Silberman is an author, a historian, and the coordinator of international programs for the Ename Center for Public Archaeology in Belgium. He thanks Marc Dewilde, Pedro Pype, Mathieu de Meyer, Frederik Demeyere, Wouter Lammens, Janiek Degryse, and Franky Wyffels of the IAP West Flanders regional office for their assistance with this article.

Germany's Nazi Past

The Past as Propaganda

How Hitler's archaeologists distorted European prehistory to justify racist and territorial goals.

Bettina Arnold

The manipulation of the past for political purposes has been a common theme in history Consider Darius I (521—486 B.C.), one of the most powerful rulers of the Achaemenid, or Persian, empire. The details of his accession to power, which resulted in the elimination of the senior branch of his family, are obscured by the fact that we have only his side of the story, carved on the cliff face of Behistun in Iran. The list of his victories, and by association his right to rule, are the only remaining version of the truth. Lesson number one: If you are going to twist the past for political ends, eliminate rival interpretations.

The use of the past for propaganda is also well documented in more recent contexts. The first-century Roman historian Tacitus produced an essay titled "On the Origin and Geography of Germany." It is less a history or ethnography of the German tribes than a moral tract or political treatise. The essay was intended to contrast the debauched and degenerate Roman Empire with the virtuous German people, who embodied the uncorrupted morals of old Rome. Objective reporting was not the goal of Tacitus's *Germania;* the manipulation of the facts was considered justified if it had the desired effect of contrasting past Roman glory with present Roman decline. Ironically, this particular piece of historical

propaganda was eventually appropriated by a regime notorious for its use and abuse of the past for political, imperialist, and racist purposes: the Third Reich.

The National Socialist regime in Germany fully appreciated the propaganda value of the past, particularly of prehistoric archaeology, and exploited it with characteristic efficiency. The fact that German prehistoric archaeology had been largely ignored before Hitler's rise to power in 1933 made the appropriation of the past for propaganda that much easier. The concept of the *Kulturkreis,* pioneered by the linguist turned-prehistorian Gustav Kossinna in the 1920s and defined as the identification of ethnic regions on the basis of excavated material culture, lent theoretical support to Nazi expansionist aims in central and eastern Europe. Wherever an artifact of a type designated as "Germanic" was found, the land was declared to be ancient Germanic territory. Applied to prehistoric archaeology, this perspective resulted in the neglect or distortion of data that did not directly apply to Germanic peoples. During the 1930s scholars whose specialty was provincial Roman archaeology were labeled *Römlinge* by the extremists and considered anti-German. The Römisch Germanische Kommission in Mainz, founded in 1907, was the object of numerous def-

amatory attacks, first by Kossinna and later by Alfred Rosenberg and his organization. Rosenberg, a Nazi ideologue, directed the Amt Rosenberg, which conducted ethnic, cultural, and racial research.

Altered prehistory also played an important role in rehabilitating German self-respect after the humiliating defeat of 1918. The dedication of the 1921 edition of Kossinna's seminal work *German Prehistory: A Preeminently National Discipline* reads: "To the German people, as a building block in the reconstruction of the externally as well as internally disintegrated fatherland."

According to Nazi doctrine, the Germanic culture of northern Europe was responsible for virtually all major intellectual and technological achievements of Western civilization. Maps that appeared in archaeological publications between 1933 and 1945 invariably showed the Germanic homeland as the center of diffusionary waves, bringing civilization to less developed cultures to the south, west, and east. Hitler presented his own views on this subject in a dinner-table monologue in which he referred to the Greeks as Germans who had survived a northern natural catastrophe and evolved a highly developed culture in southern contexts. Such wishful thinking was supported by otherwise reputable archaeologists. The *Research Report of the Reichsbund for German Prehistory,* July to December 1941, for example, reported the nine-week expedition of the archaeologist Hans Reinerth and a few colleagues to Greece, where they claimed to have discovered major new evidence of Indogermanic migration to Greece during Neolithic times.

This perspective was ethnocentric, racist, and genocidal. Slavic peoples occupying what had once been, on the basis of the distribution of archaeological remains, Germanic territory, were to be relocated or exterminated to supply true Germans with *Lebensraum* (living space). When the new Polish state was created in 1919, Kossinna published an article, "The German Ostmark, Home Territory of the Germans," which used archaeological evidence to support Germany's claim to the area. Viewed as only temporarily occupied by racially inferior "squatters," Poland and Czechoslovakia could be reclaimed for "racially pure" Germans.

Prehistoric archaeologists in Germany who felt they had been ignored, poorly funded, and treated as second-class citizens by colleagues specializing in the more honored disciplines of classical and Near Eastern archaeology now seemed to have everything to gain by an association with the rising Nazi party. Between 1933, the year of Hitler's accession to power, and 1935, eight new chairs were created in German prehistory and funding became available for prehistoric excavations across Germany and eastern Europe on an unprecedented scale. Numerous institutes came into being during this time, such as the Institute for Prehistory in Bonn in 1938. Museums for protohistory were established, and prehistoric collections were brought out of storage and exhibited, in many cases for the first time. Institutes for rune research were created to study the *futhark,* or runic alphabet in use in northern Europe from about the third to the thirteenth centuries A.D. Meanwhile, the Römisch Germanisches Zentral Museum in Mainz became the Zentral Museum für Deutsche Vor- und Frühgeschichte in 1939. (Today it has its pre-war title once again.)

Open-air museums like the reconstructed Neolithic and Bronze Age lake settlements at Unteruhldingen on Lake Constanz were intended to popularize prehistory. An archaeological film series, produced and directed by the prehistorian Lothar Zotz, included titles like *Threatened by the Steam Plow, Germany's Bronze Age, The Flames of Prehistory* and *On the Trail of the Eastern Germans.* The popular journals such as *Die Kunde (The Message), and Germanen-Erbe (Germanic Heritage)* proliferated. The latter publication was produced by the Ahnenerbe ("Ancestor History") organization, run as a personal project of Reichsführer-SS and chief of police Heinrich Himmler and funded by interested Germans to research, excavate, and restore real and imagined Germanic cultural relics. Himmler's interests in mysticism and the occult extended to archaeology; SS archaeologists were sent out in the wake of invading German forces to track down important archaeological finds and antiquities to be transported back to the Reich. It was this activity that inspired Steven Spielberg's *Raiders of the Lost Ark.*

The popular journals contained abundant visual material. One advertisement shows the reconstruction of a Neolithic drum from a pile of meaningless sherds. The text exhorts readers to "keep your eyes open, for every *Volksgenosse* [fellow German] can contribute to this important national project! Do not assume that a ceramic vessel is useless because it falls apart during excavation. Carefully preserve even the smallest fragment!" An underlined sentence emphasizes the principal message: "Every single find is important because it represents a document of our ancestors!"

Amateur organizations were actively recruited by appeals to patriotism. The membership flyer for the official National Confederation for German Prehistory (*Reichsbund für Deutsche Vorgeschichte*), under the direction of Hans Reinerth of the Amt Rosenberg, proclaimed: "Responsibility with respect to our indigenous prehistory must again fill every German with pride!" The organization stated its goals as "the interpretation and dissemination of unfalsified knowledge regarding the history and cul-

tural achievements of our northern Germanic ancestors on German and foreign soil."

For Himmler objective science was not the aim of German prehistoric archaeology. Hermann Rauschning, an early party member who became disillusioned with the Nazis and left Germany before the war, quotes Himmler as saying: "The one and only thing that matters to us, and the thing these people are paid for by the State, is to have ideas of history that strengthen our people in their necessary national pride. In all this troublesome business we are only interested in one thing—to project into the dim and distant past the picture of our nation as we envisage it for the future. Every bit of Tacitus in his *Germania* is tendentious stuff. Our teaching of German origins has depended for centuries on a falsification. We are entitled to impose one of our own at any time."

Meanwhile archaeological evidence that did not conform to Nazi dogma was ignored or suppressed. A good example is the controversy surrounding the Externsteine, a natural sandstone formation near Horn in northern Germany In the twelfth century Benedictine monks from the monastery in nearby Paderborn carved a system of chambers into the rock faces of the Externsteine. In the mid-1930s a contingent of SS Ahnenerbe researchers excavated at the site in an attempt to prove its significance as the center of the Germanic universe, a kind of Teutonic mecca. The excavators, led by Julius Andree, an archaeologist with questionable credentials and supported by Hermann Wirth, one of the founders of the SS Ahnenerbe, were looking for the remains of an early Germanic temple at the Externsteine, where they claimed a cult of solar worshipers had once flourished. The site was described in numerous publications as a monument to German unity and the glorious Germanic past, despite the fact that no convincing evidence of a temple or Germanic occupation of the site was ever found.

So preposterous were the claims made by Andree, Wirth, and their associates that numerous mainstream archaeologists openly questioned the findings of the investigators who became popularly known as *German omanen* or "Germanomaniacs." Eventually Himmler and the Ahnenerbe organization disowned the project, but not before several hundred books and pamphlets on the alleged cult site had been published.

By 1933 the Nazis had gone a step further, initiating a movement whose goal was to replace all existing religious denominations with a new pseudopagan state religion based loosely on Germanic mythology, solar worship, nature cults, and a Scandinavian people's assembly or *thing,* from which the new movement derived its name. Central to the movement were open-air theaters or *Thingstätten,* where festivals, military ceremonies, and morality plays, known as *Thingspiele,* were to be staged. To qualify as a Thingstätte, evidence of significant Germanic occupation of the site had to be documented. There was considerable competition among municipalities throughout Germany for this honor. Twelve Thingstätten had been dedicated by September 1935, including one on the summit of the Heiligenberg in Heidelberg.

The Heiligenberg was visited sporadically during the Neolithic, possibly for ritual purposes; there is no evidence of permanent occupation. It was densely settled during the Late Bronze Age (1200–750 B.C.), and a double wall-and-ditch system was built there in the Late Iron Age (200 B.C. to the Roman occupation), when it was a hillfort settlement. Two provincial Roman watchtowers, as well as several Roman dedicatory inscriptions, statue bases, and votive stones, have been found at the site.

When excavations in the 1930s failed to produce evidence of Germanic occupation the Heiligenberg was granted Thingstätte status on the basis of fabricated evidence in the published excavation reports. Ironically, most of the summit's prehistoric deposits were destroyed in the course of building the open-air arena. The Heiligenberg Thingstätte actually held only one Thingspiel before the Thing movement was terminated. Sensing the potential for resistance from German Christians, the Ministry of Propaganda abandoned the whole concept in 1935. Today the amphitheater is used for rock concerts.

Beyond its convenience for propaganda and as justification for expansion into countries like Czechoslovakia and Poland, the archaeological activities of the Amt Rosenberg and Himmler's Ahnenerbe were just so much window dressing for the upper echelons of the party. There was no real respect for the past or its remains. While party prehistorians like Reinerth and Andree distorted the facts, the SS destroyed archaeological sites like Biskupin in Poland. Until Germany's fortunes on the eastern front suffered a reversal in 1944, the SS Abhenerbe conducted excavations at Biskupin, one of the best-preserved Early Iron Age (600–400 B.C.) sites in all of central Europe. As the troops retreated, they were ordered to demolish as much of the site's preserved wooden fortifications and structures as possible.

Not even Hitler was totally enthusiastic about Himmler's activities. He is quoted by Albert Speer, his chief architect, as complaining: "Why do we call the whole world's attention to the fact that we have no past? It's bad enough that the Romans were erecting great buildings when our forefathers were still living in mud huts; now Himmler is starting to dig up these villages of mud huts and enthusing over every potsherd and stone axe he finds. All we prove by that is that we were still throwing stone hatchets and crouching around open fires when Greece and Rome had already reached the highest stage of culture. We should really do our best to keep quiet about this past. Instead Himmler makes a great fuss about it all. The present-day Romans must be having a laugh at these revelations."

"Official" involvement in archaeology consisted of visits by Himmler and various SS officers to SS-funded and staffed excavations, like the one on the Erdenburg in the Rhineland, or press shots of Hitler and Goebbels viewing a reconstructed "Germanic" Late Bronze Age burial in its tree-trunk coffin, part of the 1934 "Deutsches Volk—Deutsche Arbeit" exhibition in Berlin. Party appropriation of prehistoric data was evident in the use of Indo-European and Germanic design symbols in Nazi uniforms and regalia. The double lightning bolt, symbol of Himmler's SS organiza-

tion, was adapted from a Germanic rune. The swastika is an Indo-European sun symbol which appears in ceramic designs as early as the Neolithic in western Europe and continues well into early medieval times.

German archaeologists during this period fall into three general categories: those who were either true believers or self-serving opportunists; those (the vast majority) who accepted without criticism the appropriation and distortion of prehistoric archaeology; and those who openly opposed these practices.

Victims of the regime were persecuted on the basis of race or political views, and occasionally both. Gerhard Bersu, who had trained a generation of post–World War I archaeologists in the field techniques of settlement archaeology, was prematurely retired from the directorship of the Römisch Germanische Kommission in 1935. His refusal to condone or conduct research tailored to Nazi ideological requirements, in addition to his rejection of the racist Kossinna school, ended his career as a prehistorian until after World War II. The official reason given for the witchhunt, led by Hans Reinerth under the auspices of the Amt Rosenberg, was Bersu's Jewish heritage. By 1950 Bersu was back in Germany, again directing the Römisch Germanische Kommission.

It should be noted that some sound work was accomplished during this period despite political interference. The vocabulary of field reports carefully conformed to the dictates of funding sources, but the methodology was usually unaffected. Given time this would have changed as politically motivated terms and concepts altered the intellectual vocabulary of the discipline. In 1935, for example, the entire prehistoric and early historic chronologies were officially renamed: the Bronze and pre-Roman Iron Ages became the "Early Germanic period," the Roman Iron Age the "Climax Germanic period," the Migration period the "Late Germanic period," and everything from the Carolingians to the thirteenth century the "German Middle Ages."

It is easy to condemn the men and women who were part of the events that transformed the German archaeological community between 1933 and 1945. It is much more difficult to understand the choices they made or avoided in the social and political contexts of the time. Many researchers who began as advocates of Reinerth's policies in the Amt Rosenberg and Himmler's Ahnenerbe organization later became disenchanted. Others, who saw the system as a way to develop and support prehistory as a discipline, were willing to accept the costs of the Faustian bargain it offered. The benefits were real, and continue to be felt to this day in the institutions and programs founded between 1933 and 1945.

The paralysis felt by many scholars from 1933 to 1945 continued to affect research in the decades after the war. Most scholars who were graduate students during the 12-year period had to grapple with a double burden: a humiliating defeat and the disorienting experience of being methodologically "deprogrammed." Initially there was neither time nor desire to examine the reasons for the Nazi prostitution of archaeology. Unfortunately prehistoric archaeology is the only German social-science discipline that has still to publish a self-critical study of its role in the events of the 1930s and 1940s.

The reluctance of German archaeologists to come to terms with the past is a complex issue. German prehistoric archaeology is still a young discipline, and first came into its own as a result of Nazi patronage. There is therefore a certain feeling that any critical analysis of the motives and actions of the generation and the regime that engendered the discipline would be ungrateful at best and at worst a betrayal of trust. The vast majority of senior German archaeologists, graduate students immediately after the war, went straight from the front lines to the universities, and their dissertation advisers were men whose careers had been determined by their connections within the Nazi party.

The reluctance of German archaeologists to come to terms with the past is a complex issue.

The German system of higher education is built upon close bonds of dependence and an almost medieval fealty between a graduate student and his or her dissertation advisor. These bonds are maintained even after the graduate student has embarked on an academic career. Whistle-blowers are rare, since such action would amount to professional suicide. But in the past decade or so, most of the generation actively involved in archaeological research and teaching between 1933 and 1945 have died. Their knowledge of the personal intrigues and alliances that allowed the Nazi party machine to function has died with them. Nonetheless, there are indications that the current generation of graduate students is beginning to penetrate the wall of silence that has surrounded this subject since 1945. The remaining official documents and publications may allow at least a partial reconstruction of the role of archaeology in the rise and fall of the Nazi regime.

The future of prehistoric archaeology in the recently unified Germany will depend on an open confrontation with the past. Archaeologists in the former East Germany must struggle with the legacy of both Nazi and Communist manipulation of their discipline. Meanwhile, the legacy of the Faustian bargain struck by German archaeologists with the Nazi regime should serve as a cautionary tale beyond the borders of a unified Germany: Archaeological research funded wholly or in part by the state is vulnerable to state manipulation. The potential for political exploitation of the past seems to be greatest in countries experiencing internal instability. Germany in the years following World War I was a country searching for its own twentieth-century identity. Prehistoric archaeology was one means to that end.

Reprinted with permission from *Archaeology* magazine, July/August 1992, pp. 30–37. © 1992 by the Archaeological Institute of America.

Earth Movers

Archaeologists say Brazil's rain forest, once thought to be inhospitable to humans, fostered huge ancient civilizations. The proof is in the dirt.

MARION LLOYD

IRANDUBA, BRAZIL

HIGH ALONG BLUFFS overlooking the confluence of the mighty Negro and Solimões Rivers here, supersize eggplants, papayas, and cassava spring from the ground.

Their exuberance defies a long-held belief about the Amazon. For much of the last half century, archaeologists viewed the South American rain forest as a "counterfeit paradise," a region whose inhospitable environment precluded the development of complex societies. But new research suggests that prehistoric man found ways to overcome the jungle's natural limitations—and to thrive in this environment in large numbers.

The secret, says James B. Petersen, an archaeologist at the University of Vermont who has spent the past decade working in the Brazilian Amazon, is found in the ground beneath his feet. It is a highly fertile soil called *terra preta do indio,* which is Portuguese for "Indian black earth." By some estimates, this specially modified soil covers as much as 10 percent of Amazonia, the immense jungle region that straddles the Amazon River. And much of that area is packed with potsherds and other signs of human habitation.

"This was one of the last archaeological frontiers on the planet. It's as if we know nothing about it," says Mr. Petersen, as he analyzes the discovery of the day, a series of circular carbon deposits that might indicate the outline of a prehistoric house.

Scientists are now working to determine whether *terra preta,* which contains high levels of organic matter and carbon, was deliberately created by pre-Columbian civilizations to improve upon the notoriously poor rain-forest soil, or whether the modified earth was an accidental byproduct of sustained habitation by large groups of people.

Either way, Mr. Petersen believes it likely that pre-Columbian societies in the Amazon were not the primitive tribal societies they were once thought to be, but highly complex chiefdoms.

"We're providing the proof," he says during a several-week-long dig in August near the Brazilian jungle city of Manaus. His team of American and Brazilian archaeologists, who call themselves the Central Amazon Project, have excavated more than 60 sites rich in *terra preta* near where the Negro and Solimões Rivers merge to form the Amazon River proper.

One of the group's founders, Michael J. Heckenberger of the University of Florida, is bolstering the new findings with research on large prehistoric earthworks farther east along the upper Xingu River. Studying this area, which now is inhabited by the Kuikuru Indians, has allowed him to compare data of prehistoric land management with modern ethnographic studies.

On some pre-Columbian sites explored by Mr. Petersen and his team, several miles of earth are packed with millions of potsherds. The archaeologists have also found evidence that they say points to the existence of giant plazas, bridges, and roads, complete with curbs, and defensive ditches that would have taken armies of workers to construct.

Intriguingly, the earliest evidence of large, sedentary populations appears to coincide with the beginnings of *terra preta.*

"Something happened 2,500 years ago, and we don't know what," says Eduardo Góes Neves, a Brazilian archaeologist at the Federal University of São Paulo, who is co-director of the Central Amazon Project. He dusts off the flanged edge of a bowl from around 400 BC that one of his Brazilian graduate students pulled from a layer of *terra preta* eight feet down. The team got lucky when the landowner at Açutuba, the largest of their excavation sites, bulldozed a huge pit in one of his fields. The "swimming pool," as the team jokingly calls the 15-yard-wide hole, is giving them a rare chance to compare levels of *terra preta* over a large area.

The research has implications not only for history, but also for the future of the Amazon rain forest. If scientists could discover how the Amerindians transformed the soil, farmers could use the technology to maximize smaller plots of land, rather than cutting down ever larger swaths of jungle. The benefits of what Mr. Petersen calls this "gift from the past" are already well known to farmers in the area, who plant their crops wherever they find *terra preta*.

Rich in Controversy

The claims made for *terra preta* extend far beyond a legacy passed down from farmer to farmer. The archaeologists now reject the idea that pre-contact Amerindians were—as one team member says, ironically—"Stone Age primitives frozen at the dawn of time."

"It's made by pre-Columbian Indians and it's still fertile," says Bruno Glaser, a soil chemist from the University of Bayreuth, in Germany, who was taking samples of *terra preta* from another site discovered by Mr. Petersen's team. "If we knew how to do this, it would be a model for agriculture in the whole region."

> "It's made by pre-Columbian Indians and it's still fertile. If we knew how to do this, it would be a model for agriculture in the whole region."

Ideally what researchers dub "slash and char" agriculture, the indigenous technique that returns nutrients to the soil by mixing in organic waste and carbon, could replace slash-and-burn, a contemporary technique that consumes tens of thousands of acres of rain forest every year. Mr. Glaser is part of an international team of scientists studying the chemical composition of *terra preta* in an effort to recreate it.

The research into *terra preta* fuels a revisionist school of scientists who argue that pre-Columbian Amazonia was not a pristine wilderness, but rather a heavily managed forest teeming with human beings. They believe that advanced societies existed in the Amazon from before the time of Christ until a century after the European conquest in the 1500s decimated Amerindian populations through exploitation and disease. The theory is also supported by the accounts of the first Europeans to travel the length of the Amazon in 1542. They reported human settlements with tens of thousands of people stretching for many miles along the river banks.

But not everyone working in the field of Amazonian research buys the new theory.

"The idea that the indigenous population has secrets that we don't know about is not supported by anything except wishful thinking and the myth of El Dorado," says the archaeologist Betty J. Meggers, who is the main defender of the idea that only small, tribal societies ever inhabited the Amazon. "This myth just keeps going on and on and on. It's amazing."

Ms. Meggers, director of the Latin American Archaeology Program at the Smithsonian Institution's Museum of Natural History, in Washington, has spent her life trying to prove that Amazonia is a uniquely untrammeled and hostile wilderness. Now 82, Ms. Meggers has been working in the field since the late 1940s, when she and her husband, Clifford Evans, now deceased, began pioneering fieldwork on Marajó Island, at the mouth of the Amazon. She summarized their findings in a seminal 1954 article, "Environmental Limitation on the Development of Culture," which was published in *American Anthropologist*.

Ms. Meggers's 1971 book, *Amazonia: Man and Culture in a Counterfeit Paradise* (Aldine-Atherton), converted her views into gospel for a generation of Amazonian archaeologists. In it, she argued that modern Amerindian groups, generally composed of a few hundred people, follow ancient practices of infanticide and other population-control measures to exist in a hostile environment.

"It had a huge impact," says Susanna B. Hecht, a geographer at the University of California at Los Angeles who has spent three decades studying traditional farming practices in Amazonia. "Virtually every Anthropology I class read that book." Ms. Hecht's most recent research is with the Kayapó Indians in the upper Xingu River, the same region where Mr. Heckenberger is working. To her surprise, she discovered the Indians were creating a version of *terra preta* by burning excess vegetation and weeds and mixing the charcoal into the soil.

"One of the things we found rather unusual was how much burning was going on all the time," she says. "It wasn't catastrophic burning. It was that the whole landscape was smoldering all the time."

Ms. Hecht says the technique was probably more widespread before Indian societies were devastated by the arrival of the Europeans, who introduced measles, typhoid, and other diseases to which the Indians had no resistance. By some estimates, 95 percent of the Amerindians died within the first 130 years of contact. While their numbers were once estimated in the millions, there are now roughly 250,000 Amerindians living in Brazil.

"I think you could have had very dense populations, and what you had was a real holocaust in various forms," she says. However, Ms. Hecht notes, little was known about the impact of those epidemics when Ms. Meggers was first writing, and her persuasive arguments against large civilizations discouraged archaeologists from probing deeper into the Amazon. "Everyone said, 'Nobody was there anyway. Why bother?'" says Ms. Hecht.

The difficulty and dangers of conducting research in the Amazon also played a part. The region was largely impassible until the 1960s, when the Brazilian government began encouraging settlement in the jungle's interior.

A few researchers did challenge Ms. Meggers's theories early on. The most outspoken figure was Donald Lathrap, a University of Illinois archaeologist who worked in the Peruvian Amazon in the 1950s. He argued that Amazonia could and did support complex societies with advanced technology, and that the cradle of those civilizations was very likely in the central Amazon, where Mr. Petersen is working.

Another pioneer was William M. Denevan, a geographer emeritus at the University of Wisconsin, whose discovery of huge earthworks in lowland Bolivia in the early

1960s suggested that pre-Columbian peoples modified their environment for large-scale agriculture. In a 1992 article, "The Pristine Myth: The Landscape of the Americas in 1492," he argued that the modern Amazon rain forest was the result of human management over millennia, not a virgin wilderness.

"The key issue here can be summed up in two words: environmental determinism," he says, referring to the once-popular school of thought, favored by Ms. Meggers, that says environment dictates man's ability to progress. "We are saying people always have options," he says. "We can farm in outer space. And we can farm in the Antarctic. Or we can crop in the driest part of the Sahara Desert. It may be very expensive, but that's a different issue."

Building a Mystery

Other researchers working in Amazonia go even further. They suggest that prehistoric man may have created cities that rivaled those of the Aztecs and Maya. Again, they say, the proof is in the dirt.

William I. Woods, a geographer at Southern Illinois University at Edwardsville, has been studying *terra preta* deposits extending over 100,000 acres around the Brazilian jungle city of Santarém, where the Tapajós River meets the Amazon. He believes as many as 500,000 people might once have inhabited the area, implying a civilization larger than the Aztec capital of Tenochtitlán, once the largest city in the Americas.

"There is some fussing about the magnitude, from" he says. "But I don't think there are too many scholars who have any problems with chiefdoms existing and lots of people being supported for long times in various places in the Amazon."

Ms. Meggers has not taken challenges to her life's work lying down. In a 2001 article in *Latin American Antiquity*, she accuses the revisionist camp of endangering the rain forest by suggesting that large-scale farming was feasible in the region. Her view is shared by some biologists and environmentalists.

"Adherence to 'the lingering myth of Amazonian empires' not only prevents archaeologists from reconstructing the prehistory of Amazonia, but makes us accomplices in the accelerating pace of environmental degradation," she writes.

Mr. Neves, the Brazilian archaeologist, disagrees. "It's not like loggers are revving up the chainsaws after reading our articles," he says as he walks along a winding dirt road littered with pre-Columbian potsherds on his way to the dig site at Açutuba, a jungle-shrouded stretch of farmland overlooking the Negro River. "Deforestation through ranching isn't how the Amerindian interacted with the landscape," he says. "The Amerindians weren't destroying the environment. They were enriching it."

The rain forest is not inherently hostile to man, says Mr. Neves. He argues that pre-Columbian peoples knew how to use the huge diversity of species to their advan-

tage, through a combination of farming, fishing, and managed tree harvesting. Cassava, a starchy root that grows well in the acidic rain-forest soil, was probably the Amerindians' main food source, which the Indians could have supplemented with corn and other vegetables grown on *terra preta*. But they also relied heavily on fish and turtles for protein, he says.

Blowing Dust From the Pages

Terra preta proponents also argue that historical accounts support their theories. The Rev. Gaspar de Carvajal, a Spanish priest who accompanied the first exploratory expedition down the Amazon in 1542, reported seeing hundreds of tortoises kept in corrals and "an abundance of meat and fish . . . that would have fed 1,000 men for a year." The friar also recounts an ambush by more than 10,000 Indians at a point in the river just west of modern-day Manaus, suggesting that the area was heavily populated as recently as the 16th century. He also describes armies of Indians who repelled attempts by the Spaniards to come ashore near modern-day Santarém.

> "They have not done enough work to establish whether it was a single large settlement or a result of intermittent occupation over longer periods of time."

Ms. Meggers is skeptical. "How could these people, when they're fleeing, count 10,000 warriors?" she says. "It's silly." She notes that other portions of Father Carvajal's account, in particular his description of female Amazon warriors, which gave the river its name, have since been dismissed by historians as inventions to impress the Spanish crown.

She also challenges estimates by the Central Amazon Project that between 5,000 and 10,000 people may have once inhabited Açutuba, possibly the largest site under excavation in the Brazilian Amazon. "They have not done enough work to establish whether it was a single large settlement or a result of intermittent occupation over longer periods of time," she says. She also accuses the group of ignoring the results of surveys in the region backed by the Smithsonian Institution over several decades.

Mr. Petersen shrugs off the criticism. "We're not here to fight Betty Meggers," he says, while taking a break from digging under the broiling jungle sun. "We're here to build on her work and refine it." He says that Ms. Meggers made a major contribution to the field by highlighting the enormous challenges involved in inhabiting the Amazon rain forest, even if he argues that later research shows that pre-Columbian peoples found ways of overcoming those natural limitations.

His team has several dozen radiocarbon dates from potsherds and carbon deposits collected throughout Açutuba, which they say show that the entire site was continuously inhabited during two waves from about 360 BC to as late as 1440 AD. The evidence also supports the existence of stratified societies, says Mr. Petersen. He picks up an ornate, white- and black-painted potsherd from the *terra preta* under a field of glistening eggplants. "This is probably from about AD 800, and look how sophisticated it is. It's like fine dinnerware," he says, comparing the sherd with that from a coarser vessel from about the same period, which he calls "everyday china." His team has unearthed more than 100,000 potsherds dating from 500 BC to about AD 1500 at the three-square-mile site, including roughly a dozen burial urns.

Digging through earth packed with tons of pottery is slow going. Particularly when you only have about eight pairs of hands.

"We've been working here nine years, and we've barely scratched the surface," says Mr. Neves, who has raised the bulk of the money from his university and the São Paulo state government. He estimates that there are at least 100 unexcavated sites within their research area, which extends over 40 square miles around the town of Iranduba. Some of the sites might be even larger than Açutuba.

Ecological Edge

Unlike the Maya in northern Central America, the inhabitants of the Amazon lacked stone for building. So they had to resort to organic and man-made materials. As a result there are few permanent markers of earlier civilizations, forcing archaeologists to extrapolate from small scraps of evidence.

"The only reason that everyone accepts large, socially complex societies in Maya land is that they have surviving pyramids and stelae," says Mr. Petersen. "If the Maya and others had used mostly organic perishables in their architecture, like the Amazon people, then I would bet there would be much more mystery and debate about the

nature of pre-Columbian Amerindians in Central America, too."

At a nearby site, called Hatahara, the team recently excavated 11 human skeletons dating to about AD 800 from one nine-yard trench dug into a large burial mound. Believing it unlikely that they would have stumbled upon the only evidence in the mound, they estimate there may be hundreds more bodies buried there, suggesting a population of at least a few thousand people.

The skeletons provided the team with other insights into the previous inhabitants. "These were not famine-stricken people," Mr. Neves says, noting that the skeletons measured about 5-foot-7. In contrast, modern indigenous inhabitants often do not grow taller than five feet, a fact used by earlier archaeologists to argue that the jungle was unsuited for human habitation. "I don't think there were ever severe limitations here," says Mr. Neves.

He points at the acres of glistening vegetables that seem to grow effortlessly throughout the Açutuba site. Settlers throughout the Iranduba area take advantage of the abundant *terra preta* deposits to grow vegetables and fruit for the nearby city of Manaus, supplying much of the produce consumed by its 1.4 million people.

"I know *terra preta* is very good and that it was made by the Indians," says Edson Azevedo Santos, a 48-year-old farmer drenched in sweat from weeding his zucchini patch. Unlike the acidic soil found in most of the rain forest, which can only sustain crops for a three-year period, *terra preta* plots can withstand constant farming for decades, if properly managed.

Even more striking, *terra preta* may have the capacity to regenerate itself, says Mr. Woods, the Southern Illinois geographer. He recently tested that possibility by removing a large section of *terra preta* on a plot near Santarem. To his amazement, the soil grew back within three years. "I suggested that the soil should be treated as living organism and that microorganisms are the secret," he says, adding that more research is needed to allow scientists to repeat the process. "This is very sophisticated stuff."

From *The Chronicle of Higher Education*, December 3, 2004, pp. A16–A19. Copyright © 2004 by Marion Lloyd. Reprinted by permission of the author.

Whither the Neanderthals?

Richard G. Klein

The Neanderthals are the longest known and best understood of all fossil humans. In 1856, quarry workers cleaning out a limestone cave in the Neander Valley, Germany, found a partial skeleton for which the group is named. Today, several thousand Neanderthal bones are known from more than 70 individual sites. Yet, paleoanthropologists still debate just how much the Neanderthals differed from living humans and whether the differences help explain why the Neanderthals disappeared.

Most Neanderthal specimens are isolated skeletal elements, especially teeth and jaws, but nearly every part of the skeleton is represented in multiple copies. There are also more than 20 partial skeletons from individuals of both sexes and different ages.[1] More than 300 archaeological sites have yielded artifacts and broken-up animal bones that illuminate Neanderthal behavior and ecology.[2]

The Neanderthals evolved in Europe. Some of their distinctive anatomical features already mark European fossils that are more than 350,000 years old.[3] Through a process of natural selection and random genetic drift, they emerged in full-blown form by 130,000 years ago. From then on, they were distributed more or less continuously from Spain to southern Russia; by 80,000 years ago, they had extended their range to western Asia (see the figure). They persisted in Europe and western Asia until at least 50,000 years ago and perhaps in some places until 30,000 years ago.

Everywhere they lived, the Neanderthals were the immediate predecessors of modern humans, and it has often been suggested that they were ancestral to living populations. However, at the same time that the Neanderthals occupied Europe and western Asia, other kinds of people lived in the Far East and Africa.[4] The Africans were anatomically much more modern than the Neanderthals, and are therefore more plausible ancestors of living humans. Furthermore, surveys show that variants of mitochondrial DNA[5] and the Y chromosome[6] in living Eurasian humans derive exclusively from African variants that probably existed no more than 100,000 years ago.

Further support for this argument comes from mitochondrial DNA extracted from Neanderthal bones. The data indicate that the last shared ancestor of Neanderthals and living humans lived 500,000 to 600,000 years ago.[7] Non-sex chromosomes of living humans may conceivably retain some Neanderthal genes,[8] but the combined fossil and genetic evidence suggests that any Neanderthal contribution to living populations was small. The Neanderthals may thus be regarded as a fascinating but extinct side branch of humanity.

Modern humans invaded the west Asian part of the Neanderthal range about 45,000 years ago. They subsequently swept northward and westward through Europe, swamping or replacing the Neanderthals within 10,000 to 15,000 years. The modern human triumph depended on technological, economic, and demographic advantages that were apparently grounded in an enhanced ability to innovate. This ability probably appeared first in Africa, but debate continues on how rapidly it evolved and whether it was rooted in biological change or in population growth and social reorganization. Fossils and artifacts are unlikely to resolve this issue, but genes underlying cognition might.

Neanderthal Physical Form

The Neanderthals were distinguished by large heads, massive trunks, and relatively short, powerful limbs.[1] Their average brain size equaled or exceeded that of modern humans, but their skulls also exhibit specializations that are unknown in any other people, fossil or living.[9] These unique features underscore the likelihood that the Neanderthals represent a divergent evolutionary lineage.

The specializations include the extraordinary forward projection of the face along the midline, the tendency for the braincase to bulge outwards at the sides, a depressed elliptical area of roughened bone on the back of the skull, and an array of bumps and crannies in the vicinity of the mastoid process. In addition, high-resolution computed tomography has revealed a singular configuration of the bony labyrinth of the inner ear.[10]

These features apparently had a genetic basis, because they are already visible in young children. The labyrinth configuration was fixed even before birth. There is no indication that the specialized features attenuated through time: The latest Neanderthals, 60,000 to 30,000 years ago, express them just as strongly as their more remote ancestors. Modern humans completely lack them. The skull alone then is sufficient to preclude a major Neanderthal contribution to living human populations.

High activity levels and a strenuous life-style explain the power of Neanderthal limbs. The short limbs and massive trunk, which would conserve body heat, were probably an adaptive response to the mostly glacial climatic conditions under which the Neanderthals evolved. Among living humans, such features particularly characterize Arctic peoples. The Neanderthals had even more massive trunks and shorter limbs, yet never faced true Arctic cold. The degree to which they adapted physically may reflect their limited ability to adapt culturally.

Neanderthal Behavior and Ecology

The modern successors to the Neanderthals are often known colloquially as the Cro-Magnons, after a French site where their bones were uncovered in 1868. In general, Neanderthal bones occur with artifact assemblages that archaeologists assign to the Middle Paleolithic cultural (or artifactual) complex, whereas Cro-Magnon bones occur with artifacts of the succeeding Upper Paleolithic complex. The use of separate names for the physical types and the artifact complexes allows for deviations from the usual rule of association.

Middle and Upper Paleolithic people shared many advanced behaviors, including a refined ability to flake stone, burial of the dead (at least on occasion), an interest in naturally occurring mineral pigments, full control over fire, and a heavy dependence on meat (probably obtained mainly through hunting). Both Neanderthal and Cro-Magnon skeletal remains sometimes reveal debilitating disabilities, indicating that both kinds of peoples cared for the old and the sick. There could be no more compelling indication of shared humanity.

Yet, archaeology also suggests many important behavioral differences. Unlike Upper Paleolithic Cro-Magnons, Middle Paleolithic Neanderthals left little compelling evidence for art or jewelry. Their graves contain nothing to suggest burial ritual or ceremony. They produced a much smaller range of readily distinguishable stone tool types; much more rarely crafted artifacts from plastic substances like bone, ivory, shell, or antler; and left no evidence for projectile (as opposed to thrusting) weapons. Their cave sites are generally poorer in cultural debris and richer in bones of bears and other cave dwellers (suggesting less dense human populations). They failed to build structures durable enough to leave an archaeological trace, and were confined to relatively mild, temperate latitudes. Finally, the Middle Paleolithic artifact assemblages that Neanderthals produced varied little through time and space. The Upper Paleolithic assemblages that Cro-Magnons made varied far more and are the oldest from which we can infer identity-conscious ethnic groups.

Hence, only the Upper Paleolithic anticipates the material record of historic hunter-gatherers, and only Upper Paleolithic people were fully modern in the sense that all historic people were.

Neanderthal/Cro-Magnon Contact

Consistent with an African origin for the Cro-Magnons, radiocarbon dating suggests that they displaced the Neanderthals about 45,000 years ago in western Asia and only 5000 to 15,000 years later in Europe. In Europe, the Neanderthals may have succumbed much earlier in the far east (Russia) than the far west (Iberia), but the supporting dates are sparse. There is also the ever-present possibility of minute, undetectable contamination with recent carbon, which can make a sample that is 50,000 to 40,000 radiocarbon years old appear 20,000 to 10,000 years younger.

Such contamination may explain radiocarbon dates that suggest the survival of Neanderthals in southern Russia,[11] Croatia[12], and Spain[13] for 7000 years or more after Cro-Magnons had appeared nearby. Only the alternation of Neanderthal and Cro-Magnon layers within a single site could provide unequivocal evidence for substantial chronological overlap. No known site provides such alternation. Wherever Middle Paleolithic and early Upper Paleolithic layers occur in the same site, the Upper Paleolithic layers directly overlie the Middle Paleolithic ones, with no indication for a significant gap in time. The implication is that in most places the Neanderthals disappeared abruptly.

Neanderthal/Cro-Magnon interbreeding has been suggested from occasional fossils, including a recently discovered Upper Paleolithic child's skeleton from Portugal.[14] However, in each case, the anatomical indications are at best ambiguous, and few experts recognize any hybrids. Evidence for cultural contact is also sparse, except for one well-documented case from central France. Here, a site occupied by Neanderthals shortly before their disappearance has provided an undeniable mix of Middle and Upper Paleolithic artifact types, including well-made bone tools and jewelry.[10] It also contains the only indisputable house ruin from a Neanderthal site.

The mix may mean that Neanderthals could imitate Upper Paleolithic/Cro-Magnon neighbors. But if Upper Paleolithic technology allowed more effective use of natural resources and larger human populations, it is puzzling that Neanderthals failed to adopt it more widely. If they had done so, then their unique skeletal traits and genes would be more obvious in succeeding populations.

Cognition and Neanderthal Extinction

Except for the French site just cited, there is little to suggest that Neanderthals could behave in a modern, Upper Paleolithic way. This inability may explain why they disappeared so quickly and completely. However, Neanderthal brains were no smaller than those of modern humans. If there was a difference in brain function, it resided in soft tissue that cannot be inferred from empty skulls. Hence, neither archaeology nor fossils can reveal Neanderthal cognitive capacity.

This issue is important not only for illuminating Neanderthal disappearance. Fossils show that between 130,000 and 50,000 years ago, the African contemporaries of the Neanderthals were more modern in anatomy, but archaeology suggests that they closely resembled the Neanderthals in behavior. [4] A change in brain function about 50,000 years ago could explain why modern Africans subsequently expanded to Eurasia.

The discovery that FOXP2, a gene involved in speech and language, achieved its modern sequence less than 200,000 ago years ago[15] provides tentative support for such a change in brain function. A truly persuasive case may depend on the isolation of genes that are expressed differently in the brains of apes and people.[16] Many human gene variants will turn out be very ancient, but if there was a brain change around 50,000 years ago, one or more variants should coalesce to about this time. Fossil bones could provide a further test, now that some have been shown to retain organic compounds that bear on brain function.[17]

The longest continuous debate in paleoanthropology is nearing resolution. Modern humans replaced the Neanderthals with little or no gene exchange. Almost certainly, the Neanderthals succumbed because they wielded culture less effectively. The main question that remains open is whether Neanderthal genes explain their failure to compete culturally.

References

1. E. Trinkaus, P. Shipman, *The Neandertals: Changing the Image of Mankind* (Knopf, New York, 1993).

2. P. A. Mellars, *The Neanderthal Legacy: An Archaeological Perspective from Western Europe* (Princeton Univ. Press, Princeton, NJ, 1996).

3. J. L. Bischoff et al., *J. Archaeol. Sci.* **30**, 275 (2003).

4. R. G. Klein, *The Human Career: Human Biological and Cultural Origins* (Univ. of Chicago Press, Chicago, ed. 2, 1999).

5. M. Ingman, H. Kaessmann, S. Pääbo, U. Gyllensten, *Nature* 408, 708 (2000)

6. P. A. Underhill et al., *Nature Genet.* **26**, 358 (2000).

7. M. Hofreiter, D. Serre, H. N. Poinar, M. Kuch, S. Pääbo, *Nature Rev. Genet.* **2**, 353 (2001).

8. A. R. Templeton, *Nature 416,* **45** (2002)

9. A. P. Santa Luca, *J. Hum. Evol.* **7**, 619 (1978).

10. J.-J. Hublin, F. Spoor, M. Braun, F. Zonneveld, *Nature* **381**, 224 (1996)

11. I. V. Ovchinnikov et al., *Nature* **404**, 490 (2000).

12. F. H. SMITH, E. TRINKAUS, P. B. PETTITT, I. KARANOVIC, M. PAUNOVIC, Proc. Natl. Acad. Sci. U.S.A. **96**, 12281 (1999).

13. J.-J. Hublin et al., *C. R. Acad. Sci. Paris Ser. IIA* **321**, 931 (1995).

14. C. Duarte et al., *Proc. Natl. Acad. Sci. U.S.A.* **96**, 7604 (1999).

15. W. Enard et al., *Nature* **418**, 869 (2002).

16. W. Enard et al., *Science* **296**, 340 (2002).

17. H.-H. Chou et al., *Proc. Natl. Acad. Sci. U.S.A.* **99**, 11736 (2002).

The author is with the Program in Human Biology, Stanford University, Stanford, CA 94305, USA. E-mail: rklein@stanford.edu

The New Neandertal

Virtual fossils and real molecules are changing how we view our enigmatic cousin.

Jean-Jacques Hublin

Next year will mark the 150th anniversary of the discovery at Neandertal, a little valley near Düsseldorf in western Germany, of the first recognized fossil humans. The occasion will be commemorated with conferences and exhibitions at major German museums. As a warm-up for this "Neandertal Year," two dozen scholars gathered at New York University this past January, in a Manhattan suffering near-glacial conditions, to exchange views on the latest advances in the field.

Our fascination with Neandertals is well founded. They were the first known example of an extinct species of human, they evolved mostly in Europe, and we now have an unrivaled fossil record accumulated by a century and a half of research. Because there are more specimens of Neandertals than any other premodern human, any new techniques or approaches in paleoanthropology are usually applied to them first. And in recent years we have learned a great deal about these humans that once seemed unattainable, including aspects of their biology such as genetics. Studies have also revealed unexpected features of their growth, development, and life history. Even more traditional approaches, such as the comparison of Neandertal and modern human bone shapes, continue to yield new data.

Visions of the Neandertals as brutish cave dwellers prevailed for many years following their discovery. The first reconstruction, in 1908, was based on the partial skeleton of an old male found at La Chappelle aux Saints in France, but the individual had been stooped from arthritis. That fact, and its projecting face, heavy brow, and generally robust bones gave rise to our earliest, though inaccurate, view of Neandertals. But in the last decades of the twentieth century, the pendulum began to swing in the opposite direction. For some, Neandertals appeared only as a slightly different population of our own species, adapted to the cooler climates of the Paleolithic world. The most politically correct version saw them as almost indistinguishable from modern humans in abilities and behaviors, and hardly differing in many anatomical aspects. The New York conference provided a more balanced picture of a "New Neandertal" that is both very similar to and very different from us.

Emblematic of this New Neandertal is a composite skeleton created at the American Museum of Natural History in New York and discussed at the conference by Ian Tattersall, one of its curators. Most scholars have focused on analyzing particular parts of the skeleton, such as the skull or pelvis, so the reconstruction is our first look at an entire one. It is a large male, built from casts of bones from several individuals (most are from two finds, one at La Ferrassie, France, and the other at Kebara, Israel). Tattersall emphasized how different it is from our own skeletons, not only in the anatomy of the skull, which is well known, but in entire body shape. If any living Neandertals had come to the conference dressed in a suit and tie, they still would have stood out. But this composite skeleton was only one of many innovative approaches to finding the new Neandertal that were presented in New York.

VIRTUAL FOSSILS

Human fossils are precious and fragile, and to study them scientists have embraced or developed new methods in recent years. CT scanning, for example, is used with increasing frequency to assess fine internal details of specimens, such as the inner ear of Neandertals. Imaging techniques, combined with sophisticated software for manipulating digitized fossils, allow us to work with virtual objects rather than the originals. One can now reconstruct fragmentary specimens, piecing them together on the computer and supplying missing parts. If a skull's right side is damaged, the left can be copied and a mirror image of it substituted instead. Even specimens warped and distorted in the fossilization process can be straightened out.

The new methods of "virtual paleoanthropology" have been used to investigate how modern humans and Neandertals differ even in childhood. At the New York meeting, Marcia Ponce de Leon and Christoph Zollikofer of the University of Zurich presented a computer model and simulation comparing skull growth, showing the divergence of shape began early in development and reflected different growth patterns in the bones. Another comparison of Neandertal and modern human childhood development was recently undertaken by Fernando Ramirez–Rozzi of the French Centre National de la Recherche Scientifique in Paris and José Maria Bermudez de Castro of Madrid's Natural History Museum. They looked at tooth enamel, which has microscopic striations that can be counted like the growth rings in a tree trunk, and concluded that Neandertals reached adulthood at about 15 rather than 18 years of age, as in present-day human populations. Further analysis will confirm whether or not this was the case.

Modern human specimens are also being digitized, allowing us to assess bone shape and size variations and understand their significance in anatomical evolution. In a remarkable contribution at the conference, Katerina Harvati and Tim Weaver of the Max Planck Institute for Evolutionary Anthropology in Leipzig, Germany, looked at skull variation in modern humans from different climates and cultures. They found that the shape of the face is linked to local environmental conditions, which fits well with the current belief that the Neandertal's projecting face is a cold-climate adaptation. By contrast, the shape of the brain case, particularly the temporal bone (on the side of the skull), proved to be a good indicator of genetic closeness among populations.

REAL MOLECULES

Meanwhile, the genuine specimens have been the object of increased attention through the study of DNA, proteins, and chemical elements that can be found in bones and teeth—giving us a completely new source of valuable information about our remote relatives' biology and their daily lives.

In 1997, a fragment of DNA was reconstructed from the same bones that the quarry workers found in Neandertal in 1856. The DNA of the Neandertal fell outside modern human variation, and suggested a divergence between the ancestors of Neandertals and modern humans nearly half a million years ago. Since the original DNA study, nine other Neandertal individuals have yielded some genetic information, all similar to one another yet distinct from that of modern humans. Although this number is small, the evidence gives us insight into the demography of the Neandertals. The limited variability of their DNA suggests that there were times perhaps during glacial advances, when their population was greatly reduced, resulting in genetic bottlenecking. The population recovered in size afterward but with fewer surviving

different genetic lines. In this respect, humans—modern, Neandertal, and others—strongly contrast with African apes which evolved in a much less stressful environment during the last several hundred thousand years, and therefore have much greater genetic variability. Interestingly, while we can now study Neandertal DNA, it is very difficult to analyze DNA from the early modern humans who replaced them between 40,000 and 30,000 years ago. Because Neandertal DNA is different from our own, modern contamination (from excavators, museum curators, or laboratory personnel) can be identified and discounted. With fossils of our own forebears, however, differentiating ancient DNA from recent contamination is virtually impossible. Such research can only be undertaken with new fossil finds that are kept in sterile conditions from the field to the lab.

There is no evidence that the last Neandertals were evolving toward a physical appearance like our own, but the issue of the possible contribution of Neandertals to the modern European genetic makeup is still fervently debated. Even if Neandertals represented a distinct, although very close, species separate from modern humans, we know that in nature, hybridization is a common process under such circumstances. At the conference, Trenton Holliday of Tulane University surveyed the zoological evidence, pointing out many hybrids among large mammals including members of the camel, horse, dog, and cat families. Did Neandertals and modern humans interbreed? It is quite possible in some instances, but it had no major biological results.

Proteins can now be recovered from bones and examined with methods similar to those used with DNA. This year, for the first time, Christina Nielsen-Marsh of the Max Planck Institute was able to extract and analyze a protein from Neandertal teeth from Shanidar, Iraq. In Neandertals, this particular protein (osteocalcin) displays a sequence similar to that of modern humans, indicating it has changed little over a long period of time. In the near future, extraction and sequencing of fossil proteins may open new ways to study evolutionary relationships between extinct species, and may allow us to go farther back in time than is possible with ancient DNA, which is more complex and degrades more quickly.

Scientists are investigating other molecules and chemical elements found in

Neandertal bones. Collagen, routinely extracted from bone today for radiocarbon dating, yields carbon and nitrogen, while strontium and calcium can be sampled from the mineral parts of bone. These four elements can give us indications of an individual's diet, since they come from foods. Studies by Herve Bocherens of the Centre National de la Recherche Scientifique in Montpellier and Michael Richards of the Max Planck Institute suggest the European Neandertals were highly carnivorous, a pattern not unlike that observed in modern hunter-gatherers in cold regions. In the future, such analyses may also reveal indicators of population movements, since bone chemistry also reflects, for example, specific elements in ground water that vary from region to region.

THE LAST NEANDERTALS

The possible interactions between Neandertals and modern invaders between 40,000 and 30,000 years ago in Europe remains one of paleoanthropology's most debated issues, so it was no surprise that it surfaced in New York. There is little doubt that the presence of another group of humans in Europe played a major role in the extinction of the Neandertals, through competition for resources if nothing else. But other factors in the Neandertals' demise have been discussed recently. For example, Chris Stringer of the Natural History Museum, London, has shown that this period was characterized by repeated and extreme climatic changes occurring in rapid succession. Although Neandertals had faced and survived severe climatic crises along the course of their evolution, the coincidence of this climatic instability with the invasion of the European territory by modern humans presented a double challenge for the last Neandertals. Both groups must have tried adapting during this confrontation in a very difficult environment. At the conference, Shara Bailey of the Max Planck Institute and I showed that Neandertals at the French cave site of Arcy-sur-Cure are indisputably associated with stone tools and bone ornaments formerly thought to have been made only by modern humans. The acquisition during this period of new techniques and habits, such as the use of body ornaments, by the last Neandertals is much debated by specialists. Many scholars believe it may have resulted from their encounters with modern humans, who had developed this behavior more than 100,000 years ago, even before leaving Africa. These contacts, they argue, may have been seldom, but resulted in imitation by the Neandertals or even trade between the two populations. But modern humans might have been affected as well. It has been proposed that the burst of artistic expression—cave art, figurines, and the like—observed in our forebears at this time relates to group identification and may have resulted from the interaction with these indeed human, but very different, beings.

Because Neandertals are the best-known group of fossil humans, they are the group that always raises the most questions. As the last branching of the human evolutionary tree and our closest relatives in the recent past, they will remain an object of popular fascination as well as scientific interest. In fact, how we envision Neandertals may tell us as much about the way we see ourselves as about them. With the "New Neandertal" we have definitively shed two such images, one in which our ancient cousin was brutish and far different from us, the other in which we were nearly identical. But perhaps our newfound knowledge, from virtual fossils and molecular studies, is taking us to a deeper understanding of Neandertals.

Jean-Jacques Hublin, *director of the Department of Human Evolution at the Max Planck Institute in Leipzeig, has led fieldwork in France, Spain, and Morocco, and is now participating in an international project at Dikika, Ethiopia.*

SPACE

THE FINAL [ARCHAEOLOGICAL] FRONTIER

During a preliminary survey of late twenty-first-century mining outposts in the asteroid belt, Dr. Gan Shishu, director of the Institute for Space Archaeology at the China National Space Administration, recognized a unique opportunity. Leaving her field team as they continued to document the massive Halliburton gantry on asteroid Q36, she piloted her team's one-person archaeoprobe *L.S.B. Leakey* toward a strange-looking artifact nearby that had been drifting in heliocentric orbit for more than two centuries.

P. J. Capelotti

SCIENCE FICTION? NOT ANY LONGER. The notion of archaeological research and heritage management in space is an idea whose time has already arrived.

It's been more than 20 years since Brown University archaeologist Richard Gould proposed that aircraft wrecks might yield important data—laying the foundation for systematic archaeological studies of sites from the history of human flight. Then, in 1993, University of Hawaii anthropologist Ben Finney, who for much of his career has explored the technology and techniques used by Polynesians to colonize islands in the Pacific, suggested that it would not be premature to begin thinking about the archaeology of Russian and American aerospace sites on the Moon and Mars. Finney pointed out that just as today's scholars use the archaeological record to investigate how Polynesians diverged culturally as they explored the Pacific, archaeologists will someday study off-earth sites to trace the development of humans in space. He was certainly clear-eyed about the improbability of anyone being able to conduct fieldwork anytime soon, but he was equally convinced that one day such work would be done.

There is a growing awareness, however, that it won't be long before both corporate adventurers and space tourists reach the Moon and Mars. The Russians already carry very-high-paying tourists to the International Space Station, and the recent launch by the private company Scaled Composites of the three-passenger *SpaceShipOne* has shown that corporate space travel will soon be feasible. "There's a wealth of important archaeological sites from the history of space exploration on the Moon and Mars and protective cultural heritage regimes need to be in place before these people get there. Otherwise, we must be prepared to someday see pieces of *Apollo 11* listed for sale on Ebay.

In 1999, a company called Lunacorp proposed a robotic lunar rover mission beginning at the site of Tranquility Base and rumbling across the Moon from one archaeological site to another, from the wreck of the *Ranger 8* probe and a *Surveyor* spacecraft to *Apollo 17*'s landing site and a lost Soviet *Lunakhod* rover. The mission, which would leave more than 600 miles of tread marks at some of the most famous sites from the history of exploration, was promoted as a form of theme-park entertainment. In addition to the threat from profit-seeking corporations, scholars cite other potentially destructive forces such as wanton souvenir hunting as well as uncontrolled or unmonitored scientific sampling, like that which has occurred in explorations of remote polar regions.

According to the vaguely worded United Nations Outer Space Treaty of 1967, what it terms "space junk" remains the property of the country that sent the craft or probe into space. But the treaty doesn't explicitly address protection of sites like Tranquility Base, and equating the remains of human exploration of the heavens with "space junk" leaves them vulnerable to scavengers. Another problem arises through other treaties that proclaim that land in space cannot be owned by any country, or individual. This presents some interesting dilemmas for the aspiring manager of extraterrestrial cultural resources. If the U.S. owns the archaeological remains of *Apollo 11* but not the ground underneath it, how to protect the former without disturbing the latter? Does America own Neil Armstrong's famous first footprints on the Moon but not the lunar dust in which they were recorded? Surely those footprints are as important as those left by hominids at Laetoli, Tanzania, in the story of human development. But unlike the Laetoli prints, which have survived for 3.5 million years encased in cement-like ash, those at Tranquility Base could be swept away with a casual brush of a space tourist's hand.

In what may be the first instance of funded space archaeology research, a team led by Beth O'Leary, a New Mexico State University archaeologist, is studying legal ownership of artifacts and structures in space, and how one might go about documenting and preserving them. O'Leary's group argues that even though the United States cannot, by treaty, own the land on which the lunar module *Eagle's* descent stage rests, U.S. federal preservation laws and regulations nonetheless apply to the objects left there. They see the base as a natural candidate for the National Register of Historic Places, as a National Historic Landmark, and, potentially, as the first extraterrestrial site on UNESCO's World Heritage List.

Unless procedures and protocols are developed for evaluating and registering sites and artifacts, "there will be uncontrolled sampling and even outright treasure hunting," says John Campbell, an archaeologist at James Cook University in Queensland, Australia, who has been responsible for organizing recent international seminars on the subject of preserving space heritage. Federal cultural resource management legislation, he notes, has the potential to lift aerospace archaeology away from the profiteers and souvenir hunters and into its proper bailiwick within the discipline of historical archaeology.

As a first step in that direction and with funding from the New Mexico Space Grant Consortium, O'Leary's group of archaeologists, curators, and physicists have researched and documented an archaeological assemblage of dozens of artifacts and features at Tranquility Base alone. Using this data, they have drawn up a preliminary site plan, one that, thanks to the Moon's lack of atmosphere, will doubtless remain unchanged for centuries, provided looters leave the site untouched.

The challenges of surveying and preserving old spacecraft discarded on the surface of Mars will be greater. Dust storms could damage landers or even bury them beneath the red Martian soil. And since Mars has no protective ozone layer, ultraviolet energy from the Sun could damage the spacecraft. It may be necessary to deploy shields over such sites to protect them from the continual abrasion and decay caused by extreme temperatures, radiation, wind, and dust.

Eventually, the *Viking* landers (1976), the Mars *Pathfinder* (1997), and the *Spirit* and *Opportunity* rovers (2004) might need to be moved indoors to protect them from the Martian environment that they helped explore. And, of course, field survey teams—human or robotic—will need to be dispatched to Mars' North Pole to answer the mystery of what became of NASA's lost 1997 *Polar Lander*, and to the Isidis Planitia basin in search of the European Space Agency's ill-fated *Beagle II* (2003).

Yet it is one thing for a few archaeologists to realize the almost unlimited potential of archaeological studies in space, and quite another to do something about it. When O'Leary and her team approached various federal agencies responsible, such as NASA, to discuss legal issues related to space and national historic place designations, they were rebuffed by terse bureaucratese: "Placing Tranquility Base under protection might imply that the U.S. intended to exert sovereignty over the Moon." "Our office does not have jurisdiction." "Our office does not have the inclination." Similar problems cropped up with regard to the use of UNESCO's World Heritage List, since Tranquility Base can be seen as not so much a global cultural achievement as another battle in the Cold War.

O'Leary believes it may be time to look to new kinds of worldwide treaties for the preservation of old structures on the new frontier that would bypass the cultural baggage associated with UNESCO's World Heritage List and the vague, contradictory possession clauses of the UN's space treaty. She points out that an archaeologist on Earth needs a permit from a relevant authority prior to conducting any intrusive research. If no authority can own property in space, what authority would issue such permits for the extraterrestrial archaeologist? The problem requires the creation of new international administrative structures unlike anything archaeologists have to contend with on Earth.

The Cold War, which provided so much of the backdrop to the race for the Moon, is replete with failures that may never be examined until archaeology takes them up. The site where the Soviet *Luna 5* probe crash-landed onto the surface of the Moon on May 9, 1965, may one day provide excellent archaeological opportunities for the study of the secretive *Luna* series of unmanned probes launched in an era of intense super-power competition for priority on the Moon. The questions that could be asked of such a site are almost limitless. Does its location correspond with archival records of its guidance and trajectory? Does the composition of the craft match its specifications? Is there any instrumentation or technology on board—Cold War or otherwise—that was never announced, recorded, or used on Earth?

Dozens of sites exist on the Moon where operational spacecraft have been discarded, whether by mission requirements, accident, or obsolescence. The *Apollo* program alone left six lunar module descent stages fixed at

Gan's doctoral work on the rise and fall of the American Empire had taken her to several aerospace museums around the world. But museums, she knew, were of limited use to the archaeologist, since they frequently reinforced an established order while, consciously or not, shifting the attention of museum visitors away from manifest failures in the technological and social history of that established order. Now, as the *Leakey's* robot arm reached out and snared the slowly tumbling artifact, Gan viewed the only surviving lunar module of the American *Apollo* program, the first (and ultimately only) successful attempt to put humans on the Moon prior to permanent Chinese colonization in 2043. Of the eight lunar modules sent into space, only one survived destruction—and Gan was about to board it.

As she crossed from the *Leakey* to the primitive lunar module, Gan recognized the faded red, white, and blue symbol that represented the classic fifty-state alliance at the height of its global preeminence, a time of technological triumph, social unrest, and dietary disaster. She noted the fine coating of dust that covered the lunar module ascent stage and took great pains not to disturb it, except for one small patch. There, she wiped clear a small area to reveal the image of stylized dog with a long snout. Above the dog was the word "Snoopy."

Gan was the first human to touch the command module since it was abandoned by pilot Eugene A. Cernan and mission commander Thomas P. Stafford on May 24, 1969, 236 years earlier. Having studied it for this mission she and her team had developed a field tool that now enabled her to loosen the hatch cover that once connected *Snoopy*, the lunar module, to the command module, *Charlie Brown*. As it swung free, Gan squeezed through the narrow passage, leaving the year 2205 and entering a chamber of technology, language, and culture untouched for more than two centuries.

For two hours, Gan recorded the instrument settings and the arrangement of discarded clipboards with their innumerable checklists, marveling at how many functions humans had to attend to manually back in 1969—functions long since given over to the computers of the Central Bureau. Then, as she prepared to leave *Snoopy* and return to *Leakey*, she uncovered a small bag that held a minuscule amount of bright orange residue. She removed a tiny sample and placed it in her portable gas chromatograph mass spectrometer. The results were confusing. Though she read the English words on the bag as "Breakfast Drink, Orange," all the mass spec revealed was sugar, fructose, titanium dioxide (which apparently accounted for the bright orange color), xanthum gum, cellulose gum, and two chemicals she knew had been listed as poisons for more than a century—Yellow 5 and Yellow 6.

Sealing the hatch of *Snoopy*, Gan returned to her own research vessel, backed it away, and set the ancient space artifact adrift once again on its orbit around the sun. As it floated out of sight, she entered the results of the mass spec analysis into *Leakey's* computer. She discovered that the orange substance she had tested was known in the 1969 vernacular as "Tang." As she navigated her way back to her field team on Q36, she suddenly remembered from her food history that it would be another half century before Americans realized—too late—that such sugar- and corn syrup-based foods had led their nation into cultural and physical obesity. In her mind, she was already spinning a new hypothesis. The same processed foods that had led America to the Moon had led to its downfall. She would later present it at the next Interplanetary Archaeology Congress. She would call it her "NAPA" hypothesis: North America Pre-Atkins.

base camps, and another six ascent stages were deliberately discarded and impacted on the lunar surface after they had delivered their crews back to the mission's command module. (The exact impact sites of two of these wrecks, *Apollo 11's Eagle* and *Apollo 16's Orion*, have never been located.)

If one accepts the idea of archaeological research on sites from the history of human exploration in space, it is hardly a giant leap to consider the potential for archaeological fieldwork on the evidence of extraterrestrial civilizations. The late biochemist and science fiction writer Isaac Asimov once speculated that the galaxy may contain 325 million planets with traces of civilizations in ruins. Perhaps our astronomers and their SETI stations are hearing only static through their radio telescopes because they are, in effect, listening for a message from the extraterrestrial equivalent of the ancient Maya or the Sumerians—dead civilizations that can speak to us now only

through archaeology. Constructing a catalog of visual signatures of advanced civilizations will someday be within the province of aerospace archaeology. And with a potential cultural resource database of 325 million planets with civilizations in ruins, there sure is a lot of fieldwork to do "out there."

The Moon, with its wealth of sites, will surely be the first destination of archaeologists trained to work in space. But any young scholars hoping to claim the mantle of history's first lunar archaeologist will be disappointed. That distinction is already taken.

On November 19, 1969, astronauts Charles "Pete" Conrad and Alan Bean made a difficult manual landing of the *Apollo 12* lunar module in the Moon's Ocean of Storms, just a few hundred feet from an unmanned probe, *Surveyor 3*, that had soft-landed in a crater on April 19, 1967. Unrecognized at the time, this was an important moment in the history of science. Bean and Conrad were about to conduct the first archaeological studies on the Moon.

After the obligatory planting of the American flag and some geological sampling, Conrad and Bean made their way to the artifact made accessible by their brilliant piloting. They observed that *Surveyor 3* had bounced after touchdown and carefully photographed the impressions made by its footpads. Conrad noted the artifact's brownish tint, and learned from Mission Control engineers in Houston that the probe had been white when it was launched. The photographic system's mirror was warped and the whole spacecraft covered in dust, perhaps kicked up by the landing.

Conrad and Bean used a cutting tool to remove the probe's television camera, remote sampling arm, and pieces of tubing. The astronaut-archaeologists bagged and labeled these artifacts, stowed them on board their lunar module, and returned them to Earth. The Johnson Space Center in Houston, Texas, and the Hughes Air and Space Corporation in El Segundo, California, later analyzed the changes in these aerospace artifacts left on the Moon for more than two years.

Published by NASA in 1972 as *Analysis of* Surveyor 3 *Material and Photographs Returned by* Apollo 12 (NASA SP-284, 1972), this sophisticated multidisciplinary investigation of the *Surveyor 3* artifacts focused on the ways the retrieved components had been changed by the craft's voyage through the vacuum of space. As such, the mission of *Apollo 12* provided the first example of aerospace archaeology, extraterrestrial archaeology, and—perhaps more significant for the history of the discipline—formational archaeology, the study of environmental and cultural forces upon the life history of human artifacts in space.

A piece of the television camera, subjected to a microbiological examination, revealed evidence of the bacteria *Streptococcus mitis*. For a moment it was thought Conrad and Bean had discovered evidence for life on the Moon. As all other competing hypotheses were systematically eliminated, the origin of the seemingly extraterrestrial life became apparent. While the camera was being readied for launch, someone had sneezed on it. The resulting virus had traveled to the Moon, remained in an alternating freezing/boiling vacuum for two and a half years, and returned promptly to life upon reaching the safety of a petri dish back on Earth.

Lunar archaeology had made its first great discovery. Not even the vastness of space can stop humans from spreading a sore throat.

P. J. CAPELOTTI is a senior lecturer in anthropology and American studies at Penn State University Abington College in Abington. He is the author of Sea Drift: Rafting Adventures in the Wake of Kon-Tiki, By Airship to the North Pole: An Archaeology of Human Exploration, *and a forthcoming textbook,* The Exploring Animal: An Introduction to Archaeology from Seafarers to Spacefarers.

Index

Index

Index